AF752259

Your Study of
The

Doctrine and Covenants Made Easier

Part 1
Section 1 through Section 42

SECOND EDITION

Your Study of The Doctrine and Covenants Made Easier

Part 1
Section 1 through Section 42

SECOND EDITION

BONUS SECTION

A Brief Chronology
of Major Characters
in Early Church History

David J. Ridges

CFI, an imprint of
Cedar Fort
Publishing & Media
Springville, Utah

© 2020 David J. Ridges
All rights reserved.

No part of this book may be reproduced in any form whatsoever, whether by graphic, visual, electronic, film, microfilm, tape recording, or any other means, without prior written permission of the publisher, except in the case of brief passages embodied in critical reviews and articles.

This book is not an official publication of The Church of Jesus Christ of Latter-day Saints. The opinions and views expressed herein belong solely to the author and do not necessarily represent the opinions or views of Cedar Fort, Inc. Permission for the use of sources, graphics, and photos is also solely the responsibility of the author.

ISBN 13: 978-1-4621-4888-2

Published by CFI, an imprint of Cedar Fort, Inc.
2373 W. 700 S., Springville, UT, 84663
Distributed by Cedar Fort, Inc., www.cedarfort.com

Library of Congress Control Number: 2020945612

Cover design by Shawnda T. Craig
Cover design © 2020 Cedar Fort, Inc.

Printed in the United States of America

10 9 8 7 6 5 4 3 2 1

Printed on acid-free paper

Dedication

To my wife, Janette, who
is my greatest blessing.

CONTENTS

PREFACE

The Doctrine and Covenants is the Savior's book to us in our day. In it, He personally teaches us the "doctrines" and "covenants" necessary to live a righteous, rewarding life, and to successfully walk along the covenant path toward eventual exaltation in the highest degree of glory in the celestial kingdom. In the October 1986 general conference of the Church, in reference to the importance of understanding the doctrines of the gospel, Elder Boyd K. Packer said:

> True doctrine, understood, changes attitudes and behavior. The study of the doctrines of the gospel will improve behavior quicker than a study of behavior will improve behavior. ("Little Children," *Ensign*, Nov. 1986)

Briefly put, "doctrines" are the teachings of the plan of salvation, the answers to questions about the meaning and purpose of life, instructions, rules, facts, hows, whys, and commandments that, if followed, will lead to exaltation. In D&C 10:62, the Lord tells us that He is going to "bring to light the true points" of His doctrine. The Doctrine and Covenants does this. It also includes covenants required for celestial glory and exaltation.

This study guide is a brief, to-the-point help to a better understanding of the Doctrine and Covenants with its accompanying doctrines of the gospel and the ordinances of salvation required for celestial exaltation. The style is somewhat conversational to help you feel as if you were being guided through the Doctrine and Covenants in one of my classes. It is designed, in many cases, to give you instant understanding of basic doctrines and principles, as well as to provide you with the background to apply them in your life, which, in turn, will help you develop a deeper understanding and testimony of the gospel. Remember that the Holy Ghost is THE teacher. He will enlighten your mind and warm your heart as you pray and study this, the Savior's book directly to us.

INTRODUCTION

Welcome to the Second Edition of *Your Study of the Doctrine and Covenants Made Easier.* As was the case with the first edition, this second edition comes in three volumes. This is part 1. In compiling this second edition, I have incorporated many updates and much additional historical information and corrections based on recent research made available through the Joseph Smith Papers Project. I have added thousands of brief clarifications and helps to my notes and commentary for the first edition of this study guide. I have used the 2013 edition of the Doctrine and Covenants, as published by The Church of Jesus Christ of Latter-day Saints, as the basic text. References to the Bible come from the King James Version, as published by The Church of Jesus Christ of Latter-day Saints. JST references refer to the Joseph Smith Translation of the Bible.

Every verse of the Doctrine and Covenants, from section 1 through section 42, is included in this volume, Part 1. All the remaining verses of the Doctrine and Covenants are contained in Parts 2 and 3. All three volumes have background and setting notes for each section, as well as brief notes of explanation between and within the verses to clarify and help you learn and grow in your appreciation and understanding of this sacred volume of scripture. The notes within the verses are printed in italics and enclosed in brackets in order to make it easy for you to distinguish between the actual scripture text and my teaching comments. Notes between the verses are indented and are printed in a different font than the scripture text. **Bold** is often used to highlight things for teaching purposes.

You may be aware that, as a result of recent research, including for *The Joseph Smith Papers* publications, there are a number of changes to the section headings in the 2013 printing of the Doctrine and Covenants compared to previous editions. Such adjustments, most of them minor, have been made to 78 sections. One example of this is found in sections 39 and 40, where the name "James Covel" is now used rather than "James

Covill." The Second Edition of *Doctrine and Covenants Made Easier* incorporates these changes. You can read more about these changes by going online to Gospel Library/Study Helps/About the Scriptures/Adjustments to the Scriptures, browsing down the page to "Doctrine and Covenants and Pearl of Great Price," and continuing to read from that point on.

This work is intended to be a user-friendly, "teacher in your hand" introductory study of this portion of the Doctrine and Covenants, as well as a refresher course for more advanced students of the scriptures. It is also designed to be a quick-reference resource which will enable readers to look up a particular passage of scripture for use in lessons, talks, or personal study as desired. It is my hope that you will write some of the notes given in this book in your own scriptures, whether paper copy or on digital devices, to assist you in reading and studying this portion of the Doctrine and Covenants in the future. Thus, your own scriptures will become one of your best tools in your continued study of the gospel.

—David J. Ridges

SECTION 1

Background

This section is not the first revelation, chronologically, in the Doctrine and Covenants. In fact, the Lord had already given over 60 recorded revelations to the Church and individuals by this time. The Lord gave this revelation as "my preface unto the book of my commandments" (D&C 1:6). Thus, section 1 was to be the Lord's preface to the revelations already given and still serves that purpose for us with our edition of the Doctrine and Covenants. This revelation was given on November 1, 1831, at a special conference of elders of the Church, held in Hiram, Ohio, at the home of John and Elsa Johnson. At this point, the Church was just over one and one-half years old (having been officially organized on April 6, 1830), and the Prophet Joseph Smith was 25 years of age. One of the matters considered at this conference was that of publishing the revelations received thus far in book form. This publication was to be known as the "Book of Commandments," and the decision was made to print 10,000 copies. Later, it was decided to print 3,000 copies. It would contain 65 sections (what we now know as D&C, sections 2 through 66).

The Joseph Smith Papers publications inform us that, during the conference, a committee consisting of Sidney Rigdon, Oliver Cowdery, and William E. McLellin was asked to write a preface for the Book of Commandments (see *The Joseph Smith Papers, Documents, Volume 2, July 1831–January 1833*, ed. Matthew C. Godfrey and others [2013], 104). When they presented their work to the conference, the group rejected it, and they asked Joseph Smith to go to the Lord for help. Here again, *The Joseph Smith Papers* publications help.

"After [Joseph Smith] and the elders bowed in prayer, [Joseph], who was 'sitting by a window,' dictated the preface 'by the Spirit,' while [Sidney] Rigdon served as scribe. 'Joseph would deliver a few sentences and Sidney would write them down [recalled William E. McLellin], then read them aloud, and if correct, then Joseph would proceed and deliver more'" (in *The Joseph Smith Papers, Documents, Volume 2, July 1831–January 1833*, 104).

Preparations to print the Book of Commandments were made, and by the summer of 1833, the printing was well under way in Missouri. However, in the course of events, the printing press and most of the copies of the Book of Commandments were destroyed by mobs and the printing was held up for a time.

By the summer of 1835, the Prophet Joseph had received a number of additional revelations from the Lord. In a conference of the Church, held on August 17, 1835, approval was given to print the 65 revelations in the Book of Commandments again, and to include 37 new revelations also in this publication. Rather than calling this printing the "Book of Commandments," it was named "The Doctrine and Covenants." It had a total of 102 sections and is known as the 1835 edition of the Doctrine and Covenants.

As mentioned above, section 1 was given by the Lord as His preface to the Doctrine and Covenants. Sixty-five sections precede this one chronologically, but this revelation is listed first, because it is the Savior's preface to His book of scripture to us, namely, the Doctrine and Covenants. It is also interesting to note that section 133 was given at the same special conference of elders in Hiram, Ohio. It was given two days after section 1, on November 3, 1831, and was first included in the Doctrine and Covenants as an appendix (see heading to section 133). Thus, in a sense, sections 1 and 133 serve as "bookends" to this sacred book of scripture.

We will move ahead now in our study of section 1. As you will see, in addition to being the Lord's preface, it can also be viewed as the Savior's personal testimony to all of us.

Many doctrines and principles are taught in this section. We will point out many of these through the use of **bold**, for emphasis in the scripture text itself, as well as through indented notes between verses and the use of explanatory notes in [*brackets*] within the verses.

Note: In section 10, verse 62, the Savior specifically told us that He was going to restore "the true points of my doctrine." "Doctrines" are eternal truths, facts, things in the plan of salvation that do not change, such as:

- Faith, repentance, baptism, gift of the Holy Ghost.
- The Godhead consists of the Father, the Son, and the Holy Ghost.
- The members of the Godhead are three separate beings.
- There are three kingdoms of glory, namely, the telestial, terrestrial, and celestial.
- In the celestial kingdom, there are three degrees.
- The highest degree of glory in the celestial is called "exaltation."
- Those who attain exaltation will live in their own eternal family unit and ultimately become gods.
- Heavenly Father is completely

fair, thus everyone will ultimately get a perfect opportunity before the final judgment to hear, understand, and then accept or reject the gospel.

- The sins we have repented of will not even be mentioned on Judgment Day.
- Little children who die before the years of accountability will receive exaltation.
- Ordinance work for the dead is part of the Father's plan of happiness for His children.
- We are spirit children of Heavenly Parents.
- The Atonement of Christ works for our shortcomings and imperfections as well as our sins.
- Baptism is required for entrance into the celestial kingdom, except in the case of little children who die before the age of accountability and the intellectually handicapped who do not have sufficient understanding to be accountable.
- God will not allow His living prophets to lead us astray.
- And many, many more wonderful doctrines that help us understand the whats, whys, and hows of the Father's plan of salvation for us, His children.

In the Doctrine and Covenants, the Lord has indeed restored many true doctrines, which, among other things, enable us to better live the gospel because we better understand it. Throughout these three study guides for the Doctrine and Covenants, I will often add extra notes to point out and summarize the many doctrines given by the Savior for us, as He said He would. You will see an example of this before verse one, next.

Just one more thing. As you can see, the very first word in this revelation, given by the Savior, is "hearken." This is a powerful word meaning to both "listen" and "obey." President Russell M. Nelson, of the Quorum of the Twelve Apostles at the time, explained that "the Hebrew language of the Old Testament in most instances uses **the same term for both hearkening** (to the Lord) **and obedience** (to His word)" ("Listen to Learn," *Ensign*, May 1991, 24).

Doctrine

Verse 1. God always knows what we are doing.

1 **HEARKEN** [*a strong word, often used in scriptures to mean "listen and obey," as in 1 Nephi 4:32, Genesis 3:17, 21:12, and Acts 27:21*], O ye people of my church, saith the voice of him [*Jesus Christ*] who dwells on high, and **whose eyes are upon all men**; yea, verily I say: Hearken ye people from afar; and ye that are upon the

islands of the sea, listen together.

One of the major messages given in verse 2, next, is that God is completely fair. Everyone will be given a perfect opportunity, before the final judgment, to both hear and understand the gospel. Then, each can use personal agency to accept or reject it. We will use **bold** to emphasize this fact.

Doctrine

Verse 2. Everyone will ultimately get a perfect opportunity before the final Judgment Day, to hear, understand, and then accept or reject the gospel.

2 For verily **the voice of the Lord is unto all** men, and there is **none** to **escape**; and there is **no eye** that **shall not see, neither ear that shall not hear, neither heart that shall not be penetrated**.

As you can see from verse 2, above, it is not enough to physically "hear" the gospel or "see" things related to it. Rather, each "heart" must be "penetrated." In other words, each of God's children must have the opportunity to truly understand it. For many, that opportunity comes in this mortal life. For many others, it will not come until they hear the gospel preached in the spirit world (see D&C 138, especially verses 32–34). After the gospel has "penetrated" the heart, each can accept it or rebel against it. Thus, each will be treated fairly at the final judgment while individual agency is preserved.

Doctrine

Verse 3. All sins that have not been repented of will eventually be exposed and brought to light.

3 **And the rebellious shall be pierced with much sorrow**; for **their iniquities** [*wickedness*] **shall be spoken upon the housetops** [*all wicked deeds will be exposed; perhaps this might include news media reports and gossip in our day, as well as unrepented-of evil being revealed on Judgment Day*], and **their secret acts shall be revealed**.

Doctrine

Verse 4. The gospel will go forth to all people.

4 And the **voice of warning shall be unto all people**, by the mouths of my disciples [*faithful leaders and members of the Church*], whom I have chosen in these last days.

As you can see in verse 5, next, the Savior is very emphatic that nothing will stop the spread of the gospel in the last days.

5 And **they shall go forth and none shall stay** [*stop*] **them**, for I the Lord have commanded them.

Next, the Savior tells us that the Doctrine and Covenants is His instruction to us and to all the world.

6 Behold, **this is mine authority** [*perhaps referring back to "the voice of the Lord," verse 2, and "the voice of warning," verse 4*], **and the authority of my servants** [*perhaps meaning these revelations are authorized by the Lord; can also include the authority of the priesthood, under which the work goes forth; see footnote 6a*], and **my preface unto the book of my commandments, which I have given them to publish unto you, O inhabitants of the earth**.

Joseph Fielding Smith commented on verse 6, above, as follows:

"The Doctrine and Covenants is distinctively peculiar and interesting to all who believe in it, [in] that **it is the only book in existence which bears the honor of a preface given by the Lord himself**. . . . It was not written by Joseph Smith, but was dictated by Jesus Christ, and contains his and his Father's word to the Church and to all the world that faith in God, repentance from sin, and membership in his Church might be given to all who will believe, and that once again the New and Everlasting covenant might be established" (*Church History and Modern Revelation*, 1:252).

Next, Jesus bears His own personal witness to us that every prophesy in the Doctrine and Covenants will be fulfilled.

Doctrine

Verse 7. The words and promises of God will all be fulfilled, guaranteed.

7 Wherefore, fear and tremble, O ye people, for what I the Lord have decreed in them [*the revelations in the Doctrine and Covenants*] **shall be fulfilled.**

Verses 8–11, next, refer to the power "to seal both on earth and in heaven" (verse 8). In the context of this section, this refers particularly to the wicked who reject the gospel. In the larger context of the scriptures, this sealing power can refer to the specific sealing power and priesthood keys held by modern prophets and apostles. These verses as well as others in this section are a "voice of warning" (see verse 4) to all the world.

Doctrine

Verse 8. The official acts of God's authorized servants are valid in heaven as well as on earth.

8 And verily I say unto you, that **they who go forth**, bearing these tidings unto the inhabitants of the earth, **to them is power given to seal both on earth and in heaven**, the unbelieving and rebellious [*the wicked; see verse 9*];

Doctrine

Verse 9. The preaching of the gospel to the world makes the wicked accountable and unable to avoid the punishments of God (unless they repent).

9 Yea, verily, **to seal them up** [*to make them accountable*] **unto the day when the wrath of God** [*the punishments of God*] **shall be poured out upon the wicked without measure** [*without limit*]—

Next, in verse 10, we are taught that we are, in effect, writing part of the script for our own judgment day, based on the way we treat others.

Doctrine

Verse 10. How we treat others will have a significant impact on how we are rewarded or punished by the Lord on the day of final judgment.

10 Unto the day when the Lord shall come to recompense [*pay; reward*] unto every man according to his work, and **measure** [*give out; pay; reward*] **to every man according to the measure which he has measured to** [*according to what he has done to*] **his fellow man.**

11 Wherefore **the voice of the Lord is unto the ends of the earth** [*the gospel will be preached to all the world*], **that all that will hear** [*so that all who want to hear*] **may hear**:

Doctrine

Verse 12. The Second Coming of Christ is getting close.

12 Prepare ye, prepare ye for that which is to come, for **the Lord is nigh** [*the Second Coming is getting close; see D&C 1:12, footnote b*];

Along with the doctrine given us by the Lord, Himself, that His coming is close, comes the caution not to set a time in our own minds for this great event. Matthew 24:36 tells us: "But of that day and hour knoweth no *man,* no, not the angels of heaven, but my Father only." Therefore, while we know that we live in the last days and that the Savior's coming is "nigh," we must continue with living and not postpone some things in anticipation of it.

Doctrine

Verses 13 and 14. The wicked will be destroyed at the time of the Second Coming.

In verse 13, next, we see the phrase, ". . . his sword is bathed in heaven." Isaiah 34:5–6 gives us a possible explanation of this phrase as used in the Doctrine and Covenants. If you read these verses from Isaiah, you will see that the imagery involved is that of the sword of destruction, wielded by the powers of heaven, in harmony with the law of justice. The sword is bathed in the blood of the wicked, who are destroyed by the coming of Christ. We will include these Isaiah verses here for you to read now, then go on to verse 13.

Isaiah 34:5–6

5 **For my sword shall be bathed** [*bathed in blood; see verse 6, next*] in heaven [*in other words, the wicked will be destroyed*]: behold, **it shall come down upon Idumea** [*Edom; the world—see D&C 1:36; means the wicked and rebellious in the world*], and upon the people of my curse [*who have cursed themselves through personal wickedness*], to judgment.

6 **The sword of the LORD is filled with blood** [*bathed in blood*], it is made fat with fatness [*covered with fat like a knife used in animal sacrifices*], and with the blood of lambs and goats, with the fat of the kidneys of rams: for the LORD hath a sacrifice in Bozrah [*the capital of Edom, a country southeast of Palestine; symbolic of the world and the wickedness of its inhabitants*], and a great slaughter in the land of Idumea [*the wicked world; in other words, the sword of the Lord is going to come down upon the wicked of the world*].

13 And the anger of the Lord is kindled, and **his sword is bathed in heaven, and it shall fall upon the inhabitants** [*the wicked inhabitants*] **of the earth**.

In D&C 133:46–51, we find similar imagery referring to the blood of the wicked. In this case, the blood of the wicked is "sprinkled upon my [*Christ's*] garments" (verse 51) as the wicked are destroyed at His coming. In other words, His clothing is "dyed red" (verses 46 and 48), symbolically, by the blood of the wicked, as they are destroyed at the Second Coming.

We understand the "wicked," referred to here, to be those who are living at or below a telestial lifestyle (briefly described in D&C 76:103), who are turned over to Satan to suffer for their own sins, and who will not be resurrected until the end of the Millennium (see D&C 76:84–85; 88:100–101).

Next, the "voice of warning" continues as the Savior explains that there will ultimately be a complete separation of the righteous from the wicked.

14 And **the arm** [*symbolic of power, as used in scriptural symbolism*] **of the Lord shall be revealed**; and the day cometh that **they who will not** [*who refuse to*] **hear the voice of the Lord, neither the voice of his servants, neither give heed to the words of the prophets and apostles, shall be cut off** from among the people;

President Henry B. Eyring taught the great value of heeding the words of the prophets. "Every time in my life when I have chosen to delay following inspired counsel or decided that I was an exception, I came to know that I had put myself in harm's way. Every time that I have listened to the counsel of prophets, felt it confirmed in prayer, and then followed it, I have found that I moved toward safety" ("Finding Safety in Counsel," *Ensign*, May 1997, 25).

Next, in verses 15 and 16, we are warned about what some people do that gets them cut off from the Lord's covenant people.

15 For they have **strayed from mine ordinances**, and have **broken mine everlasting covenant** [*among other things, this can mean that they have broken their eternal covenants which, if kept, lead to peace and happiness, on earth as well as in eternity*];

16 **They seek not the Lord to establish his righteousness** [*they do not want to do God's will or they ignore it; their motives are often evil*], but **every man walketh in his own way** [*everyone does his own thing, makes his own rules; spiritual anarchy*], and after the image of his own god [*sets his own priorities in life*], whose image is in the likeness of the world [*gets caught up in worldliness*], and whose substance is that of an idol [*worldliness is like idol worship*], which waxeth [*grows*] old and shall perish in Babylon [*the wicked will die in their sins*], even Babylon the great [*Satan's kingdom; spiritual wickedness; see D&C 133:14*], which shall fall.

Next, the Savior tells us what He has available for us, as well as all the inhabitants of the world, so that we do not get caught up in the ways of the world, as explained in the previous verses.

First, Jesus bears His own personal witness to us that Joseph Smith was called of God and taught to be the prophet of the Restoration.

Doctrine

Verse 17. Joseph Smith was a true prophet, called of God.

17 **Wherefore, I the Lord**, knowing the calamity [*disasters, destructions*] which should [*will*] come upon the inhabitants of the earth, **called upon my servant Joseph Smith, Jun., and spake unto him from heaven, and gave him commandments**;

Doctrine

Verse 18. Many Church leaders and members will successfully take the blessings of the gospel restored by Joseph Smith to all the world.

18 **And also gave commandments to others** [*including early leaders of the Church who assisted Joseph Smith in the Restoration, as well as missionaries and members in our day*], **that they should proclaim these things unto the world**; and all this that it might be fulfilled, which was written by the prophets [*for instance, in 1 Corinthians 1:27*]—

19 **The weak things of the world** [*including the missionaries and all Church members*] **shall come forth and break down the mighty and strong ones** [*ultimately, the gospel truths will triumph over all falsehood and error, no matter how "strong" and "mighty" they are made to look*], that man should not counsel his fellow man [*so that we do not have to rely solely on the philosophies of men*], neither trust in the arm of flesh—

Next, in verses 20–23, we are taught four specific benefits of having the gospel of Jesus Christ in our lives and hearts.

20 But **that every man might speak in the name of God the Lord, even the Savior of the world**; [*including the privilege of having a testimony and speaking and teaching by the power of the Holy Ghost; see 2 Nephi 32:2–3*]

21 **That faith also might increase** in the earth;

22 **That mine everlasting covenant** [*the full gospel of Jesus Christ, with its truths, covenants, and ordinances*] **might be established**;

23 **That the fulness of my gospel might be proclaimed by the weak and the simple unto the ends of the world, and before kings and rulers.**

The phrase "the weak and the simple," in verse 23, above, is comforting. It is a reminder that one does not have to have advanced educational degrees or power and position in society to effectively preach and spread the gospel.

In the beginning of verse 24, next, the Savior reminds us again (as in verse 6) that this "preface" to the Doctrine and Covenants is given by His authority. Then, in verses 24–28, He goes on to give us five specific purposes of the Doctrine and Covenants. We will number these and point them out through the use of **underlined bold**.

24 Behold, **I am God and have spoken it; these commandments are of me**, and were given unto my servants in their weakness, after the manner of their language, **(1) that they might come to understanding** [*we must understand the gospel before we can live it and obtain its marvelous blessings*].

25 And **(2) inasmuch as they erred it might be made known** [*if we are in error, in actions or thoughts, we can't change unless we are taught correct doctrines and principles*];

26 And **(3) inasmuch as they sought wisdom they might be instructed** [*wisdom means, among other things, to make decisions in the present that will make a better future; those who desire to be wise need and desire instruction from wiser and higher sources*];

27 And **(4) inasmuch as they sinned they might be chastened** [*told what they are doing wrong*], **that they might repent** [*we can't repent and come unto Christ unless we are made aware of our sins*];

28 And **(5) inasmuch as they were humble they might be made strong, and blessed from on high, and receive knowledge from time to time** [*one of the great blessings of faithful membership in the Church is receiving on-going revelation, strength, and blessings from on high*].

Next, in verse 29, Jesus again bears record to us of Joseph Smith, His prophet, and bears witness that the Book of Mormon is true.

29 And after having received the record of the Nephites [*the gold plates*], yea, even **my servant Joseph Smith, Jun., might have power to translate** through the mercy of God, **by the power of God, the Book of Mormon**.

It would seem to this author that President Russell M. Nelson, with his world-wide contacts in the world of medicine, has played and continues to play a major role in fulfilling the prophecy given in verse 30, next; namely that the Church will be brought "forth out of obscurity." The word "obscure" means that few people know about it. Under President Nelson's direction, the Church has taken very significant strides in being widely known, not only for its missionary work, but also for its humanitarian aid and construction of temples.

Doctrine

Verse 30. The Church will continue going forth, becoming more and more prominent throughout the world.

30 And also those to whom these commandments were given, might have power to lay the foundation of this church, and to bring it forth out of obscurity and out of darkness, the only true and living [*having ongoing revelation and true priesthood authority, as well as the gift of the Holy Ghost*] **church upon the face of the whole earth**, with which I, the Lord, am well pleased, speaking unto the church collectively and not individually—

Verses 31–32, next, form a vital and beautiful "mini sermon." The Savior, in effect, tells us that while He "cannot look upon sin with the least degree of allowance," He can look upon sinners with a great degree of compassion because of His Atonement, if they repent.

Doctrine

Verses 31 and 32. Sin, itself, is, ultimately, completely unacceptable, as far as the eternal laws governing returning to God's presence are concerned. However, because of the Atonement of Christ, through proper repentance and living the gospel thereafter, sins can be forgiven completely and one can return to the presence of God completely sinless, pure, and clean.

31 For I the Lord cannot look upon sin with the least degree of allowance;

32 **Nevertheless, he that repents and does the commandments of the Lord** [*it is not enough to merely stop sinning, but we must start doing good, including keeping the commandments*] **shall be forgiven;**

Perhaps you've noticed, on occasion, that people who once had a testimony, but who turn to sin, lose much more than their testimony if they do not repent. They also lose the "light" in their countenance, as well as the light of gospel knowledge. They can hardly engage in a gospel conversation like they once could. It is as if something has been taken out of their soul. It has, according to verse 33, next.

Doctrine

Verse 33. It is possible to have one's testimony and gospel knowledge taken away.

33 And he that repents not, from him shall be taken even the light which he has received; for my Spirit shall not always strive with man, saith the Lord of Hosts.

> Next, in verse 34 and in the first part of verse 35, Jesus tells us again, as He did in verse 2, that He will make sure that all people, no matter who or where they are, will receive the opportunity to be taught the gospel. This counteracts a common false philosophy among some groups and cultures that some people, no matter what, will be held in higher position by the Lord than all others. This belief, often referred to as "predestination," seemed to be very prominent among the Jews at the time of Christ's ministry on earth. See Matthew 3:9.

Doctrine

Verses 34 and 35. The Lord considers all people to have equal worth and value, and thus all will ultimately have an equal opportunity to hear and understand the gospel of Jesus Christ before final judgment.

34 And again, verily I say unto you, O inhabitants of the earth: I the Lord am willing to make these things known unto all flesh [*all people*];

35 For **I am no respecter of persons** [*the Lord considers one person just as important as another; one soul is just as valuable as another*], and will that [*desire that*] all men shall know that **the day speedily cometh**; **the hour** is not yet [*in 1831, at the time of this revelation*], but **is nigh at hand, when peace shall be taken from the earth, and the devil shall have power over his own dominion**.

> The last lines of verse 35, above, combined with the first lines of verse 36, next, prophesy, in effect, that in the last days, there will not be much "gray area." It appears that people will have to choose sides. The devil will have great and wide-open power over his followers, and the humble followers of Christ will have great power and blessings come upon them. No one will be successful in stopping the progress of the Church and the blessings of God from coming upon His Saints (see also verse 5, above). People will either be swept along in the flood of evil, or they will become stronger and stronger in living the gospel. There will be little middle ground left.

36 And also **the Lord shall have power over his saints, and shall**

reign in their midst, and shall come down in judgment upon Idumea, or the world.

Finally, the Savior invites us to be nourished and strengthened by the revelations contained in the Doctrine and Covenants and promises that the Holy Ghost will attend those who study them. He also teaches the vital lesson that the words of His prophets are to be considered His own. A passage of scripture with the same basic message can be found in D&C 124:45–46.

37 **Search these commandments**, for they are true and faithful [*perhaps meaning that they will not disappoint nor let you down*], and **the prophecies and promises which are in them shall all be fulfilled**.

Doctrine

Verse 38. There is no difference in authority between the words of the Lord and the words of His authorized servants.

38 **What I the Lord have spoken, I have spoken, and I excuse not myself**; and though the heavens and the earth pass away, **my word shall not pass away, but shall all be fulfilled, whether by mine own voice or by the voice of my servants, it is the same.**

39 For behold, and lo, the Lord is God, and **the Spirit beareth record,** and **the record is true** [*the Savior is bearing His testimony directly to you and me*], and **the truth abideth** [*lasts*] **forever and ever** [*whereas false philosophies ultimately are exposed by truth and come to an end*]. Amen.

SECTION 2

Background

Chronologically, this section is the earliest in the Doctrine and Covenants and was given September 21, 1823, by the angel Moroni. Imagine how satisfying it must have been for Moroni to appear to Joseph Smith in 1823 and begin the great work of bringing forth the Book of Mormon after having waited approximately 1400 years (since he finished engraving on the gold plates and buried them In the Hill Cumorah about A.D. 421)!

On the evening of September 21, 1823 (about three and one-half years after the First Vision), as Joseph Smith, then seventeen, prayed for forgiveness of his sins and to learn his standing with God, Moroni appeared to him, telling him of the gold plates and showing him a vision of where they were deposited in the Hill Cumorah (see Joseph Smith—History 1:29–42). During this appearance, Moroni taught him much and quoted many scriptures, including the three verses that comprise this section of the Doctrine and Covenants.

As Joseph Smith tells us in Joseph Smith—History 1:36–39, Moroni quoted from Malachi 4:5–6, "but with a little variation from the way it reads in our Bibles" (Joseph Smith—History 1:36). In order for you to see the different wording used by Moroni, we will include Malachi 4:5–6 here, from the Bible, along with section 2 of the Doctrine and Covenants. We will use **bold** to point out some of the differences in Moroni's wording compared to the wording in the Bible. Then we will go through section 2 again and add some commentary.

D&C 2:1

1 **Behold, I will reveal unto you the Priesthood, by the hand of Elijah the prophet**, before the coming of the great and dreadful day of the Lord.

Malachi 4:5

5 Behold, I will send you Elijah the prophet before the coming of the great and dreadful day of the LORD:

D&C 2:2–3

2 And he shall **plant in the hearts of the children the promises made to the fathers**, and **the hearts of the children shall turn to their fathers.**

3 **If it were not so, the whole earth would be utterly wasted at his coming.**

Malachi 4:6

6 And he shall turn the heart of the fathers to the children, and the heart of the children to their fathers, lest I come and smite the earth with a curse.

Now, as stated above, we will go through section 2 again, adding some brief commentary.

The fulfillment of the promise given in D&C 2:1, next, took place on Easter Sunday, April 3, 1836, in the Kirtland Temple, as recorded in D&C 110. Elijah appeared to Joseph Smith and Oliver Cowdery and committed to them the priesthood keys of sealing families together for eternity.

Elder David A. Bednar, of the Quorum of the Twelve Apostles, explained who Elijah was and why he returned in our day:

"Elijah was an Old Testament prophet through whom mighty miracles were performed. He sealed the heavens, and no rain fell in ancient Israel for 3½ years. He multiplied a widow's meal and oil. He raised a young boy from the dead, and he called down fire from heaven in a challenge to the prophets of Baal. (See 1 Kings 17–18.) At the conclusion of Elijah's mortal ministry, he 'went up by a whirlwind into heaven' (2 Kings 2:11) and was translated.

"'We learn from latter-day revelation that Elijah held the sealing power of the Melchizedek Priesthood and was the last prophet to do so before the time of Jesus Christ' (Bible Dictionary, 'Elijah'). . . .

"Elijah appeared with Moses on the Mount of Transfiguration (see Matthew 17:3) and conferred this authority upon Peter, James, and John. Elijah appeared again with Moses and others on April 3, 1836, in the Kirtland Temple and conferred the same keys upon Joseph Smith and Oliver Cowdery" ("The Hearts of the Children Shall Turn," *Ensign* or *Liahona*, Nov. 2011, 24).

In the Bible Dictionary, in the back of our LDS Bible, under "Elijah," we are told the following (**bold** added for emphasis):

"We learn from latter-day revelation that **Elijah held the sealing power of the Melchizedek Priesthood** and was the last prophet to do so before the time of Jesus Christ. He appeared on the Mount in company with Moses (also translated) and conferred the keys of the priesthood on Peter, James, and John (Matt. 17:3). **He appeared again, in company with Moses and others, on April 3, 1836, in the Kirtland (Ohio) Temple and conferred the same keys upon Joseph Smith and Oliver Cowdery**. All of this was in preparation for the coming of the Lord, as spoken of in Malachi 4:5–6 (D&C 110:13–16). As demonstrated by his miraculous deeds, **the power of Elijah is the sealing power of the priesthood** by which things bound or loosed on earth are bound or loosed in heaven. Thus **the keys of this power are once again operative on the earth and are used in performing all the ordinances of the gospel for the living and the dead**."

Doctrine

Verses 1–3. The sealing power of the priesthood is necessary in order for ordinances, including eternal marriage, to be valid in eternity.

1 BEHOLD, I will reveal unto you the Priesthood [*the sealing keys and power of the Melchizedek Priesthood*], **by the hand of Elijah the prophet**, before the coming of the great and dreadful day of the Lord [*before the Second Coming of Christ with its accompanying tremendous and dreaded-by-the-wicked destruction*].

The change in wording given by Moroni for verse 2, next, indicates that in the last days people will have a great interest in studying and learning about their ancestors, which will be placed in the hearts of people by the Lord. Certainly, this is happening now, as people throughout the world respond to this desire to study their ancestry. Millions access the Church's family history website and come to family history centers to search for information about their family trees. This feeling in the heart is often referred to as "the Spirit of Elijah" and includes the desire among members of the Church to do the temple work for their ancestors.

In a Priesthood Genealogy Seminary, held in 1973, Harold B. Lee said that this uniting of families through the sealing keys restored by Elijah applies also to living families.

2 And **he** [*Elijah*] **shall plant in the hearts of the children the promises made to the fathers, and the hearts of the children shall turn to their fathers.**

Joseph Fielding Smith explained the phrase "the promises made to the fathers" in verse 2, above, as follows:

"This expression has reference to certain promises made to those who died without a knowledge of the Gospel, and without the opportunity of receiving the sealing ordinances of the Priesthood in matters pertaining to their exaltation. According to these promises, the children in the latter days are to perform all such ordinances in behalf of the dead" (*Improvement Era*, July 1922, 829–31).

President Russell M. Nelson of the Quorum of the Twelve Apostles explained what the promises or covenants were that God made with Abraham and others:

"The covenant God made with Abraham and later reaffirmed with Isaac and Jacob is of transcendent significance. It contained several promises, including

"• Jesus the Christ would be born through Abraham's lineage.

"• Abraham's posterity would be numerous, entitled to an eternal increase, and also entitled to bear the priesthood.

"• Abraham would become a father of many nations.

"• Certain lands would be inherited by his posterity.

"• All nations of the earth would be blessed by his seed.

"• And that covenant would be everlasting—even through 'a thousand generations' [*Deuteronomy 7:9; 1 Chronicles 16:15; Psalm 105:8*].

"Some of these promises have been fulfilled; others are still pending. . . .

". . . We have received, as did they of old, the holy priesthood and the everlasting gospel. We have the right to receive the fulness of the gospel, enjoy the blessings of the priesthood, and qualify for God's greatest blessing—that of eternal life.

"Some of us are the literal seed of Abraham; others are gathered into his family by adoption. The Lord makes no distinction. Together we receive these promised blessings—if we seek the Lord and obey His commandments" ("Covenants," *Ensign* or *Liahona*, Nov. 2011, 87–88).

Finally, in the last verse of section 2, we are taught how absolutely vital the sealing power of the Melchizedek Priesthood is as restored by Elijah. Without this, the earth would be "wasted" and would fail to fulfill its ultimate purpose. Among possible ways to interpret verse 3, next, we will consider one, as follows:

In Moses 1:39, the Lord tells us that His whole purpose is to "bring to pass the **immortality** and **eternal life** of man."

"Immortality" means living forever as a resurrected being. All who have ever lived or who will live as mortals will be resurrected because of Christ's resurrection and Atonement (see 1 Corinthians 15:22).

"Eternal life" means exaltation in the highest degree of glory in the celestial kingdom, which means living in the family unit forever (see D&C 131:1–4 and 132:19–20). Without the sealing power of the Melchizedek Priesthood, we could not be sealed together as families forever; therefore, we could not attain eternal life, which is exaltation. Thus, the "work and . . . glory" of God (Moses 1:39) would be frustrated, and the earth would fail to fulfill its purposes. In other words, as far as uniting families together eternally, the earth would be "wasted."

3 If it were not so [*if worthy families were not sealed together eternally through the sealing power of the priesthood*], **the whole earth would be utterly wasted at his coming.**

Joseph Smith taught the following concerning the message in verse 3, above:

"The greatest responsibility in this world that God has laid upon us is to seek after our dead. The Apostle says, 'They without us cannot be made perfect;' (Heb. 11:40) for it is necessary that the sealing power should be in our hands to seal our children and our dead for the fulness of the dispensation of times—a dispensation to meet the promises made by Jesus Christ before the foundation of the world for the salvation of man.

"Now, I will speak of them. I will meet Paul half way. I say to you,

Paul, you cannot be perfect without us. It is necessary that those who are going before and those who come after us should have salvation in common with us; and thus hath God made it obligatory upon man. Hence, God said, 'I will send you Elijah the prophet before the coming of the great and dreadful day of the Lord; and he shall turn the heart of the fathers to the children, and the heart of the children to their fathers, lest I come and smite the earth with a curse.' (*Mal. 4:5.*)" (*Teachings of the Prophet Joseph Smith,* 356).

SECTION 3

Background

This section was given in July 1828 at Harmony, Pennsylvania. In December 1827, Joseph Smith and his wife, Emma, had moved from the Palmyra, New York, area to Harmony, Pennsylvania, to the home of Emma's parents in order for Joseph to work on translating the gold plates in a peaceful environment. They soon purchased a small home nearby from Emma's brother, Jesse, which was located on 13 acres next to the Susquehanna River, where Joseph could continue the work. By this time, they were expecting their first of nine children.

In February 1828, Martin Harris, a prominent Palmyra businessman and friend of Joseph and his family, came and served as scribe for him as he translated. Martin's assistance was welcomed, and the work of translation went forward at a good pace. By June 14, 1828, they had 116 manuscript pages of translation written on what was called "foolscap" paper (roughly the dimensions of legal-sized paper today).

During the translation of the plates, Martin had asked Joseph if he could take the pages of translation to Palmyra, where he hoped to use them as evidence to stop the wagging tongues of his wife, Lucy, and others who had spread damaging rumors about him and his association with Joseph Smith. Being a highly respected citizen and a man of strict integrity, such reputation-damaging rumors and accusations, including that he had been deceived and had fallen under Joseph Smith's spell, were especially painful.

Joseph had asked the Lord about Martin's request through the Urim and Thummim. The Lord said not to give the pages to him. Martin persisted and asked a second time. Joseph asked the Lord again. The Lord turned down the request again. Now, with 116 pages of manuscript completed, Martin begged again, and Joseph asked the Lord for the third time, upon which he was told that Martin could take the 116 pages on the condition that he agree in writing to show them only to his "wife; his brother, Preserved Harris; his parents, Nathan and Rhoda Harris; and his wife's sister, Mary Harris Cobb (see *The Joseph Smith Papers, Documents, Volume 1: July 1828–June 1831*, ed. Michael Hubbard MacKay and others [2013], 6, footnote 25)." Martin joyfully agreed to these terms and left for Palmyra with the precious pages on June 14, 1828.

The next day, June 15, 1828, a baby boy was born to Joseph and Emma. The infant died that same day, and it was two weeks before Emma was out of danger of dying herself from the difficulties of the birth. During these trying days, Joseph stayed faithfully by her side, doing all he could to nurse her back to health. After two weeks, Emma asked if Martin had returned with the 116 pages. He hadn't. Emma was concerned, and after another week, she assured Joseph that she would be all right. She encouraged him to go to Palmyra in search of Martin and the manuscript.

Joseph left for Palmyra (actually, his parents lived in Manchester, a smaller community next to Palmyra), and upon arriving at his parents' home, sent for Martin, who lived in Palmyra. After several hours, Martin finally came, and in a traumatic scene, he explained to Joseph that the 116 pages were lost.

With a heavy heart, the young Prophet Joseph Smith returned to Harmony. There, he was met by Moroni, who took the plates and the Urim and Thummim. Shortly, the angel appeared again and gave him the Urim and Thummim, through which he received what we know as section 3 of the Doctrine and Covenants, after which Moroni took the Urim and Thummim and left.

With this as a brief background, perhaps you can understand and feel the deep impact of the lesson Joseph Smith was taught by the Lord in this revelation. As difficult as it was, Joseph learned his lesson well and never again went against the instructions of God.

By the way, this section goes with section 10. At the time section 10 was given, the gold plates and the Urim and Thummim had been returned to Joseph Smith, and he was privileged to continue the work of translation. We will discuss that background further when we get there.

There are many possible lessons for us to learn from section 3, including

1. The aftermath of disobedience to God is ugly.
2. Don't question or go against the counsel of the Lord.
3. Don't yield to peer pressure, no matter how convincing the argument, if it goes counter to God's counsel (verses 6–7).
4. Through obedience and faithfulness, we can have the help

of God in all times of trouble (verse 8).

5. God is patient and merciful and still wants us to succeed, even when we have slipped up (verse 10).

6. The definition of "wicked" doesn't always mean deeply evil (verses 12–13).

We will now go through this section verse by verse. Remember as you read that the Prophet Joseph is receiving this through the Urim and Thummim and that he has been brought to the depths of despair and humility by the loss of the 116 manuscript pages.

1 **THE works, and the designs** [*plans*], **and the purposes of God cannot be frustrated** [*stopped*], neither can they come to naught [*nothing*].

2 For **God doth not walk in crooked paths** [*implying, "like you have done, Joseph"*], neither doth he turn to the right hand nor to the left, neither doth he vary from that which he hath said [*He keeps His word*], therefore his paths are straight, and **his course is one eternal round**.

The phrase "one eternal round," as used in verse 2, above, basically means "the same," or, "God is always reliable; you can trust Him, depend on Him." An expanded definition could be that God always uses the same laws, principles, covenants, and ordinances to do His work of making exaltation available to His mortal children. Another way to look at it might be that you can always depend on God, just as you can depend on the exactness of an unvaried course, if you are going around a perfect circle. Yet another way to look at it might be that God uses the same plan of salvation for each "round" of creation, or each world to which He sends a group of His spirit children.

3 Remember, remember that **it is not the work of God that is frustrated** [*stopped; interfered with*], **but the work of men**;

One thing we can learn from verse 3, above, is that by following God, we will always succeed, but when we detour and follow the ways of man, we will be frustrated or, in other words, stopped in achieving our eternal goals.

Next, in verse 4, we see a number of paths that can take us away from God.

4 For although a man may have many revelations [*such as you, Joseph, have had, including the First Vision*], and have power to do many mighty works, yet **if he boasts in his own strength**, and **sets at naught** [*ignores*] **the counsels of God**, and **follows after the dictates of his own will** [*makes*

his own rules; does what he wants to] **and carnal desires** [*influenced by cares of the world*], he must fall and incur the vengeance of a just God upon him [*in other words, the punishment he brings upon himself is fair*].

5 Behold**, you have been entrusted with these things** [*the gold plates, the Urim and Thummim, the work of translating, and so on*], but **how strict were your commandments**; and remember also the promises which were made to you, if you did not transgress them.

In verse 5, above, the Lord refers to "strict" commandments that had been given to Joseph Smith. Among other things, we understand these to refer to Moroni's instructions to the Prophet as he told him about the gold plates and eventually turned them over to him. We will include three verses here that contain some of these commandments and warnings:

Joseph Smith—History 1:42, 46, and 59

42 Again, **he told me, that when I got those plates** of which he had spoken—for the time that they should be obtained was not yet fulfilled—**I should not show them to any person; neither the breastplate with the Urim and Thummim; only to those to whom I should be commanded to show them; if I did I should be destroyed**. While he was conversing with me about the plates, the vision was opened to my mind that I could see the place where the plates were deposited, and that so clearly and distinctly that I knew the place again when I visited it.

46 By this time, so deep were the impressions made on my mind, that sleep had fled from my eyes, and I lay overwhelmed in astonishment at what I had both seen and heard. But what was my surprise when again I beheld the same messenger at my bedside, and heard him rehearse or repeat over again to me the same things as before; and **added a caution to me**, telling me that **Satan would try to tempt me** (in consequence of the indigent circumstances [*poor financial status*] of my father's family), **to get the plates for the purpose of getting rich**. This he forbade me, saying that I must have no other object in view in getting the plates but to glorify God, and **must not be influenced by any other motive than that of building his kingdom**; otherwise I could not get them.

59 At **length the time arrived for obtaining the plates**, the Urim and Thummim, and the breastplate. On the twenty-second day of September, one thousand eight hundred and twenty-seven, having gone as usual at the end of another year to the place where they were deposited, **the same heavenly messenger delivered them up to me with this charge**: that I should be responsible for them; that **if I should let them go carelessly, or through any neglect of mine, I should be cut off**; but that if I would use all my endeavors to preserve them, until he, the messenger, should call for them, they should be protected.

We will now return to the text of section 3. These verses are certainly a lesson in parenting. The Lord is telling His young prophet the truth, with love and strictness, and with no room for misunderstanding. Yet these verses are leading up to the tenderness and encouragement of verse 10.

6 And behold, **how oft you have transgressed the commandments and the laws of God, and have gone on in the persuasions of men** [*the ways of the world*].

Verse 7, next, contains a strong warning against yielding to negative peer pressure.

7 For, behold, **you should not have feared man more than God**. Although men set at naught [*ignore*] the counsels of God, and despise his words—

8 Yet **you should have been faithful**; and **he would have extended his arm and supported you against all the fiery darts of the adversary**; and **he would have been with you in every time of trouble**.

Perhaps one important lesson we learn from verse 8, above, is that we won't be spared from trials and troubles in this life, but through faithfulness to God, we can receive His support as we go through them.

The people of Alma provide us with an example of this kind of support from God as follows:

Mosiah 24:14–15

14 And **I will also ease the burdens which are put upon your shoulders, that even you cannot feel them** upon your backs, even while you are in bondage; and this will I do that ye may stand as witnesses for me hereafter, and that ye may know of a surety that I, the Lord God, do visit my people in their afflictions.

15 And now it came to pass that **the burdens which were laid**

upon Alma and his brethren were made light; yea, the Lord did strengthen them that they could bear up their burdens with ease, and **they did submit cheerfully and with patience** to all the will of the Lord.

We return now to section 3. Notice the encouragement given in verses 9 and 10, as well as the warning in verse 11.

9 Behold, thou art Joseph, and thou wast chosen to do the work of the Lord, but because of transgression**, if thou art not aware thou wilt fall.**

Doctrine

Verse 10. God is merciful. (This may sound too simple, but some religions and people teach that God is only a God of justice, vengeance, and punishment.)

10 But **remember, God is merciful**; **therefore, repent** of that which thou hast done which is contrary to the commandment which I gave you, **and thou art still chosen, and art again called to the work**;

11 **Except thou do this, thou shalt be delivered up and become as other men, and have no more gift**.

Perhaps this is a good place to pause and consider another lesson we can learn from the above verses, combined with some of the history behind both sections 3 and 10 of the Doctrine and Covenants, which deal with the loss of the 116 manuscript pages.

The lesson is that wise parents do not always immediately restore privileges lost by disobedient children. There is wisdom in letting them go without for a period of time, during which growth and internal change can take place. It appears that the Lord used this approach on Joseph Smith at this point in the restoring of the gospel.

Rather than immediately restoring the privilege and responsibility of translating the gold plates, the Lord gave him hope and encouragement in verses 9 and 10, above, but made him wait to actually begin the work again, without knowing when the gift of translating would be restored.

Remember that the section we are studying, section 3, was given in July 1828. As mentioned previously, it was at this time that the angel took the gold plates and the Urim and Thummim from Joseph in consequence of the loss of the 116 pages. The Prophet's mother, Lucy Mack Smith, informs us that the angel returned the plates and Urim and Thummim to him on September 22, 1828. We read this in *History of Joseph Smith, by His Mother, Lucy Mack Smith*, chapter 26. Section 10 of the Doctrine and Covenants was given to the Prophet in conjunction with returning to him the privilege of translating. As you can see in the heading to section 10 in the 2013 edition of the Doctrine and Covenants, section 10 was received "likely around April, 1829, though portions may have been received as early as the summer of 1828." In section 10, Joseph is instructed on how to proceed with the translation. We will turn to his mother's account for the details, beginning with her record of what happened after Joseph found out that Martin Harris had lost the 116 manuscript pages and had returned home to Harmony, Pennsylvania. We will continue to use **bold** for teaching purposes.

> ***History of Joseph Smith by His Mother, Lucy Mack Smith*, chapter 26.**
> "On leaving you," said Joseph, "I returned immediately home. Soon after my arrival, I commenced humbling myself in mighty prayer before the Lord, and, as I was pouring out my soul in supplication to God, that if possible I might obtain mercy at his hands and be forgiven of all that I had done contrary to his will, an angel stood before me, and answered me, saying, that I had sinned in delivering the manuscript into the hands of a wicked man, and, as I had ventured to become responsible for his faithfulness, I would of necessity have to suffer the consequences of his indiscretion, and I must now give up the Urim and Thummim into his (the angel's) hands.
>
> "This I did as I was directed, and as I handed them to him, he remarked, '**If you are very humble and penitent, it may be you will receive them again; if so, it will be on the twenty-second of next September.**'"

The Prophet's mother gives additional commentary and then continues by saying that she will now continue with Joseph's account of what happened.

> "After the angel left me," said he, "I continued my supplications to God, without cessation, and **on the twenty-second of September, I had the joy and satisfaction of again receiving the Urim and Thummim**, with which I have again commenced translating, and Emma writes for me, but the angel said that the Lord would send me a scribe, and I trust his promise will be verified. The

angel seemed pleased with me when he gave me back the Urim and Thummim, and **he told me that the Lord loved me, for my faithfulness and humility."**

We will now continue with section 3. Next, the Lord will give us a definition of a "wicked man." There are certainly additional lessons for us here. We will use **bold** to point out this definition.

12 And when thou deliveredst up that which God had given thee sight and power to translate [*in other words, the 116 manuscript pages*], thou deliveredst up that which was sacred into the hands of **a wicked man** [*referring to Martin Harris*],

13 Who has **set at naught the counsels of God**, and has **broken the most sacred promises** which were made before God, and has **depended upon his own judgment** and **boasted in his own wisdom**.

14 And this is the reason that thou hast lost thy privileges **for a season**—

15 For thou hast suffered [*allowed*] the counsel of thy director to be trampled upon from the beginning.

16 **Nevertheless** [*in spite of what you have done*], **my work shall go forth**, for inasmuch as [*since*] the knowledge of a Savior has come unto the world, through the testimony of the Jews [*through the Bible*], even so shall the knowledge of a Savior come unto **my people**—

As you can see, there is a dash at the end of verse 16, and again at the end of verse 17. This alerts us to the fact that verse 17 contains the definition for "my people." The people spoken of in verse 17 are all Book of Mormon people and were descendants of Nephi and his younger brothers, Jacob and Joseph, plus Zoram, who was Laban's servant. Thus, in this context, "my people" means the descendants of the Book of Mormon people who live in these latter days.

17 And to the Nephites, and the Jacobites, and the Josephites, and the Zoramites, through the testimony of their fathers [*ancestors, such as Lehi, Sariah, Nephi, Jacob, Alma, and so on*]—

In verse 18, next, the Lord refers to the descendants of Laman, Lemuel, and Ishmael. We usually refer to these people as Lamanites. In this verse, the Lord gives a brief review of the Book of Mormon, in which the Nephites were destroyed by the Lamanites.

18 And this testimony [*the Book of Mormon*] shall come to the knowledge of the Lamanites, and the Lemuelites, and the Ishmaelites, who dwindled in unbelief because of the iniquity [*wickedness*] of their fathers, whom the Lord has suffered [*allowed*] to destroy their brethren the Nephites, because of their [*the Nephites'*] iniquities and their abominations [*extreme wickedness*].

19 And for this very purpose are these plates [*the gold plates*] preserved, which contain these records [*the account of the Lord's dealings with the peoples of the Western Hemisphere*]—that the promises of the Lord might be fulfilled, which he made to his people [*the Book of Mormon people*];

Next, the Lord gives specific things that reading and studying the Book of Mormon can do for the Lamanites. You will see many benefits for you also.

Doctrine

Verse 20. The Lamanites will come to know of God's dealings with their ancestors and of God's promises to them today.

20 And that the Lamanites might come to the knowledge of their fathers [*ancestors*], and that they might **know the promises of the Lord**, and that they may **believe the gospel** and **rely upon the merits of Jesus Christ** [*rely upon the Atonement of Christ and His gospel*], and **be glorified** [*receive exaltation in celestial glory; see footnote 20e, which refers to Moroni 7:26, where "sons of God" means exaltation, as explained in the Topical Guide*] **through faith in his name**, and **that through their repentance they might be saved**. Amen.

SECTION 4

Background

According to *The Joseph Smith Papers* publications, Joseph Smith Sr. and his son Samuel traveled from their home near Palmyra, New York, to Harmony, Pennsylvania, in January, 1829, to visit Joseph Smith Jr. and his wife, Emma. During this visit, Joseph's Father asked for a revelation concerning his possible role in God's work. (See *The Joseph Smith Papers, Documents, Volume 1: July 1828–June 1831*, ed. Michael Hubbard MacKay and others [2013], 5.)

While Father Smith was there, the Lord did indeed give him a revelation through his son, Joseph. This is the first recorded revelation given by the Lord to another person, through Joseph Smith, the

Prophet. Later in the Doctrine and Covenants, we will study many such revelations given to individuals by the Lord through the Prophet Joseph Smith.

During the years since the First Vision in the spring of 1820, Joseph's father had supported him despite severe persecution. On the evening of September 21, 1823, Moroni appeared to the seventeen-year-old Joseph Smith Jr., telling him of the gold plates buried in Hill Cumorah and teaching him of the important work he was to do. The angel appeared two more times that night and again the next day, at which time Joseph was instructed to tell his father all that had transpired during Moroni's visit. He did so, and his father replied, saying to him "that it was of God, and told me to go and do as commanded by the messenger." (See Joseph Smith—History 1:49–50.)

It must have been a tender scene as the young Prophet Joseph gave this revelation from the Savior to his father, Joseph Smith Sr. In it we find counsel and instruction which readily applies to all of us.

Verse 1 of section 4 is very similar to verse 1 of sections 6, 11, 12, and 14. It is a major theme at this point of the Restoration. The "marvelous work" spoken of is "about to come forth." It hasn't come forth yet, but is right on the threshold. The translation of the gold plates has been slowed since the loss of the 116 pages by Martin Harris but will move along rapidly once Oliver Cowdery arrives on the scene in early April 1829. The translation will be completed in late June 1829. It will be published and available for sale by March 26, 1830.

The Church is not yet organized but will be on April 6, 1830. Thus, indeed, at this point in Church history, "a marvelous work is about to come forth." We will continue to use **bold** for teaching emphasis.

1 NOW behold, **a marvelous work is about to come forth** among the children of men [*among the people of the earth*].

Verse 2, while given to Joseph Smith Sr., certainly applies to all of us. There are many things we can learn from it, including that we need to be one hundred percent committed to the Lord. A partial commitment won't do. Another thing is the comforting fact that our best is good enough to enable us to be free of sin on the final day of judgment.

Doctrine

Verse 2. If we do our best in serving God, we will indeed be made free from sin and thus stand clean and pure before the Savior on the day of final judgment. In other words, because of our best

effort, coupled with the Savior's Atonement, we will be worthy to enter celestial glory. Our best will be good enough.

2 Therefore, O ye that embark [*go forth*] **in the service of God**, see that ye **serve him with all** your **heart**, **might**, **mind** and **strength**, **that ye may stand blameless before God at the last day** [*final Judgment Day*].

In conjunction with verse 2, above, perhaps you have noticed that some people are afflicted with what might be termed "the re-deciding syndrome." In other words, their commitment to the Lord and to the Church, their covenants, and so on, are not one hundred percent. As a result, they find themselves constantly "re-deciding" whether or not to go to church, whether or not to pay tithing, minister to their assigned families, read scriptures, avoid inappropriate media, movies, music, and so on. Such "re-deciding" promotes stagnation, stifles progress, and causes instability.

3 Therefore, **if ye have desires to serve God ye are called to the work**;

The question sometimes arises with respect to verse 3, above, as to whether or not it refers to formal callings in the Church, including full-time missionaries, or what? As you have no doubt noticed, proper interpretation of verses of scripture depends on the context in which the verse is found.

In this case, there is no Church yet at this time In Church history. The priesthood has not been restored yet. There are no formal callings in the Church yet. The context is that of missionary work. The "field is white, already to harvest" (verse 4).

George Albert Smith, who later became the eighth president of the Church, explained that this verse applies to missionary work as follows:

"It is not necessary for you to be called to go into the mission field in order to proclaim the truth. Begin on the man who lives next door by inspiring confidence in him, by inspiring love in him for you because of your righteousness, and your missionary work has already begun" (In Conference Report, Oct. 1916, 50–51).

Verse 4, next, can be seen as the beginning of the fulfillment of the prophecy given in Daniel 2:35, 44–45, which foretells the spreading of the gospel to fill the whole earth. The "field is white," meaning ready to harvest. The grain (the "wheat," symbolic of faithful converts) is ready to be harvested and brought into the Lord's "barn." See Matthew 13:24–30, which is the parable of the wheat and the tares, and in which "barn" symbolizes the Church and kingdom of

God—ultimately, celestial glory.

Verse 4 also explains the reward of personal salvation that comes to those who faithfully help with the "harvest" of souls by bringing people to Christ, who brings them to the Father.

4 For behold **the field is white already to harvest**; and lo, **he that thrusteth in his sickle** [*a cutting tool, used anciently to harvest grain*] **with his might**, the same layeth up in store [*stores up personal blessings*] that he perisheth not [*spiritually*], but **bringeth salvation to his soul**;

There are many possible approaches to studying verses 5 and 6, next. First, we will **bold** the personal qualities we need to develop in order to successfully "thrust in [our] sickle" in the latter-day harvesting of souls.

5 And **faith**, **hope, charity** and **love**, with an **eye single to the glory of God** [*having pure motives, not doing it for personal profit or gain*], qualify him for the work.

6 Remember **faith, virtue, knowledge, temperance, patience, brotherly kindness, godliness, charity, humility, diligence**.

Next, we will go through verses 5 and 6 again, this time adding a bit more commentary.

5 And **faith** [*a principle of action, doing; actual movement on our part*], **hope** [*optimism, confidence that there is good in people, and that there will be some who will listen; also, humble confidence in ourselves, that we can do the work, with the help of the Lord*], **charity and love** [*inspired, Christlike love for people, which radiates from the member-missionary and touches hearts*], **with an eye single to the glory of God** [*while there are many personal benefits to those who share the gospel, the chief motivation for sharing it should be bringing joy to God*], **qualify him for the work**.

6 Remember **faith** [*keeps us trying when otherwise we might give up*], **virtue** [*personal purity; uplifting thoughts about others*], **knowledge** [*of the doctrines and principles of the gospel, plan of salvation, and so on*], **temperance** [*self-control; using wisdom*], **patience** [*it often requires much patience over long periods of time to bring people to Christ*], **brotherly kindness** [*kind acts are often the very best method of "preaching"*], **godliness** [*trying our best to reflect God in our behaviors and thoughts*], **charity** [*"the pure love of Christ"—see Moroni 7:47*], **humility** [*the opposite of arrogance and the "holier than thou" attitude which quickly alienates others*], **diligence** [*wise persistence;*

not giving up; missionary work often requires hard work].

Finally, we will go through verses 5 and 6 one more time, pointing out another possible lesson learned from them. One of the wonderful things about studying and restudying the scriptures is that there are many different messages imbedded in them. One time we see this message. Another time through, we see that message. The Holy Ghost inspires and directs our minds and hearts such that, over a lifetime of study, we can receive a multitude of personal instructions and messages from the same passage of scripture.

This time through verses 5 and 6, we will point out that verse 5 emphasizes personal qualities needed in order for us to do the work. Verse 6 emphasizes "people skills," or, in other words, how to work successfully with others in promoting and furthering the work of the Lord. Another way to put it might be to say that verse 6 shows us how to lead others in a Christlike way. You can come up with many more definitions, as well as counsel for leaders, from the words in verse 6.

5 And faith, hope, charity and love, with an eye single to the glory of God, **qualify him** for the work.

6 Remember **faith** [*in others*], **virtue** [*so that others will respect you*], **knowledge** [*so that others can look up to you, trust you, and so that you can teach them correctly*], **temperance** [*not given to wild mood swings, etc., that destroy confidence in leaders*], **patience** [*allowing people to fail and try again until they succeed*], **brotherly kindness** [*is felt as much or more than observed; instills confidence in followers*], **godliness** [*when they watch you, they understand God better*], **charity** [*radiates to and encourages others; gives them strength to succeed*], **humility** [*helps people want to follow you; they know you know you are not perfect*], **diligence** [*they know you are going to keep helping them until they succeed; thus they are less likely to give up*].

In verse 7, next, the Lord exemplifies verses 5 and 6, above. He encourages Joseph Smith Sr., as well as all of us, to turn constantly to Him. In other words, He says, "Turn to Me and I will help you. Thus, your work will become My work."

They are strong words of assurance.

Doctrine

Verse 7. Action is often required on our part to access God's help.

7 **Ask**, and ye shall **receive**; **knock**, and it shall be **opened** unto you. Amen.

SECTION 5

Background

This revelation was given to the Prophet Joseph Smith at the request of Martin Harris. About 7–8 months before, Martin had lost the 116 manuscript pages. Now, in March 1829, several months after the angel had returned the plates and the Urim and Thummim to Joseph, Harris came to Harmony, Pennsylvania, to visit the Prophet and to request the privilege of seeing the gold plates (see verses 1 and 24).

Many years ago, when I was first studying the background and history of this section of the Doctrine and Covenants and realized that Martin Harris had actually come back to make such a request, I was appalled that he would be so bold as to return to where he had caused so much trouble and heartache, let alone make such a request.

However, as I thought about it, my heart changed, and I found myself grateful that Martin Harris had returned. I realized that all of us make mistakes and that each of us can humble ourselves, come back, and receive rich blessings precluded by previous behaviors. I became aware of a tremendous lesson to be found in section 5; namely that the Savior is infinitely forgiving. He will counsel, instruct, help, and offer the previously lost blessings again.

Much of the instruction in section 5 is to Joseph Smith, telling him just what to say to Martin (starting with verse 2). As you can understand, this was a kindness of the Lord to Joseph, who was in a rather awkward situation with this influential friend of the Smith family. Harris was a prominent Palmyra businessman, who was 23 years older than the young Prophet, and who had provided substantial financial help and support that had significantly helped Joseph to proceed with the work.

First, in verse 1, we see that a major purpose of Martin's visit was to actually verify that Joseph had the gold plates.

1 BEHOLD, I say unto you, that
as my servant **Martin Harris has
desired a witness** at my hand,
**that you, my servant Joseph
Smith, Jun., have got the plates**
of which you have testified and
borne record that you have received of me;

2 And now, behold, **this shall you
say unto him—he who spake
unto you, said unto you** [*in other
words, in effect, tell him that I told you
to tell him . . .*]: I, the Lord, am God,
and have given these things unto
you, **my servant** [*a kind reassurance to Joseph of his standing with the
Lord*] **Joseph Smith, Jun.**, and have
commanded you that you should
stand as a witness of these things;

3 And I have caused you that you should enter into **a covenant** with me, **that you should not show them except to those persons to whom I commanded you**; and **you have no power over them except** [*unless*] **I grant it unto you**.

4 And **you have a gift to translate the plates**; and this is the first gift that I bestowed upon you; and I have commanded that you should **pretend to no other gift until my purpose is fulfilled in this**; for I will grant unto you **no other gift until it** [*the translation of the Book of Mormon plates*] **is finished**.

Remember that these are the things the Lord told Joseph to tell Martin (verse 2). The Lord is showing kindness here in helping Martin understand why Joseph is under such strict covenant and obligation not to show anyone the plates unless commanded to do so by the Lord Himself.

In addition, Joseph himself is being taught and reminded of the importance of the work of translating and how vital strict obedience is on his part.

Next, in verses 5–7, both Joseph and Martin are reminded of the tremendous importance of this work of translation for the whole world! It is preliminary to much more that will take place in the restoration of the gospel.

Doctrine

Verse 5. Trouble and woe are the natural aftermath of refusal to obey God's commandments.

5 Verily, I say unto you, that woe shall come unto the inhabitants of the earth if they will not hearken unto [*listen to and obey*] **my words**;

6 For **hereafter** [*after you finish the translation*] **you shall be ordained** [*including being ordained an apostle; see footnote 6a, which refers to D&C 20:2*] **and go forth and deliver my words unto the children of men** [*a scriptural term meaning "people"*].

7 Behold, **if they will not believe my words** [*contained in the Book of Mormon*], **they would not believe you**, my servant Joseph, if it were possible that you should show them all these things [*including the gold plates and the Urim and Thummim*] which I have committed unto you.

8 Oh, this unbelieving and stiffnecked [*prideful; not humble; not teachable*] generation—mine anger is kindled against them.

9 Behold, verily I say unto you, I have reserved those things which I have entrusted unto you, my

servant Joseph, for a wise purpose in me, and it shall be made known unto future generations [*perhaps meaning, among other things, that great numbers in future generations will understand the importance of the Book of Mormon*];

Sometimes, members of the Church wonder why the Lord does not seem to reveal spectacular new doctrines through our modern prophets. The answer seems to be given in verse 10; namely, that He has already revealed the doctrines through the Prophet Joseph Smith. The emphasis in the revelations to our modern "prophets, seers, and revelators" is more how to implement the plan of salvation and save souls rather than the revealing of new doctrine.

Doctrine

Verse 10. Joseph Smith was the prophet chosen by the Lord to restore the doctrines of the gospel in the last days.

10 **But this generation shall have my word through you** [*Joseph Smith*];

Verse 11, next, must have quickly gained Martin's full attention. Three special witnesses were to be called by the Lord, who would be shown the things Martin desired to see.

11 And in addition to your [*Joseph Smith's*] testimony, **the testimony of three** of my servants, whom I shall call and ordain, **unto whom I will show these things** [*the things mentioned in D&C 17:1*], and they [*the words of testimony from these three witnesses*] shall go forth with my words [*especially the Book of Mormon*] that are given through you [*Joseph Smith*].

Next, the Lord gives additional details as to the special witness that will be given to the three men chosen to be witnesses to the Book of Mormon. In verse 12 we learn that Jesus will personally bear witness of these things to them from heaven.

12 Yea, **they** [*the Three Witnesses*] **shall know of a surety that these things are true**, for **from heaven will I declare it unto them**.

Next, Joseph and Martin are told that these three witnesses will literally see the things being spoken of. In D&C 17:1, we are informed that "these things" were the gold plates, breastplate, sword of Laban, Urim and Thummim, and the Liahona.

13 I will give them power that **they may behold** [*see*] and **view these things** as they are;

14 And **to none else will I grant this power, to receive this same testimony among this generation**,

in this the beginning of the rising up and the coming forth of my church out of the wilderness [*symbolic of the earth without the gospel*]—clear as the moon, and fair as the sun, and terrible as an army with banners [*symbolizing that none will stop the coming forth and spreading of the restored gospel*].

15 And **the testimony of three witnesses** will I send forth of [*as a witness for*] my word.

> Next, the Lord teaches that He will also bear witness, through the Holy Ghost, to all who will believe in the Book of Mormon. This same promise obviously applies to all His words, in other scriptures as well as through His living prophets today.

Doctrine

Verse 16. Baptism and confirmation are prerequisites to being truly "born again."

16 And behold, **whosoever believeth on my words, them will I visit with the manifestation of my Spirit**; and they shall be born of me, even of water and of the Spirit [*in other words, they will be baptized and receive the gift of the Holy Ghost, through which they will then be spiritually reborn*]—

17 And **you must wait yet a little while** [*for baptism, etc.*], for ye are not yet ordained [*you don't yet have the priesthood authority necessary*]—

18 And **their** [*the three special witnesses*] **testimony shall also go forth** unto the condemnation of [*will stand as a witness against*] this generation if they harden their hearts against them;

> The first half of verse 19, next, speaks of a devastating plague, which could easily include the withdrawal of the Spirit. The last half of the verse give us a clue as to how the wicked will be destroyed at the Second Coming of Christ.

Doctrine

Verse 19. At the Second Coming, the wicked will be destroyed by the glory of Christ as He comes. Their physical bodies cannot survive the full glory of the Savior at that time.

19 For **a desolating scourge** [*perhaps meaning spiritual sickness, which is the worst plague of all*] **shall go forth among the inhabitants of the earth**, and shall continue to be poured out from time to time, if they repent not, until the earth is empty, **and the inhabitants thereof are consumed away and utterly**

destroyed by the brightness of my coming.

As you just read at the end of verse 19, above, we are told that the wicked will be burned by the glory of the coming of Christ. They will not be able to withstand His presence as He comes in full glory, which will be the case at the Second Coming. Second Nephi tells us the same thing as follows:

2 Nephi 12:10, 19, 21

10 O ye wicked ones, enter into the rock, and hide thee in the dust, for the fear of the Lord and the glory of his majesty shall smite thee.

19 And they shall go into the holes of the rocks, and into the caves of the earth, for the fear of the Lord shall come upon them and **the glory of his majesty shall smite them**, when he ariseth to shake terribly the earth.

21 To go into the clefts of the rocks, and into the tops of the ragged rocks, for the fear of the Lord shall come upon them and the majesty of **his glory shall smite them**, when he ariseth to shake terribly the earth.

We will now return to Doctrine and Covenants, section 5. The Savior, in effect, is telling us that just as the inhabitants of Jerusalem were warned of coming destruction, so also the inhabitants of the world are being warned, and everything prophesied will come to pass.

20 Behold, **I tell you these things, even as I also told the people of the destruction of Jerusalem**; and **my word shall be verified** at this time as it hath hitherto been verified.

Next, the Lord gives Joseph Smith a strong commandment to do better, still using tender terminology ("my servant Joseph") as He does so.

21 And now I command you, my servant Joseph, to repent and **walk more uprightly** before me, and to yield to the persuasions of men no more [*certainly a strong reference, perhaps among other things, to his previous giving in to Martin Harris concerning the 116 pages*];

22 And that you **be firm in keeping the commandments** wherewith I have commanded you; and **if** you do this, behold I grant unto you eternal life [*exaltation*]**, even if you should be slain.**

We can learn more from verse 22, above. For one thing, some people have come to believe that if you were to see the Father or the Son, it is evidence that you are saved. We see here that

Joseph Smith does not yet have his calling and election made sure. In other words, he does not yet have his exaltation in celestial glory assured, even though he has seen both the Father and the Son, as well as Moroni, and several other angels. At this point in the Prophet's life, there is still an "if." By the way, in D&C 132:49, Joseph Smith will be told that his exaltation is assured.

Another thing we see here, in verse 22 (in the last phrase), is a strong hint that the Prophet will eventually give his life for the gospel.

Next, the instruction turns again from Joseph to Martin Harris. In His mercy, the Savior specifically gives Martin another chance, spelling out in considerable detail what he must do in order to qualify for the witness he desires.

23 **And now**, again, **I speak** unto you, my servant Joseph, **concerning the man** [*Martin Harris*] **that desires the witness**—

24 Behold, I say unto him, **he exalts himself** [*he is still afflicted with pride and arrogance*] and **does not humble himself sufficiently** before me; **but if he will bow down before me, and humble himself in mighty prayer and faith, in the sincerity of his heart, then will I grant unto him a view of the things which he desires to see.**

Having given Martin such tremendous and merciful encouragement, the Lord next gives strict instructions as to what he is to say by way of bearing witness to the Book of Mormon. He is to "say no more" (verse 26) than what he is told to say. Perhaps this is another chance for him to show strict obedience to the Lord's instruction, rather than giving in to his tendency to make his own rules.

25 And **then he shall** say unto the people of this generation: Behold, **I have seen the things which the Lord hath shown unto Joseph Smith, Jun.**, and **I know of a surety that they are true**, for **I have seen them**, for **they have been shown unto me by the power of God and not of man**.

26 And **I the Lord command him**, my servant Martin Harris, **that he shall say no more** unto them concerning these things, except he shall say: I have seen them, and they have been shown unto me by the power of God; and **these are the words which he shall say**.

We will pause here for a moment and turn to the Testimony of the Three Witnesses in the introductory pages of the Book of Mormon. Note how strictly Martin Harris and the other two witnesses (Oliver Cowdery and David Whitmer) held to this instruction from the Lord. We will use **bold** to point things out.

THE TESTIMONY OF THREE WITNESSES

BE IT KNOWN unto all nations, kindreds, tongues, and people, unto whom this work shall come: That **we**, through the grace of God the Father, and our Lord Jesus Christ, **have seen the plates** which contain this record, which is a record of the people of Nephi, and also of the Lamanites, their brethren, and also of the people of Jared, who came from the tower of which hath been spoken. And we also know that they have been translated by the gift and power of God, for his voice hath declared it unto us; wherefore **we know of a surety that the work is true**. And **we also testify that we have seen** the engravings which are upon the plates; and **they have been shown unto us by the power of God, and not of man**. And we declare with words of soberness, that an angel of God came down from heaven, and he brought and laid before our eyes, that we beheld and saw the plates, and the engravings thereon; and we know that it is by the grace of God the Father, and our Lord Jesus Christ, that **we beheld and bear record that these things are true**. And it is marvelous in our eyes. Nevertheless, the voice of the Lord commanded us that we should bear record of it; wherefore, to be obedient unto the commandments of God, **we bear testimony of these things**. And we know that if we are faithful in Christ, we shall rid our garments of the blood of all men, and be found spotless before the judgment-seat of Christ, and shall dwell with him eternally in the heavens. And the honor be to the Father, and to the Son, and to the Holy Ghost, which is one God. Amen.

OLIVER COWDERY
DAVID WHITMER
MARTIN HARRIS

We will now return to section 5. In verses 27–29, Joseph is told what to do and say if Martin Harris fails to comply with the strict instructions just given by the Lord.

27 But **if he deny this he will break the covenant** which he has before covenanted with me, **and** behold, **he is condemned** [*stopped in progress toward returning to live with God forever*].

In the instructions given for Martin Harris in verse 28, next, we find a concise summary of how to obtain forgiveness. Sometimes people seem to think that all that is required to obtain forgiveness is to stop committing the sin. There is more, including humbling oneself, confessing, making covenants, keeping other commandments of God, and fostering attitudes and taking actions that show faith in Christ as explained next.

28 And now, except he **humble himself** and **acknowledge unto me the things that he has done which are wrong**, and **covenant with me that he will keep my commandments**, and **exercise faith in me**, behold, I say unto him, he shall have no such views, for I will grant unto him no views of the things of which I have spoken.

In conclusion, Joseph is told to tell Martin that if he refuses to be obedient to these strict instructions, he is to have nothing more to do with the coming forth of the Book of Mormon and is to stop troubling the Lord about it.

29 And **if this be the case** [*if he declines to follow the instructions in verse 28, above*] I command you, my servant Joseph, that **you shall say unto him, that he shall do no more, nor trouble me any more concerning this matter**.

Next, the Lord tells Joseph what to do if Martin disregards this merciful offer. As you will see, in verse 31, Joseph is also warned what will happen if he himself fails to obey. As mentioned previously, this is, in effect, a "parenting scene."

30 And **if this be the case**, behold, I say unto thee Joseph, **when thou hast translated a few more pages thou shalt stop for a season, even until I command thee again; then thou mayest translate again**.

The following quote from the *Doctrine and Covenants Student Manual*, 2017 Edition, used in the Institutes of religion of the Church, gives possible Insights for verse 30, above:

"The Prophet Joseph Smith had made very little progress on the work of the translation since the Book of Mormon plates had been returned to him following the loss of the 116 manuscript pages. It is possible that during this time, both Emma Smith and her brother Reuben Hale assisted Joseph as scribes (see *The Joseph Smith Papers, Documents, Volume 1: July 1828–June 1831*, 4). When the revelation recorded in Doctrine and Covenants 5 was given in March 1829, the Lord indicated that Joseph should 'stop for a season' (D&C 5:30) and wait until He would 'provide means' to complete the translation of the Book of Mormon (D&C 5:34). This seems to have been fulfilled when Oliver Cowdery arrived in Harmony, Pennsylvania, a few weeks after Joseph received this revelation (see commentary in this manual for Doctrine and Covenants 6)."

31 And **except thou do this**, behold, **thou shalt have no more gift**, and **I will take away the things which I have entrusted with thee**.

Next, we see the Savior's kindness as He explains why He is being so strict with both Joseph and Martin. This, again, is a part of good "parenting" by explaining the reasons for the instructions given. We will see more of this when we study section 95, where the Lord disciplines His children for not having proceeded with the building of the Kirtland Temple.

32 And now, because **I foresee the lying in wait to destroy thee**, yea, **I foresee that if my servant Martin Harris humbleth not himself and receive a witness from my hand, that he will fall into transgression**;

33 And **there are many that lie in wait to destroy thee** from off the face of the earth [*many are even now plotting to kill you*]; and **for this cause, that thy days may be prolonged, I have given unto thee these commandments** [*in other words, I have given you these commandments in order to save your life*].

34 Yea, **for this cause** [*for this reason*] **I have said: Stop, and stand still until I command thee** [*as stated in verse 30*], and I will provide means whereby thou mayest accomplish the thing which I have commanded thee.

35 And **if thou art faithful in keeping my commandments, thou shalt be lifted up** [*exalted in celestial glory*] **at the last day** [*on Judgment Day*]. Amen.

SECTION 6

Background

This revelation was given to Joseph Smith and Oliver Cowdery at Harmony, Pennsylvania, in April 1829. The 5-foot, 5-inch, small-boned Oliver (see *History of Seneca County, Ohio*, by W. Lang, 365) was 22 years old at the time and had been teaching school in Manchester, New York (next to Palmyra), where Joseph's parents lived.

We can see the hand of the Lord in bringing Oliver Cowdery to teach in the school that served some of the Smith children. Joseph's mother, Lucy Mack Smith, recorded that Joseph's older brother,

Hyrum, was a trustee for the local school district and that a man by the name of Lyman Cowdery applied to him to teach in the area. He was hired, but ended up not able to come, and asked if his brother, Oliver, could teach in his stead. The trustees held a meeting and agreed to the proposal. Oliver began boarding at the Smith residence at this time. (See *History of Joseph Smith by His Mother, Lucy Mack Smith*, 138.)

For their labors, such school teachers typically received a small salary plus room and board in the homes of students' parents. Oliver received 50 cents a day, plus room and board in various homes. As mentioned above, the Smiths were the first to have him board in their home.

It was during this time that Oliver heard of the gold plates from people in the community. He consequently asked the Smiths about them. They were reluctant at first to say anything due to the difficulties they had already endured. Eventually they told him about the Book of Mormon plates and the work of translating that Joseph was doing in Harmony, Pennsylvania. After asking many questions and being told some details by Joseph Smith Sr., Oliver became desirous to meet the Prophet. Joseph's mother, Lucy Mack Smith, wrote about what happened as follows:

"Shortly after receiving this information, he [Oliver] told Mr. Smith that he was highly delighted with what he had heard, that he had been in a deep study upon the subject all day, and that it was impressed upon his mind, that he should yet have the privilege of writing for Joseph. Furthermore, that he had determined to pay him a visit at the close of the school. . . .

"On coming in on the following day, he said, 'The subject upon which we were yesterday conversing seems working in my very bones, and I cannot, for a moment, get it out of my mind; finally, I have resolved on what I will do. Samuel [Smith], I understand, is going down to Pennsylvania to spend the spring with Joseph; I shall make my arrangements to be ready to accompany him thither, . . . for I have made it a subject of prayer, and I firmly believe that it is the will of the Lord that I should go. If there is a work for me to do in this thing, I am determined to attend to it.'"

It was in April 1829 that Samuel and Oliver traveled to Harmony, Pennsylvania, to visit Joseph and Emma. The Prophet's mother wrote the following:

"Joseph had been so hurried with his secular affairs that he could not proceed with his spiritual concerns so fast as was necessary for the speedy completion of the work; there was also another disadvantage under which he labored, his wife had so much of her time taken up with the care of her house, that she could write for him but a small portion of the time. On account of these embarrassments, Joseph called upon the Lord, three days prior to the arrival of Samuel and Oliver, to send him a scribe, according to the promise of the angel; and he was informed that the same should be forthcoming in a few days. Accordingly, when Mr. Cowdery told him the business that he had come upon, Joseph was not at all surprised." (*History of Joseph Smith by His Mother, Lucy Mack Smith*, 141.)

Of special note in the above record by Joseph's mother is the information that Oliver had already received a witness of the work that Joseph was doing. Joseph Smith later recorded that the "Lord appeared unto a young man by the name of Oliver Cowd[e]ry and showed unto him the plates in a vision. . . . Therefore he was desirous to come and write for me" (in *The Joseph Smith Papers, Histories, Volume 1: Joseph Smith Histories, 1832–1844,* ed. Karen Lynn Davidson and others [2012], 16; spelling, punctuation, and capitalization standardized). This witness will be referred to in this section, especially in verses 14, 15, 22, and 23.

We will now proceed to study section 6. Verses 1–5 are nearly identical to verses 1–5 in sections 11, 12, and 14 and are similar to verses 1–4 in section 4. The message is clear. The true Church of Jesus Christ is about to be restored to the earth.

1 **A GREAT and marvelous work is about to come forth unto the children of men.**

Next, in verse 2, the word of God will be compared to a living, powerful sword, symbolic of truth from God, which cuts quickly though false doctrine and misunderstanding so that people who are honest in heart can know the truth.

2 Behold, I am God; **give heed unto my word, which is quick** [*alive*] and **powerful**, sharper than a two-edged sword, to the dividing asunder [*cutting apart*] of both joints and marrow; therefore give heed unto my words.

<u>Doctrine</u>

Verse 3. A very important benefit of missionary work is that it can save the soul of the missionary.

3 Behold, the field [*symbolic of the inhabitants of the world*] is white [*ripe, as in a field of grain*] already to harvest; therefore, whoso desireth to reap, let him thrust in his sickle [*join in the work of harvesting; missionary work, etc.*] with his might, and reap [*harvest*] while the day lasts, **that he may treasure up for his soul**

everlasting salvation in the kingdom of God.

4 Yea, whosoever will thrust in his sickle and reap, the same is called of God.

5 Therefore, **if you will ask of me you shall receive; if you will knock it shall be opened unto you.**

The endorsement and instruction from the Lord personally to Oliver, in verse 5, above, must have been gratifying to Oliver who had acted in great faith to come visit Joseph.

As the Lord specifically addresses Oliver's desires in the next verses, we will be taught much too. Verse 7, for instance, is rather well-known and is often quoted in talks and gospel lessons. You may wish to mark it by putting a box around it or underlining it in your own scriptures or marking it in your electronic scriptures.

6 Now, as you [*Oliver Cowdery*] have asked, behold, I say unto you, **keep my commandments**, and **seek to bring forth and establish the cause of Zion** [*seek to help in the restoration of the gospel*];

7 **Seek not for riches but for wisdom, and behold, the mysteries** [*the plain and simple truths, doctrines, ordinances, etc. of the gospel of Christ; compare with the information given in the Bible Dictionary, at the back of your Latter-day Saint Bible, under "Mystery"*] **of God shall be unfolded unto you, and then shall you be made rich. Behold, he that hath eternal life** [*exaltation in the highest degree of glory in the celestial kingdom*] **is rich.**

Joseph Fielding Smith said the following about the word "mysteries" as used in verse 7, above (**bold** added for emphasis):

"The Lord has promised to reveal his mysteries to those who serve him in faithfulness. . . . **There are no mysteries pertaining to the Gospel, only as we, in our weakness, fail to comprehend Gospel truth**. . . . **The 'simple' principles of the Gospel, such as baptism, the atonement, are mysteries to those who do not have the guidance of the Spirit of the Lord**" (*Church History and Modern Revelation*, 1:43).

8 Verily, verily, **I say unto you** [*Oliver*], even as you desire of me so it shall be unto you [*your desires will be granted*]; and **if you desire, you shall be the means of doing much good in this generation.**

Some people get a bit confused as they read verse 9, next, because of the phrase, "say nothing but repentance." They wonder if maybe they should only say "repent" in one form or another as they share the gospel or preach it formally. The solution to this momentary dilemma is simple: follow the Savior, follow the Brethren. Do they literally say more than "repent" as they teach and explain the gospel? Answer—yes, of course! Therefore, we come to understand that "say nothing but repentance" means to teach the gospel simply and directly, such that people have a chance to understand it and accept it. If they do, it will lead them to repentance and progress in coming unto Christ.

Joseph Fielding Smith explained this as follows:

"In the revelation to Oliver Cowdery, and to several others who came to ask what the Lord would have them do, the Lord said: 'Say nothing but repentance unto this generation; keep my commandments, and assist to bring forth my work.' We must not infer from this expression that those who went forth to preach were limited in their teachings so that all they could say was 'repent from your sins,' but in teaching the principles of the Gospel they should do so with the desire to teach repentance to the people and bring them in humility to a realization of the need for remission of sins. Even today in all of our preaching it should be with the desire to bring people to repentance and faith in God. That was the burden of John's message as he went forth to prepare the way for the Lord: 'Repent ye; for the kingdom of heaven is at hand,' he declared to the people, but he also taught them the necessity of baptism and officiated in that ordinance for all who repented of their sins. [Matt. 3:11.] (*CHMR*, 1947, 1:39–40.)" (Roy W. Doxey, *Latter-day Prophets and the Doctrine and Covenants*, 1:64–65).

9 **Say nothing but repentance** unto this generation; keep my commandments, and assist to bring forth my work, according to my commandments, and you shall be blessed.

In verse 10, next, Oliver is told by the Lord that he has a gift. There are various possibilities as to what this gift was. One possibility is that it was the "spirit of revelation," as explained in D&C 8:2–3. In D&C 8:4, Oliver is told that this is his "gift."

Another possibility is the ability and privilege of assisting in the translating of the Book of Mormon plates (see verse 25). Oliver attempted to translate but did not succeed, as explained in D&C 9.

Yet another possibility is that the gift referred to here, in D&C 6:10, is the "gift of Aaron," which is referred to in D&C 8:6–8. The *Doctrine and Covenants Student Manual*, used in the institutes of religion of the Church, 1981, page 19, contains the following quotes explaining this gift:

"There was another gift bestowed upon Oliver Cowdery, and that was the gift of Aaron. Like Aaron with his rod in his hand going before Moses as a spokesman, so Oliver Cowdery was to go before Joseph Smith. Whatever he should ask the Lord by power of this gift should be granted if asked in faith and in wisdom. Oliver was blessed with the great honor of holding the keys of this dispensation with Joseph Smith, and, like Aaron, did become a spokesman on numerous occasions. It was Oliver who delivered the first public discourse in this dispensation. (Smith, *Church History and Modern Revelation*, 1:52.)"

"Oliver Cowdery also had the 'gift of Aaron.' Aaron was the elder brother of Moses. Being prompted by the Spirit of the Lord, he met his younger brother in the wilderness and accompanied him to Egypt. He introduced him to the children of Israel in the land of Goshen. He was his spokesman before Pharaoh, and he assisted him in opening up the dispensation which Moses was commissioned to proclaim (Exodus 4:27–31). This was the gift of Aaron. In some respects, Oliver Cowdery was the Aaron of the new and last dispensation." (Smith and Sjodahl, Commentary, 44)

10 Behold **thou hast a gift**, and blessed art thou because of thy gift. Remember it is sacred and cometh from above—

11 And **if thou wilt inquire, thou shalt know mysteries** which are great and marvelous; therefore thou shalt **exercise thy gift**, that thou mayest find out mysteries [*the basics of the gospel of Christ; see note in verse 7, above*], that thou mayest bring many to the knowledge of the truth, yea, convince them of the error of their ways.

12 Make not **thy gift** known unto any save it be those who are of thy faith. Trifle not with sacred things.

Next, in verse 13, we are all reminded that there is more to being righteous and qualifying for exaltation than avoiding sins of commission. We must also do much good. In addition, in verse 13, we note that in this context, "saved" and "salvation" mean exaltation. This is often the doctrinal definition of these two words. However, one must always look carefully at the context in which these terms are used. For instance, the people spoken of in D&C 132:17 are "saved" but not "exalted."

Doctrine

Verse 13. Exaltation is the greatest gift to us from God. It means living with Heavenly Father forever, in the highest degree of glory within the celestial kingdom, in our own family units, and becoming gods ourselves, like our Heavenly Parents.

13 **If thou wilt do good**, yea, **and hold out faithful to the end,** thou shalt be **saved in the kingdom of God** [*In this context, "saved" means "exaltation"*], **which is the greatest of all the gifts of God**; for **there is no gift greater than the gift of salvation.**

In verses 14–15, next, we are reminded that we don't always realize it when we are being inspired, and it seems to take later events and experiences to confirm that we were indeed being prompted by the Spirit. Once we are aware of the fact that the Spirit spoke to us, we can think back and analyze how we felt or how we were inspired, and then learn from it to be better at recognizing how God speaks to us personally.

14 Verily, verily, I say unto thee, blessed art thou for what thou hast done; for thou hast inquired of me, and behold, **as often as thou hast inquired thou hast received instruction of my Spirit.** If it had not been so, thou wouldst not have come to the place where thou art at this time [*Harmony, Pennsylvania, to see Joseph Smith*].

15 Behold, thou knowest that thou hast inquired of me and **I did enlighten thy mind**; and now **I tell thee these things that thou mayest know that thou hast been enlightened by the Spirit of truth**;

You may have heard that Satan can't read our minds and may have wondered if this is indeed the case. Verse 16, next, gives the answer.

Doctrine

Verse 16. Satan cannot read our minds.

16 Yea, I tell thee, that thou mayest know that there is none else save God that knowest thy thoughts and the intents of thy heart.

In the context of the scriptures, we come to understand that the word "God," in verse 16, above, obviously means "members of the Godhead." Also, people may wonder how servants of the Lord can "read" peoples' minds when appropriate, as in the case of Alma and Amulek (Alma 12:3), in doing His work. The answer is simple. The Spirit can read the "thoughts and intents" of the heart and can put them in the minds of the servants of the Lord, including missionaries, teachers, parents, and others as needed when appropriate according to God's laws.

Next, the Lord confirms to Oliver that he has indeed been inspired to know that Joseph Smith has been called of God as a prophet. Oliver has obviously already begun serving as the scribe for the translation by the time this revelation is given.

17 **I tell thee these things as a witness unto thee—that the words or the work which thou hast been writing** [*as Joseph's scribe during the translating of the plates*] **are true**.

Verses 18–19 contain tender counsel to Oliver to be faithful and loyal to the Prophet, who is not perfect. This counsel applies to all of us as we, too, stand by and support our bishops and Church leaders, as well as family members and friends.

18 Therefore be diligent; **stand by my servant Joseph, faithfully**, in whatsoever difficult circumstances he may be for the word's sake.

19 **Admonish** [*counsel and advise*] **him in his faults**, and **also receive admonition of him** [*take counsel from him also*]. **Be patient**; be **sober** [*be serious about serious things*]; be **temperate**; **have patience**, **faith**, **hope** and **charity** [*all denote qualities needed in order to do the work of the Lord, as stated in D&C 4:5*].

20 Behold, thou art Oliver [*in other words, I know you personally*], and I have spoken unto thee because of thy desires; therefore treasure up these words [*the words of counsel I am now giving you*] in thy heart. **Be faithful and diligent in keeping the commandments** of God, **and I will encircle thee in the arms of my love.**

Next, the Savior personally introduces Himself to Oliver Cowdery.

21 **Behold, I am Jesus Christ, the Son of God**. I am the same that came unto mine own, and mine own received me not [*I am He whom the Jews rejected*]. **I am the light which shineth in darkness** [*spiritual darkness*], and the darkness comprehendeth it not.

Perhaps you have had the experience of being given a blessing by a faithful priesthood holder, during which blessing things were mentioned which you alone knew. Such occurrences are sweet reminders of the truthfulness of the work. In verses 22–24, next, Oliver is given such a testimony-strengthening experience.

At one point, while he was staying with the Smith family in the Manchester and Palmyra area, Oliver had prayed to the Lord concerning what he had heard about Joseph Smith and the gold plates. He had received a witness from the Lord, but had told absolutely no one about the experience. Now, through the Prophet Joseph Smith, the Savior reminds him of this witness.

22 Verily, verily, I say unto you, if you desire a further witness,

cast your mind [*look back*] **upon the night that you cried unto me in your heart, that you might know concerning the truth of these things.**

Doctrine

Verse 23. Peace is one of the greatest forms of testimony and communication that comes from God.

23 **Did I not speak peace to your mind concerning the matter? What greater witness can you have than from God**?

Joseph Smith said the following about verses 22–24 in this section:

"After we had received this revelation [D&C 6], Oliver Cowdery stated to me that after he had gone to my father's to board, and after the family had communicated to him concerning my having obtained the plates, that one night after he had retired to bed he called upon the Lord to know if these things were so, and the Lord manifested to him that they were true, but he had kept the circumstance entirely secret, and had mentioned it to no one; so that after this revelation was given, he knew that the work was true, because no being living knew of the thing alluded to in the revelation, but God and himself" (*History of the Church*, 1:35).

Also, from verse 23, above, we learn that peace is one of the greatest testimonies we can be given from God. Unfortunately, it is sometimes overlooked because of the expectation of more spectacular forms of communication from heaven.

24 And **now, behold, you have received a witness; for if I have told you things which no man knoweth have you not received a witness?**

As mentioned previously, one of the gifts given to Oliver Cowdery was the gift of translating. We see this in verses 25–28, next, and find in verse 26 that there are yet other ancient records containing the gospel that we have not yet received (compare with 2 Nephi 29:7–11).

25 And, behold, **I grant unto you a gift**, if you desire of me, **to translate, even as my servant Joseph**.

26 Verily, verily, I say unto you, that **there are records which contain much of my gospel, which have been kept back** because of the wickedness of the people;

27 And now I command you, that if you have good desires—a desire to lay up treasures for yourself in heaven—**then shall you assist in bringing to light,**

with your gift, those parts of my scriptures which have been hidden because of iniquity.

In verse 28, next, we are reminded of the law of witnesses, which is an important part of the gospel. One of the common uses of this law of witnesses is for baptism—two witnesses are required to view each baptism to assure that the person is baptized properly.

28 And now, behold, I give unto you, and also unto my servant Joseph, the keys of this gift, which shall bring to light this ministry; and **in the mouth of two or three witnesses shall every word be established.**

Next, the Savior addresses both Joseph and Oliver, giving them true perspective as to what matters most. Although what He says to them, namely that "they can do no more unto you than unto me," may at first be a bit of a shock, it is a strong reminder that whatever happens to us in mortality is but a small thing compared with eternity and will "soon" be over.

29 Verily, verily, I say unto you, if they reject my words, and this part of my gospel and ministry, blessed are ye [*in other words, you will be okay, no matter what, because you have done your part*], for **they can do no more unto you than unto me.**

30 **And even if they do** unto you even as they have done unto me, blessed are ye, for **you shall dwell with me in glory.**

31 But **if they reject not my words**, which shall be established by the testimony which shall be given, **blessed are they**, and then shall ye have joy in the fruit of your labors [*in other words, you will be all right, no matter what, but if they do heed My words, brought forth by you, it will be an extra blessing and additional joy for you*].

Next, we see that the Savior is very much involved in the day-to-day work of the kingdom here on earth.

32 Verily, verily, I say unto you, as I said unto my disciples, where two or three are gathered together in my name, as touching one thing, behold, **there will I be in the midst of them—even so am I in the midst of you.**

Next, the Lord states twice what we know as "the law of the harvest."

33 **Fear not to do good**, my sons [*a particularly tender form of addressing these men*], for **whatsoever ye sow** [*plant; in other words, the work that you do for Me*]**, that shall ye also reap** [*harvest; in other words, what you do for Me will*

come back to bless you]; therefore, **if ye sow good ye shall also reap good for your reward.**

Doctrine

Verse 34. If we build our lives upon Christ, nothing can stop us from obtaining exaltation.

34 Therefore, **fear not**, little flock; **do good; let earth and hell combine against you**, for **if ye are built upon my rock, they cannot prevail** [*ultimately win over us*].

We all have imperfections, sins, and shortcomings that can make us feel inadequate to accept callings and to do the work of the Lord. Christ's tender counsel to Joseph and Oliver, next, can give comfort to all of us. It is both reassuring and insightful as to the intended effect and power of the Atonement in our daily lives.

35 Behold, **I do not condemn you; go your ways and sin no more; perform with soberness** [*seriousness*] **the work** which I have commanded you.

36 **Look unto me in every thought; doubt not, fear not.**

We understand verse 37, next, to not be an actual appearance of the Savior to Joseph and Oliver, rather, an invitation to better understand the power of the Atonement to cleanse and heal. Thus, along with them, all of us are given power and encouragement to continue striving to keep the commandments, with optimism and confidence in the final outcome.

Doctrine

Verse 37. The Savior's suffering paid the price for us to become free from sin. Those who are faithful will receive exaltation.

37 **Behold the wounds which pierced my side, and also the prints of the nails in my hands and feet** [*reflect on My Atonement*]; **be faithful, keep my commandments, and ye shall inherit the kingdom of heaven**. Amen.

SECTION 7

Background

We know from this section in the Doctrine and Covenants that the Apostle John, often referred to as "John the Beloved," was given the privilege of remaining alive and continuing to minister and teach the gospel until the time of the Second Coming of the Savior. Thus, he is what we refer to as a "translated being." However, without the revelation here in section seven, we would be like others who only have the Bible on this subject. The problem is that the wording in the Bible, John

21:22–23, is not entirely clear and leaves readers wondering as to whether or not John would remain on earth and continue to live until the Second Coming. Those verses in John follow Peter's question to the resurrected Christ as to what John would do after the Savior's departure. We will include these verses from the New Testament here so that you can see how the question remains unanswered by them as to whether or not John was allowed to stay on earth. As you can see, in John 21:22, next, there is a big **"if."**

John 21:22–23

22 Jesus saith unto him, If I will that he tarry [*remain on earth*] till I come, what *is that* to thee? follow thou me.

23 Then went this saying [*a tradition, a rumor*] abroad among the brethren, that that disciple [*John*] should not die: **yet Jesus said not unto him** [*Peter*], **He** [*John*] **shall not die; but, If I will that he tarry till I come, what *is that* to thee?**

Joseph Smith tells us that he and Oliver Cowdery found themselves with differing opinions about whether or not John died, or is still alive on earth. Consequently, they asked the Lord through the Urim and Thummim. The Prophet said:

"During the month of April [*1829, at Harmony, Pennsylvania*] I continued to translate, and he [*Oliver Cowdery*] to write, with little cessation, during which time we received several revelations. **A difference of opinion arising between us about the account of John the Apostle, mentioned in the New Testament, as to whether he died or continued to live**, we mutually agreed to settle it by the Urim and Thummim" (*History of the Church*, 1:35–36).

Section 7 was given in response to their question. As you will see, in the heading to section 7 in your Doctrine and Covenants, this section "is a translated version of the record made on parchment by John." We don't know whether Joseph Smith had the actual parchment in his possession and translated it, was shown it in vision, or was given its contents by revelation. Whatever the case, the answer was given in section 7, and thus we know that John the Beloved Apostle is still alive and on earth, and he will be until the Savior comes. See also *Doctrine and Covenants Student Manual*, 2018, used by the institutes of religion of the Church, under "Doctrine and Covenants 7."

As mentioned above, we understand that John is a translated being (see Bruce R. McConkie, *Mormon Doctrine*, 806). For more information about translated beings, you may wish to read 3 Nephi 28, which gives some details about the Three Nephites, who will continue to live on earth as translated beings and will die and be resurrected instantly at the time of the Savior's Second Coming.

In 1831, Joseph Smith said that at that time, John was working with the Lost Ten Tribes, preparing them for their return. See *History of the Church*, 1:176.

We will now proceed with our study of the text of section 7. Remember, as stated above, that this is taken from the writings of John, on parchment, and thus Joseph Smith is giving us John's own words here. Again, the question leading up to this revelation was whether or not John the Apostle is still alive on earth.

1 AND **the Lord said unto me: John**, my beloved, **what desirest thou?** For if you shall ask what you will [*whatever you want*], it shall be granted unto you.

2 And **I said unto him: Lord, give unto me power over death, that I may live and bring souls unto thee**.

3 And the Lord said unto me: Verily, verily, I say unto thee, because thou desirest this **thou shalt tarry** [*remain alive on earth*] **until I come in my glory** [*until the Second Coming*], and shalt prophesy before nations, kindreds, tongues and people.

4 And **for this cause** [*this is why*] **the Lord said unto Peter: If I will that he** [*John*] **tarry till I come, what is that to thee?** For **he desired of me that he might bring souls unto me**, but **thou** [*Peter*] **desiredst that thou mightest speedily come unto me in my kingdom**.

As you have just read, both Peter and John made special requests to the resurrected Savior, as He appeared and taught them on the shores of the Sea of Galilee (see John 21). As you will see, in verse 8, both of these requests were granted.

Verses 5 and 6, next, use the word "greater." Because of this, some people may tend to think that the Lord is telling Peter that John's wish was more important than his. This is not the case, according to verses 5, 6, and 8. "Greater," in this context, simply means "more" or "additional." In other words, John wants to do more work, or a "greater" work here on earth, in bringing souls unto Christ, than he has done up to now. Whereas, Peter wants to return quickly to heaven to be with the Savior, when he has finished his mission on earth.

5 I say unto thee, Peter, **this was a good desire** [*Peter's desire, as expressed at the end of verse 4, above*]; but my beloved [*John*] has desired that he might do **more**, or

a **greater work yet among men** than what he has before done.

6 Yea, he has undertaken a greater work [*additional work*]; therefore I will make him as flaming fire and a ministering angel [*he will be a translated being*]; he shall minister for those who shall be heirs of salvation who dwell on the earth.

Next, the writings of John, on this parchment, inform us that the Savior told Peter that he would be privileged to help John, from the other side of the veil, and that he, along with James and John, would continue to work as a team, holding the keys of presidency. One manifestation of this fact is their appearing to Joseph Smith and Oliver Cowdery in 1829 and restoring the keys of the Melchizedek Priesthood to them. (See *History of the Church*, 3:387. See also D&C 81:1–2.)

7 And I will make thee [*Peter*] to minister for him and for thy brother James; and **unto you three I will give this power and the keys of this ministry until I come**.

Did you notice, in verse 7, above, that Peter is told, in effect, that he would preside in this "presidency" and as such, he would "minister" to his counselors, James and John? We see this pattern today in our first presidencies.

Finally, we are taught that the Savior told both Peter and John that what they asked for was good, and that they would both be rewarded for their righteous desires.

8 Verily I say unto you, **ye shall both have according to your desires**, for ye both joy in that which ye have desired.

SECTION 8

Background

Both sections 8 and 9 deal with Oliver Cowdery's desire to assist with the actual translating of the gold plates. Oliver had been told that he had the gift to translate ancient records (see D&C 6:25–28). The Prophet Joseph Smith recorded the following with respect to Oliver's desire to do so: "Whilst continuing the work of translation, during the month of April, Oliver Cowdery became exceedingly anxious to have the power to translate bestowed upon him, and in relation to this desire the following revelations were obtained: [D&C 8–9]" (*History of the Church*, 1:36).

Section 8 was given to Oliver Cowdery in April 1829, at Harmony, Pennsylvania, where he was serving as scribe to Joseph Smith as he translated the gold plates. From it we gain valuable instruction concerning how to recognize and receive revelation.

In verse 1, next, we are taught some of the basic requirements for receiving knowledge and revelation from God.

1 OLIVER Cowdery, verily, verily, I say unto you, that assuredly as the Lord liveth, who is your God and your Redeemer, even so surely shall you receive a knowledge of whatsoever things you shall **ask in faith**, with an **honest heart** [*having pure motives*], **believing that you shall receive** a knowledge concerning the engravings of old records, which are ancient, which contain those parts of my scripture of which has been spoken by the manifestation of my Spirit.

Next, we are taught of two major ways, among others, in which the Holy Ghost communicates with us, namely, in our mind and in our heart. There is a difference between the two. In a stake presidents' training meeting, which I was privileged to attend in the fall of 2000, Elder Richard G. Scott of the Quorum of the Twelve explained that "heart" deals with general feelings and impressions, whereas "mind" refers to specific thoughts and instruction. In other words, "heart" is general and "mind" is very specific. He went on to teach us that an impression to the heart, when followed, will lead to more specific instruction to the mind.

Elder Scott used Enos, in the Book of Mormon, as an example. He pointed out that in Enos 1:3, tender feelings about the words and instructions from his father over the years sunk deep into Enos's heart. Then in Enos 1:4, Enos acted upon those feelings and left his hunting and turned to God in humble prayer. As a result, very specific teachings and instructions came into his mind. (See Enos 1:5–10, especially verse 10.)

We will now continue with section 8.

Doctrine

Verse 2. Two of the most common ways the Lord speaks to us are in our minds and in our hearts through the Holy Ghost.

2 Yea, behold, **I will tell you in your mind and in your heart, by the Holy Ghost**, which shall come upon you and which shall dwell in your heart.

Next, in verse 3, Oliver is instructed as to the "spirit of revelation" and is reminded that it is a powerful means of communication that is also used by prophets. This is a gift that all of us can enjoy. It is part of having the gift of the Holy Ghost. In verse 4, Oliver will be told that he has this gift of recognizing and understanding the voice of the Spirit, and if he carefully follows what it says, he will be spared much misery.

3 Now, behold, **this** [*being taught in your mind and heart by the Holy Ghost*] **is the spirit of revelation**; behold, this is **the spirit by which Moses brought the children of Israel through the Red Sea on dry ground**.

4 Therefore **this is thy gift**; **apply unto it, and** blessed art thou, for **it shall deliver you out of the hands of your enemies**, when, if it were not so, they would slay you and bring your soul to destruction.

President M. Russell Ballard, then of the Quorum of the Twelve Apostles, gave powerful counsel regarding the sources we use in seeking knowledge and understanding about the Church and the gospel:

"Today we live in a world in which people don't ask of God—they seem to want to ask of Google. Even when it comes to questions of faith, there are many who trust the Internet to provide accurate, fair, and balanced answers to their questions more than they trust the ultimate source of truth, our Heavenly Father. . . .

". . . Today the Internet is full of those lying in wait to deceive the uninformed and inexperienced.

"In our search for gospel truth, we not only need to find reliable sources but we also need to give the Lord equal time in our daily pursuits. We need to study the scriptures and the words of the Lord's servants. We need to be living right before God—we need to be doing His will [see John 7:16–17]. And we can never overstate the importance of taking our spiritual concerns directly to God and trusting His inspiration and guidance" ("Women of Dedication, Faith, Determination, and Action" [address given at Brigham Young University Women's Conference, May 1, 2015], 5–6; see womensconference.ce.byu.edu/transcripts).

Next, we are reminded that in order to recognize when the Holy Ghost speaks to our minds and hearts, we must be in tune by keeping the commandments of God.

5 Oh, **remember these words, and keep my commandments**. Remember, this is your gift.

Next, Oliver Cowdery is told that he has another gift, namely, the "gift of Aaron."

6 Now this is not all thy gift; for **you have another gift, which is the gift of Aaron**; behold, it has told you many things;

7 Behold, there is no other power, save the power of God, that can cause this **gift of Aaron** to be with you.

Joseph Fielding Smith explained the "gift of Aaron" as follows:

"There was another gift bestowed upon Oliver Cowdery, and that was the gift of Aaron. Like Aaron with his rod in his hand going before Moses as a spokesman, so Oliver Cowdery was to go before Joseph Smith. Whatever he should ask the Lord by power of this gift should be granted if asked in faith and in wisdom. Oliver was blessed with the great honor of holding the keys of this dispensation with Joseph Smith, and, like Aaron [Ex. 4:10–17], did become a spokesman on numerous occasions. It was Oliver who delivered the first public discourse in this dispensation." (*Church History and Modern Revelation*, 1:48. See also Doxey, *Latter-day Prophets and the Doctrine and Covenants*, 1:82.)

8 Therefore, **doubt not** [*an important ingredient of powerful faith*], for it is the gift of God; and you shall hold it in your hands [*perhaps this is symbolic, in the sense that his gift to be a spokesman for Joseph Smith would be like Aaron's rod (Exodus 7:10–12, etc.), which symbolized his authority and calling to be a spokesman for Moses*], **and do marvelous works**; and no power shall be able to take it away out of your hands, for it is the work of God.

9 And, therefore, whatsoever you shall ask me to tell you by that means, that will I grant unto you, and you shall have knowledge concerning it.

Doctrine

Verse 10. Faith in Christ is the foundation principle upon which all successful religious behavior is based.

10 Remember that **without faith you can do nothing**; therefore **ask in faith**. Trifle not with these things; do not ask for that which you ought not.

We do not know what specific ancient records are being referred to in verse 11, next. But we do know that there are many ancient records yet to be brought forth. See 2 Nephi 27:7–8; 29:11–13; 3 Nephi 26:6–11; Ether 3:22–28; 4:5–7.

11 Ask that you may know the mysteries of God, and that you may translate and receive knowledge from **all those ancient records** which have been hid up, that are sacred; and according to your faith shall it be done unto you.

From verse 12, next, we get a hint that the Savior is much involved in our lives, even though we often don't realize the extent of his involvement.

12 Behold, it is I [*Jesus Christ*] that have spoken it; and **I am the same that spake unto you from the beginning** [*see D&C 6:14–15, 22–23*]. Amen.

SECTION 9

Background

Section 9 was given to Oliver Cowdery in Harmony, Pennsylvania, in April 1829, and goes together with section 8. You may wish to review the background notes for section 8 in this study guide.

It would appear from the context of verses 1 and 2 that Oliver, who had been serving as Joseph Smith's scribe during the translating of the gold plates, had attempted to do some translating himself with the Lord's permission. In fact, in D&C 6:25, he was told, "I grant unto you a gift, if you desire of me, to translate, even as my servant Joseph."

He apparently did not understand, among other things, that translating required work (see verses 7–8), and thus failed in his effort. While it was obviously a disappointment to both Oliver and Joseph (see end of verse 12), it served as an important lesson and provides an opportunity for all of us to learn more about the process of receiving revelation.

Pay special attention to the tender words used by the Savior in addressing Oliver and encouraging him in verses 1–6, next. We feel His compassion and kindness for this powerful young man who was in rather intense training for the role he was to play in the restoration of the gospel. We will **bold** some of these terms of tenderness.

1 BEHOLD, I say unto you, **my son** [*Oliver Cowdery*], that because you did not translate according to that which you desired of me, and did commence again to write [*to serve as a scribe*] for my servant, Joseph Smith, Jun., even so I would that ye should continue until you have finished this record [*finished writing down the translation of the gold plates, which was to become the Book of Mormon*], which I have entrusted unto him.

2 And then, behold, **other records have I, that I will give unto you power that you may assist to translate.**

While we don't know what "other records" are referred to here by the Lord, we do know from the Book of Mormon that there are many such records. For instance, additional records are mentioned in 2 Nephi 27:7–8; 29:11–13; 3 Nephi 26:6–11; Ether 3:22–28 and 4:5–7.

We also have a fascinating account given by President Brigham

Young of other records, as follows:

"When Joseph got the plates, the angel instructed him to carry them back to the hill Cumorah, which he did. Oliver says that when Joseph and Oliver went there, the hill opened, and they walked into a cave, in which there was a large and spacious room. He says he did not think, at the time, whether they had the light of the sun or artificial light; but that it was just as light as day. They laid the plates on a table; it was a large table that stood in the room. Under this table there was a pile of plates as much as two feet high, and there were altogether in this room more plates than probably many wagon loads; they were piled up in the corners and along the walls. The first time they went there the sword of Laban hung upon the wall; but when they went again it had been taken down and laid upon the table across the gold plates; it was unsheathed, and on it was written these words: 'This sword will never be sheathed again until the kingdoms of the world become the kingdom of our God and his Christ.' I tell you this as coming not only from Oliver Cowdery, but others who were familiar with it, and who understood it just as well as we understand coming to this meeting, enjoying the day, and by and by we separate and go away, forgetting most of what is said, but remembering some things." (*Journal of Discourses*, 19:38. See also Doxey, *Latter-day Prophets and the Doctrine and Covenants*, 1:87.)

3 **Be patient, my son**, for it is wisdom in me, and it is not expedient that you should translate at this present time.

Next, Oliver is told to continue serving as scribe for Joseph Smith. We will have to wait for further information as to what "continue as you commenced" refers to in verse 5.

4 Behold, the work which you are called to do is to write for my servant Joseph.

5 And, behold, it is because that you did not continue as you commenced, when you began to translate, that I have taken away this privilege from you.

6 **Do not murmur** [*complain*]**, my son**, for it is wisdom in me [*I know what I am doing*] that I have dealt with you after this manner.

While verses 7–12 are very specific to Oliver's attempt to translate, we can nevertheless learn some principles regarding how to prepare for and qualify for receiving revelation by studying them.

First of all, in verse 7, combined with the beginning of verse 8, we learn that effort is required on our part. We will use **bold** to point this out.

Doctrine

Verses 7 and 8. Receiving revelation often requires work and preparation on our part.

7 Behold, you have not understood; **you have supposed that I would give it unto you, when you took no thought save it was** [*other than*] **to ask me.**

8 But, behold, I say unto you, that **you must study it out in your mind; then you must ask me if it be right**, and if it is right I will cause that your bosom shall burn within you; therefore, you shall feel that it is right.

We must be a bit careful with the word "burn" in verse 8, above. The use of this word seems to be very specific to this context with Oliver Cowdery. Perhaps we need to wait until we have an opportunity to ask him about it in the next life to find out exactly what is meant.

In general applications, the word "peace" seems to apply to all of us as far as recognizing the Lord's approval of a course of action we have determined to take. See, for instance, D&C 6:23, where the Lord asks Oliver Cowdery, "Did I not speak peace to your mind concerning the matter?"

President Dallin H. Oaks, when he was a member of the Quorum of the Twelve Apostles, spoke about this burning in the bosom mentioned in verse 8. He taught:

"What does a 'burning in the bosom' mean? Does it need to be a feeling of caloric heat, like the burning produced by combustion? If that is the meaning, I have never had a burning in the bosom. Surely, the word 'burning' in this scripture signifies a feeling of comfort and serenity. That is the witness many receive. That is the way revelation works" ("Teaching and Learning by the Spirit," *Ensign*, Mar. 1997, 13).

Again, verse 9, next, is very specific to Oliver Cowdery and his attempts to translate.

9 But **if it be not right you shall have no such feelings, but you shall have a stupor of thought that shall cause you to forget the thing which is wrong**; therefore, you cannot write that which is sacred save it be given you from me.

In the April 1931 general conference of the Church, Elder Melvin J. Ballard showed how principles learned from the specific lessons given to Oliver Cowdery in these verses could apply to members of the Church in general. He taught:

"There is a key given in the ninth section of the book of Doctrine and Covenants, which would be very profitable for the Latter-day Saints to follow even now. You remember the circumstance of

Oliver Cowdery translating portions of the Book of Mormon, and then all became darkness to him and he could not proceed. He inquired of the Lord to know why it was, and the answer came that he had taken no thought save it was to ask the Lord, and left the burden of responsibility there. [Sec. 9:8–9, quoted.]

"You do not know what to do today to solve your financial problems, what to plant, whether to buy or sell cattle, sheep or other things. It is your privilege to study it out; counsel together with the best wisdom and judgment the Lord shall give you, reach your conclusions, and then go to the Lord with it, tell him what you have planned to do. If the thing you have planned to do is for your good and your blessing, and you are determined to serve the Lord, pay your tithes and your offerings and keep his commandments, I promise that he will fulfil that promise upon your head, and your bosom shall burn within by the whisperings of the Spirit that it is right. But if it is not right, you shall have no such feelings, but you shall have a stupor of thought, and your heart will be turned away from that thing.

"I know of nothing today that the Latter-day Saints need more than the guidance of the Holy Spirit in the solution of the problems of life" (In Conference Report, April 1931, 37–38).

Next, the Savior continues to instruct Oliver as to why he did not succeed in translating and explains that the opportunity is now past.

10 Now, **if you had known this you could have translated**; nevertheless, it is not expedient [*necessary*] that you should translate now.

11 Behold, it was expedient [*important*] when you commenced; but **you feared, and the time is past**, and it is not expedient [*necessary*] now;

12 For, do you not behold [*can't you see*] that I have given unto my servant Joseph sufficient strength, whereby it is made up? **And neither of you have I condemned**.

We understand from the last sentence in verse 12, above, that Joseph Smith must have been somewhat concerned and disappointed too when Oliver failed to translate. Perhaps he felt some responsibility himself for the failure. Whatever the case, we see the kindness of the Lord in assuring both of them that "neither of you have I condemned." The word "condemned," in this context, can mean "put a stop to your eternal progression."

In other words, all is not lost, and it is important to move ahead according to the Lord's instructions. If they do, they will "prosper," as they are told in verse 13, next. In fact, according to verses 13 and 14, if they move past this failure and follow God's counsel in the future, nothing will be lost as far as their eternal exaltation is concerned. This is perhaps one of the most important lessons for all of us in this section.

13 **Do this thing which I have commanded you, and you shall prosper.** Be faithful, and yield to no temptation.

14 **Stand fast in the work** wherewith I have called you, and a hair of your head shall not be lost [*a symbolic phrase, meaning that the Lord will take good care of you completely and lead you to exaltation*], and **you shall be lifted up** [*be exalted; receive the highest degree of glory in the celestial kingdom*] at the last day [*on the day of final judgment*]. Amen.

SECTION 10

Background

Sections 3 and 10 go together. They both deal with the loss of the 116 manuscript pages of the Book of Mormon translation by Martin Harris. For more background information, you may wish to read the notes given in this study guide at the beginning of section 3.

By way of brief review, Martin Harris came to Harmony, Pennsylvania, in February 1828, and served as scribe for Joseph Smith as he translated from the gold plates. By June 14, 1828, they had 116 handwritten pages (called "manuscript pages") containing the translation of the Book of Mormon plates up to that point. After repeated requests by Martin, and contrary to the Lord's initial instruction, Joseph finally let him take the manuscript back to Palmyra, New York. Martin's hope, among other things, was to convince his wife and others that he was not wasting his time with a false prophet.

Martin broke serious promises made with respect to safeguarding the precious manuscript pages, and they were lost. After about three weeks, when Martin had not returned to Joseph and Emma's home in Harmony with the 116 pages, Joseph went to Palmyra to check concerning the manuscript. Upon finding that the pages had been lost, he returned to Harmony, dejected and very discouraged.

After returning home, the Urim and Thummim was taken from the Prophet by Moroni, referred to as "an angel" by his mother in her account (see *History of Joseph Smith by His Mother,* pages 133–36). Shortly thereafter, it was returned to Joseph, at which point he received the revelation we now have as section 3 of the Doctrine and Covenants. Afterward, the Urim and Thummim, as well as the gold plates, were taken from him.

After a time, both the plates and the Urim and Thummim were returned to him. Of this, the Prophet's mother wrote the following, quoting her son, Joseph Smith Jr.:

"After the angel left me," said he, "I continued my supplications to God, without cessation, and on the twenty-second of September, I had the joy and satisfaction of again receiving the Urim and Thummim, with which I have again commenced translating, and Emma writes for me, but the angel said that the Lord would send me a scribe [*Oliver Cowdery*], and I trust his promise will be verified. The angel seemed pleased with me when he gave me back the Urim and Thummim, and he told me that the Lord loved me, for my faithfulness and humility" (Lucy Mack Smith, *History of Joseph Smith by His Mother*, 135).

We will now study the revelation recorded as section 10 that Joseph received after the gold plates and the Urim and Thummim were returned to him. We will learn much about what happened to the 116 lost pages and see what the Lord told Joseph Smith to do about it.

We can learn many lessons from these verses, several of which we will point out as we go. First, we will consider verses 1–9 as a unit and simply **bold** five phrases that remind us of the reality of our accountability when we intentionally go against the counsels of God. Pay special attention to the word, "***you***," which we will **bold**, *italicize*, and underline for extra emphasis. When we finish with this, we will repeat this block of verses and do more with several of the verses.

1 NOW, behold, I say unto you, that because ***you*** **delivered up those writings which** you had power given unto you to translate by the means of the Urim and Thummim, into the hands of a wicked man, ***you*** **have lost them.**

2 And ***you*** **also lost your gift** at the same time, and your mind became darkened.

3 Nevertheless, it is now restored unto you again; therefore see that you are faithful and continue on unto the finishing of the remainder of the work of translation as you have begun.

4 Do not run faster or labor more than you have strength and means provided to enable you to translate; but be diligent unto the end.

5 Pray always, that you may come off conqueror; yea, that you may conquer Satan, and that you may escape the hands of the servants of Satan that do uphold his work.

6 Behold, they have sought to destroy you; yea, even the man in whom you have trusted has sought to destroy you.

7 And for this cause I said that he is a wicked man, for he has sought to take away the things wherewith you have been entrusted; and he has also sought to destroy your gift.

8 And because ***you*** **have delivered the writings into his hands**, behold, wicked men have taken them from you.

9 Therefore, ***you*** **have delivered them up, yea, that which was sacred, unto wickedness**.

As mentioned above, we will now start over with the first nine verses, and do many more things with them. We can see the Savior teaching His young prophet (Joseph Smith was 22 years old at this time) by giving him understanding and leading him on the path to wisdom and increased ability to do the work that has been entrusted to him. We will continue to **bold** the actual scriptural text for teaching purposes. First, in verses 1–2, the Master Teacher gives a lesson on "cause and effect."

1 NOW, behold, I say unto you, that **because you delivered up those writings** [*the 116 manuscript pages*] which you had power given unto you to translate by the means of the Urim and Thummim, **into the hands of a wicked man** [*Martin Harris*], **you have lost them**.

2 And **you also lost your gift** at the same time, **and your mind became darkened** [*an immediate result of intentional disobedience*].

Next, Christ teaches a lesson on mercy and hope, explaining how Joseph can successfully complete the work of translating. In other words, His Atonement allows and enables us to move ahead after having been stopped by our own poor choices.

Doctrine

Verse 3. Through our repentance, the Atonement of Christ allows and enables us to resume progress on the covenant path toward exaltation after having been stopped by our own wrong choices.

3 Nevertheless, it [*the gift of translating*] **is now restored unto you again**; therefore **see that you are faithful** and **continue on unto the finishing of the remainder of the work of translation** as you have begun.

Verse 4, next, is a rather well-known verse in the Doctrine and Covenants, and is often quoted in lessons, conversations and sermons. In context, it contains a number of insights and vital lessons for each of us.

First of all, having been given another chance, after having "feared man [*Martin Harris*] more than God" (D&C 3:7), it would be highly likely that Joseph would have worn himself out and ruined his health and ability to serve by spending all his time and energy in resuming the work. He could easily have been too anxious and thus neglected his family, his health, and other responsibilities.

In addition, being too anxious can give Satan power over us because we become too hard on ourselves. It is possible that Joseph may indeed have been too hard on himself or this verse and its message would not have been included here by the Lord.

Being unreasonably hard on ourselves can become a serious deterrent to personal progress and can lead to discouragement and maybe even giving up as far as hopes of exaltation are concerned. Elder Marvin J. Ashton of the Quorum of the Twelve Apostles gave counsel regarding this as follows: ". . . the speed with which we head along the straight and narrow path isn't as important as the direction in which we are traveling" (April 1989 general conference). You may wish to read his entire talk. It is full of wisdom and encouragement on this issue.

For those who wish to be faithful in all things, the phrase "means provided," in verse 4, could even include things such as health, finances, time, family situation, and more. Having said this, we will now proceed to verse 4.

4 **Do not run faster or labor more than you have strength and means provided to enable you to translate; but be diligent unto the end.**

Mosiah 4:27 is an especially significant cross-reference for verse 4, above. We will include this counsel from King Benjamin here.

Mosiah 4:27

27 And see that all these things are done in wisdom and order; for it is not requisite [*required by the Lord*] **that a man should run faster than he has strength.** And again, it is expedient [*necessary*] that he should **be diligent**, that thereby he might win the prize [*exaltation in celestial glory*]; therefore, **all things must be done in order.**

Next, verse 5 teaches us the importance of prayer in gaining personal victory over Satan and his evil followers.

5 **Pray always**, that you may come off conqueror; yea, that you may conquer Satan, and that you may escape the hands of the servants of Satan that do uphold his work.

There are many ways we can apply the counsel to "pray always" as given in verse 5, above. We will list a few here.

1. Constantly remember God and your covenants with Him, no matter what you are doing.
2. Maintain a constant feeling of gratitude and reverence for God and His creations.
3. Have a constant prayer in your heart that you will be guided and directed to do right, no matter what others do.
4. Always be ready to ask, "What would Jesus do?" as you face temptations in daily living.
5. Say many little prayers throughout the day, including expressions of gratitude for kindnesses as well as pleas for help.
6. Have a constant awareness of who you are and your covenant to "stand as [*a witness*] of God at all times and in all things, and in all places" (Mosiah 18:9).

President Henry B. Eyring gave counsel regarding "pray always." "The Lord hears the prayers of your heart. The feelings in your heart of love for our Heavenly Father and for His Beloved Son can be so constant that your prayers will ascend always" ("Always," *Ensign*, Oct. 1999, 12).

President Marion G. Romney of the First Presidency taught the importance of taking time to ponder. He said, "Pondering is, in my feeling, a form of prayer" (April 1973 general conference). Therefore, "praying always" could include taking time to ponder the things of God, thus giving the Holy Ghost a chance to teach, inspire, and direct you more effectively.

Next, beginning with verse 6, the Lord explains to Joseph Smith why he called Martin Harris a "wicked" man and tells him what has happened to the lost 116 pages of the Book of Mormon translation.

6 Behold, **they** [*the wicked people who now have the 116 pages*] **have sought to destroy you**; yea, even **the man** [*Martin Harris*] in whom **you have trusted has sought to destroy you.**

7 And for this cause [*this is why*] I said that he is a wicked man, for **he has sought to take away the things wherewith you have been entrusted**; and he has also sought to destroy your gift [*of translating the gold plates—see D&C 10:2–3*].

8 And because you have delivered the writings [*the 116 manuscript pages*] into his hands, behold, **wicked men have taken them** from you.

9 Therefore, **you** have delivered

them up, yea, that which was sacred, unto wickedness.

Next, Joseph is told of the plot which has been hatched in the minds of the evil men who now have the 116 pages. He learns that they have changed the wording on the manuscript pages with the intent to get him to retranslate from the gold plates. If they can get him to do so, they will then produce the stolen pages and compare them with the retranslation. They will make sure that the stolen pages do not agree with the retranslation, thus attempting to discredit the Prophet and make themselves popular with local people who oppose Joseph Smith and his work. We will use **bold** to summarize what Joseph is told by the Lord.

10 And, behold, **Satan hath put it into their hearts to alter the words** which you have caused to be written, or which you have translated, which have gone out of your hands [*which you have lost*].

11 And behold, I say unto you, that **because they have altered the words, they read contrary from that which you translated** and caused to be written;

12 And, on this wise [*this is how*], **the devil has sought to lay a cunning plan, that he may destroy this work**;

13 For he hath put into their hearts to do this, that **by lying they may say they have caught you in the words which you have pretended to translate**.

14 Verily, I say unto you, that **I will not suffer** [*allow*] **that Satan shall accomplish his evil design** in this thing.

Next, we get a specific insight as to one way in which Satan works with people to accomplish his evil goals with them.

15 For behold, **he has put it into their hearts** to get thee to tempt the Lord thy God, in asking to translate it over again.

16 **And then**, behold, **they say and think in their hearts—We will see if God has given him power to translate; if so, he will also give him power again**;

Did you notice in verse 16, above, how cunning Satan is? He is not telling these wicked men that there is no God. In fact, he has them so deceived and dulled spiritually and intellectually as to be thinking up a plan to destroy Joseph and work against God, even if God helps him translate again!

17 And **if God giveth him power again**, or if he translates again, or, in other words, **if he bringeth forth the same words**, behold, we have the same [*the original*

translation on the 116 pages] with us, and we have altered them;

18 Therefore they will not agree [*the two translations will not agree, because of what we do with the original*], and **we will say that he has lied in his words, and that he has no gift, and that he has no power** [*in other words, we will say that he is not a prophet*];

19 **Therefore we will destroy him, and also the work**; and we will do this **that we may not be ashamed** [*embarrassed*] in the end, and **that we may get glory of the world** [*so that we will be praised by wicked and foolish people*].

20 Verily, verily, I say unto you, that **Satan has great hold upon their hearts**; he **stirreth them up to iniquity** [*wickedness*] **against that which is good**;

Satan is a master of deception. One of his strongest "tools" is that of stirring up feelings and emotions that go against and defy rational thought. For instance, as the Lord points out to Joseph in verse 21, next, these men did not even ask God in prayer if Joseph Smith has indeed been called as a prophet and is in fact translating ancient scripture. Because the devil has stirred up their hearts (feelings) so effectively, they haven't even taken time to "ask of me" (verse 21). Thus, we are taught that wickedness does not promote rational thought.

If Satan can get people to act according to feelings of hatred, jealousy, prejudice, and so forth as he has these men; or, in other words, if he can stir up wicked feelings within their hearts, he can usually ruin their ability to think clearly and thus successfully trap them.

21 And **their hearts** [*center of feelings*] **are corrupt**, and **full of wickedness and abominations** [*extreme wickedness*]; and **they love darkness rather than light**, because **their deeds are evil**; therefore **they will not ask of** me [*they won't approach Me in prayer about this*].

Next, we are clearly shown a major goal and tactic used by the devil. He loves to destroy destroyers.

22 Satan stirreth them up, **that he may lead their souls to destruction.**

23 And thus **he has laid a cunning plan**, thinking to destroy the work of God; but **I will require this at their hands** [*these men will be held accountable for what they are attempting to do*], and **it shall turn to their shame** [*what they were trying to avoid in verse 19, above*] **and condemnation** [*being stopped in progress toward exaltation*] in the day of judgment.

Next, we are given another lesson and review how Satan works against people.

24 Yea, **he stirreth up their hearts to anger** against this work.

25 Yea, **he saith unto them**: **Deceive** and **lie in wait to catch, that ye may destroy**; behold, **this is no harm**. And **thus he flattereth them, and telleth them that it is no sin to lie that they may catch a man in a lie, that they may destroy him**.

26 And thus **he flattereth them**, and **leadeth them along** until he **draggeth their souls down to hell**; and thus **he causeth them to catch themselves in their own snare** [*they get caught in their own trap*].

27 And **thus he** [*Satan*] **goeth up and down, to and fro in the earth, seeking to destroy the souls of men.**

28 Verily, verily, I say unto you, **wo be unto him that lieth to deceive because he supposeth that another lieth to deceive**, for such are not exempt from the justice of God.

Next, the Savior reminds Joseph Smith again (see verse 11, above) that these men have altered the 116 pages. He instructs him not to retranslate the portion of the gold plates from which the lost manuscript pages came.

29 Now, behold, **they have altered these words, because Satan saith unto them** [*the men who have the 116 pages*]: **He** [*Joseph Smith*] **hath deceived you**—and thus he flattereth them away to do iniquity, to get thee to tempt the Lord thy God.

30 Behold, I say unto you, that **you shall not translate again those words** [*the lost 116 pages*] which have gone forth out of your hands;

31 For, behold, **they shall not accomplish their evil designs in lying against those words**. For, behold, **if you should bring forth the same words** [*if you were to retranslate them*] **they will say that you have lied** and that you have pretended to translate, but that you have contradicted yourself.

32 And, behold, **they will publish this** [*their lies about you and the translation*], and **Satan will harden the hearts of the people** to stir them up to anger against you, that they will not believe my words.

33 Thus **Satan thinketh to overpower your testimony in this generation**, that the work may not come forth in this generation.

Next, Jesus tells Joseph what to do instead of retranslating. He also tells him not to make this plan public knowledge until the Book of Mormon is completed.

34 But behold, **here is wisdom** [*here is wise counsel regarding the plan for replacing the lost 116 pages*], and because I show unto you wisdom, and give you commandments concerning these things, what you shall do, **show it not unto the world until you have accomplished the work of translation.**

35 **Marvel not** [*don't be surprised and don't question it*] that I said unto you: Here is wisdom, show it not unto the world—[*here is why I said it*] **for I said, show it not unto the world, that you may be preserved** [*to save your life*].

36 Behold, I do not say that you shall not show it unto the righteous;

Remember that in verse 34, above, the Lord told Joseph that He would teach him wisdom. There is very wise counsel in verse 37, next. It will help the Prophet avoid being deceived by people who appear to be righteous but are not. It is a reminder that Joseph Smith, as a prophet, is still learning. Such is the case, of course, with all of us.

37 But as you cannot always judge [*discern*] the righteous, or **as** [*since*] **you cannot always tell the wicked from the righteous**, therefore I say unto you, **hold your peace** [*keep this plan to yourself*] until I shall see fit to make all things known unto the world concerning the matter.

Next, the Lord tells Joseph exactly what to do to replace the lost 116 pages. You may recall from your study of the Book of Mormon that Nephi was instructed to make an additional set of plates (known as the small plates of Nephi—see 1 Nephi 9:2–3). Nephi did not know why he was so instructed (1 Nephi 9:5) but was obedient, pointing out to us that the Lord "knoweth all things from the beginning; wherefore, he prepareth a way to accomplish all his works among the children of men" (1 Nephi 9:6).

Now we know why. In the set of gold plates delivered to Joseph Smith by Moroni, there was a small set—the small plates of Nephi. Joseph will now be instructed to translate them to address the same period of time covered by the lost 116 pages. These small plates are what we have today as the books of 1 Nephi, 2 Nephi, Jacob, Enos, Jarom, and Omni in the Book of Mormon.

Thus, knowing what would happen, the Lord had prepared for the loss of the 116 pages by having Nephi make another set of plates, which He explains to the Prophet Joseph in the following verses.

38 And now, verily I say unto you, that **an account of those things that you have written** [*translated; the lost 116 pages*], **which have gone out of your hands** [*which have been lost*], **is engraven upon the plates of Nephi** [*the large plates of Nephi—see Words of Mormon 1:3–7*];

39 Yea, and you remember it was said in those writings [*1 Nephi 9:1–4; 2 Nephi 5:28–33*] that a more particular account was given of these things upon the plates of Nephi [*the small plates of Nephi*].

40 And now, **because the account which is engraven upon the plates of Nephi** [*the small plates*] **is more particular** [*has more detail about spiritual things—see, for instance, Words of Mormon 1:4*] concerning the things which, in my wisdom, I would bring to the knowledge of the people in this account—

41 Therefore, **you shall translate the engravings which are on the plates of Nephi** [*the small plates of Nephi*], **down even till you come to the reign of king Benjamin** [*which starts in Words of Mormon and continues in Mosiah, chapters 1–6*], or until you come to that which you have translated, which you have retained;

42 And behold, **you shall publish it as the record of Nephi** [*coming from the small plates of Nephi*]; and **thus I will confound** [*stop; thwart*] **those who have altered my words.**

43 I will not suffer [*permit*] that they shall destroy my work; yea, **I will show unto them that my wisdom is greater than the cunning of the devil.**

44 Behold, **they have only got a part**, or an abridgment [*a condensed version*] **of the account of Nephi.**

With respect to the "abridgment" spoken of in verse 44, above, Words of Mormon 1:3 contains Mormon's explanation that he had "made an abridgment from the plates of Nephi [*the large plates of Nephi*] down to the reign of this King Benjamin." Thus, what the men who stole the 116 pages actually had was limited in what it covered.

Verse 45, next, explains that what Joseph Smith was to translate now to replace the lost 116 pages had a much richer and fuller account of that period of time among the Nephites.

45 Behold, **there are many things engraven upon the plates of Nephi** [*the small plates of Nephi*] **which do throw greater views**

upon my gospel; therefore, it is wisdom in me that you should translate this first part of the engravings of Nephi [*consisting of 1 Nephi, 2 Nephi, Jacob, Enos, Jarom, and Omni*], and send forth in this work.

From what the Savior explained to His young Prophet, Joseph, in the foregoing verses, it is interesting to note that we, as students of the Book of Mormon, actually came out ahead as far as the loss of the 116 manuscript pages are concerned. Elder Jeffrey R. Holland explains:

"At least six times in the Book of Mormon, the phrase 'for a wise purpose' is used in reference to the making, writing, and preserving of the small plates of Nephi (see 1 Ne. 9:5; [Words of Mormon] 1:7; Alma 37:2, 12, 14, 18). We know one such wise purpose—the most obvious one—was to compensate for the future loss of 116 pages of manuscript translated by the Prophet Joseph Smith from the first part of the Book of Mormon (see D&C 3; 10).

"But it strikes me that there is a 'wiser purpose' than that, or perhaps more accurately, a 'wiser purpose' *in* that. The key to such a suggestion is in D&C 10:45. As the Lord instructs Joseph Smith on the procedure for translating and inserting the material from the small plates into what had been begun as the translation of the abridged large plates, he says, 'Behold, there are many things engraven upon the [small] plates of Nephi which do throw greater views upon my gospel' (emphasis added).

"So clearly this was not a *quid pro quo* in the development of the final Book of Mormon product. It was not tit for tat, this for that—116 pages of manuscript for 142 pages of printed text. Not so. We got back more than we lost. And it was known from the beginning that it would be so. We do not know exactly what we have missed in the 116 pages, but we do know that what we received on the small plates was the personal declarations of the three great witnesses [Nephi, Jacob, and Isaiah], three of the great doctrinal voices of the Book of Mormon, testifying that Jesus is the Christ" ("For a Wise Purpose," *Ensign*, Jan. 1996, 13–14).

Next, the Savior points out that many Book of Mormon prophets prayed that these records might come forth in the last days.

46 And, behold, all the remainder of this work [*the Book of Mormon*] does contain all those parts of my gospel which **my holy prophets, yea, and also my disciples, desired in their prayers** [*for example, Enos in Enos 1:13*] **should come forth unto this people**.

47 And **I said unto them, that**

it should be granted unto them according to their faith in their prayers;

48 Yea, and **this was their faith—that my gospel**, which I gave unto them that they might preach in their days, **might come unto their brethren the Lamanites, and also all that had become Lamanites because of their dissensions**.

49 Now, **this is not all**—their faith in their prayers was that this gospel should be made known also, if it were possible that other nations should possess this land;

50 And thus **they did leave a blessing upon this land in their prayers, that whosoever should believe in this gospel in this land might have eternal life** [*exaltation*];

51 Yea, **that it might be free unto all** of whatsoever nation, kindred, tongue, or people they may be.

Some members of the Church have a tendency to want to belittle or tear down the teachings and convictions of other religions. According to verse 52, next, this should not be. The proper approach to bringing the gospel to others is given by the Lord at the end of the verse.

52 And now, behold, according to their faith in their prayers [*the prayers of ancient Book of Mormon prophets*] will I bring this part of my gospel [*the Book of Mormon*] to the knowledge of my people. Behold, **I do not bring it to destroy that which they have received, but to build it up.**

As you no doubt noticed in verse 52, above, the proper approach to teaching the gospel is to compliment people on what they do have and believe, and to offer the full and true gospel of Jesus Christ to fill in the gaps and complete the picture for them.

53 And for this cause have I said: If this generation harden not their hearts, I will establish my church among them.

54 Now I do not say this to destroy my church [*as defined in verses 67 and 69*], but I say this to build up my church;

Next, the Lord teaches the contrast between those who join His Church and keep His commandments, and the wicked, including those who pretend to set up churches of God but have selfish and wicked motives in so doing. As you will see, fear and lack of fear is a major part of this contrast.

55 Therefore, whosoever belongeth to my church **need not fear**, for such shall inherit the kingdom of heaven.

56 But it is **they who do not fear me** [*who do not respect and obey God and his commandments*], neither keep my commandments **but build up churches unto themselves to get gain**, yea, **and all those that do wickedly and build up the kingdom of the devil**—yea, verily, verily, I say unto you, that **it is they that I will disturb, and cause to tremble and shake to the center**.

> Next, the Master emphasizes who He is, using many descriptive phrases from the Bible, and explaining that the Book of Mormon peoples were the "other sheep" of which he spoke in John 10:16.

Doctrine

Verse 57. Jesus is the Christ, the Son of God.

57 Behold, I am Jesus Christ, the Son of God. I came unto mine own, and mine own received me not [*John 1:11*].

Doctrine

Verse 58. Jesus is the light of the world (see also verse 70). People who are caught up in spiritual darkness do not comprehend spiritual things.

58 **I am the light which shineth in darkness, and the darkness comprehendeth it not** [*John 1:5*].

59 **I am he who said—Other sheep have I which are not of this fold** [*John 10:16*]—unto my disciples, and many there were that understood me not.

> Next, the Savior describes some of the purposes of the Book of Mormon as He briefly reviews what he did for these "other sheep."

60 And **I will show unto this people** [*in our day, via the Restoration through Joseph Smith*] **that I had other sheep** [*the people of the Book of Mormon*], and that they were a branch of the house of Jacob [*they were a part of the house of Israel, the covenant people*];

61 And **I will bring to light their marvelous works** [*the works of these "other sheep" as recorded in the Book of Mormon*], which they did in my name;

62 Yea, and **I will also bring to light my gospel which was ministered unto them**, and, behold, they shall not deny that which you have received [*the words and teachings of the Book of Mormon will not contradict what I have given you, Joseph*], but they shall build it up, and shall bring to light the true **points of my doctrine**, yea, and the only doctrine which is in me.

The phrase, "points of my doctrine," as found in both verse 62, above, and verse 63, below, are of particular significance. The word "points" denotes clear, well-defined, and specific as opposed to "foggy," "blurry," "poorly defined," and "vague." Perhaps you've noticed that Satan has scored major victories among most people in the world today in terms of destroying clear doctrines. It is indeed a fact, as stated in 1 Nephi 13:26, that "they have taken away from the gospel of the Lamb many parts which are plain and most precious; and also many covenants of the Lord."

As we continue our study of the Doctrine and Covenants, we will see example after example of the restoration of clear, beautiful doctrines of the plan of salvation, along with the restoration of priesthood covenants.

63 And this I do that I may establish my gospel, that there may not be so much contention [*doing away with contention is one of the sweet results of understanding pure doctrine*]; yea, Satan doth stir up the hearts of the people to contention concerning the **points of my doctrine**; and in these things they do err, for they do wrest [*twist, misinterpret*] the scriptures and do not understand them.

64 Therefore, I will unfold unto them this great mystery [*perhaps including that the Lord will restore the gospel with its "points of doctrine," thus reducing contention and confusion among the honest in heart*];

65 For, behold, **I will gather them** [*the latter-day gathering of Israel*] **as a hen gathereth her chickens under her wings**, if they will not harden their hearts;

66 Yea, **if they will come, they may, and partake of the waters of life** [*the gospel of Jesus Christ as explained by the Savior to the woman at the well; John 4:7–14*] **freely**.

Next, in verses 67–69, Jesus explains how one can "partake of the waters of life freely" as invited in verse 66, above.

<u>Doctrine</u>

Verse 67. Repentance is essential in coming unto Christ, as well as remaining a strong member of His Church.

67 Behold, this is my doctrine—whosoever repenteth and cometh unto me, the same is my church.

<u>Doctrine</u>

Verse 68. It is dangerous to subject the gospel to personal interpretations that divert away from the Savior's intent in giving it.

68 **Whosoever declareth more or less than this** [*a warning not to dilute, add to, or take away from the pure gospel*], the same is not of me, but is against me; therefore he is not of my church.

69 And now, behold, **whosoever is of my church, and endureth** of my church **to the end**, him will I establish upon my rock [*the absolutely safe and secure gospel of Jesus Christ*], and the gates of hell shall not prevail [*win*] against them.

The Savior's closing words to Joseph Smith can easily apply to all of us.

70 And now, **remember the words of him who is the life and light of the world, your Redeemer, your Lord and your God**. Amen.

Just a quick review of how the translation of the gold plates progressed after the Urim and Thummim and the gold plates were returned to Joseph Smith prior to his receiving the revelation that we have just studied, section 10.

As mentioned in the notes at the beginning of section 10, Joseph Smith's wife, Emma, served as a scribe during part of the translation after the plates and Urim and Thummim were returned to her husband. Martin Harris, who had served as a scribe from February 1828 to June 14, 1828 (at which time they had 116 manuscript pages of the translation) was out of the picture, although he came back to visit the Prophet in February 1829 (see notes in this study guide at the beginning of section 5).

The translation proceeded very slowly until the arrival of Oliver Cowdery, who began serving as scribe on April 7, 1829. After Oliver was sent by the Lord to assist the work, things moved quickly such that the translation was completed near the end of June 1829.

SECTION 11

Background

This revelation, received through the Urim and Thummim, was given through the Prophet Joseph Smith at Harmony, Pennsylvania, to his older brother Hyrum in the latter part of May 1829. Hyrum (born February 9, 1800) was almost 6 years older than Joseph (born December 23, 1805) and was about 4 inches taller at 6 feet, 4 inches in height. The tender relationship between these two great men of God is exemplary. They supported each other throughout their lives and died together in Carthage Jail on June 27, 1844.

To me, this sweet relationship is like that between Nephi and his older brother Sam in the Book of Mormon. Sam was generally in the background, never seeking center stage and always faithful and supportive of his younger brother, the Prophet Nephi. So it was with Hyrum, never seeking to draw attention away from Joseph and faithfully supporting his younger brother, the Prophet of the Restoration.

One of the reasons we know that Hyrum Smith was about 6 feet, 4 inches tall is that the suit he was wearing when he was martyred in Carthage jail is still in existence (in the possession of Hyrum's descendants), and it would take a man of that height to wear it properly according to the fashions of that day. I have seen this suit and felt the great spirit and goodness of this humble man.

Hyrum will be baptized by his brother Joseph in Seneca Lake sometime in June 1829. He will become one of the Eight Witnesses and will bring the first installment of the Book of Mormon manuscript (24 pages) to the typesetter, John H. Gilbert, who will set the type for the printing of the Book of Mormon at Grandin Press in Palmyra, New York.

At the time this revelation was given, the Aaronic Priesthood had already been conferred upon Joseph Smith and Oliver Cowdery by John the Baptist. That took place on May 15, 1829 (see heading to D&C 13). At the time of the restoration of the Aaronic Priesthood, Joseph and Oliver had also been baptized, with John the Baptist as their instructor (see Joseph Smith—History 1:68–74).

Sometime after the coming of John the Baptist, Hyrum had journeyed to Harmony to visit Joseph and Emma. The Prophet recorded the background to section 11, noting that being baptized had had a significant effect upon their ability to understand the scriptures. Joseph gave the following (**bold** added for emphasis):

"Our minds being now enlightened, we began to have the Scriptures laid open to our understandings, and the true meaning and intention of their more mysterious passages revealed unto us in a manner which we never could attain to previously, nor ever before had thought of. In the meantime we were forced to keep secret the circumstances of having received the Priesthood and our having been baptized, owing to a spirit of persecution which had already manifested itself in the neighborhood. . . .

"After a few days, however, feeling it to be our duty, we commenced to reason out of the Scriptures with our acquaintances and friends, as we happened to meet with them. About this time my brother Samuel H. Smith came to visit us. . . .

"**Not many days afterwards, my brother Hyrum Smith came to us** to inquire concerning these things, when at his earnest request, I inquired of the Lord through the Urim and Thummim, and received for him the following: [D&C 11]" (*History of the Church*, 1:43–45).

We will now proceed to study section 11. First of all, you will perhaps notice that it seems like you have read verses 1–9 before. You have. With the exception of two words, two punctuations, and one capitalization, these verses are the same as verses 1–9 of section 6, given to Oliver Cowdery, who was also anxious to assist with the work. We will point out these differences with **bold**.

1 A GREAT and marvelous work is about to come forth **among** the children of men.

2 Behold, I am God; give heed to my word, which is quick and powerful, sharper than a two-edged sword, to the dividing asunder of both joints and marrow; therefore give heed unto my **word**.

3 Behold, the field is white already to harvest; therefore, whoso desireth to reap **[*section 6 has a comma here*]** let him thrust in his sickle with his might, and reap while the day lasts, that he may treasure up for his soul everlasting salvation in the kingdom of God.

4 Yea, whosoever will thrust in his sickle and reap, the same is called of God.

5 Therefore, if you will ask of me you shall receive; if you will knock it shall be opened unto you.

6 Now, as you have asked, behold, I say unto you, keep my commandments, and seek to bring forth and establish the cause of Zion.

7 Seek not for riches but for wisdom; and, behold, the mysteries of God shall be unfolded unto you, and then shall you be made rich. Behold, he that hath eternal life is rich.

8 Verily, verily, I say unto you, even as you desire of me so it shall be done unto you; and, if you desire, you shall be the means of doing much good in this generation.

9 Say nothing but repentance unto this generation**.** Keep **[*section 6 has a semicolon here and "keep" is not capitalized*]** my commandments, and assist to bring forth my work, according to my commandments, and you shall be blessed.

You may wish to review the notes for the above verses as given in section 6 in this study guide. They are a reminder that the same basic message from the Lord applied to many who were to assist as the restoration of the gospel got underway. A similar message is given in the initial verses of sections 4, 12, and 14.

Also, you may wish to review the note preceding verse 9 in section 6 of this study guide, which explains the instruction to preach "nothing but repentance unto this generation" in verse 9 of this section (section 11).

We will now proceed with the rest of section 11. First, we will note that the first five words in verse 10, next, are identical to the words the Lord spoke to Oliver Cowdery in D&C 6:10. This is perhaps a reminder that each member is given one or more spiritual gifts by the Lord (see D&C 46:11). Verse 10 also reminds us that these gifts of the Spirit require personal righteousness and faith.

10 **Behold, thou hast a gift**, or thou shalt have a gift if thou wilt desire of me in **faith**, with an **honest heart**, believing in the power of Jesus Christ, or in my power which speaketh unto thee;

Joseph Fielding Smith sheds additional light upon Hyrum's "gift" as follows:

"The Lord declared that Hyrum Smith had a gift. The great gift which he possessed was that of a tender, sympathetic heart; a merciful spirit. The Lord on a later occasion said: 'Blessed is my servant Hyrum Smith; for I, the Lord, love him because of the integrity of his heart, and because he loveth that which is right before me, saith the Lord.' (D&C 124:15.) This great gift was manifest in his jealous watch care over the Prophet lest some harm come to him" (*Church History and Modern Revelation*, 1:57).

Next, the Savior assures Hyrum that He is the one giving this revelation.

11 For, behold, **it is I that speak**; behold, I am the light which shineth in darkness, and by my power **I give these words unto thee.**

Verses 12–13, next, teach us some of the ways we can tell when we are feeling the Spirit.

<u>Doctrine</u>

Verses 12–13. You can tell when the Spirit is with you by paying attention to what the Spirit does to you and for you.

12 And now, verily, verily, I say unto thee, put your trust in that Spirit which **leadeth to do good**—yea, to **do justly**, to **walk humbly**, to **judge righteously**; and **this is my Spirit.**

13 Verily, verily, I say unto you, I will impart unto you of **my Spirit**, which **shall enlighten your mind**, which **shall fill your soul with joy**;

Some people still have difficulty recognizing when they are feeling the Spirit. Did you notice the two specific ways mentioned in verse 13, above, as to how you can recognize that the Spirit is with you and inspiring you? Your mind works better and you are filled with joy.

Next, in verse 14, we are taught how significant and meaningful these simple instructions can be when followed.

14 And then shall ye know, or **by this shall you know, all things whatsoever you desire of me**, which are pertaining unto things of righteousness, **in faith believing in me that you shall receive**.

From the context of verses 15–26, especially verse 26, we understand that Hyrum Smith was anxious to begin preaching the gospel, which was being restored by his brother Joseph. As we watch what the Lord told him at this time, among other things, we are taught an important lesson, namely, that we need to be prepared before we go out to preach. This certainly can apply to missionaries and members today in teaching and preaching the gospel. In these verses, Hyrum was told to wait to preach until he was better prepared in several ways. We will use **bold** to point them out and then repeat these verses for additional teachings. By the way, Hyrum will finally get the go ahead to preach in D&C 23:3, about 11 months later in April 1830.

15 Behold, I command you that **you need not suppose that you are called to preach until you are called**.

16 **Wait a little longer**, until you shall have my word, my rock, my church, and my gospel, that you may know of a surety my doctrine.

17 And then, behold, according to your desires, yea, even according to your faith shall it be done unto you.

18 Keep my commandments; **hold your peace**; appeal unto my Spirit;

19 Yea, cleave unto me with all your heart, that you may assist in bringing to light those things of which has been spoken—yea, the translation of my work; be patient until you shall accomplish it.

20 Behold, this is your work, to keep my commandments, yea, with all your might, mind and strength.

21 **Seek not to declare my word, but first seek to obtain my word**, and then shall your tongue be loosed; then, if you desire, you shall have my Spirit and my word,

yea, the power of God unto the convincing of men.

22 **But now hold your peace; study my word** which hath gone forth among the children of men, and also study my word which shall come forth among the children of men, or that which is now translating, yea, until you have obtained all which I shall grant unto the children of men in this generation, and then shall all things be added thereto.

23 Behold thou art Hyrum, my son; seek the kingdom of God, and all things shall be added according to that which is just.

24 Build upon my rock, which is my gospel;

25 Deny not the spirit of revelation, nor the spirit of prophecy, for wo unto him that denieth these things;

26 Therefore, **treasure up in your heart until the time** which is in my wisdom **that you shall go forth**.

As mentioned previously, we will now repeat verses 15–26, gleaning many additional insights from them, and then we will continue to the end of the section.

First of all, in verse 15, next, we are reminded that God's kingdom is a kingdom of order, which makes it a kingdom we can trust and understand. Hyrum is taught here that we do not take positions and callings in the Lord's Church until we are properly called by those in authority.

15 Behold, I command you that **you need not suppose that you are called to preach until you are called.**

In verses 16–19, next, Hyrum is again taught the lesson of "first things first." In other words, as stated above, there is order in the way the Lord runs things, and we, as workers in the kingdom, must abide by this order. In this case, we must prepare properly before we undertake to do His work.

16 **Wait** a little longer, **until you shall have my word, my rock, my church, and my gospel, that you may know of a surety my doctrine** [*you must understand the doctrine before you can preach it*].

17 **And then**, behold, **according to your desires**, yea, even **according to your faith shall** it **be done unto you**.

18 **Keep my commandments**; hold your peace [*don't start yet*]; **appeal unto my Spirit** [*first, learn more from the Spirit*];

19 Yea, **cleave unto** [*hold on to*] **me with all your heart**, that you

may assist in bringing to light those things of which has been spoken—yea, the translation of my work [*the Book of Mormon*]; **be patient** until you shall accomplish it.

In verse 20, next, Hyrum is taught the importance of keeping the commandments as a means of personal preparation to serve the Lord.

20 Behold, **this is your work, to keep my commandments**, yea, with all your might, mind and strength.

Verse 21, next, is quite often quoted in lessons and sermons. You may wish to mark it in your own scriptures. It applies wonderfully to missionaries as well as teachers and speakers in church. It again reminds us all that we must study and do our part to qualify for the help of the Spirit in teaching and explaining the gospel. When we do, the Spirit then carries our words into the hearts and souls of others who are ready to hear them.

21 Seek not to declare my word, but first seek to obtain my word, and then shall your tongue be loosed [*then you will be given the ability to teach*]**; then, if you desire, you shall have my Spirit and my word** [*a powerful combination!*]**, yea, the power of God unto the convincing of men.**

22 **But now hold your peace** [*don't start preaching, yet*]; **study my word** which hath gone forth among the children of men [*the Bible plus what Joseph Smith has taught so far*], and also study my word which shall come forth among the children of men, or that which is now translating [*the Book of Mormon; see footnote 22d, for this section*], yea, until you have obtained all which I shall grant unto the children of men in this generation, and **then shall all things be added thereto.**

23 Behold **thou art Hyrum, my son** [*these are terms of tenderness and endearment used by the Lord*]; **seek the kingdom of God, and all things shall be added according to that which is just.**

According to verse 24, next, a vital part of Hyrum's preparation is to build his life upon the gospel of Jesus Christ. This applies, of course, to all of us. The symbolism of "rock" is that of a completely firm, immovable foundation, one that you can completely trust.

24 **Build upon my rock, which is my gospel**;

As you are no doubt aware, a basic doctrine or teaching of some religions is that revelation has ceased. As we see in verse 25, next, that is a very serious false doctrine.

25 **Deny not the spirit of revelation, nor the spirit of prophecy,** for wo [*trouble, sadness, misery will come*] unto him that denieth these things;

Yet again, in verse 26, next, Hyrum is told to keep studying and learning until the time is right for him to start preaching the restored gospel. As stated previously, he will be called to go forth and preach in D&C 23:3, which is about 11 months from the time this revelation was received.

26 Therefore, **treasure up in your heart until the time which is in my wisdom that you shall go forth.**

In verse 27, next, we are reminded that what the Lord says to specific individuals can often apply to all of us.

27 Behold, **I speak unto all** who have good desires, and have thrust in their sickle to reap.

28 Behold, **I am Jesus Christ, the Son of God. I am the life and the light of the world.**

You may wish to read D&C 88:41 to catch a glimpse of the extent to which Jesus Christ is "the life and the light of the world" in terms of the physical universe. Not only is He our life and light (verse 28, above), but His power and influence are also the means by which the physical universe is held in place.

29 **I am the same who came unto mine own and mine own received me not** [*I am the one who was rejected by the people in the Holy Land*];

As the Savior closes this revelation to Hyrum Smith, we are reminded that through Christ, we can receive exaltation in the highest degree of glory within the celestial kingdom. The phrase "become the sons of God," in verse 30, means full heirs of all God has, or, in other words, exaltation. Thus, the phrase "become his sons and his daughters" (Mosiah 5:7) is another way of saying the same thing. One more example is from D&C 76:24 where it explains to us that people on Heavenly Father's other worlds are also given the opportunity for exaltation through the Atonement of our Savior. It uses the phrase "begotten sons and daughters unto God" to denote exaltation, which means to obtain the highest degree of glory in the celestial kingdom. We will quote that verse of section 76 here, using **bold** for emphasis.

D&C 76:24

24 That by him [*Jesus Christ*], and through him, and of him, the worlds are and were created, and the inhabitants thereof are begotten sons and daughters unto God.

We will now conclude our study of section 11 as we read verse 30.

30 But verily, verily, I say unto you, that **as many as receive me**, to them will I give power to **become the sons of God**, even to them that believe on my name. Amen.

One last comment about the term "sons of God" in verse 30, above. It is an important phrase in gospel doctrinal vocabulary. Once in awhile, a student of the scriptures will become a bit confused on this point, thinking, "Wait a minute—we are all sons and daughters of God. We were all born to our Heavenly Parents as spirit children. It says so right in the proclamation on the family, second paragraph (given September 23, 1995). So, what does it mean to *become* a son or daughter of God?"

Well, the fact is that we are indeed all spirit sons and daughters of God. But the term "become sons of God" or "become daughters of God," as used in the scriptures in the context of final judgment and the eternity which lies ahead of us, means to be "born again" through Christ and to ultimately receive exaltation.

SECTION 12

Background

This revelation was given in Harmony, Pennsylvania, in May 1829. It was given through Joseph Smith to Joseph Knight Sr.

Joseph Knight was born on November 3, 1772, making him almost 33 years older than the Prophet Joseph Smith. At this point in history, Joseph Smith was 23 years old and Joseph Knight was 56.

Father Knight, as he was sometimes called, had first met Joseph Smith in 1826 when he hired him to do some work at his farm and grist mill in Colesville, New York, about 130 miles southeast of Palmyra. By this time, the 20-year-old prophet had already seen the Father and Son during the First Vision and had also seen Moroni and had learned of the gold plates. In fact, he had already returned to the Hill Cumorah twice, as instructed by Moroni, on September 22 each year since 1823.

Joseph Smith boarded with the Knight family while working for them, and he eventually told them of his visions and spiritual experiences. Joseph Knight Sr. believed, along with other members of his family, including his wife, Polly, and sons, Joseph Knight Jr. and Newel Knight.

Father Knight assisted Joseph Smith on numerous occasions, supplying provisions and money, which enabled the Prophet and his scribe to continue the work of translating. Among other things, Brother Knight gave Joseph money to buy paper for his scribe to write on during the translating of the gold plates. Father Knight was baptized on June 28, 1830.

The Prophet Joseph Smith gave us the background to the receiving of this section as follows:

"About the same time an old gentleman came to visit us of whose name I wish to make honorable mention—Mr. Joseph Knight, Sen., of Colesville, Broome county, New York, who, having heard of the manner in which we were occupying our time, very kindly and considerately brought us a quantity of provisions, in order that we might not be interrupted in the work of translation by the want of such necessaries of life; and I would just mention here, as in duty bound, that he several times brought us supplies, a distance of at least thirty miles, which enabled us to continue the work when otherwise we must have relinquished it for a season.

"Being very anxious to know his duty as to this work, I inquired of the Lord for him, and obtained the following: [D&C 12]" *(History of the Church*, 1:47–48).

As we study this section, you will probably notice that the first 6 verses sound familiar. You have already seen almost identical counsel from God in the first six verses of sections 6 and 11, and you will see it again in the first six verses of section 14. This counsel, given to Joseph Knight and others, is obviously very important counsel to all of us who seek to help build up the kingdom of God in these last days.

You may wish to review the notes given for verses 1–6 in section 6 in this book.

1 **A GREAT and marvelous work** [*the restoration of the gospel in the last days, before the Second Coming of Christ*] **is about to come forth among the children of men** [*the people of the world*].

2 **Behold** [*see, pay attention*], **I am God; give heed to my word**, which is quick [*living, alive*] and powerful, sharper than a two-edged sword [*which is effective in all directions*], to the dividing asunder [*separating*] of both joints and marrow [*symbolic of cutting through false doctrines and philosophies, exposing them to the light of truth*]; therefore, **give heed unto my word**.

3 Behold, **the field** [*the world*] **is white already to harvest** [*ready for the final preaching of the gospel before the Second Coming of Christ*]; **therefore, whoso desireth to reap** [*to help with the harvesting*] **let him thrust in his sickle with his might**, and reap while the day lasts, **that he may treasure up for his soul everlasting salvation**

in the kingdom of God [*that he may save his own soul*].

4 Yea, **whosoever will** [*has the desire and will take action to do so*] thrust in his sickle and reap, the same **is called of God.**

5 Therefore, **if you will ask of me you shall receive; if you will knock it shall be opened unto you** [*constant revelation is available to those who help with this work*].

Next, the Lord will respond directly to Joseph Knight's request for counsel as to what the Lord would have him do in helping with the work of restoring the gospel. It is interesting to note that, just as was the case with Hyrum Smith (section 11), the Lord emphasizes personal preparation first as a top priority. We will use **bold** to point this out. The Lord will give Brother Knight additional instruction in section 23.

6 Now, as you [*Joseph Knight Sr.*] have asked, behold, I say unto you, **keep my commandments**, and **seek to bring forth and establish the cause of Zion**.

7 Behold, **I speak** unto you, and also **to all** those who have desires to bring forth and establish this work;

8 And no one can assist in this work except he shall **be humble** and **full of love**, **having faith, hope, and charity, being temperate** in all things, whatsoever shall be entrusted to his care.

The Savior concludes by personally introducing Himself to Joseph Knight.

9 Behold, **I am the light and the life of the world, that speak these words**, therefore give heed with your might, and then you are called. Amen.

SECTION 13

Background

This is a very short section, consisting of just one verse, but it has tremendous significance. It deals with the coming of John the Baptist as a resurrected being on May 15, 1829, to confer the Aaronic Priesthood upon Joseph Smith and Oliver Cowdery. John the Baptist told Joseph and Oliver that he was working under the direction of Peter, James, and John, and that the time would soon come that they would receive the Melchizedek Priesthood (see heading to section 13 in your Doctrine and Covenants).

We will study more about the Aaronic Priesthood in sections 20 and 107. Those who hold this priesthood are authorized to administer in the outward ordinances of the gospel. For instance, deacons can pass the sacrament. Teachers can do the above, plus prepare and pass the sacrament. Priests can do the above, plus bless the sacrament and perform baptisms. The Aaronic Priesthood and its associated ordinances prepare us to enjoy the blessings and benefits of the Melchizedek Priesthood ordinances.

At the time of this great event in the Restoration, Joseph and Oliver had been working on the translation of the Book of Mormon in Harmony, Pennsylvania. The Book of Mormon teaches that one must be baptized in order to be saved (see, for example, 3 Nephi 11:33–34). As Joseph and Oliver got to this point in the translating, they became concerned that they, themselves, had not been baptized. We will quote from the Institute of Religion Church history student manual, *Church History in the Fullness of Times*, 2003, page 55, chapter 5, for more about this (**bold** added for emphasis):

"Joseph and Oliver were thrilled as such doctrines as the resurrected Savior's visit to the inhabitants of the Western Hemisphere and his teachings about baptism were unfolded during the translation (see 3 Nephi 11:18–38). **At this point their souls were driven to mighty prayer to learn how they could obtain the blessing of baptism**. On 15 May 1829, Joseph and Oliver went into the nearby woods along the Susquehanna River to pray."

Imagine for a moment what a special occasion this would have been for John the Baptist, who ministered during his mortal mission by virtue of the Aaronic Priesthood and was beheaded by Herod after almost a year in prison (see Mark 6:17–29). We know that John was resurrected with the Savior (see D&C 133:55). Imagine how he must have felt as Joseph and Oliver walked to the banks of the Susquehanna River near Joseph's home to pray about baptism, knowing that the time had finally arrived when he could restore the Aaronic Priesthood to the earth. And imagine what feelings must have swelled up in his heart as he actually laid his hands upon their heads and conferred upon Joseph and Oliver this sacred Aaronic Priesthood and instructed them in the mode of proper baptism so that they could baptize each other (see Joseph Smith—History 1:68–72).

The words used by John are full of meaning and doctrine. We will study them now, making several notes as we go along, and repeating the verse several times. You will see that there are many powerful principles and much authority associated with this priesthood.

First of all, we note that the "Priesthood of Aaron," referred to in this section, is what we normally refer to as the "Aaronic Priesthood." It was named after Aaron, who was Moses's brother. He and his sons were called upon to officiate as priests in the rites and sacrifices that belonged to the Aaronic Priesthood among the Children of Israel as Moses led them in the wilderness (see Exodus 28).

1 UPON you my fellow servants, in the name of Messiah I confer **the Priesthood of Aaron**, which holds the keys of the ministering of angels, and of the gospel of repentance, and of baptism by immersion for the remission of sins; and this shall never be taken again from the earth, until the sons of Levi do offer again an offering unto the Lord in righteousness.

Next, we see that this priesthood holds "keys." Three specific keys are mentioned:

1. The ministering of angels.
2. The gospel of repentance.
3. Baptism by immersion for the remission of sins.

Doctrine

Verse 1. The blessings that come to us through the Aaronic Priesthood include repentance, baptism, and the ministering of angels, whether behind the scenes or by direct appearance.

Doctrine

Verse 1. Baptism is an Aaronic Priesthood ordinance.

1 UPON you my fellow servants, in the name of Messiah I confer the Priesthood of Aaron [*the Aaronic Priesthood*]**, which holds the keys of the ministering of angels**, and of **the gospel of repentance**, and **of baptism by immersion for the remission of sins**; and this shall never be taken again from the earth, until the sons of Levi do offer again an offering unto the Lord in righteousness.

In the wording used by John the Baptist in verse 1, above, you can see that repentance and baptism are closely associated with the ministering of angels. We will first consider the keys of the ministering of angels and of repentance, with Moroni as our instructor, and then turn to President Dallin H. Oaks, then a member of the Quorum of the Twelve Apostles, for more on how these three keys work together for our good. Concerning the ministering of angels, Moroni taught:

Moroni 7:29–31

29 And because he hath done this, my beloved brethren, have miracles ceased? Behold I say unto you, Nay; neither have angels ceased to minister

unto the children of men.

30 For behold, they are subject unto him [*Christ*], to minister according to the word of his command, **showing themselves unto them of strong faith** and a firm mind in every form of godliness.

31 And **the office of their ministry is to call men unto repentance**, and to fulfil and **to do the work of the covenants of the Father** [*example: Peter, James, and John restoring the Melchizedek Priesthood*], which he hath made unto the children of men, **to prepare the way** among the children of men, by **declaring the word of Christ unto the chosen vessels of the Lord**, that they may bear testimony of him.

As mentioned above, Elder Dallin H. Oaks spoke on the subject of the Aaronic Priesthood and the ministering of angels in the priesthood session of the October 1998 general conference as follows (**bold** added for emphasis):

"The scriptures recite numerous instances where an angel appeared personally. Angelic appearances to Zacharias and Mary (see Luke 1) and to King Benjamin and Nephi, the grandson of Helaman (see Mosiah 3:2; 3 Ne. 7:17–18) are only a few examples. **When I was young, I thought such personal appearances were the only meaning of the ministering of angels**. As a young holder of the Aaronic Priesthood, I did not think I would see an angel, and **I wondered what such appearances had to do with the Aaronic Priesthood**.

"But **the ministering of angels can also be unseen**. Angelic messages can be **delivered by a voice** or merely by **thoughts** or **feelings communicated to the mind**. President John Taylor described 'the action of the angels, or messengers of God, upon our minds, so that the heart can conceive . . . revelations from the eternal world' (*Gospel Kingdom*, sel. G. Homer Durham [1987], 31).

"Nephi described three manifestations of the ministering of angels when he reminded his rebellious brothers that (1) they had '**seen an angel**,' (2) they had '**heard his voice from time to time**,' and (3) also that an angel had '**spoken** unto [them] **in a still small voice**' though they were 'past feeling' and 'could not feel his words' (1 Ne. 17:45). The scriptures contain many other statements that angels are sent to teach the gospel and bring men to Christ (see Heb. 1:14; Alma 39:19; Moro. 7:25, 29, 31–32; D&C 20:35). **Most angelic communications are felt or heard rather than seen**.

"How does the Aaronic Priesthood hold the key to the

ministering of angels? The answer is the same as for the Spirit of the Lord.

"**In general, the blessings of spiritual companionship and communication are only available to those who are clean**. As explained earlier, through the Aaronic Priesthood ordinances of **baptism** and the **sacrament**, we are cleansed of our sins and promised that if we keep our covenants we will always have His Spirit to be with us. **I believe that promise not only refers to the Holy Ghost but also to the ministering of angels**, for 'angels speak by the power of the Holy Ghost; wherefore, they speak the words of Christ' (2 Ne. 32:3). So it is that **those who hold the Aaronic Priesthood open the door for all Church members who worthily partake of the sacrament to enjoy the companionship of the Spirit of the Lord and the ministering of angels**" (Dallin H. Oaks, "The Aaronic Priesthood and the Sacrament," *Ensign*, Nov. 1998, 39).

Before we move on to section 14, we will take a closer look at the phrase, "until the sons of Levi do offer again an offering unto the Lord in righteousness."

1 UPON you my fellow servants, in the name of Messiah I confer the Priesthood of Aaron, which holds the keys of the ministering of angels, and of the gospel of repentance, and of baptism by immersion for the remission of sins; and this shall never be taken again from the earth, **until the sons of Levi do offer again an offering unto the Lord in righteousness.**

There seem to be many possibilities as to what this phrase means, and we will not venture to give a final answer. Rather, we will give some possibilities by way of quotes from the scriptures and Church leaders.

Joseph Fielding Smith addresses the question as to whether or not the Aaronic Priesthood will remain on earth now as follows:

"We may be sure that the Aaronic Priesthood will never be taken from the earth while mortality endures, for there will always be need for temporal direction and the performance of ordinances pertaining to 'the preparatory Gospel'" (*Church History and Modern Revelation*, 1:62).

Oliver Cowdery's account uses the word "that" instead of "until." Thus, in Oliver's rendition, it reads "that the Sons of Levi may yet offer an offering unto the Lord in righteousness!" (See Pearl of Great Price, 1989 edition, page 59, last phrase of the second to last paragraph.) With this in mind, it could be that the phrase means, in effect, that the Aaronic Priesthood is being restored and "shall never be taken again from the earth" in order that authorized Aaronic Priesthood ordinances such as the sacrament and baptism can once again be offered to the Lord by sincere Saints.

Third Nephi 24:3 also uses the word "that" in the context of the sons of Levi offering an offering. We will quote it here, using **bold** for emphasis:

3 Nephi 24:3

And he shall sit as a refiner and purifier of silver; and he shall purify the sons of Levi, and purge them as gold and silver, **that they may offer unto the Lord an offering in righteousness.**

D&C 128:24 also uses the word "that" and seems to indicate that the faithful members of the Church are, in a sense, the "sons of Levi." We will quote this verse here, again using **bold** for emphasis.

D&C 128:24

24 Behold, the great day of the Lord is at hand; and who can abide the day of his coming, and who can stand when he appeareth? For he is like a refiner's fire, and like fuller's soap; and he shall sit as a refiner and purifier of silver, and he shall purify the sons of Levi, and purge them as gold and silver, **that they may offer unto the Lord an offering in righteousness**. Let **us**, therefore, **as a church** and **a people**, and **as Latter-day Saints**, offer unto the Lord an offering in righteousness; and let us present in his holy temple, when it is finished, a book containing the records of our dead, which shall be worthy of all acceptation.

Having noted above that the faithful members of the Church could be one definition of "sons of Levi" in a broad sense, we will continue, suggesting that modern priesthood holders could also be considered to be the "sons of Levi." In the days of Moses, the sons of Levi were the ones who officiated in the Aaronic Priesthood ordinances among the Children of Israel. Thus, symbolically, "sons of Levi" could mean those who hold the priesthood today and officiate in priesthood ordinances. This seems to be the meaning of "sons of Moses and Aaron," who were of the tribe of Levi, in D&C 84:31–32. In this revelation, the Lord is addressing a number of elders who had gathered in Kirtland, Ohio, after returning from their missions in the eastern states. In these verses, He uses the phrase "sons of Moses and also the sons of Aaron." These would be the same as "sons of Levi." In verse 32, He tells these priesthood holders that they are the sons of Moses and Aaron. We will quote these two verses here and use **bold** to point things out.

D&C 84:31–32

31 Therefore, as I said concerning the sons of Moses—for the sons of Moses and also the sons of Aaron [*sons of Levi*] **shall offer an acceptable offering** and sacrifice in the house of the Lord, which house [*the Kirtland Temple*] shall be built unto the Lord in this generation, upon the consecrated spot as I have appointed—

32 And **the sons of Moses and of Aaron** shall be filled with the glory of the Lord, upon Mount Zion in the Lord's house, **whose sons are ye** [*you are the "sons of Moses and of Aaron"*]; and also many whom I have called and sent forth to build up my church.

And finally, In the 2018 *Doctrine and Covenants Student Manual*, used by the institutes of religion of the Church, in chapter 6 we read (**bold** added for emphasis): "In ancient times, God commanded His people to offer up animal sacrifices as part of their worship. The purpose of shedding the blood of an animal was to help people look forward in faith to the time when the blood of Jesus Christ would be shed to atone for their sins. From Moses's time to the death of Jesus Christ, the law of Moses dictated that animal sacrifices and burnt offerings be performed by priests officiating at the tabernacle or temple. These priests were descendants of Levi who were designated by the Lord to serve in the sanctuary (see Numbers 18:20–21). Thus **the term 'sons of Levi' refers to holders of the priesthood."**

The question is often asked as to whether or not sacrifice will be offered again as a part of the restoration of all things in the last days. We will conclude our study of section 13 by quoting the Prophet Joseph Smith on this subject and then quoting Joseph Fielding Smith (**bold** added for emphasis):

"It is generally supposed that sacrifice was entirely done away when the Great Sacrifice [i.e.,] the sacrifice of the Lord Jesus was offered up, and that there will be no necessity for the ordinance of sacrifice in the future; but those who assert this are certainly not acquainted with the duties, privileges and authority of the Priesthood, or with the Prophets.

"The offering of sacrifice has ever been connected and forms a part of the duties of the Priesthood. It began with the Priesthood, and will be continued until after the coming of Christ, from generation to generation. . . .

"These sacrifices, as well as every ordinance belonging to

the Priesthood, will, when the Temple of the Lord shall be built, and the sons of Levi be purified, be fully restored and attended to in all their powers, ramifications, and blessings. This ever did and ever will exist when the powers of the Melchizedek Priesthood are sufficiently manifest; else how can **the restitution of all things** spoken of by the Holy Prophets be brought to pass. **It is not to be understood that the law of Moses will be established again with all its rites and variety of ceremonies**; this has never been spoken of by the prophets; **but those things which existed prior to Moses' day, namely, sacrifice, will be continued**" (*Teachings of the Prophet Joseph Smith*, 172–73).

Joseph Fielding Smith explained that "we are living **in the dispensation of the fulness of times** into which all things are to be gathered, and **all things are to be restored since the beginning**. Even this earth is to be restored to the condition which prevailed before Adam's transgression. Now in the nature of things, **the law of sacrifice will have to be restored, or all things which were decreed by the Lord would not be restored**. It will be necessary, therefore, for the sons of Levi, who offered the blood sacrifices anciently in Israel, to offer such a sacrifice again to round out and complete this ordinance in this dispensation. Sacrifice by the shedding of blood was instituted in the days of Adam and of necessity will have to be restored.

"The sacrifice of animals will be done to complete the restoration when the temple spoken of is built; **at the beginning of the millennium, or in the restoration, blood sacrifices will be performed long enough to complete the fulness of the restoration in this dispensation. Afterwards sacrifice will be of some other character**" (*Doctrines of Salvation*, 3:94).

SECTION 14

Background

Sections 14–16 go together in the sense that they are given to three brothers, David Whitmer, John Whitmer, and Peter Whitmer Jr., all of whom desired to know what the Lord wanted them to do at this point in the restoration of the gospel. These three brothers were sons of Peter Whitmer Sr. and Mary Whitmer of Fayette, New York, who would play a prominent role in enabling the Prophet to complete the translation of the Book of Mormon.

It is interesting to see how the Lord prepares things in advance in order for His work to proceed. Joseph Smith had previously become acquainted with the Whitmer family. Oliver Cowdery had become especially good friends with David Whitmer after having met him in Palmyra. He had developed a special interest in David's sister, Elizabeth, whom he will later marry. As Joseph and Oliver continued the work of translating the Book of Mormon in Harmony, Pennsylvania, persecution began to increase. As a result, Oliver wrote to David Whitmer, requesting that he come and take him and Joseph to the home of David's father, Peter Whitmer Sr., in Fayette where they could continue the translation in peace. Peter Whitmer Sr. invited them to stay as long as was needed to complete the work. David came and picked up Joseph, Emma, and Oliver and transported them back to Fayette in his two-horse wagon. The translation was thus completed rapidly, under peaceful circumstances, at the home of Peter Whitmer Sr. in Fayette, New York.

One more interesting note reminds us of the miracles that accompanied this part of the work of the Restoration. As soon as David Whitmer received the letter from Oliver Cowdery asking him to come get Joseph, Emma, and Oliver, he wanted to leave right away with a wagon and go to Harmony and get them. But it was springtime, and preparation of the soil for spring planting could not be delayed. Consequently, he hurriedly set out to plow the soil on the farm. "At the end of a day of plowing he found he had accomplished in one day what normally would have taken two days to do. David's father was likewise impressed with this apparent miracle. Peter Whitmer Sr. said, 'There must be an overruling hand in this, and I think you would better go down to Pennsylvania as soon as your plaster of paris is sown.' (Plaster of paris was used to reduce the acidity of the soil.) The next day David went to the fields to sow the plaster, but to his surprise he found the work had been done. His sister, who lived near the field, said that her children had called her to watch three strangers the day before spread the plaster with remarkable skill. She assumed they were men David had hired.

"Grateful for this divine intervention, David Whitmer hurried off on the three-day journey to Harmony. Joseph Smith and Oliver Cowdery met him as he approached the town. Although David had not told them exactly when he was coming, Joseph had seen in vision the details of David's trip to Harmony" (*Church History in the Fulness of Times*, 2003, 56–57).

We will now study section 14, which was given through Joseph Smith to David Whitmer in Fayette, New York, in June 1829. By the way, David was born on January 7, 1805, and thus was a little over 11 months older than Joseph Smith. He will become one of the Three Witnesses to the Book of Mormon. The Prophet gave the background to this section as follows:

". . . in the beginning of the month of June, his [Peter Whitmer, Sr.,] son, David Whitmer, came to the place where we were residing, and brought with him a two-horse wagon, for the purpose of having us accompany him to his father's place, and there remain until we should finish the work. It was arranged that we should have our board free of charge, and the assistance of one of his brothers to write for me, and also his own assistance when convenient. Having much need of such timely aid in an undertaking so arduous, and being informed that the people in the neighborhood of the Whitmers were anxiously awaiting the opportunity to inquire into these things, we accepted the invitation, and accompanied Mr. Whitmer to his father's house, and there resided until the translation was finished and the copyright secured. Upon our arrival, we found Mr. Whitmer's family very anxious concerning the work, and very friendly toward ourselves. They continued so, boarded and lodged us according to arrangements; and John Whitmer, in particular, assisted us very much in writing during the remainder of the work.

"In the meantime, David, John and Peter Whitmer, Jun., became our zealous friends and assistants in the work; and being anxious to know their respective duties, and having desired with much earnestness that I should inquire of the Lord concerning them, I did so, through the means of the Urim and Thummim, and obtained for them in succession the following revelations: [D&C 14–16]" (*History of the Church*, 1:48–49).

Again, verses 1–6 may seem quite familiar to you, because very similar wording was used by the Lord at the beginning of sections 4, 6, 11, and 12.

1 **A GREAT and marvelous work** [*the restoration of the gospel*] **is about to come forth unto the children of men.**

2 Behold, **I am God; give heed to my word**, which is **quick** [*alive; living; continuing revelation*] and **powerful, sharper than a two-edged sword**, to the dividing asunder [*separating; symbolic of cutting through false philosophies and doctrines, separating truth from error*] of both joints and marrow; therefore **give heed unto my word**.

3 Behold, **the field** [*the world*] **is white already to harvest** [*the time for the final gathering of Israel has arrived*]; therefore, **whoso desireth to reap** [*to join in the harvest*] **let him thrust in his sickle with his might, and reap while the day lasts** [*while the opportunity is still available*], **that he may treasure up for his soul everlasting salvation in the kingdom of God**

[*that he may save his own soul in exaltation in celestial glory*].

4 Yea, **whosoever will thrust in his sickle and reap, the same is called of God**.

5 Therefore, if you will **ask** of me you shall **receive**; if you will **knock** it shall be **opened** unto you.

6 Seek to bring forth and establish my Zion. **Keep my commandments in all things**.

Doctrine

Verse 7. Exaltation, obtained through keeping the commandments, is the greatest of all God's gifts to us.

7 And, **if you keep my commandments** and **endure to the end you shall have eternal life** [*exaltation*], which gift is **the greatest of all the gifts of God**.

Next, David Whitmer is told that if he is faithful, he can have the privilege of teaching by the power of the Holy Ghost, as well as hearing and seeing marvelous things.

Doctrine

Verse 8. The Holy Ghost enables us to bear witness effectively.

8 And it shall come to pass, that if you shall ask the Father in my name, in faith believing, you shall receive the Holy Ghost, which giveth utterance, that you may stand as a witness of the things of which you shall both hear and see, and also that **you may declare repentance** [*preach the gospel of Jesus Christ, which leads to repentance and cleansing through the Atonement*] unto this generation.

9 Behold, **I am Jesus Christ**, the Son of the living God, who created the heavens and the earth, a light which cannot be hid in darkness;

10 Wherefore, **I must bring forth the fulness of my gospel from the Gentiles unto the house of Israel**.

The question comes up as to who the "Gentiles" are in verse 10, above. Perhaps you have already noticed that the term "Gentile" is very context sensitive. According to the Bible Dictionary, page 679, the word has various meanings, depending on context. For instance, it can mean non-Jews, non-Israelites, nonmembers of the Church, Israelites who don't have the gospel, and so forth.

As used in verse 10, above, "Gentiles" refers to Joseph Smith and the early members of the Church, as well as faithful members now, who are taking the gospel to all the world in the final gathering of Israel. They are considered to be Gentiles because they are not inhabitants of the Holy Land now. President Wilford Woodruff explained this as follows (**bold** added for emphasis):

"Sometimes our neighbors and friends think hard of us because we call them Gentiles; but, bless your souls, **we are all Gentiles**. **The Latter-day Saints are all Gentiles in a national capacity**. The Gospel came to us among the Gentiles. **We are not Jews, and the Gentile nations have got to hear the Gospel first**. The whole Christian world have got to hear the Gospel, and when they reject it, the law will be bound and the testimony sealed, and it will turn to the house of Israel. Up to the present day we have been called to preach the Gospel to the Gentiles, and we have had to do it. For the last time we have been warning the world, and we have been engaged in that work for forty-five years" (*Journal of Discourses*, 18:112).

As the Lord closes this revelation to David Whitmer, he is counseled to "assist." This is especially significant in view of the fact that later in life he rejected Joseph Smith's authority, claiming to be president of the Church in Missouri (see *Joseph Smith and the Restoration*, 371), which led, among other things, to his excommunication in April 1838.

11 And behold, thou art **David**, and **thou art called to assist**; which thing **if ye do, and are faithful, ye shall be blessed both spiritually and temporally**, and great shall be your reward. Amen.

SECTION 15

Background

As mentioned in the background to section 14, John Whitmer, brother of David Whitmer, wanted to know what the Lord desired him to do at this point of his life. In June 1829, the Lord gave him this revelation through the Prophet Joseph Smith in Fayette, New York.

1 HEARKEN, my servant John, and **listen to the words of Jesus Christ**, your Lord and your Redeemer.

2 For behold, **I speak unto you with sharpness and with power**, for mine arm is over all the earth.

3 And I will tell you that which no man knoweth save me and thee alone—

Sometimes we worry that it is too selfish to ask what will be of most benefit to us personally in doing the work of the Lord. While it is true that we must avoid becoming self-centered, verses 4–6, next, suggest that within proper limits, it is appropriate to consider the benefits to ourselves that come from participating in the work of the Lord.

4 For **many times you have desired of me to know that which would be of the most worth unto you.**

5 Behold, **blessed are you for this thing** [*it was appropriate for you to ask about this*], and for speaking my words which I have given you according to my commandments.

Doctrine

Verse 6. Serving missions and teaching the gospel to others is one of the most beneficial things we can do for ourselves.

6 And now, behold, I say unto you, that **the thing which will be of the most worth unto you will be to declare repentance unto this people**, that you may bring souls unto me, that you may rest with them in the kingdom of my Father. Amen.

SECTION 16

Background

This section was given to Peter Whitmer Jr. under the same circumstances as those for his brothers, David and John, as explained in the background for sections 14 and 15.

Since this section is exactly the same as section 15 except for the name "Peter," the question comes up as to why the Lord would use the same wording for two different people. While we don't know the answer for sure, there are many possibilities. One likely answer is simply that they were both wondering the same thing and that the answer was exactly the same for both; namely, that the preaching of the gospel in missionary efforts would be of most worth to them personally at this point in their lives. This same answer could be given to thousands of potential young missionaries today, as well as to many thousands of potential senior missionaries.

Since sections 15 and 16 are identical except for the names John and Peter, we will review a few scriptural terms as we study section 16.

1 **HEARKEN** [*listen carefully with the Intent to obey*], my servant Peter, and listen to the words of Jesus Christ, your Lord and your Redeemer.

2 For behold, I speak unto you with **sharpness** [*pointedly, with a specific answer to your question*] and with power, for mine **arm** [*in scriptural symbolism, "arm" means power and authority*] is over all the earth.

Doctrine

Verses 3–5. Only members of the Godhead can know the deepest thoughts of your heart. See also D&C 6:16.

3 And I will tell you that which **no man knoweth save me and thee alone**—

4 For **many times you have desired of me to know that which would be of the most worth unto you.**

5 Behold, **blessed are you for this thing**, and for speaking my words which I have given unto you according to my commandments.

We will define three more scriptural vocabulary words and phrases in verse 6, next.

6 And now, behold, I say unto you, that the thing which will be of the most worth unto you will be to **declare repentance** [*preach the gospel in its simplicity, which leads to repentance*] unto this people, that you may bring souls unto me, that you may **rest** [*the word "rest" is defined in D&C 84:24 as the "fulness" of God's glory, or, in other words, exaltation*] with them in the **kingdom of my Father** [*the celestial kingdom*]. Amen.

SECTION 17

Background

During the translation of the gold plates, it became apparent that they would be shown by the power of God to three special witnesses, who would then bear witness to the world that the Book of Mormon is the work of God. We see this in the Book of Ether as follows (**bold** used for emphasis):

Ether 5:2–4

2 And behold, ye [*Joseph Smith*] **may be privileged that ye may show the plates unto those** [*the Eight Witnesses*] **who shall assist to bring forth this work**;

3 And **unto three shall they be shown by the power of God**; wherefore they shall know of a surety that these things are true.

4 And **in the mouth of three witnesses shall these things be established**; and the testimony of three, and this work, in the which shall be shown forth the power of God and also his word, of which the Father, and the Son, and the Holy Ghost bear record—and all this shall stand as a testimony against the world at the last day.

Another place in the Book of Mormon where the Three Witnesses are mentioned is 2 Nephi 27:12. We will quote that verse here and again use **bold** to point things out.

2 Nephi 27:12

12 Wherefore, at that day when the book [*the gold plates*] shall be delivered unto the man [*Joseph Smith*] of whom I have spoken, the book shall be hid from the eyes of the world, that the eyes of none shall behold it save it be that **three witnesses shall behold it, by the power of God**, besides him to whom the book shall be delivered; and they shall testify to the truth of the book and the things therein.

Furthermore, Joseph Smith and Martin Harris had been told, as recorded in section 5, that there would be three special witnesses who would be shown these things by the power of God, and who would literally hear the voice of the Lord declaring the truthfulness thereof. We will quote those verses here and use **bold**, as usual, for emphasis:

D&C 5:11–13

11 And in addition to your testimony, the testimony of three of my servants, whom I shall call and ordain, **unto whom I will show these things**, and they shall go forth with my words that are given through you.

12 Yea, **they shall know of a surety that these things are true, for from heaven will I declare it unto them**.

13 I will give them power that **they may behold and view these things as they are**;

As the translation of the Book of Mormon continued, in June 1829, Oliver Cowdery, David Whitmer, and Martin Harris, who had come to Fayette to visit the Prophet, expressed a deep desire to be the three witnesses spoken of. At their continued urging, Joseph finally agreed to inquire of the Lord through the Urim and Thummim and received section 17 as a result. Imagine the feelings in their hearts as they heard the following from the Savior, including the specific things they would be privileged to see as witnesses:

1 BEHOLD, I say unto you, that **you must rely upon my word**, which **if you do** with full purpose of heart, **you shall have a view of the plates**, and also of **the breastplate**, the **sword of Laban**, the **Urim and Thummim**, which were given to the brother of Jared upon the mount, when he talked with the Lord face to face, and **the miraculous directors** [*the*

Liahona] which were given to Lehi while in the wilderness, on the borders of the Red Sea.

The Joseph Smith Papers publications give additional insights as to what these three witnesses saw. Later in his life, David Whitmer testified "We not only saw the plates of the B[ook] of M[ormon] but also the Brass plates, the Plates of the Book of ether [sic], the Plates containing the Record of the wickedness of the people of the world, and many other plates" (in *The Joseph Smith Papers, Documents, Volume 1: July 1828–June 1831*, 380).

2 And **it is by your faith that you shall obtain a view of them**, even by that faith which was had by the prophets of old.

3 And **after that you have obtained faith, and have seen them** with your eyes, **you shall testify of them**, by the power of God;

4 And **this you shall do that my servant Joseph Smith, Jun., may not be destroyed**, that I may bring about my righteous purposes unto the children of men in this work.

Next, the Lord gives them very specific commandments as to what they are to testify of as the Three Witnesses.

5 And **ye shall testify that you have seen them**, even as my servant Joseph Smith, Jun., has seen them; for it is by my power that he has seen them, and it is because he had faith.

6 **And he has translated the book**, even that part which I have commanded him, **and** as your Lord and your God liveth **it is true**.

7 Wherefore, **you have received the same power**, and **the same faith**, and **the same gift like unto him**;

We will include the Testimony of the Three Witnesses here so that you can see that they held very tightly to these instructions of the Lord given in verses 5–7, above. As usual, we will use **bold** for emphasis.

THE TESTIMONY OF THREE WITNESSES

BE IT KNOWN unto all nations, kindreds, tongues, and people, unto whom this work shall come: That **we**, through the grace of God the Father, and our Lord Jesus Christ, **have seen the plates** which contain this record, which is a record of the people of Nephi, and also of the Lamanites, their brethren, and also of the people of Jared, who came from the tower of which hath been spoken. And **we also know that they have been translated by the gift and power of God**, for **his voice hath declared it unto us**; wherefore **we know of a surety that the work is true**. And **we also testify that we have seen the engravings which are upon the plates**; and **they have been shown unto us by the power of God, and not of man**. And we declare with words of soberness, that **an angel of God came down from heaven, and he brought and laid before our eyes, that we beheld and saw the plates, and the engravings** thereon; and **we know** that it is by the grace of God the Father, and our Lord Jesus Christ, that **we beheld and bear record that these things are true**. And it is marvelous in our eyes. Nevertheless, the voice of the Lord commanded us that we should bear record of it; wherefore, to be obedient unto the commandments of God, **we bear testimony of these things**. And we know that if we are faithful in Christ, we shall rid our garments of the blood of all men, and be found spotless before the judgment-seat of Christ, and shall dwell with him eternally in the heavens. And the honor be to the Father, and to the Son, and to the Holy Ghost, which is one God. Amen.

OLIVER COWDERY
DAVID WHITMER
MARTIN HARRIS

As this revelation comes to a close, we see an "if, then" clause, meaning that "if" they do their part, "then" the Lord will be enabled to do His part. Furthermore, as we apply this to ourselves, we see that "if" we do our best, the "grace" or help of the Lord will be sufficient for us to attain exaltation at the final judgment. This is a very encouraging and comforting fact.

8 And **if you do these last commandments** of mine, which I have given you, **the gates of hell shall not prevail against you**; for **my grace is sufficient for you**, and **you shall be lifted up** [*exalted*] **at the last day** [*at the final judgment*].

9 And **I, Jesus Christ, your Lord and your God, have spoken it** unto you, that I might bring about my righteous purposes unto the children of men. Amen.

Since the Three Witnesses are such an important part of Church history and the coming forth of the Book of Mormon, we will take extra time here to give some follow-up history to this revelation that informed Oliver Cowdery, David Whitmer, and Martin Harris that they could serve as the Three Witnesses. We have fascinating and wonderful accounts of how and what the Three Witnesses saw and heard. The Prophet Joseph Smith wrote the following:

"Not many days after the above commandment [*section 17*] was given, we four, viz., Martin Harris, David Whitmer, Oliver Cowdery and myself, agreed to retire into the woods, and try to obtain, by fervent and humble prayer, the fulfilment of the promises given in the above revelation—that they should have a view of the plates. We accordingly made choice of a piece of woods convenient to Mr. Whitmer's house, to which we retired, and having knelt down, we began to pray in much faith to Almighty God to bestow upon us a realization of these promises.

"According to previous arrangement, I commenced by vocal prayer to our Heavenly Father, and was followed by each of the others in succession. We did not at the first trial, however, obtain any answer or manifestation of divine favor in our behalf. We again observed the same order of prayer, each calling on and praying fervently to God in rotation, but with the same result as before.

"Upon this, our second failure, Martin Harris proposed that he should withdraw himself from us, believing, as he expressed himself, that his presence was the cause of our not obtaining what we wished for. He accordingly withdrew from us, and we knelt down again, and had not been many minutes engaged in prayer, when presently we beheld a light above us in the air, of exceeding brightness; and behold, an angel stood before us. In his hands he held the plates which we had been praying for these to have a view of. He turned over the leaves one by one, so that we could see them, and discern the engravings thereon distinctly. He then addressed himself to David Whitmer, and said, 'David, blessed is the Lord, and he that keeps His commandments;' when, immediately afterwards, we heard a voice from out of the bright light above us, saying, 'These plates have been revealed by the power of God, and they have been translated by the power of God. The translation of them which you have seen is correct, and I command you to bear record of what you now see and hear.'

"I now left David and Oliver, and went in pursuit of Martin Harris, whom I found at a considerable distance, fervently engaged in prayer. He soon told me, however, that he had not yet prevailed with the Lord, and earnestly requested me to join him in prayer, that he also might realize the same blessings which we had just received. We accordingly joined in prayer, and ultimately obtained our desires, for before we had yet finished, the same vision was opened to our view, at least it was again opened to me, and I once more beheld and heard the same things; whilst at the same moment, Martin Harris cried out, apparently in an ecstasy of joy, 'Tis enough; tis enough; mine eyes have beheld; mine eyes have beheld;' and jumping up, he shouted, 'Hosanna,' blessing God, and otherwise rejoiced exceedingly" (*History of the Church*, 1:54–55).

Elders Orson Pratt and Joseph F. Smith (who later became the President of the Church) interviewed David Whitmer on September 7, 1878, and asked him questions about his experience as one of the Three Witnesses. Their account of this interview is as follows:

"On Saturday morning, Sept. 7 [1878], we met Mr. David Whitmer (at Richmond, Ray Co., Mo.), the last remaining one of the Three Witnesses of the Book of Mormon.

"Elder O. Pratt to David Whitmer: 'Do you remember what time you saw the plates?'

"D. Whitmer: It was in June, 1829, the latter part of the month, and the eight witnesses saw them, I think, the next day or the day after (i.e., one or two days after). Joseph showed them the plates himself, but the angel showed us (the Three Witnesses) the plates, as I suppose to fulfill the words of the book itself. Martin Harris was not with us at this time; he obtained a view of them afterwards (the same day). Joseph, Oliver, and myself were together when I saw them. We not only saw the plates of the Book of Mormon, but also the brass plates, the plates of the Book of Ether, the plates containing the records of the wickedness and secret combinations of the people of the world down to the time of their being engraved, and many other plates. The fact is, it was just as though Joseph, Oliver and I were sitting just here on a log, when we were overshadowed by a light. It was not the light of the sun, nor like that of a fire, but more glorious and beautiful. It extended away round us, I cannot tell how far, but in the midst of this light about as far off as he sits (pointing to John C. Whitmer, sitting a few feet from him), there appeared as it were a table with many records or plates upon it, besides the plates of the Book of Mormon, also the sword of Laban, the directors (i.e., the ball which Lehi had) and the interpreters. I saw them just as plain as I see this bed (striking the bed beside him with his hand), and I heard the voice of the Lord, as distinctly as I ever heard anything in my life, declaring that the records of the plates of the Book of Mormon were translated by the gift and power of God" (*Historical Record, Church Encyclopedia,* Book I, May 1887, 207–208; see also Doxey, *Latter-day Prophets and the Doctrine and Covenants*, 1:153).

Joseph Smith's mother, Lucy Mack Smith, writes of the relief felt by her son now that three others had a sure witness that the work he was doing was of God. She wrote (**bold** added for emphasis):

"AS SOON as the Book of Mormon was translated, Joseph despatched a messenger to Mr. Smith, bearing intelligence of the completion of the work, and a request that Mr. Smith and myself should come immediately to Waterloo [*near Fayette and the Peter Whitmer Sr. farm*].

"The same evening, we conveyed this intelligence to Martin Harris, for we loved the man, although his weakness had cost us much trouble. Hearing this, he greatly rejoiced, and determined to go straightway to Waterloo to congratulate Joseph upon his success. Accordingly, the next morning, we all set off together, and before sunset met Joseph and Oliver at Mr. Whitmer's.

"The evening was spent in reading the manuscript, and it would be superfluous for me to say, to one who has read the foregoing pages, that we rejoiced exceedingly. It then appeared to those of us who did not realize the magnitude of the work, as if the greatest difficulty was then surmounted; but Joseph better understood the nature of the dispensation of the Gospel which was committed unto him.

"The next morning, after attending to the usual services, namely, reading, singing and praying, Joseph arose from his knees, and approaching Martin Harris with a solemnity that thrills through my veins to this day, when it occurs to my recollection, said, 'Martin Harris, you have got to humble yourself before God this day, that you may obtain a forgiveness of your sins. If you do, it is the will of God that you should look upon the plates, in company with Oliver Cowdery and David Whitmer.'

"In a few minutes after this, Joseph, Martin, Oliver and David, repaired to a grove, a short distance from the house, where they commenced calling upon the Lord, and continued in earnest supplication, until he permitted an angel to come down from his presence, and declare to them, that all which Joseph had testified of concerning the plates was true.

"When they returned to the house it was between three and four o'clock p.m. (David Whitmer indicated that they left the house about 11 a.m. Therefore, it appears that they were gone from the house between four and five hours.) Mrs. Whitmer, Mr. Smith and myself, were sitting in a bedroom at the time. **On coming in, Joseph threw himself down beside me, and exclaimed, 'Father, mother, you do not know how**

happy I am: the Lord has now caused the plates to be shown to three more besides myself. They have seen an angel, who has testified to them, and they will have to bear witness to the truth of what I have said, for now they know for themselves, that I do not go about to deceive the people, and I feel as if I was relieved of a burden which was almost too heavy for me to bear, and it rejoices my soul, that I am not any longer to be entirely alone in the world.' Upon this, Martin Harris came in: he seemed almost overcome with joy, and testified boldly to what he had both seen and heard. And so did David and Oliver, adding that no tongue could express the joy of their hearts, and the greatness of the things which they had both seen and heard" (*History of Joseph Smith by His Mother*, 151).

In conclusion, we will include one more quote, this time from Richard Lloyd Anderson's fascinating research, combining several documented interviews with David Whitmer into one "composite" interview, providing a number of additional details about the heavenly manifestation given the Three Witnesses. Brother Anderson put this composite of several interviews with David Whitmer into a question and answer format as follows:

Q: Is your published testimony accurate?

A: "As you read my testimony given many years ago, so it stands as my own existence, the same as when I gave it, and so shall stand throughout the cycles of eternity."

Q: When did this event take place?

A: "It was in June, 1829, the very last part of the month."

Q: What was the approximate time of day?

A: "It was about 11 a.m."

Q: What were the circumstances of the vision?

A: "[We] went out into the woods nearby, and sat down on a log and talked awhile. We then kneeled down and prayed. Joseph prayed. We then got up and sat on the log and were talking, when all at once a light came down from above us and encircled us for quite a little distance around, and the angel stood before us."

Q: Describe the angel.

A: "He was dressed in white, and spoke and called me by name and said, 'Blessed is he that keepeth His commandments.' This is all that I heard the angel say."

Q: Did the angel have the Book of Mormon plates?

A: "[He] showed to us the plates, the sword of Laban, the Directors, the Urim and Thummim, and other records. Human language could not describe heavenly things and that which we saw."

Q: Did the vision take place under natural circumstances?

A: "The fact is, it was just as though Joseph, Oliver and I were sitting right here on a log, when we were overshadowed by a light. It was not like the light of the sun, nor like that of a fire, but more glorious and beautiful. It extended away round us, I cannot tell how far, but in the midst of this light, immediately before us, about as far off as he sits (pointing to John C. Whitmer, who was sitting 2 or 3 feet from him) there appeared, as it were, a table, with many records on it—besides the plates of the Book of Mormon, also the sword of Laban, the Directors, and the Interpreters. I saw them as plain as I see this bed (striking his hand upon the bed beside him), and I heard the voice of the Lord as distinctly as I ever heard anything in my life declaring that they were translated by the gift and power of God."

Q: Can you explain the supernatural power that surrounded you?

A: "All of a sudden I beheld a dazzlingly brilliant light that surpassed in brightness even the sun at noonday, and which seemed to envelop the woods for a considerable distance around. Simultaneous with the light came a strange entrancing influence which permeated me so powerfully that I felt chained to the spot, while I also experienced a sensation of joy absolutely indescribable."

Q: "Did you see the Urim and Thummim?"

A: "I saw the Interpreters in the holy vision; they looked like whitish stones put in the rim of a bow—looked like spectacles, only much larger."

Q: Did you see an actual table?

A: "You see that small table by the wall? . . . Well, there was a table about that size, and the heavenly messenger brought the several plates and laid them on the table before our eyes, and we saw them."

Q: Did you handle the plates?

A: "I did not handle the plates—only saw them. Joseph, and I think Oliver and Emma told me about the plates, and described them to me, and I believed them, but did not see except at the time testified of."

Q: How clearly could you see the plates?

A: "[T]he angel stood before us, and he turned the leaves one by one." "[H]e held the plates and turned them over with his hands, so that they could be plainly visible."

Q: "Did the angel turn all the leaves before you as you looked on it?"

A: "No, not all, only that part of the book which was not sealed, and what there was sealed appeared as solid to my view as wood."

Q: "Can you describe the plates?"

A: "They appeared to be of gold, about six by nine inches in size, about as thick as parchment, a great many in number and bound together like the leaves of a book by massive rings passing through the back edges. The engraving upon them was very plain and of very curious appearance."

Q: Is it possible that you imagined this experience?

A: "[O]ur testimony is true. And if these things are not true, then there is no truth; and if there is no truth, there is no God; and if there is no God, there is no existence. But I know there is a God, for I have heard His voice and witnessed the manifestation of his power."

Q: "Do you remember the peculiar sensation experienced upon that occasion?"

A: "Yes, I remember it very distinctly. And I never think of it, from that day to this, but what that spirit is present with me" (*Investigating the Book of Mormon Witnesses*, 80).

SECTION 18

Background

This section is perhaps most well known and oft-quoted for its teaching about the worth of souls (verses 10–16). It has this and much more to teach us. It was given to Joseph Smith, Oliver Cowdery, and David Whitmer in June 1829 at the Peter Whitmer Sr. residence in Fayette, New York.

When John the Baptist restored the Aaronic Priesthood to Joseph Smith and Oliver Cowdery on May 15, 1829 (see D&C 13), he told them that he was acting under the direction of Peter, James, and John, and that, in due time, they would receive the Melchizedek Priesthood (see heading to D&C 13). Peter, James, and John did indeed come and confer the Melchizedek Priesthood as promised by John the Baptist, but the date was not recorded. It does appear, though, that by the time section 18 was given, the Melchizedek Priesthood had been restored. Research from the Joseph Smith Papers given in the *Doctrine and Covenants Student Manual*, 2018, chapter 6, confirms this thinking (**bold** added for emphasis).

"In June 1829, Joseph Smith and Oliver Cowdery continued the translation of the Book of Mormon in the home of Peter Whitmer Sr. in Fayette, New York. During this time, Joseph and Oliver also sought to know how to exercise **the keys of the Melchizedek Priesthood that had been recently conferred upon them by heavenly messengers**. While praying in a room of the Whitmer home, the word of the Lord came to them and directed them to exercise the priesthood to ordain elders, administer the sacrament, and bestow the gift of the Holy Ghost by the laying on of hands. However, the Lord instructed them to wait to perform these ordinances until a group of believers could be assembled. (See *The Joseph Smith Papers, Histories, Volume 1: Joseph Smith Histories, 1832–1844*, ed. Karen Lynn Davidson and others [2012], 326, 328.)

Joseph Smith gives us a bit more background to section 18. From his writings, we learn that sometime in June 1829, Oliver Cowdery and David Whitmer had joined with him in desiring additional instruction with regard to the Melchizedek Priesthood. Joseph tells what occurred as they sought the Lord in prayer in the chamber of Peter Whitmer's house. Note how the Lord is patiently teaching them about proper order and procedure in His true Church, including the principle of having members sustain their leaders as well as sustaining priesthood ordinations:

"We had for some time made this matter a subject of humble prayer, and at length we got together in the chamber of Mr. Whitmer's house, in order more particularly to seek of the Lord what we now so earnestly desired; and here, to our unspeakable satisfaction, did we realize the truth of the Savior's promise—'Ask, and it shall be given you; seek, and ye shall find; knock, and it shall be opened unto you'—for we had not long been engaged in solemn and fervent prayer, when the word of the Lord came unto us in the chamber, commanding us that I should ordain Oliver Cowdery to be an Elder in the Church of Jesus Christ; and that he also should ordain me to the same office; and then to ordain others, as it should be made known unto us from time to time. We were, however, commanded to defer this our ordination until such times as it should be practicable to have our brethren, who had been and who should be baptized, assembled together, when we must have their sanction to our thus proceeding to ordain each other, and have them decide by vote whether they were willing to accept us as spiritual teachers or not; when also we were commanded to bless bread and break it with them, and to take wine, bless it, and drink it with them; afterward proceed to ordain each other according to commandment; then call out such men as the Spirit should dictate, and ordain them; and then attend to the laying on of hands for the gift of the Holy Ghost, upon all those whom we had previously baptized, doing all things in the name of the Lord. The following commandment will further illustrate the nature of our calling to this Priesthood, as well as that of others who were yet to be sought after: [D&C 18]" (*History of the Church*, 1:60–62).

First, in section 18, the Lord specifically addresses Oliver Cowdery, acknowledging that He is aware of a matter Oliver has had on his mind, and assuring him that he does have a testimony, especially of the Book of Mormon manuscript. This may sound a bit strange because of the great spiritual experiences Oliver has already had. But perhaps you know from personal experience or from the experiences of others that a testimony needs constant nourishment. Thus, we see the Lord's kindness here in strengthening Oliver's testimony. We will use **bold** to point this out.

1 NOW, behold, **because of the thing which you, my servant Oliver Cowdery, have desired to know of me, I give unto you these words**:

2 Behold, **I have manifested unto you, by my Spirit in many instances, that the things which you have written** [*as a scribe during the translation of the gold plates*] **are true**; wherefore **you know that they are true** [*you do have a testimony of the Book of Mormon*].

Doctrine

Verses 3–4. Studying the scriptures and strictly living by the things contained in them is vital for our salvation.

3 **And if you know that they are true,** behold, I give unto you a commandment, that you **rely upon the things which are written**;

Specifically, Oliver is being reminded of the benefits which will come to him personally through studying the scriptures and sticking strictly to the teachings contained in them.

4 For **in them are all things written concerning the foundation of my church, my gospel, and my rock**.

The word "rock," used in verse 4, above, can have various meanings depending on context. Obviously, it symbolizes something that is solid and safe to build our lives upon. Three of many scriptural definitions are as follows:

1. "Build upon my rock, which is my gospel" (D&C 11:24).
2. "Jesus in His teachings says, 'Upon this rock I will build my Church, and the gates of hell shall not prevail against it [Matt. 16:18].' What rock? Revelation" (*History of the Church*, 5:258).
3. Jesus Himself is "the Rock" upon which we are invited to build. For example, "I am the good shepherd, and the stone of Israel. He that buildeth upon this rock shall never fall" (D&C 50:44).

Some members of the Church hesitate or decline to accept callings. What the Savior tells Oliver Cowdery next in verse 5 applies to all of us and reminds us that if we accept and fulfill callings, thus helping to "build up" the Church, the "gates of hell" will not ultimately win against us. This is a great benefit of being faithfully engaged in our church responsibilities.

5 Wherefore, **if you shall build up my church**, upon the foundation of my gospel and my rock, **the gates of hell shall not prevail** [*win*] **against you**.

Next, the Lord tells Oliver that the world is getting more and more wicked. The phrase "ripening in iniquity" involves the imagery of fruit ripening toward the point that it becomes completely rotten and falls off the tree.

6 Behold, **the world is ripening in iniquity** [*moving toward complete wickedness*]; **and it must needs be** [*it is necessary*] **that the children of men** [*the inhabitants of the earth*] **are stirred up unto repentance**, both the Gentiles [*non-Israelites*] and also the house of Israel [*descendants of Abraham, Isaac, and Jacob (Israel, who was the father of the Twelve Tribes of Israel)*].

From the context of verses 7 and 8, next, it appears that Oliver may have had a tendency to be critical of the Prophet Joseph because of his imperfections. The counsel given to Oliver in verse 8 applies to all of us as we sustain our church leaders.

Doctrine

Verses 7–8. The Lord knows what He is doing when He calls certain individuals to be leaders in His church. (So, don't be critical of them.)

7 Wherefore, as thou hast been baptized by the hands of my servant Joseph Smith, Jun., according to that which I have commanded him, he **hath fulfilled the thing which I commanded him**.

8 And now, **marvel not** [*don't wonder or be surprised*] **that I have called him** unto mine own purpose, which purpose is known in me; wherefore, **if he shall be diligent in keeping my commandments he shall be blessed unto eternal life**; and his name is Joseph [*I know him perfectly well. (By the way, in Hebrew, "Joseph" means "he who gathers for God")*].

There can be much additional significance to the Lord's saying "and his name is Joseph" in verse 8, above. For instance, Oliver would likely be familiar with the prophecy of Joseph, who was sold into Egypt, about a great latter-day prophet named Joseph, through whom the Lord would restore the gospel. (See 2 Nephi 3:13–15.) Thus, we can easily see the Savior saying to Oliver, in effect, that Joseph Smith is *the* Joseph spoken of in prophecy.

Next, as mentioned in the introductory notes to this section, the Lord refers to these men's callings as that of Apostles. Quoting from the *Doctrine and Covenants Student Manual* used in the Institutes of Religion of the Church, 1981 edition, page 35, we read the following:

"Brigham Young taught that Joseph Smith, Oliver Cowdery, and David Whitmer were the first Apostles of this dispensation (see *Journal of Discourses*, 6:320). To these, according to Heber C. Kimball, Martin Harris was later added (see *Journal of Discourses*, 6:29). These men were instructed to find and ordain twelve others who would form the Quorum of the Twelve."

The Lord is telling these men that they have the same calling as Paul the Apostle. Included in this holy calling is the responsibility of preaching the gospel and crying "repentance unto this people" (see verse 14 of this section). And in order to fulfill this calling, they must understand the true worth of each soul.

9 And now, Oliver Cowdery, I speak unto you, and also unto David Whitmer, by the way of commandment; for, behold, I command all men everywhere to repent, and I speak unto you, even as unto Paul mine apostle, for you are called even with that same calling with which he was called.

As mentioned previously, verses 10–16, next, are oft-quoted in the Church. The message is vital and sweet, for it deals with the foundational doctrine and truth that each soul, each individual person, is of incalculable worth. Tyrants and despots, whether widely known or appearing as bullies in small settings, are inspired by Satan to violate this eternal principle.

Doctrine

Verse 10. The worth of each individual soul is great in the sight of God.

10 Remember the worth of souls is great in the sight of God;

Next, we are taught that the Savior's Atonement itself is a supreme measure of the worth of souls.

Doctrine

Verse 11. The Savior suffered for all of the sins of all people. (Then, if they repent, they accept His gift. If they don't repent, they, in effect, reject His payment, and thus suffer

for their own sins—see D&C 19:17.)

11 **For, behold, the Lord your Redeemer suffered death in the flesh**; wherefore [*for this reason*] **he suffered the pain of all men, that all men might repent and come unto him.**

12 And **he hath risen again from the dead, that he might bring all men unto him, on conditions of repentance.**

Doctrine

Verse 13. When we repent, it brings the Savior great personal joy.

13 And **how great is his joy in the soul that repenteth!**

14 **Wherefore** [*this is why*], **you** [*Oliver Cowdery and David Whitmer*] **are called to cry repentance unto this people.**

Did you notice the exclamation point at the end of verse 13, above? Also take note of them at the end of verses 15 and 16, next. They are reminders of the pure joy felt by the Savior, as well as by us when we help bring souls to Him.

15 **And if it so be that you should labor all your days in crying repentance unto this people, and bring, save it be one soul unto me, how great shall be your joy with him in the kingdom of my Father!**

16 **And now, if your joy will be great with one soul that you have brought unto me into the kingdom of my Father, how great will be your joy if you should bring many souls unto me!**

We often think of missionaries when we read these two verses, and rightly so. But we must not limit the application to full-time missionary service. For instance, what about the parents who teach their children the gospel such that their souls are saved? And what about the individual member who brings a spouse back into activity or is the motivation for a friend to return to the Church?

Or what about the kind act or the show of respect that plants a "seed" that takes years to begin to grow, eventually does grow, and ultimately leads to conversion and coming unto Christ? In other words, there are virtually infinite applications for these verses in our lives.

Next, we see the Master Teacher providing training to these men as to how best to go about preaching the gospel. First, He assures them that they have His true gospel with its stability and power to save souls. Then He gives them additional instructions and cautions.

17 Behold, **you have my gospel** before you, and **my rock**, and **my salvation.**

18 **Ask the Father in my name, in faith believing** that you shall receive, **and you shall have the Holy Ghost**, which manifesteth [*shows and teaches*] all things which are expedient [*necessary*] unto the children of men. [*In other words, obtain the help of the Holy Ghost and you will be given all the assistance you need to be effective in saving souls.*]

19 And **if you have not faith, hope, and charity, you can do nothing**.

20 **Contend against no church, save** [*except*] **it be the church of the devil**.

The advice in verse 20, above, is critical for missionary success. The word "church" can mean any organization, group or individual. The "church of the devil" refers to anything that would tend to lead someone away from God. In 1 Nephi 14:10, Nephi was taught, "Behold there are save **two churches only**; the one is **the church of the Lamb of God**, and the other is **the church of the devil**; wherefore, whoso belongeth not to the church of the Lamb of God belongeth to that great church, which is the mother of abominations; and she is the whore of all the earth."

For successful missionary work, we must show respect and courtesy toward others and that which is sacred to them. Yet, when the Holy Ghost inspires and prompts, we must help people understand things that lead away from God.

Thus, the instruction to "contend against no church, save it be the church of the devil" can include not getting caught up in endless and worthless debates with other religions or philosophies, nor debating and quarreling with others over matters of personal preference and opinion.

Next, the "missionary training" of these early brethren continues with the caution to be serious about sacred things.

21 **Take upon you the name of Christ** [*keep your covenants and represent Christ properly*], and **speak the truth in soberness** [*be serious about serious and sacred things*].

Doctrine

Verse 22. Being saved is a very simple process. Baptism is essential for salvation (except, of course, in the case of children under age eight—see D&C 29:46–47; 68:25—and the handicapped who are not able to understand the gospel

sufficiently—see D&C 29:50).

22 And as many as **repent** and are **baptized** in my name, which is Jesus Christ, and **endure to the end**, the same shall **be saved**.

Doctrine

Verses 23–25. There is absolutely no other way to be saved other than through the gospel of Jesus Christ.

23 Behold, **Jesus Christ is the name** which is given of the Father, and **there is none other name given whereby man can be saved**;

24 Wherefore, **all men must take upon them the name which is given of the Father**, for in that name shall they [*those who are to be saved in celestial glory*] be called at the last day [*on the day of final judgment*];

25 Wherefore [*therefore*], **if they know not the name by which they are called, they cannot have place in the kingdom of my Father** [*the celestial kingdom*].

The imagery of the **bolded** part of verse 25, above, is that of a common scene in the Holy Land at the time of Christ's earthly ministry. Shepherds gave their sheep individual names and the sheep recognized their own name and the voice of their shepherd. In the evening, several shepherds would bring their sheep to a common enclosure for safe-keeping during the night. Thus, the sheep of many shepherds mingled together throughout the night, kept safe by one or two guards.

In the morning, each shepherd would come to the gate of the enclosure and call out the names of his sheep to come to him and follow him out to pasture. His sheep recognized their master and "the name by which they were called." They came out of the crowd unto the shepherd and followed him to their reward of nourishment and protection during the day.

The "name by which we are called" is the name of Christ, which we have taken upon ourselves by covenant. If we are faithful to the gospel, we keep that name and recognize the voice of our "Good Shepherd" when He calls us to come out from the ways of the world. We thus follow Him to the safety and joy of righteousness on earth, and eventually, of celestial glory.

Beginning with verse 26 and continuing to the end of section 18, the topic switches to the calling of twelve men who will serve as the first Quorum of the Twelve Apostles in this dispensation. The Lord instructs Oliver Cowdery and David Whitmer to find twelve men who will qualify for this holy calling. Later, Martin Harris will also be called to assist them in this responsibility. By way of additional background, we will quote from the Church History student manual used by our institutes of religion entitled *Church History in the Fulness of Times*. We will use **bold** for teaching purposes.

"One of the most important events in the restoration of the Savior's church was the formation of the Quorum of the Twelve Apostles. Even before the Church was organized, the members had anticipated this significant step. Joseph Smith and Oliver Cowdery had received the authority of the apostleship (see D&C 20:2–3) probably as early as **1829. During that same year, a revelation [D&C 18] directed Oliver Cowdery and David Whitmer to search out the twelve** who would be 'called to go into all the world to preach my gospel unto every creature' (D&C 18:28). **Later Martin Harris was also called to assist in this selection**. This meant that the Three Witnesses to the Book of Mormon, under the direction and consent of the First Presidency, would choose the Twelve Apostles who were to serve as special witnesses of the Savior in this dispensation" (*Church History in the Fulness of Times*, 2003, 153–54).

It will be almost six years before these twelve special witnesses will be selected. It will be done at a meeting held in Kirtland, Ohio, on Saturday, February 14, 1835, to which those men who participated in the march of Zion's Camp were invited. From these faithful men, who had been tried and proven, came the majority of the members of the leading quorums of the Church.

We will list the original members of the Quorum of Twelve Apostles in order of seniority and age (which determined their order of seniority since they were all called at the same time): Thomas B. Marsh (35), David W. Patten (35), Brigham Young (33), Heber C. Kimball (33), Orson Hyde (30), William E. McLellin (29), Parley P. Pratt (27), Luke S. Johnson (27), William B. Smith (23), Orson Pratt (23), John F. Boynton (23), Lyman E. Johnson (23).

With the above as background, we will now study the rest of the section.

Next, Oliver and David are given some of the criteria that will apply when it comes time to select the Twelve. They are also instructed as to the duties of these twelve Apostles.

26 And now, behold**, there are others who are called** [*perhaps meaning "foreordained," since these twelve won't be officially called here on earth for almost six years*] **to declare my gospel, both unto Gentile and unto Jew**;

27 Yea, even twelve; and **the Twelve shall be my disciples**, and **they shall take upon them my name**; and the Twelve are they who **shall desire to take upon them my name with full purpose of heart**.

28 And if they desire to take upon them my name with full purpose of heart, **they are called to go into all the world to preach my gospel unto every creature**.

29 And **they are they who are ordained of me to baptize in my name**, according to that which is written;

30 And **you have that which is written before you**; wherefore, **you must perform it according to the words which are written**.

Next, the Savior speaks in advance to the twelve men who will be chosen, and who will understandably be quite intimidated and humbled by such a calling from God.

31 And now I speak unto you, the Twelve—Behold, **my grace is sufficient for you** [*I will help you carry out your sacred duties*]**; you must walk uprightly before me and sin not**.

32 And, behold, **you are they who are ordained of me to ordain priests and teachers; to declare my gospel, according to the power of the Holy Ghost which is in you, and according to the callings and gifts of God unto men;**

33 And **I, Jesus Christ, your Lord and your God, have spoken it**.

34 **These words are not of men nor of man, but of me**; wherefore, **you shall testify they are of me and not of man**;

Next, in verses 35–36, as the Savior continues to instruct the Twelve, we, ourselves, are taught a beautiful and simple principle, namely that we can hear the voice of the Lord by reading the scriptures. S. Dilworth Young spoke of this fact in the April 1963 general conference as follows:

"The thing that impresses me about this is, and I have never thought of it before, when I read a verse in the Doctrine and Covenants, I am hearing the voice of the Lord as well as reading his words, if I hear by the Spirit.

"Now I have heard it said many times by men that they have often asked the Lord for a special testimony and oftentimes haven't had it. They seem to want to hear the voice of the Lord. I confess I have often wanted to hear the voice of the Lord, without knowing that all these years I have been hearing it with deaf ears. This woke me up" (In Conference Report, April 1963, 74).

35 For **it is my voice which speaketh them** [*the scriptures*] unto you; for **they are given by my Spirit** unto you, and **by my power you can read them one to another;** and save it were by my power you could not have them;

36 **Wherefore, you can testify that you have heard my voice**, and know my words.

Next comes the specific instruction to Oliver Cowdery and David Whitmer (who, as noted previously, will also be joined by Martin Harris in this assignment) to search out the twelve men who will become the first Quorum of Twelve in this dispensation.

37 And now, behold, **I give unto you, Oliver Cowdery, and also unto David Whitmer, that you shall search out the Twelve, who shall have the desires of which I have spoken**;

38 And **by their desires and their works you shall know them**.

39 **And when you have found them** you shall **show these things** [*this revelation, including what I say next*] **unto them**.

The remainder of the verses in this section are to the Twelve, who will be called in just under six years in February 1835. They are to hear these verses especially at this time. According to the following quote from S. Dilworth Young, Oliver Cowdery read section 18 to them at the time of their calling.

"In 1835 the Twelve were chosen, as you know, and on one occasion they were called together and given their instructions. Oliver Cowdery was the spokesman; and after having given them some very powerful and heartwarming instruction, so moved was he, himself, that he had to stop two or three times to weep. He finally read the revelation [now designated as section 18]" (*Doctrine and Covenants Student Manual*, 1981, 36).

40 And **you** [*the Twelve*] **shall fall down** [*humble yourselves*] **and worship the Father in my name.**

41 And **you must preach unto the world**, saying: You must repent and be baptized, in the name of Jesus Christ;

42 For all men must repent and be baptized, and not only men, but women, and children who have arrived at the years of accountability [*this is in preparation for D&C 68:25, in which the age of eight will be given as the age for baptizing children*].

43 And now, after that you have

received this, **you must keep my commandments in all things**;

44 And **by your hands I will work a marvelous work among the children of men**, unto the convincing of many of their sins, that they may come unto repentance, and that they may come unto the kingdom of my Father.

45 Wherefore, **the blessings which I give unto you are above all things**.

46 And **after that you have received this, if you keep not my commandments you cannot be saved in the kingdom of my Father**.

47 Behold, **I, Jesus Christ, your Lord and your God, and your Redeemer, by the power of my Spirit have spoken it.** Amen.

SECTION 19

Background

Research for *The Joseph Smith Papers* publications has resulted in a change for the date given in the heading for this revelation. If you have a Doctrine and Covenants printed before the most recent edition (2013), the date given in the heading to section 19 is "March 1830." However, the date given in the 2013 edition of the scriptures is "likely in the summer of 1829." We will Include a quote from the *Doctrine and Covenants Student Manual*, 2018, chapter 8, which explains this change:

"Note: Earlier editions of the Doctrine and Covenants give the date of the revelation recorded in Doctrine and Covenants 19 as March 1830. Recent research suggests that the revelation was likely received during the summer of 1829. This date is reflected in the 2013 edition of the scriptures and in this chapter.) On August 25, 1829, Martin Harris mortgaged his property to Grandin as payment for the publication (see *The Joseph Smith Papers, Documents, Volume 1: July 1828–June 1831*, ed. Michael Hubbard MacKay and others [2013], 86–89)."

Section 19 is one of the great revelations on the Atonement of Christ. In it, He teaches us about the extreme difficulty of His suffering for us and urgently invites us to repent so that we can be forgiven through His atoning gift and will not have to suffer the penalties for our own sins, which suffering will be far beyond our ability now to comprehend.

This revelation was given in the form of a commandment through Joseph Smith to Martin Harris at Manchester, New York. You may remember that Martin Harris lived in Palmyra, which was next to Manchester where Joseph Smith's parents lived.

Martin Harris had signed a contract that mortgaged his farm to guarantee payment for the printing of the Book of Mormon. The printer, 23-year-old Egbert B. Grandin, was manager and principal owner of the *Wayne Sentinel*, which was a newspaper printed in Palmyra. There was much local opposition to the printing of the Book of Mormon, and the only way Grandin would agree to proceed with the printing was if the printing costs were secured in this way. The plan had been to sell copies of the Book of Mormon and pay for the printing in that manner. But with opposition building, the only way Grandin would continue printing was through Martin's legal guarantee to pay the costs within eighteen months of the time printing began if sales failed to cover the amount owed. The agreement called for the printing of 5,000 copies for $3,000.

As the printing proceeded, opposition increased. In fact, a mass meeting was held by the people of Palmyra and the surrounding area in which it was agreed to boycott the purchase of Books of Mormon and to use their influence to prevent others likewise from buying it. The first completed copies of the Book of Mormon were ready for sale on March 26, 1830, according to an ad in the *Wayne Sentinel*. (See *Joseph Smith and the Restoration*, 114–17.)

With this as background, it doesn't take much imagination to suggest that Martin Harris was getting worried that he might actually end up losing some of his prime farm acreage to pay the debt and perhaps was beginning to hesitate to keep his part of the agreement. It is indeed a credit to him that he obeyed the word of the Lord in verses 26, 34, and 35, wherein he was told "Impart of thy property . . . Pay the debt." He did so, selling 151 acres of the approximately 240 to 300 acres that he owned to pay the $3,000 printing debt.

Martin Harris had seen the angel who brought the gold plates to the Three Witnesses, by permission of the angel had handled each of the plates that had been translated, had seen the Urim and Thummim, the breastplate, the sword of Laban, the Liahona (see D&C 17:1), and also the brass plates, the plates of Ether, and several other plates (see note after section 17, verse 1, in this study guide). He had also heard the voice of the Lord. Even with witnessing all of this, at the time of this revelation, he was still having difficulties keeping the commandments as you will sense from the context of the verses in this section. Still, one of the encouraging and endearing things about Martin Harris is that despite troubles along the way, including leaving the Church for several years, he came back and was faithful to the end of his life. This is a sweet reminder to each of us that the Lord keeps helping us in spite of our weaknesses and failures. This can give us great hope and encouragement along the way.

As indicated previously, this revelation is unusual in the sense that it is given as a commandment (see heading to section 19 in your Doctrine and Covenants). As you will see, the Savior is direct and to the point with Martin Harris, commanding him frequently on several different matters. As we study it, we will be taught many doctrines and principles that can bless our lives also.

The first thing we will do by way of studying section 19 is to go through the entire section **bolding** several of the gospel vocabulary words and phrases, doctrines, commandments, principles, gospel concepts, and counsel in order to get a better idea and feeling for how much is packed into these forty-one verses. Then we will repeat the verses, taking time to study several of them.

Doctrine

Verses 1–2. Under the Father's direction, Jesus is in charge of all things on earth.

1 **I AM Alpha and Omega** [*the beginning letter and the ending letter in the Greek alphabet*], Christ the Lord; yea, even I am he, **the beginning and the end**, the **Redeemer of the world**.

2 **I**, having accomplished and **finished the will of** him whose I am, even **the Father**, concerning me—having done this **that I might subdue all things unto myself**—

Doctrine

Verse 3. Jesus will overcome Satan completely and will be our final judge—see also John 5:22.

3 **Retaining all power**, even to the **destroying of Satan and his works at the end of the world**, and the **last great day of judgment, which I shall pass upon the inhabitants** thereof, **judging every man according to his works and** the **deeds** which he hath done.

Doctrine

Verses 4–5. All of us must repent of our sins or suffer for them.

4 And surely **every man must repent or suffer**, for **I, God, am endless**.

5 Wherefore, I revoke not the judgments which I shall pass, but **woes shall go forth, weeping, wailing and gnashing of teeth,**

yea, to those who are found on my left hand. [*In scriptural symbolism, "left hand" is often symbolic of the wicked, whereas, "right hand" or "covenant hand," is symbolic of the righteous, those who make and keep covenants with God.*]

Doctrine

Verses 6–12. "Endless torment" does not last forever.

6 Nevertheless, it is not written that there shall be no end to this torment, but it is written *endless torment*.

7 Again, it is written ***eternal damnation;*** wherefore it is more express than other scriptures, that it might work upon the hearts of the children of men, altogether for my name's glory.

8 Wherefore, **I will explain unto you this mystery**, for it is meet unto you to know even as mine apostles.

9 I speak unto you that are chosen in this thing, even as one, that you may enter into **my rest** [*celestial glory*].

10 For, behold, the mystery of godliness, how great is it! For, behold, **I am endless**, and **the punishment which is given from my hand is endless punishment,** for **Endless is my name**. Wherefore—

11 **Eternal punishment is God's punishment**.

12 **Endless punishment is God's punishment**.

13 Wherefore, **I command you to repent**, and keep the commandments which you have received by the hand of my servant Joseph Smith, Jun., in my name;

14 And it is by my almighty power that you have received them;

Doctrine

Verses 15–18. We cannot begin to imagine or comprehend the suffering endured by the Savior as He paid for our sins.

15 Therefore **I command you to repent**—repent, **lest** I smite you by **the rod of my mouth**, and by my wrath, and by my anger, and **your sufferings be sore**—how sore you know not, **how exquisite** you know not, yea, **how hard to bear** you know not.

16 For behold, **I, God, have suffered these things for all, that they might not suffer if they would repent**;

__Doctrine__

If we do not repent, we will have to suffer for our own sins.

17 But **if they would not repent they must suffer even as I**;

18 **Which suffering caused myself, even God, the greatest of all, to tremble because of pain, and to bleed at every pore, and to suffer both body and spirit—and would that I might not drink the bitter cup, and shrink—**

19 Nevertheless, glory be to the Father, and **I partook and finished my preparations unto the children of men.**

__Doctrine__

Verse 20. Confession is a necessary part of qualifying for forgiveness of sins.

__Doctrine__

Verse 20. Part of the suffering endured by the Savior for our sins was the withdrawal of the Spirit from Him so that He was alone without that help and support.

20 Wherefore, **I command you again to repent**, lest I humble you with my almighty power; and that you **confess your sins, lest you suffer these punishments** of which I have spoken, of which in the smallest, yea, even in the least degree **you have tasted at the time I withdrew my Spirit**.

21 And **I command you** that you preach naught but repentance, and show not these things unto the world until it is wisdom in me.

22 For **they cannot bear meat now, but milk** they must receive; wherefore, they must not know these things, lest they perish.

23 **Learn of me, and listen to my words; walk in the meekness of my Spirit, and you shall have peace in me.**

__Doctrine__

Verse 24. Christ works under the direction of the Father and carried out His will in every detail.

24 I am Jesus Christ; I came by the will of the Father, and I do his will.

25 And again, **I command thee** that thou shalt not covet thy neighbor's wife; nor seek thy neighbor's life.

__Doctrine__

Verse 26. The Book of Mormon contains the word of God.

26 And again, **I command thee** that **thou shalt not covet thine own property, but impart it freely to the printing of the Book of Mormon**, which **contains the truth and the word of God**—

27 Which is my word to the **Gentile**, that soon it may go to the **Jew**, of whom the **Lamanites are a remnant**, that they may believe the gospel, and look not for a Messiah to come who has already come.

__**Doctrine**__

Verse 28. Public prayer as well as private prayer are part of proper worship.

28 And again, **I command thee** that thou shalt **pray vocally as well as in thy heart**; yea, before the world as well as in secret, in public as well as in private.

29 And thou shalt declare glad tidings, yea, **publish it upon the mountains**, and upon every high place, and among every people that thou shalt be permitted to see.

30 And thou shalt do it with all humility, trusting in me, **reviling not against revilers**.

31 And of **tenets** thou shalt not talk, but thou shalt declare **repentance** and **faith** on the Savior, and remission of sins by **baptism**, and by fire, yea, even the **Holy Ghost**.

32 Behold, this is a great and the last commandment which I shall give unto you concerning this matter; for this shall suffice for thy daily walk, even unto the end of thy life.

33 And **misery** thou shalt receive **if** thou wilt **slight these counsels, yea,** even the **destruction** of thyself and property.

34 Impart a portion of thy property, yea, even part of thy lands, and all save the support of thy family.

35 **Pay the debt** thou hast contracted with the printer. **Release thyself from bondage**.

36 Leave thy house and home, except when thou shalt desire to see thy family;

37 And **speak freely to all**; yea, **preach**, **exhort**, **declare the truth**, even with a loud voice, with a sound of rejoicing, crying—**Hosanna**, hosanna, blessed be the name of the Lord God!

38 **Pray always**, and I will pour out my Spirit upon you, and great shall be your blessing—yea, even more than if you should obtain treasures of earth and **corruptibleness** to the extent thereof.

39 Behold, canst thou read this without rejoicing and lifting up thy heart for gladness?

40 Or **canst thou run about longer as a blind guide?**

41 Or canst thou be humble and meek, and conduct thyself wisely before me? Yea, **come unto me thy Savior**. Amen.

Having looked at many of the gospel concept words and phrases contained in these 41 verses as stated previously, we will now go through and add notes and do a detailed study of many of the teachings contained in this section. First of all, in verses 1–3, next, the Savior introduces Himself. The names and titles He uses are often used elsewhere in the scriptures. Through them, we learn more about Him in His various stewardships and powers as our Savior and Redeemer. For instance, in verse 1, we see five titles by which He is identified in the scriptures and through which He teaches us much about Himself. We will **bold** them and add explanatory notes.

1 I AM **Alpha and Omega** [*the first and last letters of the Greek Alphabet; in other words, "I am the first and the last, the beginning and the end"; for instance, He created the earth in the beginning, under the Father's direction, and will be there at the end, as our final judge*], **Christ** [*the "Anointed One," the "Messiah" whom the prophets promised would come*] **the Lord** [*the God of this world, under the Father's direction*]; yea, even I am he, **the beginning and the end** [*same as Alpha and Omega*], the **Redeemer of the world** [*the Savior of all*].

As Jesus Christ continues introducing Himself in verses 2 and 3, next, we are taught much more about Him.

2 I, **having accomplished and finished the will of him whose I am, even the Father, concerning me** [*He carried out the Atonement and all aspects of His mortal mission perfectly, as assigned by the Father; see also verse 19*]—having done this **that I might subdue all things unto myself** [*having carried out the Atonement perfectly gave Christ personal power over all things (see verse 3) such that he could save all who are willing to come unto Him for salvation*]—

3 **Retaining all power, even to the destroying of Satan and his works at the end of the world** [*the "end of the world" is defined as "the destruction of the wicked" in Joseph Smith—Matthew 1:4*], and **the last great day of judgment** [*the final judgment*], **which I shall pass upon the inhabitants thereof** [*Christ is our final judge. John 5:22 tells us that "the Father*

judgeth no man, but hath committed all judgment unto the Son."], **judging every man according to his works and the deeds which he hath done.** [*Christ will judge us according to our works. In D&C 137:9, Jesus informs us that He will also judge us according to the desires of our hearts.*]

Some people wonder at times if there is any chance that Satan might win out in the end. The answer, at the beginning of verse 3, above, is clear. There is absolutely no chance at all of this happening. The devil and his evil hosts will ultimately be "cast away into their own place, that they shall not have power over the saints any more at all." See D&C 88:114. This absolute truth is most comforting.

Next, the Savior teaches Martin Harris (and us) about the suffering of those who choose not to repent. He will use the terms, "endless," and "eternal." Pay close attention to them and how He defines them. You will see that they are not the same in this context.

First of all, He will make two simple statements in verse 4, next.

4 And surely **every man must repent or suffer**, for **I, God, am endless.**

The first **bolded** statement in verse 4, above, needs no clarification, because it is an established and obvious fact.

For the last statement, we will quickly convene an English grammar class and review the use of adjectives. Adjectives describe a noun. For instance, in the sentence, "Go get the blue ball," the word "blue" is an adjective describing the noun "ball."

If we had a sentence describing God, we might have several adjectives. Example: "We worship a kind, loving, endless God." "Kind," "loving," and "endless" are all adjectives describing God. Let's take it one step farther. Supposing we were describing God's punishment of Laman and Lemuel and the others who had rebelled on the ship and tied Nephi up (1 Nephi 18:8–11), we could say it was "God's" punishment. We could say the same thing in our context here by saying it was "kind" punishment (because it was designed by God to help save their souls), or "loving" punishment, or "endless" punishment (meaning coming from God). In this case, "endless" would have nothing to do with how long it lasts (because the punishment was a raging storm which lasted four days [1 Nephi 18:15]); rather, it would be simply stating that the punishment came from God. "Endless" describes Him. Therefore, **"endless" can be used as an adjective to describe blessings or punishments that come from Him**. Just tuck this thinking into your mind for a moment and you will soon see where we are going with this.

Continuing, the Savior says that nothing will stop the punishments which will come upon the unrepentant.

5 Wherefore, **I revoke** [*cancel*] **not the judgments** [*punishments*] **which I shall pass**, but woes shall go forth, **weeping, wailing and gnashing of teeth** [*extreme misery*], yea, to those who are found on **my left hand.** [*"Left hand" is a scriptural term which refers to those who will have to suffer for their own sins. "Right hand" refers to those who have made and kept covenants ("right hand" is symbolic of covenant making), and are thus forgiven through the Savior's Atonement.*]

In verse 6, next, we come back to the idea that "endless" can sometimes be used simply as an adjective describing God, and thus describing punishments or blessings which come from Him. In this type of context, it is not describing the duration of things.

6 Nevertheless, **it is not written that there shall be no end to this torment, but it is written *endless torment*.**

Before we move on, let's do a bit more with "suffer," verse 4, "weeping, wailing and gnashing of teeth," verse 5, and "endless torment," verse 6. We have just been told in verse 6 that this suffering and punishment doesn't last forever. So, when does it take place?

For the most part, the answer is that this punishment and suffering will take place when people who refuse to repent are turned over to Satan to suffer for their own sins. Generally speaking, this takes place while the Millennium is going on upon the earth. We don't know where Satan is at that time (he is not on earth tempting people, see D&C 101:28), but the wicked will be turned over to him, "thrust down to hell! These are they who shall not be redeemed from the devil until the last resurrection, until the Lord, even Christ the Lamb, shall have finished his work [the end of the Millennium—see D&C 76:84–85; compare with 88:100–101]."

Concerning being turned over to Satan to be punished, Apostle Bruce R. McConkie taught that it means to be turned over to Satan "with all the protective power of the priesthood, of righteousness, and of godliness removed so that Lucifer is free to torment, persecute and afflict such a person without let or hindrance" (*Mormon Doctrine*, 108).

Continuing, we know from the scriptures that the only ones who will spend eternity with Satan are sons of perdition. Thus, we know that the rest of the wicked who do not qualify for outer darkness will be among those spoken of in D&C

76:84–85 (quoted above) who will eventually be "redeemed from the devil" and will be completely free from his influence as they go to the telestial kingdom, which is so nice that it "surpasses all understanding." See D&C 76:89.

So, by way of summarizing all of the above concerning "endless" punishment, we see that it is the punishment, among other things, of being turned over to the buffetings of Satan to suffer for one's own sins, having refused to repent, and that it does not last forever. So, Martin Harris is being told, in very strong and serious terms, that unless he repents, he will suffer "endless" punishment, or God's punishments, and that he would do very well to reconsider some of the things he is doing, along with some of his attitudes and the commitments he ought to keep.

In fact, as you will see as we move on to verse 7, next, the Lord specifically tells Martin that He is using terminology designed to get Martin's full attention.

7 Again, **it is written** *eternal damnation;* wherefore **it is more express than other scriptures, that it might work upon the hearts of the children of men**, altogether for my name's glory.

As you noticed, the term "eternal damnation" is used in verse 7, above. The term "eternal punishment" will be used in verse 11. There is a difference between "damnation" and "punishment." We will quote from the *Doctrine and Covenants Student Manual*, 1981, page 37. Elder James E. Talmage is quoted there, explaining what "eternal punishment" means (**bold** added for emphasis):

"That is a direful expression; but in his mercy the Lord has made plain what those words mean. 'Eternal punishment,' he says, is God's punishment, for he is eternal; and that condition or state or possibility will ever exist for the sinner who deserves and really needs such condemnation; but **this does not mean that the individual sufferer or sinner is to be eternally and everlastingly made to endure and suffer. No man will be kept in hell** (turned over to the buffetings of Satan; see D&C 76:84–85) **longer than is necessary to bring him to a fitness for something better**. When he reaches that stage the prison doors will open and there will be rejoicing among the hosts who welcome him into a better state. The Lord has not abated in the least what he has said in earlier dispensations concerning the operation of his law and his gospel, but he has made clear unto us his goodness and mercy through it all, for it is his glory and his work to bring about the immortality and eternal life of man" (In Conference Report, April 1930, 97).

Again, quoting from the student manual mentioned above, page 37, we will see what "eternal damnation" means. Elder Bruce R. McConkie is quoted as follows (**bold** added for emphasis):

"**Eternal damnation is the opposite of eternal life**, and all those who do not gain eternal life, or exaltation in the highest heaven within the celestial kingdom, are partakers of **eternal damnation**. **Their eternal condemnation is to have limitations imposed upon them so that they cannot progress to the state of godhood and gain a fulness of all things**.

"They 'remain separately and singly, without exaltation, . . . to all eternity; and from henceforth are not gods, but are angels of God forever and ever.' (D&C 132:17.) **Their** kingdom or **progress has an 'end,'** and **they 'cannot have an increase**.' (D&C 131:4.) **Spirit children are denied to them to all eternity**, and they inherit 'the deaths,' meaning an absence of posterity in the resurrection. (D&C 132:16–25.)

"**They are never** redeemed from their spiritual fall and **taken back into the full presence and glory of God**. Only the obedient are 'raised in immortality unto eternal life.' The disobedient, 'they that believe not,' are raised in immortality 'unto eternal damnation; for they cannot be redeemed from their spiritual fall, because they repent not.' (D&C 29:42–44.)" (*Mormon Doctrine*, 234).

With the above as background, we will listen as the Lord explains these important concepts to Martin Harris.

8 Wherefore, **I will explain unto you this mystery**, for it is meet [*necessary*] unto you to know even as mine apostles.

9 I speak unto you that are chosen in this thing, even as one, **that you may enter into my rest** [*exaltation in celestial glory, the "fulness of his glory"; see D&C 84:24*].

10 For, behold, the mystery of godliness, how great is it! For, **behold, I am endless, and the punishment which is given from my hand is endless punishment, for Endless is my name**. Wherefore—

11 **Eternal punishment is God's punishment**.

12 **Endless punishment is God's punishment**.

13 Wherefore [*this is why*], **I command you to repent**, and keep the commandments which you have received by the hand of my servant Joseph Smith, Jun., in my name;

14 And it is by my almighty power that you have received them;

Verses 15–19, next, are quite well-known and often-quoted in sermons and lessons. You may wish to mark them in your own scriptures. In them, the Savior explains how difficult His suffering was, and pleads with all of us to accept His gift so that we don't have to "suffer even as I" (verse 17).

15 Therefore **I command you to repent**—repent, **lest I smite** [*punish*] **you by the rod** [*power and authority*] **of my mouth**, and **by my wrath**, and **by my anger, and your sufferings be sore** [*extremely severe*]—how sore you know not, how **exquisite** [*extremely difficult*] you know not, yea, how **hard to bear** you know not.

16 For behold, **I, God, have suffered these things for all, that they might not suffer if they would repent**;

17 **But if they would not repent they must suffer even as I;**

As you are perhaps aware, because of the wording in Luke 22:44, many Bible scholars and students have doubts as to whether or not Jesus actually bled from every pore. It reads as follows:

<u>Luke 22:44</u>

44 And being in an agony he prayed more earnestly: and his sweat was as it were [*as if it were*] great drops of blood falling down to the ground.

In verse 18, next, in which the Savior describes the suffering required by His Atonement, He, Himself, tells us that He did, indeed, bleed from every pore because of the suffering He took upon Himself for the sins of all mankind.

18 **Which suffering caused myself, even God**, the greatest of all [*who have lived as mortals on this earth*], **to tremble because of pain**, and to **bleed at every pore**, and to **suffer both body and spirit**—and **would** [*desire*] **that I might not drink the bitter cup** [*follow through with the Atonement*], and **shrink** [*hesitate*]—

From the above description by the Savior Himself, it would appear that when it finally came right down to it, He was somewhat taken back by how difficult it really was. All the more reason for us to be eternally grateful to Him for His following through. He did, as stated by Him in the next verse.

19 **Nevertheless**, glory be to the Father, and **I partook and finished my preparations unto the children of men** [*the Savior's work to prepare the way for us to have forgiveness available*].

The rest of the verses in this section are very specific to Martin Harris. But, as usual, we can learn much which applies to ourselves from what the Lord says here.

20 Wherefore, **I command you** [*Martin Harris*] again to **repent, lest I humble you** with my almighty power; and that you **confess your sins, lest you suffer these punishments of which I have spoken**, of which in the smallest, yea, even in the least degree you have tasted at the time I withdrew my Spirit [*referring to some past experience in Martin's life*].

21 And I command you that you **preach naught but** [*nothing but*] **repentance**, and show not these things [*possibly referring to the teachings about eternal punishment, endless punishment, and so on*] unto the world until it is wisdom in me.

22 For **they cannot bear meat now, but milk they must receive**; wherefore, they must not know these things, lest they perish [*for fear that they would be overwhelmed, and thus would lose their interest in the gospel*].

23 **Learn of me**, and **listen to my words**; **walk in** the **meekness** [*part of the definition of meekness is the attribute of not being easily irritated*] of my Spirit, and **you shall have peace in me.**

24 **I am Jesus Christ; I came by the will of the Father, and I do his will.**

From verse 25, we are given to understand that Martin was struggling with some major temptations at this point in his life.

25 And again, **I command thee that thou shalt not covet thy neighbor's wife; nor seek thy neighbor's life**.

Next, Martin is commanded (for his own good) to keep his word, and sell some of his property to pay for the printing of the Book of Mormon, as he had formerly agreed to do.

26 And again, **I command thee** that **thou shalt not covet thine own property, but impart it freely to the printing of the Book of Mormon**, which contains the truth and the word of God—

27 Which is my word to the **Gentile** [*meaning, in this context, all who are not Jews*], that soon it may go to the **Jew**, of **whom the Lamanites are a remnant** [*meaning that the Lamanites are descendants of Lehi, who came from Jerusalem; all citizens of Jerusalem, regardless of which tribe of Israel they came from, were considered to be Jews*], that they may believe the gospel, and look not for a Messiah to come

who has already come [*meaning that the Jews will someday know, through the true gospel, that Christ has already come*].

Perhaps you've heard someone criticize the practice of public prayer on the basis that Jesus taught people to avoid praying in public like the hypocrites and taught instead to "enter into thy closet" and thus pray in secret (Matthew 6:5–6). We don't know whether or not Martin felt this way, but we do see the Savior's instruction, next, that both sincere public prayer as well as private prayer are part of His gospel. This is one of the reasons this book of scripture is called the "Doctrine and Covenants," because it gives us correct doctrine on such matters.

28 And again, I command thee that thou shalt **pray vocally as well as in thy heart**; yea, **before the world as well as in secret, in public as well as in private**.

29 And thou shalt **declare glad tidings** [*preach the gospel*], yea, publish it upon the mountains [*make it available to many people*], and upon every high place [*symbolic of making it easy for people to hear you and know what you stand for*], and among every people that thou shalt be permitted to see.

30 And thou shalt **do it with all humility**, trusting in me, **reviling not against revilers** [*don't say mean things back to people who say mean things to you or about you*].

31 And of tenets thou shalt not talk [*don't get caught up in "bashing" other people's doctrines and beliefs*], but **thou shalt declare repentance** and **faith on the Savior**, and remission of sins by **baptism**, and by fire [*symbolic of how the Holy Ghost "burns" imperfections out of us, as in the refining of gold*], yea, even the **Holy Ghost**. [*In other words, don't waste time arguing and debating different ideologies, dogmas, and beliefs. Rather, teach the simple basics of the gospel*].

In verses 32–33, next, Martin is told, in effect, that this is a very important opportunity being given him by the Lord, and how he responds to it will affect him the rest of his life.

32 Behold, **this is a great and the last commandment which I shall give unto you concerning this matter**; for **this shall suffice for thy daily walk, even unto the end of thy life**.

33 And **misery thou shalt receive if thou wilt slight** [*ignore or underestimate the importance of*] **these counsels**, yea, even the **destruction of thyself and property**.

Next, the Savior once again instructs Martin to sell part of his land and pay the printing bill for the Book of Mormon. He does it, selling 151 acres to raise the $3,000 needed to pay for the printing of 5,000 Books of Mormon.

34 **Impart a portion of thy property, yea, even part of thy lands**, and all save the support of thy family.

35 **Pay the debt thou hast contracted with the printer**. Release thyself from bondage [*a simple reminder that debt is a form of bondage*].

According to the 2018 edition of the *Doctrine and Covenants Student Manual*, chapter 8, "Later in life, Martin testified that from the proceeds of the sale of the book, he recouped all of the money that he had advanced for the printing of the book. (See 'Additional Testimony of Martin Harris [One of the Three Witnesses] to the Coming forth of the Book of Mormon,' *The Latter-day Saints' Millennial Star*, vol. 21 [August 20, 1859], 545.)"

In the context of section 19, verses 36–37, next, seem to refer to missionary travel in order to preach the gospel rather than instructing Martin to leave home and never come back except on occasion to see his family.

36 Leave thy house and home [*to preach*], except when thou shalt desire to see thy family;

37 And **speak freely to all**; yea, **preach**, **exhort** [*urge people to obey the gospel*], **declare** the truth, even with a loud voice, **with a sound of rejoicing** [*be happy as you preach*], crying—Hosanna, hosanna, blessed be the name of the Lord God!

The word, "hosanna," as used in verse 37, above, means "Lord, please save now," or words to that effect. (See Bible Dictionary, under "Hosanna.") It is used in conjunction with praising the Lord and asking for his help and support, acknowledging our dependency on Him.

38 **Pray always** [*remember God constantly in your daily life, and your responsibility and opportunity to represent Him properly, and to get help from Him*], **and I will pour out my Spirit upon you**, and **great shall be your blessing**—yea, even more than if you should obtain treasures of earth and corruptibleness to the extent thereof.

39 Behold, **canst thou read this without rejoicing and lifting up thy heart for gladness?**

40 **Or canst thou run about longer as a blind guide?**

41 **Or canst thou be humble and meek, and conduct thyself wisely before me?** Yea, **come unto me thy Savior**. Amen.

The last phrase of verse 41, above, is especially tender, indicating that despite the severe reprimands Martin Harris received throughout section 19, our loving Savior wants to be his Redeemer too.

SECTION 20

Background

The heading to this section in the latest edition of the scriptures (2013) reads quite differently than in the previous editions of the Doctrine and Covenants. It is a direct result of the research for the Joseph Smith Papers Project. First, we will give the heading to recent editions prior to 2013, and then the heading for the 2013 edition.

Recent editions prior to 2013

"Revelation on Church Organization and Government, given through Joseph Smith the Prophet, April 1830. HC 1:64–70. Preceding his record of this revelation the Prophet wrote: We obtained of him [Jesus Christ] the following, by the spirit of prophecy and revelation; which not only gave us much information, but also pointed out to us the precise day upon which, according to his will and commandment, we should proceed to organize his Church once more here upon the earth."

The 2013 edition

"Revelation on Church organization and government, given through Joseph Smith the Prophet, at or near Fayette, New York. Portions of this revelation may have been given as early as summer 1829. The complete revelation, known at the time as the Articles and Covenants, was likely recorded soon after April 6, 1830 (the day the Church was organized). The Prophet wrote, 'We obtained of Him [Jesus Christ] the following, by the spirit of prophecy and revelation; which not only gave us much information, but also pointed out to us the precise day upon which, according to His will and commandment, we should proceed to organize His Church once more here upon the earth.'"

Section 20 could easily be called the first "Handbook of Instructions" for the Church. In it, the Lord tells the exact day upon which He wants His Church organized (verse 1). Among other things, He gives instructions on how people can qualify for baptism (verse 37), explains specific duties of elders, priests, teachers, deacons, and members (verses 38–69), gives instructions for people called to positions in the Church to be sustained by the members before they are ordained or set apart (verse 65), and gives instruction for blessing babies (verse 70).

Continuing, the Lord gives specific instructions on how to baptize and the exact words of the baptismal prayer (verses 73 and 74). Next, He gives instructions regarding the sacrament and the exact words of the prayers to be used by the priesthood holders in blessing the bread and wine (verses 75–79). We will discuss the use of water in the place of wine when we get to these verses in our detailed study of section 20.

The Savior goes on to give instructions on dealing with members who are involved in transgression (verse 80), instructs that membership records should be kept (verse 82), deals with excommunication (verse 83), and instructs that members moving into another area of the Church may take a signed certificate with them indicating that they are in good standing. This is somewhat similar to temple recommends today.

As you can see, this section is indeed a handbook of instructions for the early leaders of the Church in this dispensation.

Section 20 is also sometimes referred to as the "Articles and Covenants of the Church," as well as the "Constitution of the Church." It was a most important foundational revelation in the establishment of the Church through Joseph Smith and is a vital document for Church government and doctrine in our day.

Before we begin our detailed, verse-by-verse study, we will quote Joseph Smith and then Elder George Q. Cannon for a brief summary of the organization of the Church on April 6, 1830 (**bold** added for emphasis). First, Joseph Smith:

"In this manner did the Lord continue to give us instructions from time to time, concerning the duties which now devolved upon us; and among many other things of the kind, we obtained of him the following [section 20], by the spirit of prophecy and revelation; which not only gave us much information, but also **pointed out to us the precise day upon which, according to his will and commandment, we should proceed to organize his Church once more here upon the earth**" (*History of the Church*, 1:64, April 1830).

Next, George Q. Cannon:

"The Church of Jesus Christ of Latter-day Saints was organized on the 6th day of April, in the year of our Lord one thousand eight hundred and thirty, in Fayette, Seneca County, in the State of New York. Six persons were the original members: Joseph Smith the Prophet, Oliver Cowdery, Hyrum Smith, Peter Whitmer, Jun., Samuel H. Smith, and

David Whitmer. Each of the men had already been baptized by direct authority from heaven. The organization was made on the day and after the pattern dictated by God in a revelation given to Joseph Smith. The Church was called after the name of Jesus Christ; because he so ordered. Jesus accepted the Church, declared it to be his own and empowered it to minister on earth in his name.

"The sacrament, under inspiration from Jesus Christ, was administered to all who had thus taken upon them his name . . .

". . . It was necessary that God should define the mode and the principle of organization and should direct each step to be taken in this establishment of his kingdom . . .

"Joseph proceeded carefully, and exactly according to the instruction of the Almighty, and he laid the foundation of a work which will endure as long as earth shall last" (George Q. Cannon, *Life of Joseph Smith*, 1907, 52–54).

There were six original members of the Church, as stated in the George Q. Cannon quote above, which met the requirements of the state of New York for the organizing of a church. While there were several others present at the organization meeting who had likewise been baptized previously, only six were on the organization documentation, the minimum number required by state law. We will quote the Institute of Religion student manual for Church History, *Church History in the Fulness of Times*, for a brief summary of the actual organizing of the Church (**bold** added for teaching purposes):

"The meeting was simple. Joseph Smith, then twenty-four years old, called the group to order and designated five associates—Oliver Cowdery, Hyrum Smith, Peter Whitmer, Jr., Samuel H. Smith, and David Whitmer—to join him to meet New York's legal requirements for incorporating a religious society. After kneeling in solemn prayer, Joseph asked those present if they were willing to accept him and Oliver as their teachers and spiritual advisers. Everyone raised their hands in the affirmative. Although they had previously received the Melchizedek Priesthood, Joseph Smith and Oliver Cowdery then ordained each other to the office of elder. They did this to signify that they were elders **in the newly organized church**. The sacrament of the Lord's supper was administered next. The prayers used had been received through revelation (see D&C 20:75–79). **Joseph and Oliver then confirmed those who had previously been baptized as members of the Church of Jesus Christ** and bestowed upon them the gift of the Holy Ghost" (*Church History in the Fulness of Times*, 2003, 67–68).

We will now proceed with our verse-by-verse study.

1 THE rise of the Church of Christ in these last days, **being one thousand eight hundred and thirty years since the coming of our Lord and Savior Jesus Christ in the flesh** [*in other words, since the birth of Christ*], it being regularly organized and established agreeable to the laws of our country [*specifically, the laws of the state of New York*], by the will and commandments of God, in the fourth month, and on **the sixth day of the month which is called April**—

Both President Harold B. Lee and President Spencer W. Kimball explained the significance of this specific date as follows (**bold** added for emphasis):

President Lee: "**April 6**, 1973, is a particularly significant date because it commemorates not only the anniversary of the organization of The Church of Jesus Christ of Latter-day Saints in this dispensation, but also **the anniversary of the birth of the Savior**, our Lord and Master, Jesus Christ" (In Conference Report, April 1973, 4; or *Ensign*, April 1973, 2).

President Kimball: ". . . The name Jesus Christ and what it represents has been plowed deep into the history of the world, never to be uprooted. **Christ was born on the sixth of April**. Being one of the sons of God and His Only Begotten, his birth is of supreme importance" (In Conference Report, Apr. 1975, 3–4; or *Ensign*, May 1975, 4).

One more comment about April. The month of April appears to be very significant to the Savior. Not only was He born in April (in our calendar system), but He was also crucified and resurrected near this time of year.

2 Which commandments [*referred to near the end of verse 1*] were given to **Joseph Smith, Jun.**, who **was called of God**, and **ordained an apostle** of Jesus Christ, to be **the first elder of this church**;

3 And to **Oliver Cowdery**, who was also called of God, **an apostle** of Jesus Christ, to be **the second elder** of this church, and ordained under his [*Joseph Smith's*] hand;

4 And this according to the grace of our Lord and Savior Jesus Christ, to whom be all glory, both now and forever. Amen.

While the proper order of having one in charge (Joseph Smith as the "first elder" in verses 2–3, above) may seem standard procedure for us because we are used to it, this was somewhat unusual in many New England churches and congregations of Joseph Smith's day. For instance, in many religious organizations of the day, any one was considered authorized to have revelations for the entire congregation or for any individuals or groups.

God's kingdom is a "house of order" (D&C 132:8), with a living prophet at the head. And as you can see, the Lord established this principle among His Saints right at the beginning in our dispensation at the organization of His true Church.

From this point, with Joseph Smith as the first elder or presiding elder and Oliver Cowdery as the second elder, the Lord will continue to organize the leadership of the Church as the membership increases in numbers. Anthon H. Lund explained this process as follows:

"Now the Church was organized [April 1830], but not all the officers of the Church as we have them today, for the simple reason they did not have enough members in the Church to make a complete organization. Ten months after the Church was organized, Edward Partridge was ordained a Bishop to the Church, and in June following the first High Priests were ordained. In December, 1833, Joseph Smith, Senior, was ordained a Patriarch, and two months later the first High Council was organized. The Quorum of Twelve Apostles was organized [February 1835]. All the offices in the Priesthood were now established and men were ordained to fill them.

"In regard to Church government I will state that during the first thirteen months all Church business was done by conferences of Elders presided over by Joseph Smith and Oliver Cowdery. Several of the leading brethren were now ordained High Priests who afterwards formed the presiding quorum of the Church. In March, 1832, Joseph was called by revelation to be President of the Church, and a month later he was sustained as President of the High Priests' quorum. Next spring, March 18, 1833, the First Presidency was organized and sustained, consisting of three High Priests; Joseph Smith, President; Sidney Rigdon, First Counselor, and Frederick G. Williams, Second Counselor" (In Conference Report, April 1917, 14–15).

Continuing now with section 20, we will first read verse 5, next, and then read the Prophet Joseph Smith's explanation of what is meant by "entangled again in the vanities of the world."

5 After it was truly manifested unto this first elder [*Joseph Smith*] that he had received a remission of his sins [*which was one of his main concerns as he went into the grove to pray, which led to the First Vision in spring 1820*], he was entangled again in the vanities of the world;

As mentioned above, we will now turn to Joseph's account for help in understanding verse 5 (**bold** added for emphasis):

Pearl of Great Price, JS—History 1:28

"During the space of time which intervened between the time I had the vision and the year eighteen hundred and twenty-three—having been forbidden to join any of the religious sects of the day, and being of very tender years, and persecuted by those who ought to have been my friends and to have treated me kindly, and if they supposed me to be deluded to have endeavored in a proper and affectionate manner to have reclaimed me—I was left to all kinds of temptations; and, mingling with all kinds of society, I frequently fell into many foolish errors, and displayed the weakness of youth, and the foibles of human nature; which, I am sorry to say, led me into divers temptations, offensive in the sight of God. In making this confession, **no one need suppose me guilty of any great or malignant sins**. A disposition to commit such was never in my nature. But **I was guilty of levity, and sometimes associated with jovial company, etc., not consistent with that character which ought to be maintained by one who was called of God as I had been**. But this will not seem very strange to any one who recollects my youth, and is acquainted with my native cheery temperament."

Continuing with section 20, verses 6–12 refer to the appearance of Moroni to Joseph Smith and to the coming forth of the Book of Mormon.

6 But **after repenting, and humbling himself sincerely**, through faith, **God ministered unto him by an holy angel** [*Moroni*], whose countenance [*face*] was as lightning, and whose garments [*robes; clothes*] were pure and white above all other whiteness;

7 **And gave unto him** [*Joseph Smith*] **commandments which inspired him**;

Too many people look upon commandments as restrictions which they must obey or they will be in trouble. This is sad. Verse 7, above, shows us the true role of commandments from God in our lives. They are to inspire us and bless us, to provide safety, security, and happiness for us. In fact, in D&C 59:4, the Savior tells us that if we are faithful, we will be blessed "with commandments not a few."

8 And **gave him power from on high, by the means** [*including the Urim and Thummim*] **which were before prepared** [*which were prepared in advance*], **to translate the Book of Mormon**;

9 **Which contains** a record of a fallen people [*the Nephites*], and **the fulness of the gospel** of Jesus Christ **to the Gentiles and to the Jews** also;

Verse 9, above, contains three words or phrases (**bolded**) which we will pause to examine.

Fullness of the gospel

Some people wonder how the Book of Mormon can have the "fulness" of the gospel when, for instance, nothing is specifically mentioned within its pages about temple marriage, the three degrees of glory, or work for the dead. No details are given about a number of doctrines contained in the Doctrine and Covenants. Since we know that the Book of Mormon is true, whenever we see something that appears on the surface to be a contradiction, we know that it is our understanding that is flawed rather than the word of God. Therefore, whenever we come to a word or phrase we may not understand, there is wisdom in looking at other possible meanings for it, especially paying attention to the context in which it is set. When we do this, we find a number of possibilities. For instance, "fulness," in this context, could easily mean the gospel of faith, repentance, baptism, and gift of the Holy Ghost followed by the lifestyle of Christlike charity and humility which will lead to exaltation. An example of this would be the Nephites in the land of Zarahemla, who welcomed their former enemies, the Lamanites who had been converted, gave them land on which to live, and defended them with their lives. (See Alma 27:22–23.)

Charles W. Penrose, who served as a counselor in the First Presidency, explained "fulness of the gospel" as follows:

"We are told that the Book of Mormon contains the fulness of the gospel, that those who like to get up a dispute, say that the Book of Mormon does not contain any reference to the work of salvation for the dead, and there are many other things pertaining to the gospel that are not developed in that book, and yet we are told that book contains 'the fulness of the everlasting gospel.' Well, what is the fulness of the gospel? You read carefully the revelation in regard to the three glories, section 76, in the Doctrine and Covenants, and you find there defined what the gospel is [76:40–43]. There God, the Eternal Father, and Jesus Christ, his Son, and the Holy Ghost, are held up as the three persons in the

Trinity—the one God, the Father, the Word and the Holy Ghost, all three being united and being one God. When people believe in that doctrine and obey the ordinances which are spoken of in the same list of principles [20:17–28], you get the fulness of the gospel for this reason: If you really believe so as to have faith in our Eternal Father and in his Son, Jesus Christ, the Redeemer, and will hear him, you will learn all about what is needed to be done for the salvation of the living and the redemption of the dead.

"When people believe and repent and are baptized by Divine authority and the Holy Ghost is conferred upon them as a gift, they receive the everlasting gospel . . . and when the Holy Ghost as a gift is conferred upon people, young or old, as an 'abiding witness,' as a continuous gift, as a revelating spirit, they have the beginning, and I would not say the end, but they have the substance of the gospel of Jesus Christ. They have that which will bring salvation, for the gift of the Holy Ghost is such that it will highly enliven everyone who receives it" (In Conference Report, April 1922, 27–28).

Gentiles

As you no doubt have already noticed, the word, "Gentiles," has many different meanings and must be understood in context. According to the Bible Dictionary under "Gentiles," it can mean people who are not of the house of Israel or people who are of Israel but who do not have the gospel. In addition, "Gentile" can also mean someone who is not a Jew, either by blood line or by nationality. In this sense, Joseph Smith and most members of the Church are Gentiles. In the context of verse 9, above, "Gentiles" can easily refer to everyone other than the Jews.

Jews

"Jews," as used in the scriptures, usually refers to people who are blood line descendants of Judah, or to people who are residents of the Jerusalem area. Since Lehi and his family, including Laman and Lemuel, came from the Jerusalem area, they would be considered Jews, even though Lehi was from the tribe of Manasseh (Alma 10:3). Therefore, in the context of verse 9, above, "Jews" can be referring to the Lamanites, or descendants of Lehi, through Laman and Lemuel, and so on. This is clearly stated in D&C 19:27. Of course, the Jews, as we know them, will also be blessed by the teachings and testimony of Christ as contained in the Book of Mormon. This is also confirmed in D&C 19:27.

We will now continue with section 20, verses 10–16, in which the Savior tells us that angels are much involved in spreading the Book of Mormon throughout the world. He also teaches us more about the purposes of the Book of Mormon.

10 Which [*the Book of Mormon*] was given by inspiration, and is **confirmed to others by the ministering of angels**, and is declared unto the world by them—

In verse 11, next, we are taught that one of the important functions of the Book of Mormon is to bear witness of and support the Bible. Perhaps you've noticed that fewer and fewer "Christians" today seem to believe the Bible. In fact, it may well be said that members of the Church believe the Bible and the standards and principles taught in it much more than most Christians.

This is not bragging. It is a simple fact, especially when you look at the involvement of many Christians in premarital sex, homosexuality, lesbianism, and the like. The Bible preaches strongly against such behaviors, and the teachings of our Church substantiate and support the Bible.

Just one more comment regarding verse 11. The Prophet Ezekiel prophesied of the day when the Bible and the Book of Mormon would go hand-in-hand. We are living in the time of the fulfillment of that great prophecy. In fact, do you realize that the Topical Guide and Bible Dictionary, as well as the footnotes in the Book of Mormon, are a prominent part of the fulfillment of Ezekiel's prophecy? They are uniting the Bible and Book of Mormon as never before. We will quote Ezekiel here, using **bold** for emphasis:

Ezekiel 37:15–19

15 The word of the LORD came again unto me, saying,

16 Moreover, thou son of man, **take** thee **one stick** [*the Bible*], and write upon it, **For Judah, and for the children of Israel his companions**: then take **another stick** [*the Book of Mormon*], and write upon it, **For Joseph, the stick of Ephraim, and *for* all the house of Israel his companions**:

17 And **join them one to another** into one stick; and **they shall become one in thine hand**.

18 ¶ And when the children of thy people shall speak unto thee, saying, Wilt thou not **shew us what thou *meanest*** by these?

19 Say unto them, **Thus saith the Lord GOD; Behold, I will take the stick of Joseph, which *is* in the hand of Ephraim, and the tribes of Israel his fellows, and will put them with him, *even* with the stick of Judah, and make them one stick, and they shall be one in mine hand.**

As you can well see, the 1982 addition of the words "Another Testament of Jesus Christ" to the title of the Book of Mormon is very significant in light of Ezekiel's prophecy.

Again, as taught in verse 11, next, one of the significant functions of the Book of Mormon is to prove that the Bible is true. It also shows that revelation has not ceased.

11 **Proving to the world that the holy scriptures are true**, and **that God does inspire men and call them to his holy work in this age and generation, as well as in generations of old**;

12 Thereby **showing that he is the same God yesterday, today, and forever**. Amen.

Be careful not to confuse policies with doctrines as you consider verse 12, above. Some members wonder how God can be the same "yesterday, today, and forever" when He changes the age for missionaries to go on missions; changes from separate meetings for priesthood and Relief Society, Sunday School, and sacrament meetings to a meeting block for all; eliminates seventies on a stake basis and only has general authority seventies, and so on.

While policies change as needed to meet the needs of an expanding and growing church, doctrines such as faith, repentance, baptism by immersion, the gift of the Holy Ghost, celestial marriage, and all things needed for exaltation and living in the family unit forever do not change. In this sense, God is the same "yesterday, today, and forever." He is completely fair to all people through work for the living and work for the dead. The requirements for exaltation are the same and must be met, whether in this life or in the next (through the preaching of the gospel in the spirit world and work for the dead).

Among other things, verses 13–16, next, bear witness that the Book of Mormon and those who bear witness of it and the restoration of the gospel will prepare the world for the final judgment.

13 Therefore, having so great witnesses [*among other things, the Book of Mormon and those called to the work of spreading the gospel—see verse 11, above*], **by them shall the world be judged**, even as many as shall hereafter come to a knowledge of this work [*the Book of Mormon and the ensuing restoration of the true Church*].

14 And **those who receive it in faith, and work righteousness**, shall **receive** a crown [*"crown" is symbolic of becoming gods*] of **eternal life** [*"eternal life" always means exaltation in the highest degree of glory in the celestial kingdom*];

15 But **those who harden their**

hearts in unbelief, and **reject it**, it shall turn to their own **condemnation**—

"Condemnation," as used in verse 15, above, simply defined, means "stopped."

16 For **the Lord God has spoken it**; and **we, the elders of the church**, have heard and **bear witness** to the words of the glorious Majesty on high, to whom be glory forever and ever. Amen.

In verses 17–36, we will be taught about the creation, the fall, the Atonement, and several accompanying doctrines. By way of reminder, one of the obvious reasons this book of scripture is called "The Doctrine and Covenants" is that it contains many "doctrines" that can be loosely defined as true facts about God and the gospel and includes teachings and requirements for exaltation, the proper procedures for use of the priesthood, the priesthood ordinances, and so on.

We will continue to point out many "doctrines" along the way by using "**Doctrine**" to emphasize them. Some may seem almost too obvious to even mention, but remember that they are not obvious to the majority of the residents of the earth in our day.

Doctrine

Verse 17. There is a God. This earth and its inhabitants are not a biological accident careening through interstellar space.

17 By these things we know that there is a God in heaven, who is **infinite and eternal**, from everlasting to **everlasting** the same **unchangeable** [*therefore, completely reliable*] God, the framer [*the Creator*] of heaven and earth, and all things which are in them;

Doctrine

Verse 18. We are created in the image of God.

18 And that he created man, male and female, after his own image and in his own likeness, created he them;

There is an important "order" or "sequence" pointed out in verses 19 through 31, next. It is a sequence that, in a significant way, is repeated over and over in our lives (although we use the sacrament rather than being rebaptized) as we grow and progress toward returning to our Father in Heaven. We will use **bold** to highlight key words in this sequence.

As you know, we were given **agency** clear back in premortality—see D&C 29:35–36. In order to have agency mean anything at all, we must have **knowledge**. Knowledge and agency bring the possibility of both **progression** on the covenant path and **transgression** with its accompanying **accountability**. Transgression leads to the need for the **Atonement**, which is accessed through **faith**, **repentance**, **baptism**, and the **gift of the Holy Ghost**. These, in turn, all combine together to bring **justification** and **sanctification**.

We will likewise **bold** most of the doctrines in verses 19–31 so that you can quickly see them in their context. Then we will repeat these verses and do more with them.

19 And gave unto them **commandments** that they should love and serve him, the only living and true God, and that he should be the only being whom they should worship.

20 But by the **transgression** of these holy laws man became sensual and devilish, and became **fallen** man.

21 Wherefore, the Almighty **God gave his Only Begotten Son**, as it is written in those scriptures which have been given of him.

22 He suffered temptations but gave no heed unto them.

23 **He was crucified, died, and rose again the third day**;

24 And **ascended into heaven**, to sit down on the right hand of the Father, to reign with almighty power according to the will of the Father;

25 **That as many as would believe and be baptized in his holy name, and endure in faith to the end, should be saved**—

26 Not only those who believed after he came in the meridian of time, in the flesh, but all those from the beginning, even as many as were before he came, who believed in the words of the holy prophets, who spake as they were inspired by **the gift of the Holy Ghost**, who truly testified of him in all things, should have eternal life,

27 As well as those who should come after, **who should believe in the gifts and callings of God by the Holy Ghost**, which beareth record of the Father and of the Son;

28 Which **Father, Son,** and **Holy Ghost** are one God, infinite and eternal, without end. Amen.

29 And we know that all men must **repent** and **believe on the name of Jesus Christ**, and **worship the Father in his name**, and endure in **faith** on his name to the

end, or they cannot be saved in the kingdom of God.

30 And we know that **justification** through the grace of our Lord and Savior Jesus Christ is just and true;

31 And we know also, that **sanctification** through the grace of our Lord and Savior Jesus Christ is just and true, to all those who love and serve God with all their mights, minds, and strength.

As indicated above, we will now repeat verses 19 through 31 and do more with them. In these verses, the Lord gives us knowledge of many basics of the plan of salvation. Before we can exercise faith, be obedient, or even have effective agency, we must have knowledge, including knowledge of God and His commandments.

Doctrine

Verse 19. There is only one living and true God. (This is God the Father, as spoken of in Ephesians 4:6. Christ and the Holy Ghost are members of the Godhead but serve under the Father.)

19 And gave unto them commandments that they should **love and serve him, the only living and true God**, and that **he should be the only being whom they should worship**.

Doctrine

Verse 19, above. Heavenly Father is the only being we should worship. (Christ always directs us to worship the Father. We pray to the Father in the name of Jesus Christ. We reverence, love and respect the Savior, but in the strict sense of verse 19, we do not worship Him.)

Doctrine

Verse 20. The fall of Adam came through transgression. Also, we did not start out "carnal, sensual, and devilish" at birth. Rather, clean and pure at birth, all of us can "become carnal, sensual and devilish" through personal transgression.

20 But **by** the **transgression** of these holy laws **man became sensual and devilish**, and **became fallen man**.

There is a commonly taught false doctrine that we are all, by nature, evil and unclean. In fact, this is the thinking behind the false doctrine of "original sin," which, in some belief systems, states that babies are unclean at birth and must be baptized as infants. In other words, such people believe that we are "fallen" at birth, inherently unclean and evil by nature because we are human beings. Verse 20, above, contains the key word "became," showing that such thinking is not true. It says, in effect, that we can become evil through our choices. See also Alma 42:10.

Doctrine

Verse 21. Heavenly Father did give His Only Begotten Son to atone for our sins.

21 Wherefore, the Almighty God gave his Only Begotten Son, as it is written in those scriptures which have been given of him.

Some people get confused with the phrase "Only Begotten Son" because they realize that all of us are spirit sons and daughters of Heavenly Parents (see proclamation on the family, paragraph 2). They wonder how Jesus can be the "Only Begotten" when it is clear that we are all begotten spirit children of God. In other words, we are His literal spirit offspring. The answer is simple. The complete phrase is "the Only Begotten of the Father, in the flesh." Jesus is the only one born into a mortal body, begotten of the Father, in the flesh. In other words, the Father is the literal father of Christ's mortal body. President Heber J. Grant explained this as follows (**bold** added for emphasis):

"We believe absolutely that Jesus Christ is the Son of God, begotten of God, the first-born in the spirit and **the only begotten in the flesh**; that He is the Son of God just as much as you and I are the sons of our fathers" (Heber J. Grant, "Analysis of the Articles of Faith," *Millennial Star*, Jan. 5, 1922, 2).

Doctrine

Verse 22. Christ was actually tempted but did not give in to it at all.

22 **He suffered temptations** but **gave no heed unto them**.

Doctrine

Verse 23. Christ was literally resurrected.

23 **He** was crucified, **died, and rose again** the third day;

24 And ascended into heaven, to sit down on the right hand of the Father, to reign with almighty power according to the will of the Father;

The title "Doctrine and Covenants" implies that there are "covenants" as well as "doctrines" included within the pages of this sacred volume of scripture we are studying. Verse 25, next, is an example of this.

Covenant

Verse 25. Baptism is a "covenant."

25 That as many as would believe and **be baptized in his holy name**, and **endure in faith** [*live righteously*] to the end, should be **saved**—

Doctrine

Verse 26. The Atonement worked before it was actually performed by the Savior. (In other words, it is truly an "infinite" Atonement, covering present, past, and future.)

26 Not only those who believed after he came in the meridian of time, **in the flesh**, **but all those from the beginning**, even as many as were before he came, **who believed** in the words of the holy prophets, who spake as they were inspired by the gift of the Holy Ghost, who truly testified of him in all things, should have eternal life,

Doctrine

Verse 27. One of the major functions of the Holy Ghost is to bear witness to us of the Father and the Son.

27 As well as those who should come after [*all who have lived since Christ, or will live*], who should believe in the gifts and callings of God by **the Holy Ghost**, which **beareth record of the Father and of the Son**;

Doctrine

Verse 28. The Godhead consists of the Father, the Son, and the Holy Ghost. They work in complete unity and harmony with each other as "one."

28 Which Father, Son, and Holy Ghost are one God, infinite and eternal, without end. Amen.

Joseph Fielding Smith gave additional instruction on what "one God" means (verse 28, above) in reference to the Godhead:

"It is perfectly true, as recorded in the Pearl of Great Price and in the Bible, that to us there is but one God [see Moses 1:6; Mark 12:32]. Correctly interpreted God in this sense means Godhead, for **it is composed of Father, Son, and Holy Spirit**. This Godhead presides over us, and to us, the inhabitants of this world, **they constitute the only God, or Godhead**. There is none other besides them [See 1 Corinthians 8:5–6]. To them we are amenable, and subject to their authority, and there is no other Godhead unto whom we are subject. However, as the Prophet has shown, there can be, and are, other Gods" (*Answers to Gospel Questions*, 2:142).

Doctrine

Verse 29. No one can be saved except through Jesus Christ.

29 And we know that all men **must repent** and **believe on the name of Jesus Christ**, and **worship the Father in his name**, and **endure in faith on his name to the end, or they cannot be saved** in the kingdom of God.

Verses 30 and 31, next, deal with the doctrines of justification and sanctification. There are many ways to approach and define both of these words. We will intentionally keep it simple for our purposes here. We will use Moses 6:60 from the Pearl of Great Price as the basis for our discussion:

Moses 6:60

For **by the water** [*in other words, through baptism*] ye keep the commandment [*to be baptized*]; **by the Spirit** [*the Holy Ghost*] **ye are justified**, and **by the blood** [*Christ's Atonement*] **ye are sanctified**;

From Moses 6:60, quoted above, we see that the Holy Ghost "justifies" us. Perhaps one of the simplest ways to envision being "justified" is to think in terms of computers and word processing. When we are typing a document and want to "justify" the left margin, we use the proper key strokes or the correct mouse click and the left margin lines up perfectly. If we choose to "justify" both margins and give the computer the proper commands, both left and right margins line up perfectly.

Applying this analogy to ourselves as members of the Church, we are given the gift of the Holy Ghost. If we follow His promptings faithfully throughout our lives, we will gradually be "justified" or lined up in harmony with the requirements for exaltation. This will allow us to fully qualify for the cleansing and purifying "blood" [*Atonement of Christ*] by which we are "sanctified." "Sanctified" can be defined as being cleansed from sin and made pure and holy, fit to be in the presence of God in celestial glory.

Thus, "justification" comes by following the promptings of the Holy Ghost and being lined up in harmony with God through the grace of [*help of*] the Savior. Additionally, one of the functions of the Holy Ghost, who is also known as the "Holy Spirit of promise" (D&C 132:7), is to ratify and approve all covenants, etc., that we enter into with God. When we qualify for our covenants to be "sealed by the Holy Spirit of promise" (132:7), it is another way of saying that we are "justified."

"Sanctification," as mentioned above, means to be made worthy to be in the presence of God. It is to have our sins remitted through the atoning blood of the Savior; or, in other words, to have our "garments [*symbolic of our lives*] . . . made white through the blood of the Lamb" (Alma 34:36).

In summary, the Holy Ghost prompts us and guides us as we strive to follow the teachings of Christ. As we follow His promptings, we are "justified," lined up in harmony with Christ, which allows us to be "sanctified" or cleansed from sin through His Atonement. Ultimately, our lives, covenants, promises, etc., can thus be ratified, approved, and sealed by the Holy Ghost, who is also known as the Holy Spirit of promise (or the Holy Spirit who was promised by the Savior to His disciples and who came to them on the day of Pentecost—see Acts 2). Through being justified and sanctified, we will be allowed entrance into exaltation in the celestial kingdom.

Doctrine

Verses 30 and 31. In order to be saved in celestial exaltation, we must be "justified" and "sanctified."

30 And we know that justification through the grace of our Lord and Savior Jesus Christ is just and true;

31 And we know also, that **sanctification through the grace of our Lord and Savior Jesus Christ is just and true**, to all those who love and serve God with all their mights, minds, and strength.

Verses 32–34, next, are a reminder that we must be careful not to let our guard down because of past good deeds and success in being in harmony with God.

32 But **there is a possibility that man may fall from grace** and depart from the living God;

33 Therefore **let the church take heed** and pray always, **lest they fall into temptation**;

34 Yea, and even **let those who are sanctified take heed also**.

Verse 35, next, is a reference to Revelation 22:18–19, in which the Apostle John warns against adding unauthorized teachings or doctrines to or taking away from the pure gospel of Jesus Christ.

35 And we know that **these things are true and according to the revelations of John, neither adding to, nor diminishing from the prophecy of his book, the holy scriptures, or the revelations of God** which shall come hereafter by the gift and power of the Holy Ghost, the voice of God, or the ministering of angels.

36 And **the Lord God has spoken it**; and honor, power and glory be rendered to his holy

name, both now and ever. Amen.

From here to the end of the section, we see what we referred to at the beginning of this section as the first "Handbook of Instructions" of the Church. As you will see, it gives instructions on many matters concerning how to conduct and run the newly restored Church. First of all, verse 37, next, gives instructions as to how people are to qualify for baptism into the Church.

Doctrine

Verse 37. Baptism is the "gate" or entrance into the Lord's Church and onto the covenant path.

37 *And again, by way of commandment to the church concerning the manner of baptism*—All those who **humble themselves** before God, and **desire to be baptized**, and **come forth with broken hearts** and **contrite spirits** [*"contrite" means humbly desiring correction as needed*], and **witness before the church** that they have **truly repented of all their sins**, and are **willing to take upon them the name of Jesus Christ**, having a **determination to serve him to the end**, and truly **manifest by their works** that they **have received of the Spirit of Christ unto the remission of their sins, shall be received by baptism into his church**.

Verses 38 through 60 explain various duties, responsibilities, and limitations of the different priesthood offices. Perhaps you've wondered why we refer to Apostles as "elders." The answer is found in verse 38, next. In fact, "elder" is a title that can appropriately refer to any Melchizedek Priesthood holder, including general authorities. Joseph Fielding Smith explained this as follows (**bold** added for emphasis):

"We learn at this time the Lord revealed that the designation of **'Elder' is one applicable to the apostles and likewise to all others who hold the Melchizedek Priesthood**. The use of this designation makes it needless to use unnecessarily sacred terms as 'Apostle,' 'Patriarch,' 'High Priest,' etc. It is proper in general usage to speak of the apostles, the seventies and all others holding the Melchizedek Priesthood as 'elders.' Of course, the term President, in speaking of the First Presidency, is the proper designation" (*Church History and Modern Revelation*, 1:95).

38 *The duty of the elders, priests, teachers, deacons, and members of the church of Christ*—An **apostle is an elder**, and it is his calling [*the calling of an elder*] to baptize;

In the next several verses, this "handbook of instructions" will explain the various duties of certain priesthood offices.

Duties of Elders—vv. 39–45

39 And **to ordain other elders, priests, teachers, and deacons**;

40 And to **administer bread and wine—the emblems of the flesh and blood of Christ**—

41 And to **confirm those who are baptized into the church, by the laying on of hands** [*confirmation must be done by holders of the Melchizedek Priesthood and cannot be done by holders of the Aaronic Priesthood*] for the baptism of fire and the Holy Ghost [*the gift of the Holy Ghost*], according to the scriptures;

The use of the word "fire" in conjunction with the Holy Ghost (see verse 41, above) is common in the scriptures and in sermons and lessons in the Church. The imagery is that of a refiner's fire. The refiner heats the gold ore to the point of melting it, at which point the pure gold remains and the slag containing imperfections and impurities floats to the top of the crucible and is discarded. The Holy Ghost can do the same for us. He "burns" the impurities out of our minds and hearts as we listen to His promptings. Thus, we ultimately become "pure gold," worthy to live in celestial glory.

42 And **to teach**, **expound** [*explain*], **exhort** [*urge and warn as needed*], **baptize**, and **watch over the church**;

43 And **to confirm the church** [*since confirming new members is already mentioned in verse 41, above, perhaps this means to set members apart to various callings, which is a Melchizedek Priesthood function*] by the laying on of the hands, and the giving of the Holy Ghost;

44 And to **take the lead of all meetings** [*when no one with higher authority is present*].

45 The elders are to **conduct the meetings as they are led by the Holy Ghost**, according to the commandments and revelations of God.

Duties of Priests—vv. 46–52

46 The priest's duty is **to preach, teach, expound, exhort, and baptize, and administer the sacrament**,

Neither teachers nor deacons can baptize, bless the sacrament, or lay on hands (see verse 58).

47 And **visit** the house of **each member** [*as in ministering to assigned members and families*], and **exhort** them to pray vocally and in secret and attend to all family duties.

48 And he may also **ordain other priests, teachers, and deacons**.

49 And he is to **take the lead of meetings when there is no elder present**;

50 But when there is an elder present, he is only to preach, teach, expound, exhort, and baptize,

51 And visit the house of each member, exhorting them to pray vocally and in secret and attend to all family duties.

52 **In all these duties the priest is to assist the elder if occasion requires.**

Duties of Teachers—vv. 53–57

53 The teacher's duty is to **watch over the church always, and be with and strengthen them**;

54 And **see that there is no iniquity in the church, neither hardness with each other, neither lying, backbiting, nor evil speaking**;

55 And **see that the church meet together often**, and also **see that all the members do their duty**.

56 And he is to **take the lead of meetings in the absence of the elder or priest**—

57 And is **to be assisted** always, in all his duties in the church, **by the deacons, if occasion requires**.

Duties of Deacons—vv. 57–59

58 But **neither teachers nor deacons have authority to baptize, administer the sacrament, or lay on hands**;

59 They are, however, to **warn, expound, exhort, and teach, and invite all to come unto Christ**.

Verse 60, next, among other things, reminds us that the one ordaining another to an office in the priesthood should seek the guidance of the Holy Ghost as he does so in order that the ordination and accompanying blessing might be specific to that person.

60 Every elder, priest, teacher, or deacon **is to be ordained according to the gifts and callings of God unto him**; and **he is to be ordained by the power of the Holy Ghost, which is in the one who ordains him**.

Next, this "handbook of instructions" deals with the topic of what we now refer to as "stake conferences." For many years, these stake conferences were held on a quarterly basis. Now, they are held every six months. A reminder that this is a "policy," not a "doctrine," and that we are led by living prophets.

Stake Conferences—vv. 61–62

61 The several elders composing this church of Christ are to **meet in conference once in three months, or from time to time as said conferences shall direct or appoint**;

62 And said conferences are to do whatever church business is necessary to be done at the time.

Sustainings—vv. 63, 65–67

63 The elders are to receive their licenses [*recommends to perform ordinances or function in their priesthood callings*] from other elders, **by vote of the church** [*the church unit, such as branches, wards, districts, stakes*] **to which they belong, or from the conferences**.

Recommends to Perform Priesthood Ordinances and Duties—vv. 64

64 Each priest, teacher, or deacon, who is ordained by a priest, may **take a certificate** [*recommend to perform ordinances and so on*] from him at the time, **which certificate**, when presented to an elder, shall entitle him to a license, which **shall authorize him to perform the duties of his calling**, or he may receive it from a conference.

No Secret Ordinations—v. 65

65 **No person is to be ordained to any office** in this church, where there is a regularly organized branch of the same, **without the vote of that church**;

The instruction in verse 65, above, that no one is to be ordained without being sustained by the members of his appropriate church unit, is far more important that many members realize. It is a vital safeguard against apostasy. Perhaps you are aware that many so-called break-offs from the Church claim that their leaders were secretly ordained and thus have authority to carry on the work of God. Such claims are in direct violation of the above instructions from the Savior Himself.

66 But the **presiding elders, traveling bishops, high councilors, high priests, and elders, may have the privilege of ordaining, where there is no branch of the church that a vote may be called.**

67 Every president of the high priesthood (or presiding elder), bishop, high councilor, and high priest, **is to be ordained by the direction of a high council or general conference**.

Verse 37 listed requirements for people to qualify for baptism. Once a person has been baptized, there is to be a waiting period before he or she is confirmed and begins partaking of the sacrament.

Waiting Period Between Baptism and Confirmation—vv. 68–69

68 *The duty of the members after they are received by baptism*—The **elders or priests are to have a sufficient time to expound all things concerning the church of Christ to their understanding, previous to their partaking of the sacrament and being confirmed** by the laying on of the hands of the elders, **so that all things may be done in order**.

69 And **the members shall manifest** before the church, and also before the elders, **by a godly walk and conversation, that they are worthy of it**, that there may be works and faith agreeable to the holy scriptures—walking in holiness before the Lord.

Blessing Babies—v. 70

70 Every member of the church of Christ having children is to bring them unto the elders before the church, who are to lay their hands upon them in the name of Jesus Christ, and **bless them in his name**.

No Infant Baptisms—v. 71

71 **No one** can be received [*baptized*] into the church of Christ **unless he has arrived unto the years of accountability** before God [*which is age eight; see D&C 68:25*], **and is capable of repentance.**

Baptismal Prayer and How to Baptize—vv. 72–74

72 Baptism is to be administered in the following manner unto all those who repent—

Doctrine

Baptism is to be performed by immersion—vv. 73–74.

73 The **person who** is called of God and **has authority** from Jesus Christ to baptize, **shall go down into the water with the person** who has presented himself or herself for baptism, and **shall say, calling him or her by name: Having been commissioned of Jesus Christ, I baptize you in the name of the Father, and of the Son, and of the Holy Ghost. Amen.**

74 Then shall he **immerse him or her in the water**, and come forth again out of the water.

The baptismal prayer, given in verse 73, above, is the one that is used today. Perhaps you are aware that a baptismal prayer is given in 3 Nephi 11:25, which was used by the Nephites. Its wording is just a bit different than the prayer given here.

In preparation for my first baptism as a young missionary in Austria, I memorized the baptismal prayer in German as given in 3 Nephi 11:25 rather than the one in D&C 20:73. I didn't know any better, and I never thought to ask my senior companion. I'm sure that he assumed that since I was from Utah, I would know to use the prayer given in the Doctrine and Covenants.

When the time of the actual baptism arrived, I nervously went down into the water with the man I was to baptize, got situated, and began saying the prayer from Third Nephi. The witnesses quickly corrected me, which did away with any composure I had left, and so they had to say almost each word or phrase of the prayer, which I repeated in halting German, in order to complete the ordinance. As you can imagine, I have always used the correct prayer since then.

If a person were to ask why we can't use the baptismal prayer given in Third Nephi, the answer is simple. The Lord gave us the prayer He wants us to use in our day, which is recorded in D&C 20:73, and we don't seek to counsel the Lord.

Also, some members wonder why we can't baptize someone in a bathtub or other container which is just large enough for the candidate for baptism to fit in and be successfully immersed. Again, we find the answer in verse 73, above. Both the priesthood holder and the candidate for baptism must go down into the water. In fact, I had an acquaintance who had to be rebaptized at age twelve when it was brought up that he was baptized at age eight in a watering trough at the farm, with the man performing the baptism standing on the ground outside the trough.

Sacrament Prayers and How to Conduct the Sacrament—vv. 75–79

75 It is expedient [*necessary, vital*] **that the church meet together often to partake of bread and wine in the remembrance of the Lord Jesus**;

As you know, we use water in place of wine in our sacrament services today. We will discuss this when we study section 27, verses 1–4. As we come to the sacrament prayers themselves, verses 77 and 79, we will use **bold** to point out the covenants we make and the promises the Lord gives us in return.

76 And **the elder** [*a Melchizedek Priesthood holder*] **or priest shall administer it**; and after this

manner shall he administer it—he shall kneel with the church and call upon the Father in solemn prayer, saying:

77 O God, the Eternal Father, we ask thee in the name of thy Son, Jesus Christ, to bless and sanctify this bread to the souls of all those who partake of it, that they may **eat in remembrance of the body of thy Son**, and **witness** unto thee, O God, the Eternal Father, **that they are willing to take upon them the name of thy Son**, and **always remember him** and **keep his commandments** which he has given them; **that they may always have his Spirit to be with them**. Amen.

78 The manner of administering the wine—he shall take the cup also, and say:

79 O God, the Eternal Father, we ask thee in the name of thy Son, Jesus Christ, to bless and sanctify this wine to the souls of all those who drink of it, that they may **do it in remembrance of the blood of thy Son, which was shed for them**; that they may **witness** unto thee, O God, the Eternal Father, **that they do always remember him**, that they may **have his Spirit to be with them**. Amen.

Thus, from verses 77 and 79, above, we see that when partaking of the sacrament, we do it in remembrance of His body and blood that were given for us, and make covenants to (1) take upon us the name of Jesus Christ, (2) to constantly remember Him and our commitments to Him, and (3) we promise to keep His commandments. In return, He promises that we will "always have his Spirit to be with" us, which is a most powerful promise. When we strive to keep our covenants, and thus have the strong influence of the Spirit with us, we will consistently be guided and directed toward exaltation!

Perhaps you've heard someone ask if we are renewing covenants or making covenants when we partake of the sacrament. The answer is that we do both. We make the same covenants again and again each time we partake of the sacrament. We also, in effect, renew these covenants as well as our covenants of baptism and other covenants we have made. This includes temple covenants, as explained by President Dallin H. Oaks in a talk about the sacrament. (**Bold** added for emphasis.)

"Our witness that we are willing to take upon us the name of Jesus Christ has several different meanings. . . .

". . . We take upon us the name of Christ when we are baptized in his name, when we belong to his Church and profess our belief in him, and when we do the work of his kingdom. . . .

"It is significant that when we partake of the sacrament we do not witness that we *take upon* us the name of Jesus Christ. We witness that we are *willing* to do so. (See D&C 20:77.) The fact that we only witness to our willingness suggests that something else must happen before we actually take that sacred name upon us in the most important sense. . . .

"Willingness to take upon us the name of Jesus Christ can . . . be understood as willingness to take upon us the authority of Jesus Christ. According to this meaning, **by partaking of the sacrament we witness our willingness to participate in the sacred ordinances of the temple** and to receive the highest blessings available through the name and by the authority of the Savior when he chooses to confer them upon us. . . .

". . . **When we witness our willingness to take upon us the name of Jesus Christ, we are signifying our commitment to do all that we can to achieve eternal life in the kingdom of our Father**. We are expressing our candidacy—our determination to strive for—exaltation in the celestial kingdom" ("Taking upon Us the Name of Jesus Christ," *Ensign*, May 1985, 80–82).

President Spencer W. Kimball explained that the covenants we renew in partaking of the sacrament include all of our covenants to live righteously:

"The Savior emphasized that the tangible bread and water of the Sacrament were to remind us continually of the sacrifice he made for us and **for renewal of our covenants of righteousness**" (*Teachings of Spencer W. Kimball*, 220).

Church Discipline, Including Excommunication—vv. 80 and 83

80 **Any member** of the church of Christ **transgressing**, or being overtaken in a fault, **shall be dealt with as the scriptures direct**.

Membership Records—vv. 81, 82, and 84

81 It shall be the duty of the several churches, composing the church of Christ, to send one or more of their teachers to attend the several conferences held by the elders of the church,

82 With a list of the names of the several members uniting themselves with the church since the last conference; or send by the hand of some priest; so that **a regular list of all the names of the whole church** may be **kept in a book by one of the elders**, whomsoever the other elders shall appoint from time to time;

83 And also, **if any have been expelled from the church** [*excommunication*], so that their **names** may be **blotted out** of the general church record of names.

84 All members removing from the church where they reside, if going to a church where they are not known, may take **a letter certifying that they are regular members and in good standing**, which certificate may be signed by any elder or priest if the member receiving the letter is personally acquainted with the elder or priest, or it may be signed by the teachers or deacons of the church.

SECTION 21

Background

This revelation was received by Joseph Smith on Tuesday, April 6, 1830, at the home of Peter Whitmer Sr. in Fayette, New York, during the actual meeting in which the Church was officially organized.

There were about sixty people present in Father Whitmer's home to witness this marvelous event. As the meeting began, the twenty-four-year-old Prophet Joseph designated five others to join him in order to meet the requirements of the state of New York for the organization of a church. The five were Oliver Cowdery, Hyrum Smith, Peter Whitmer Jr., Samuel H. Smith, and David Whitmer.

The meeting was opened with prayer, after which Joseph Smith asked those present to sustain him and Oliver Cowdery as their leaders in the kingdom of God. Everyone present raised their hands in support of this action. Unanimous approval was also given to organize the Church of Jesus Christ. Joseph recorded what followed these actions:

"I then laid my hands upon Oliver Cowdery, and ordained him an Elder of the 'Church of Jesus Christ of Latter-day Saints;' after which, he ordained me also to the office of an Elder of said Church. [*They had previously received the Melchizedek Priesthood but were told to wait to ordain each other to the office of elder until the Church was organized. See* History of the Church*, 1:61).*] We then took bread, blessed it, and brake it with them; also wine, blessed it, and drank it with them. We then laid our hands on each individual member of the Church present, that they might receive the gift of the Holy Ghost, and be confirmed members of the Church of Christ. The Holy Ghost was poured out upon us to a very great degree—some prophesied, whilst we all praised the Lord, and rejoiced exceedingly. Whilst yet together, I received the following commandment: [D&C 21]" (*History of the Church*, 1:77–78).

After the meeting concluded, a number of people were baptized, including Orrin Porter Rockwell and Martin Harris, as well as Joseph Smith Sr. and Lucy Mack Smith, the parents of the Prophet.

As we begin our study of the verses in this section, which was given during the meeting in which the Church was officially organized, we will see that the Lord gave several instructions to the new members of the Restored Church. The very first phrase, in verse 1, emphasizes the importance of keeping records, which will include a history of the Church and a record of the revelations received.

1 BEHOLD, **there shall be a record kept among you**; and in it thou [*Joseph Smith*] shalt be called a seer, a translator, a prophet, an apostle of Jesus Christ, an elder of the church through the will of God the Father, and the grace of your Lord Jesus Christ,

We will repeat verse 1, this time emphasizing what the Lord teaches us about the role of the living prophet.

1 BEHOLD, there shall be a record kept among you; and in it **thou shalt be** called a **seer**, a **translator**, a **prophet**, an **apostle** of Jesus Christ, an **elder** of the church through the will of God the Father, and the grace [*help, mercy*] of your Lord Jesus Christ,

The Institute of Religion *Doctrine and Covenants Student Manual, 1981,* defines the above terms as follows (**bold** added for emphasis and text rearranged slightly for use here):

Seer

Elder John A. Widtsoe defined a seer as "one who **sees with spiritual eyes. He perceives the meaning of that which seems obscure to others**; therefore he is an interpreter and clarifier of eternal truth. He **foresees the future** from the past and the present. This he does by the power of the Lord operating through him directly, or indirectly with the aid of divine instruments such as the Urim and Thummim. In short, he is one who sees, who walks in the Lord's light with open eyes" (Mosiah 8:15–17) (*Evidences and Reconciliations*, 1:205–6; see also Moses 6:36).

Translator

The title "translator" may refer to one who has received two blessings given a prophet by the spirit of God: (1) The power to convert the written or spoken word into another language (see D&C 20:8). (2) The power to give a clearer meaning to a given language.

Through the gift of translation, a prophet does not merely convey in the language of the reader the words that were recorded by the writer, but by revelation, he also **preserves for the reader the thoughts or intent of the original writer**.

Prophet

According to Elder Widtsoe, "**A prophet is a teacher. That is the essential meaning of the word**. He teaches the body of truth, the gospel, revealed by the Lord to man; and under inspiration explains it to the understanding of the people. He is an expounder of truth. Moreover, he shows that the way to human happiness is through obedience to God's law. He calls to repentance those who wander away from the truth. He becomes a warrior for the consummation of the Lord's purposes with respect to the human family. The purpose of his life is to uphold the Lord's plan of salvation. All this he does by close communion with the Lord, until he is 'full of power by the spirit of the Lord' (Micah 3:8; see also D&C 20:26; 34:10; 43:16).

"In the course of time the word 'prophet' has come to mean, perhaps chiefly, a man who receives revelations and directions from the Lord. **The principal business of a prophet has mistakenly been thought to foretell coming events, to utter prophecies, which is only one of the several prophetic functions**.

"In the sense that a prophet is a man who receives revelations from the Lord, the titles 'seer and revelator' merely amplify the larger and inclusive meaning of the title 'prophet'" (*Evidences and Reconciliations*, 1:204–5).

Scriptural insights into the role of a prophet are found in Exodus 4:15–16; 7:1–2.

Apostle

An Apostle is a special witness of Jesus Christ to all the world (see D&C 107:23). The Prophet Joseph Smith explained the important calling of an Apostle by asking a question and then giving the answer:

"What importance is there attached to the calling of these Twelve Apostles, different from the other callings or officers of the Church? . . .

"They are the Twelve Apostles, who are called to the office of the Traveling High Council, who are to preside over the churches of the Saints, among the Gentiles, where there is a presidency established; and they are to travel and preach among the Gentiles, until the Lord shall command them to go to the Jews. They are to hold the keys of this ministry, to unlock the door of the Kingdom of heaven unto all nations, and to preach the Gospel to every creature. This is the power, authority, and virtue of their apostleship" (*History of the Church*, 2:200).

Elder

The name of an office in the Melchizedek Priesthood, elder is also the general title used to address one who bears this priesthood. Elder Bruce R. McConkie added that an elder is a representative of the Lord:

"What is an elder? An elder is a minister of the Lord Jesus Christ. He holds the holy Melchizedek Priesthood. He is commissioned to stand in the place and stead of his Master—who is the Chief Elder—in ministering to his fellowmen. He is the Lord's agent. His appointment is to preach the gospel and perfect the Saints" ("Only an Elder," *Ensign*, June 1975, 66). (End of quote from the *Doctrine and Covenants Student Manual*, 1981 edition, 44.)

Before we move on, we will give one more quote, this time from the Prophet Joseph Smith, concerning the role of a "seer." As usual, we will use **bold** for emphasis.

"Wherefore, we again say, search the revelations of God; study the prophecies, and rejoice that God grants unto the world **Seers and Prophets**. They are **they who saw** the mysteries of godliness; **they saw** the flood before it came; **they saw** angels ascending and descending upon a ladder that reached from earth to heaven; **they saw** the stone cut out of the mountain, which filled the whole earth; **they saw** the Son of God come from the regions of bliss and dwell with men on earth; **they saw** the deliverer come out of Zion, and turn away ungodliness from Jacob; **they saw** the glory of the Lord when he showed the transfiguration of the earth on the mount; **they saw** every mountain laid low and every valley exalted when the Lord was taking vengeance upon the wicked; **they saw** truth spring out of the earth, and righteousness look down from heaven in the last days, before the Lord came the second time to gather his elect; **they saw** the end of wickedness on earth, and the Sabbath of creation crowned with peace; **they saw** the end of the glorious thousand years, when Satan was loosed for a little season; **they saw** the day of judgment when all men received according to their works, and **they saw** the heaven and the earth flee away to make room for the city of God, when the righteous receive an inheritance in eternity" (*Teachings of the Prophet Joseph Smith,* 12–13).

In this quote from Joseph Smith, we are taught that seers "see" the future. They "see" by the power of God and then tell us what they see. They are "watchmen on the tower," which is a scriptural phrase referring to guards who stand high upon towers where they can "see" a long way off and warn the citizens of the city when danger is coming. Thus, our modern "prophets, seers, and revelators" have been, in effect, called of God to stand upon high "towers" and are given spiritual sight to "see" when danger is coming and to warn us of it. For instance, in "The Family: A Proclamation to the World," our "prophets, seers, and revelators" have strengthened us and warned us of coming dangers and of dangers that have already come among us in our day.

Continuing with section 21, we hear the Lord bearing witness of Joseph Smith and his role in restoring the Church in the last days (verses 2 and 3).

2 **Being inspired of the Holy Ghost to lay the foundation thereof** [*the Church*], and to build it up unto the most holy faith.

3 Which church was organized and **established in** the year of your Lord **eighteen hundred and thirty**, in the **fourth month**, and on the **sixth day** of the month which is called **April**.

Next, in verses 4–6, we are clearly taught the importance of following the living prophet. In fact, we are specifically taught that if we do, there is not a chance that Satan's forces can succeed in ultimately taking us from God. Apostates and detractors do not seem to be able to comprehend this simple doctrine.

Doctrine

Verses 4–6. If we faithfully follow the living prophet, we are assured of exaltation.

4 Wherefore, meaning the church [*in other words, the members of the Church*], **thou shalt give heed unto all his words and commandments** which he shall give unto you as he receiveth them, walking in all holiness before me;

5 For **his word ye shall receive, as if from mine own mouth**, in all patience and faith.

6 For **by doing these things the gates of hell shall not prevail** [*win*] **against you**; yea, and the Lord God will disperse the powers of darkness from before you, and cause the heavens to shake for your good, and his name's glory.

Elder Harold B. Lee reminded us that the Lord will never allow our living Prophet to lead us astray. He taught (**bold** added for emphasis):

"We are not dependent only upon the revelations given in the past as contained in our standard works—as wonderful as they are . . . We have a mouthpiece to whom God does and is revealing his mind and will. **God will never permit him to lead us astray**. As has been said [D&C 43:3–4], God would remove us out of our place if we should attempt to do it. You have no concern. Let the management and government of God, then, be with the Lord. Do not try to find fault with the management and affairs that pertain to him alone and by revelation through his prophet—his living prophet, his seer, and his revelator. (*The Place of the Living Prophet* [address delivered to seminary and institute of religion personnel], 8 July 1964, 16.)" (*Doctrine and Covenants Student Manual*, 1981, 45).

In the remaining verses of this section, the Savior continues to instruct and bear witness to the members of the Church as to the importance and validity of the calling of Joseph Smith.

7 For thus saith the Lord God: **Him have I inspired to move the cause of Zion in mighty power for good**, and his diligence I know, and his prayers I have heard.

8 Yea, **his weeping for Zion I have seen**, and I will cause that he shall mourn for her no longer; for **his days of rejoicing are come unto the remission of his sins**, and the manifestations of my blessings upon his works.

9 For, behold, I will bless **all those who labor in my vineyard** with a mighty blessing, and they **shall believe on his words**, which are given him through me by the Comforter [*the Holy Ghost*], which manifesteth that Jesus was crucified by sinful men for the sins of the world, yea, for the remission of sins unto the contrite [*humble and willing to be corrected as needed*] heart.

As previously mentioned, during the organization of the Church in the Peter Whitmer Sr. home, Oliver Cowdery ordained Joseph Smith an elder, and then Joseph ordained Oliver an elder, as instructed by the Lord. Next, we see these instructions.

10 Wherefore it behooveth me [*it is My desire*] that **he** [*Joseph Smith*] **should be ordained by you, Oliver Cowdery** mine apostle;

11 This being an ordinance unto you, that you are an elder under his hand, **he being the first** unto you [*Joseph Smith presides, is the highest officer in the Church, and is over you*], that you might be an elder unto this church of Christ, bearing my name—

12 And **the first preacher of this church** unto the church, and before the world, yea, before the Gentiles; yea, and thus saith the Lord God, lo, lo! to the Jews also. Amen.

SECTION 22

Background

Given through the Prophet Joseph Smith at Manchester, New York, in April 1830, this revelation addresses the issue of whether or not converts need to be baptized if they were previously baptized in their old church.

The Lord speaks clearly and to the point, as you can see in verses 2 and 4. It almost sounds like a parent speaking to children who keep bringing up the same question, even though they have already been told the answer.

First, in verses 1 and 2, next, the Lord explains the reason for requiring that all who desire to enter His true Church do so through proper, authorized baptism. Among other things, He explains that this is a new covenant, not an existing one contained in other religious organizations that is just being revised or updated. In other words, this is a "restoration" of the true Church, not a revitalization of an existing sect or church.

1 BEHOLD, I say unto you that **all old covenants** [*such as in the Law of Moses*] **have I caused to be done away in this thing** [*in the restoration of the Church of Jesus Christ through Joseph Smith*]; and **this is a new and an everlasting covenant** [*"new" for this dispensation (the last days), because all other churches have gone into apostasy and have no priesthood authority*], **even that which was from the beginning** [*this is a restoration of the true Church, with the power and authority that Adam had at the beginning of things on this earth; see Moses 6:64–68*].

The phrase "the new and everlasting covenant," seen in verse 1, above, is an important point of doctrine for anyone who understands the gospel. President Joseph Fielding Smith explained it as follows:

"The new and everlasting covenant is the fulness of the gospel. It is composed of 'All covenants, contracts, bonds, obligations, oaths, vows, performances, connections, associations, or expectations' that are sealed upon members of the Church by the Holy Spirit of promise, or the Holy Ghost, by the authority of the President of the Church who holds the keys. . . .

"Marriage for eternity is **a** new and everlasting covenant. Baptism is also **a** new and everlasting covenant, and likewise ordination to the priesthood, and every other covenant is everlasting and **a part** of **the new and everlasting covenant** which **embraces all things**" (*Answers to Gospel Questions*, 1:65).

2 Wherefore [*this is why*], **although a man should be baptized an**

hundred times it availeth him nothing [*it does him no good*], for **you cannot enter in at the strait** [*narrow*] **gate by the law of Moses** [*in other words, even the Law of Moses can't get you into the celestial kingdom*], **neither by your dead works** [*other religions and churches of the day don't have the necessary power and authority either*].

Next, in verse 3, the Lord explains that none of the existing churches of the day have the power and authority to save souls. In other words, the apostasy was universal.

3 For **it is because of your dead works** [*baptisms and other ordinances in existing churches that have no power or authority to perform them*] **that I have caused this last covenant and this church to be built up** unto me, even as in days of old [*just like I did in previous dispensations and restorations of the gospel*].

4 Wherefore, **enter ye in at the gate** [*be baptized by immersion by proper authority; it is the gate to the covenant path*], **as I have commanded, and seek not to counsel your God**. Amen.

SECTION 23

Background

This revelation (which is a series of five brief revelations) was given through Joseph Smith at Manchester, New York (which was located next to Palmyra), in April 1830. These revelations were given to five men, Oliver Cowdery, Hyrum Smith (Joseph's older brother), Samuel H. Smith (Joseph's younger brother), Joseph Smith Sr. (Joseph's father), and Joseph Knight Sr. Shortly after the official organization of the Church, on Tuesday, April 6, 1830, all five men had come to the Prophet to have him inquire of the Lord for them as to their duties. These 5 individual revelations were later combined to become section 23.

Joseph Smith recorded the following that led up to these revelations:

"The following persons being anxious to know of the Lord what might be their respective duties in relation to this word, I enquired of the Lord, and received for them the following:" (*History of the Church,* 1:80).

As you read this section, you may wish to pay attention to which of the five men listed above that is not told that he is under no condemnation.

The first message is to Oliver Cowdery, consisting of verses 1 and 2. At this point, he was the "second elder" of the Church and was a prominent and important player in the Restoration. However, he is warned about pride, which will ultimately lead to his excommunication in 1838. (He will return to the Church ten years later.)

1 BEHOLD, **I speak unto you, Oliver**, a few words. Behold, **thou art blessed, and art under no condemnation** [*Oliver is doing well at this point*]. **But beware of pride**, lest thou shouldst enter into temptation.

2 Make known thy calling unto the church, and also before the world, and **thy heart shall be opened to preach the truth** from henceforth and forever. Amen.

We will include just a bit here about the charges that led to Oliver Cowdery's excommunication in 1838 in Missouri. We will quote from the *Church History in the Fulness of Times* student manual, 2003, used by our institutes of religion:

"A much more serious matter was the case of Oliver Cowdery. He was charged by the high council for persecuting Church leaders with vexatious lawsuits, seeking to destroy the character of Joseph Smith, not abiding ecclesiastical authority in temporal affairs, selling lands in Jackson County, and leaving his calling as Assistant President of the Church and turning to the practice of law. Oliver refused to appear before the council, but he answered by letter. He denied the Church's right to dictate how he should conduct his life and asked that his fellowship with the Church be ended. The high council excommunicated him 12 April 1838. He spent a decade outside the Church, but later humbly submitted himself for rebaptism in October 1848 in Kanesville, Iowa" (*Church History in the Fulness of Times*, 2003, 186).

Next, the Lord speaks to Hyrum, who is five years older than his brother, Joseph. Perhaps you will remember, from section 11, that Hyrum Smith was anxious to go forth and preach the gospel. At that time, he was told to wait. Now, in this brief message, he is told that the time has come for his tongue to be "loosed" and that he can now "exhort" and "strengthen the church." Imagine his gratitude and feelings as he realizes that his obedience to the Lord's instructions in section 11 have paid off and he can now begin preaching.

Something in verse 3 appears to be prophetic, namely, "thy duty is unto the church." This would seem to be a reference to Hyrum's later being called to serve as patriarch to the Church. (See D&C 124:124.)

3 Behold, **I speak unto you, Hyrum**, a few words; for **thou also art under no condemnation**

[*the same as Oliver Cowdery in verse 1*], and **thy heart is opened, and thy tongue loosed** [*you can go forth and preach now; see section 11*]**; and thy calling is to exhortation, and to strengthen the church continually**. Wherefore **thy duty is unto the church forever**, and this because of thy family. Amen.

The next message is to Joseph's younger brother by about three years, Samuel, who is considered to be one of the first missionaries of the Church. He traveled to Lima, New York, in April 1830, where he preached the gospel. He was ordained an elder at the first conference of the Church held June 9, 1830.

His missionary efforts included selling a copy of the Book of Mormon in April 1830 to Phineas Young, a brother of Brigham Young. Brigham gave the book to his sister, Fanny Young Murray, who was the mother-in-law of Heber C. Kimball. All of these people were eventually baptized. (See *Church History in the Fullness of Times*, 1989 edition, 75.)

Samuel also left a copy of the Book of Mormon with a minister named John P. Greene, whose wife, Rhoda, was Brigham Young's sister. They, too, joined the Church.

4 Behold, **I speak a few words unto you, Samuel**; for **thou also art under no condemnation**, and **thy calling is to exhortation** [*teaching and explaining the gospel*]**, and to strengthen the church**; and thou art **not as yet called to preach before the world**. Amen.

Next, the Lord speaks to Joseph Smith's father. He was born on July 12, 1771, and was 59 years old at the time of this revelation.

5 Behold, **I speak a few words unto you, Joseph;** for **thou also art under no condemnation,** and **thy calling also is to exhortation, and to strengthen the church**; and this is thy duty from henceforth and forever. Amen.

In the introduction to this section, we invited you to note which of the five men addressed by the Lord in these brief revelations was not told that he was under no condemnation. It is Joseph Knight Sr. The reason is that the other four have already been baptized, but Father Knight has not yet agreed to be baptized. Thus, he is under "condemnation," which is a word that basically means "stopped from progressing farther." Also, he apparently has not brought himself to pray yet.

You may wish to review the background notes for section 12 in this study guide for more information about Joseph Knight.

6 Behold, I manifest unto you [*a*

bit stronger wording than used with the other four men], Joseph Knight, by these words, that **you must take up your cross,** in the which **you must pray** vocally before the world as well as in secret, and in your family, and among your friends, and in all places.

7 And, behold, **it is your duty to unite with the true church** [*you must be baptized*], and give your language to exhortation continually, that you may receive the reward of the laborer. Amen.

Joseph Knight Sr. was baptized on June 28, 1830, by Oliver Cowdery. It was the same day that Emma Smith, the Prophet's wife, was baptized. For a bit more background on this, we quote the following:

"In the latter part of June 1830, the Prophet, accompanied by his wife, Oliver Cowdery, and John and David Whitmer, visited the Knight family in Colesville, New York. Joseph Knight, Sr., who had read the Book of Mormon and was satisfied it was true, and a number of others in the area desired baptism. On Saturday, 26 June, the brethren dammed a stream to make a pond suitable for baptisms. That night a mob, incited by leaders of some area churches who feared losing members, demolished the dam. On Sunday the brethren proceeded with the meeting. The Prophet related, 'Oliver Cowdery preached, and others of us bore testimony to the truth of the Book of Mormon, the doctrine of repentance, baptism for the remission of sins, and laying on of hands for the gift of the Holy Ghost.' Some members of the mob attended the meeting and afterward harassed those in attendance.

"Early the next day, 28 June, the brethren repaired the dam and held the baptismal service. Thirteen people were baptized, including Emma Smith. Many neighbors mocked them, asking if they 'had been washing sheep'" *(Church History in the Fulness of Times*, 2003, 71).

SECTION 24

Background

Section 24 was given to Joseph Smith and Oliver Cowdery in July 1830 in Harmony, Pennsylvania, where Joseph and Emma were living on a small farm. In the approximately four months since the organization of the Church on April 6, 1830, persecution had increased significantly.

We know that during these months since the organization of the Church, there had been much harassment of the Saints and a number of lawsuits against Joseph based on trumped-up charges. He had been arrested more than once and hauled off to court. Although he was acquitted each time, it still was terribly time consuming and disruptive and had to be discouraging to him and his wife and the members of the Church.

George Q. Cannon, who served as a counselor in the First Presidency under Presidents John Taylor, Wilford Woodruff, and Lorenzo Snow, gave the following, which helps us understand the setting and background for sections 24–26:

"Accompanied by his wife and three of the Elders, he [Joseph Smith] went again to Colesville [New York, in late June 1830]. Here they found many people awaiting baptism. Joseph prepared to accede to their demand. A suitable portion of a little stream in that locality was prepared for the purpose of the administration of the ordinance; but in the night sectarian priests, fearful of losing their congregations and their hire, instigated evil men to desecrate the spot and to destroy all the preparations of the Elders. . . . A few days later the ordinance was administered by Oliver Cowdery to thirteen persons at Colesville. . . .

"While the baptisms were in progress an angry mob collected, and threatened destruction to the Elders and believers. The mob surrounded the house of Joseph Knight and his son Newel and railed with devilish hatred at the inmates. The Prophet spoke to them and made an effort to calm their passions, but without avail. Wearied with their own impotent wrath, the mobs departed; but only to concoct new plots.

"That night a meeting was to be held, and when the believers and sympathizers had assembled, and Joseph was about to offer them instruction and consolation, a constable approached and arrested him on a warrant charging him with being a disorderly person, for setting the country in an uproar by circulating the Book of Mormon and by preaching a gospel of revelation.

"A court was convened to consider the strange charges brought against the young man, Joseph Smith; and hateful lies, of every form which the father of falsehood could devise, were circulated to create popular dislike. . . . The bitter feeling of endangered priestcraft was visible throughout the trial; but all the accusations which were made were but lies, and none were sustained. The court declared an acquittal. The evidence in the trial was a high tribute to the character of Joseph Smith. . . .

"This paper [a warrant] was secured on the oath of a sectarian bigot; and no sooner was Joseph acquitted by the court in Chenango County than he was seized under the new warrant and dragged back to Colesville.

"When the morning came, Joseph was arraigned before the magistrate's court of Colesville. Arrayed against him were some of the people who had been discomfited at the trial in Chenango County. This time they were determined to secure a conviction. By the side of the Prophet were his friends and advocates who had aided him in the former trial. Despite the vindictive effort of the mob, the court discharged the Prophet, declaring that nothing was shown to his dishonor" (*Life of Joseph Smith the Prophet*, 64–67).

The Prophet, himself, does not give any specific reason for this revelation, but does write the following by way of general background to sections 24, 25, and 26:

"After our departure from Colesville [*in April 1830*], after the trial [*based on false charges and held in South Bainbridge, New York; see* Church History in the Fulness of Times*, 2003, 71–73*], the Church there were very anxious, as might be expected, concerning our again visiting them, during which time Sister Knight, wife of Newel Knight, had a dream, which enabled her to say that we would visit them that day, which really came to pass, for a few hours afterwards we arrived; and thus was our faith much strengthened concerning dreams and visions in the last days, foretold by the ancient Prophet Joel; and although we this time were forced to seek safety from our enemies by flight, yet did we feel confident that eventually we should come off victorious, if we only continued faithful to Him who had called us forth from darkness into the marvelous light of the everlasting Gospel of our Lord Jesus Christ.

"Shortly after our return home, we received the following commandments [sections 24, 25, and 26]:" (*History of the Church*, 1:101).

With this background in mind, we will now watch as the Lord comforts the Prophet and counsels him in verses 1–9.

1 BEHOLD, **thou wast called and chosen to write** [*translate*] **the Book of Mormon**, and to my ministry; and **I have lifted thee up out of thine afflictions**, and have counseled thee, that **thou hast been delivered from all thine enemies**, and **thou hast been delivered from the powers of Satan and from darkness!**

The last phrase of verse 1, above, can refer to Satan's attempts to disrupt the work of restoration referred to in the background notes above, and could well also include the powers of darkness that overtook Joseph in the Sacred Grove preceding the First Vision.

Joseph is still not perfect, as the Lord reminds him in verse 2, next, but the encouragement, kindness, and power of the Atonement are made clear in the second half of the verse.

2 Nevertheless, **thou art not excusable in thy transgressions; nevertheless, go thy way and sin no more.**

Verse 3, next, reminds us that Joseph had the normal responsibilities of a husband and father to provide for his family.

3 Magnify thine office [*serve well in the calling you have*]; and **after thou hast sowed** [*planted*] **thy fields** and secured them, go speedily unto the church [*members of the Church*] which is in Colesville, Fayette, and Manchester, and they shall support thee; and I will bless them both spiritually and temporally;

As is the case with full-time general authorities and missionaries in our day, Joseph Smith was also to receive some support for him and his family from the members of the Church as explained in verse 3, above. Just as some members today decline to pay tithes and offerings, so also did some members in the early Church fail to give of their means to the Church, and thus came under condemnation as explained in verse 4, next.

4 But **if they receive thee not, I will send upon them a cursing instead of a blessing.**

In section 21, verses 1, 4, and 5, Joseph's role as the Prophet was briefly described by the Lord. In verse 5, next, he is told to continue in this role as Prophet and teacher to the Church. By the way, you can tell from the wording in verse 5 that the Savior is speaking.

5 And thou shalt continue in calling upon God [*the Father*] **in my name** [*Jesus Christ*], and writing the things [*the revelations and instructions*] which shall be given thee by the Comforter [*the Holy Ghost*], and expounding [*teaching and explaining*] all scriptures unto the church.

Verse 6, next, reminds us that the companionship of the Holy Ghost is a powerful help from God, and we can receive inspiration at the very moment we need it.

Also, in the last half of verse 6, we are reminded of the consequences to us as members if we ignore the words of our living Prophet.

6 And **it shall be given thee in the very moment what thou shalt speak and write**, and **they** [*the members of the Church*] **shall hear it** [*be obedient to it*], **or I will send unto them a cursing instead of a blessing.**

In verses 7 and 9, next, Joseph Smith is told that he will have the help of the Lord in serving well as the Prophet, but that he will not become wealthy financially.

7 For thou shalt devote all thy service in Zion; and **in this thou shalt have strength.**

8 **Be patient in afflictions**, for thou shalt have many; but endure them, for, lo, **I am with thee**, even unto the end of thy days.

9 And **in temporal labors** [*pursuing wealth and worldly status*] **thou shalt not have strength, for this is not thy calling.** Attend to thy calling [*as the Prophet*] and thou shalt have wherewith [*the means necessary*] to magnify thine office, and to expound all scriptures, and continue in laying on of the hands and confirming the churches [*strengthening the branches of the Church; see Acts 15:41*].

Regarding the first sentence in verse 9, above, President Dallin H. Oaks, of the Quorum of the Twelve Apostles at the time, explained that: "[Joseph Smith] was almost continually on the edge of financial distress. In the midst of trying to fulfill the staggering responsibilities of his sacred calling, he had to labor as a farmer or merchant to provide a living for his family. He did this without the remarkable spiritual gifts that sustained him in his prophetic calling. The Lord had advised him that 'in temporal labors thou shalt not have strength, for this is not thy calling' (D&C 24:9)" ("Joseph, the Man and the Prophet," *Ensign*, May 1996, 71).

Next, the Savior gives Joseph counsel for Oliver Cowdery. He is to continue in preaching the gospel and is warned against slacking off in the work to which he has been called. He is also warned again against pride (see D&C 23:1) and seeking glory for himself rather than for the Lord. Great promises are given to him if he will follow this counsel.

10 And thy brother [*in the gospel*] **Oliver shall continue in bearing my name before the world, and also to the church**. And **he shall not suppose that he can say enough in my cause**; and lo, I am with him to the end.

11 **In me he shall have glory, and not of himself**, whether in weakness or in strength, whether in bonds or free;

12 And at all times, and in all places, **he shall open his mouth and declare my gospel** as with the voice of a trump, both day and night. **And I will give unto him strength such as is not known among men.**

Perhaps you have noticed that "the voice of a trump," verse 12, above, is a phrase used frequently in the scriptures. It carries with it the imagery of a message that is clear and simple, easy to pick out from other sounds. Thus, Oliver is to teach the gospel simply and clearly and is to make his voice reach far and wide to be heard by many.

Next, counsel is given regarding expecting and requesting miracles, except for those that naturally go along with the work of serving in the Church as a priesthood holder and as a missionary. People who demand miracles are, in effect, tempting the Lord to prove His power, and thus place themselves in a dangerous position. See Matthew 4:7, where the devil is told by the Savior, "Thou shalt not tempt the Lord thy God."

13 **Require not miracles, except** [*unless*] **I shall command you, except** casting out devils, healing the sick, and against poisonous serpents, and against deadly poisons;

The miracles listed in verse 13, above, are listed in Mark 16:17–18 and are associated with missionary work (see Mark 16:15) and faithful membership in the Church. We will quote Mark here (**bold** added for emphasis):

Mark 16:15–18

15 And he said unto them, **Go ye into all the world, and preach the gospel to every creature**.

16 He that believeth and is baptized shall be saved; but he that believeth not shall be damned.

17 And **these signs shall follow them that believe**; In my name shall they **cast out devils**; they shall speak with new tongues;

18 They shall **take up serpents**; and **if they drink any deadly thing, it shall not hurt them**: they shall **lay hands on the sick, and they shall recover**.

One example of "casting out devils," in verse 13 of section 24, above, occurred in behalf of Newel Knight, a son of Joseph Knight Sr. as follows:

"Newel, a son of Joseph Knight, became much interested in the Prophet's words. Many serious conversations ensued, and Newel became so far convinced of the divinity of the work that he gave a partial promise that he would arise in meeting and offer supplication to God before his friends and neighbors. But at the appointed moment he failed to respond to Joseph's invitation. Later he told the Prophet that he would pray in secret, and thus seek to resolve his doubts and gain strength. On the day following, Newel went into the woods to offer his devotions to heaven; but was unable to give utterance to his feelings, being held in bondage by some power which he could not define. He returned to his home ill in body, and depressed in mind. His appearance alarmed his wife, and in a broken voice he requested her to quickly find the Prophet and bring him to his bedside. When Joseph arrived at the house, Newel was suffering most frightful distortions of his visage and limbs, as if he were in convulsions. Even as the Prophet gazed at him, Newel was seized upon by some mysterious influence and tossed helpless about the room. Through the gift of discernment, Joseph saw his friend was in the grasp of the evil one, and that only the power of God could save him from the tortures under which he was suffering. He took Newel's hand and gently addressed him. Newel replied, 'I am possessed of a devil. Exert your authority, I beseech you, to cast him out.' Joseph replied, 'If you know that I have power to drive him from your soul, it shall be done.' And when these words were uttered, Joseph rebuked the destroyer and commanded him in the name of Jesus Christ to depart. The Lord condescended to honor his servant, in thus exercising the power which belonged to his Priesthood and calling, for instantly Newel cried out with joy that he felt the accursed influence leave him and saw the evil spirit passing from the room.

"Thus was performed the first miracle of the Church. . . . Since that hour thousands of miracles have been performed by the Elders of the Church, through the power of the Priesthood restored from heaven and in fulfillment of the promises made by the Lord Jesus" (*Life of Joseph Smith*, 61–63).

As we continue with verse 14, next, we see an important matter in conjunction with administering to the sick that is sometimes misunderstood by members of the Church. It is that Melchizedek Priesthood holders are not to solicit opportunities to give blessings and administer to the sick. Such blessings are to be requested by those who desire them, which is clearly stated in this verse.

14 And **these things ye shall not do, except it be required of you by them who desire it**, that the scriptures might be fulfilled; for ye shall do according to that which is written [*in the scriptures*].

One example of "do according to that which is written," at the end of verse 14, above, is found in James 5:14. We will quote James here, using **bold** to emphasize the principle that the one needing the blessing should be the one asking for it:

James 5:14

Is any sick among you? **let him call for the elders of the church**; and let them pray over him, anointing him with oil in the name of the Lord:

A serious difficulty that can arise when the proper order given in verse 14, above, is not followed, is that a blessing or administration could be imposed upon a member who does not feel comfortable having one. In such cases, damage can be done and embarrassment and alienation from the Church could occur. Obviously, in the case of a faithful member who is unconscious or a child who does not know enough to ask for a blessing, family or friends could properly ask that he or she be administered to. It is also appropriate, when the Spirit so prompts, for family or friends to ask an ill individual if he or she would like to be administered to. This still leaves it up to the sick person to "call for the elders."

We will continue now with section 24, verse 15. Many people have heard, in one form or another, the term, "casting off the dust of your feet against them." Such terminology is used many places in the scriptures. (See Topical Guide under "Dust.") We will first read verse 15, using **bold** for emphasis, and then include a quote from Joseph Fielding Smith about this matter.

15 And in whatsoever place ye shall enter, and they receive you not in my name, ye shall leave a cursing instead of a blessing, by **casting off the dust of your feet against them as a testimony**, and cleansing your feet by the wayside.

As you can see, in verse 15, above, "casting off the dust of your feet" is basically a witness or testimony that the missionary has tried to teach them the gospel but was rejected by them. The *Doctrine and Covenants Student Manual*, 1981, 130–31, explains this and quotes Joseph Fielding Smith as follows (**bold** added for emphasis):

"The ordinance of washing the dust from one's feet was practiced in New Testament times and was reinstituted in this dispensation. (See D&C 88:139–40; John 11:2; 12:3; 13:5–14.) **The action of shaking or cleansing the dust from one's feet is a testimony against those who refuse to accept the gospel.** (See D&C 24:15; 84:92; 99:4.) Because of the serious nature of this act, Church leaders have directed that it be done only at the command of the Spirit. President Joseph Fielding Smith explained the significance of the action as follows: 'The cleansing of their feet, either by washing or wiping off the dust, would be recorded in heaven as a testimony against the wicked. This act, however, was not to be performed in the presence of the offenders, "lest thou provoke them, but in secret, and wash thy feet, as a testimony against them in the day of judgment." The missionaries of the Church who faithfully perform their duty are under the obligation of leaving their testimony with all with whom they come in contact in their work. This testimony will stand as a witness against those who reject the message, at the judgment.' (*Church History and Modern Revelation*, 1:223.)"

Perhaps you have found yourself wondering why it seems that the wicked get away with their evil deeds and don't seem to get punished by the Lord, while their victims suffer. The scriptures are clear that they will be punished, but there is a key phrase in verse 16, next, which explains the delay.

16 And it shall come to pass that whosoever shall lay their hands upon you by violence, ye shall command to be smitten in my name; and, behold, I will smite them according to your words, **in mine own due time**.

No doubt one of the key reasons for the Lord's waiting to "smite" the wicked is that there is still a chance that they might repent and come unto Christ. Think of how many times you, yourself, may have deserved "smiting" but it didn't happen to you, and then it becomes easier to let the Lord smite others in His "own due time."

17 And **whosoever shall go to law with thee** [*takes you to court*] shall be cursed by the law [*perhaps meaning that they will eventually be caught up with, either by the laws of the land or the laws of God*].

The Joseph Smith Papers publications shed additional light on the severe persecutions faced by the early Church at this point, including vexatious law suits ("whosoever shall go to law with thee" in verse 17, above) as shown by a quote from the 2019 *Doctrine and Covenants Student Manual*, chapter 10, as follows:

"In late June 1830, Joseph Smith, Emma Smith, Oliver Cowdery, David Whitmer, and John Whitmer traveled from Harmony, Pennsylvania, to visit Church members and other believers in Colesville, New York. On Saturday, June 26, a stream was dammed to prepare for baptisms the next day (Sunday), but a hostile mob destroyed the dam during the night. Early Monday morning, the dam was rebuilt and 13 people were baptized, including Emma Smith. By the time the baptisms were completed, however, a mob of nearly 50 men gathered, insulting and threatening to harm the Saints. That evening, the Saints met to confirm those who had been baptized earlier that day, but before the confirmations could be performed, Joseph was arrested on charges of "being a disorderly person, of setting the country in an uproar by preaching the Book of Mormon" (in *The Joseph Smith Papers, Histories, Volume 1: Joseph Smith Histories, 1832–1844*, ed. Karen Lynn Davidson and others [2012], 396).

The terms "purse" and "scrip," in verse 18, next, are important for understanding this verse as well as other passages of scripture where they are used. Some people tend to think that "scrip" is a short form of "scriptures." It is not. We will read the verse and then turn to the Bible Dictionary for help.

18 And thou shalt **take no purse nor scrip**, neither staves, neither two coats, **for the church shall give unto thee in the very hour what thou needest** for food and for raiment [*clothing*], and for shoes and for money, and for scrip.

The Bible Dictionary, under "Scrip," defines both "scrip" and "purse" as follows (**bold** added for emphasis):

Bible Dictionary, under "Scrip"

"**Scrip.** A bag used by shepherds or by travelers (1 Sam. 17:40; Matt. 10:10; Mark 6:8; Luke 9:3; 10:4; 22:35–36). The **bag** was usually made of leather and was **used for carrying bread and other food**. It should not be confused with a **money bag**, which **was called a purse**."

As you can see from the above definitions, Joseph and Oliver were instructed to rely completely on the Lord for their upkeep while going out among the members and preaching to the world.

Finally, in verse 19, next, we see that this is indeed the last dispensation (the last time the gospel is to be restored before the Second Coming of Christ). We see the imagery of pruning or cutting out false philosophies and false doctrines from people's lives so that they can enjoy the true gospel of Christ. We also see, at the end of the verse, that many of the counsels and instructions given in this section provide a pattern for others who have joined the Church and are assisting Joseph and Oliver in the work of the Restoration.

19 For **thou art called to prune my vineyard** [*the world*] with a mighty pruning, yea, even **for the last time** [*compare with Jacob 5:69 and 71*]; yea, and **also all those whom thou hast ordained**, and they **shall do even according to this pattern**. Amen.

SECTION 25

Background

Section 25 is perhaps best-known, because in it, Emma Smith is requested by the Lord to make a collection of sacred hymns, which became the first hymn book for the Church. See verse 11.

As noted in the background to section 24 in this book, this revelation was given through the Prophet Joseph Smith while at Harmony, Pennsylvania, in July 1830. It is directed to the Prophet's wife, Emma.

At this time, Joseph was 25 years old and Emma was 26. She was born on July 10, 1804, in Harmony, the seventh of nine children born to Isaac and Elizabeth Hale. Joseph was born on December 23, 1805.

Joseph and Emma had met in late 1825. He and some other men worked for about a month not far from the Hale residence in Harmony, Pennsylvania, as employees of Mr. Josiah Stowell. During this time, Joseph boarded at the Hale residence and was attracted to their daughter. She was also attracted to him.

Emma is described on page 50 of the *Doctrine and Covenants Student Manual, 1981,* as follows:

"Emma was a beautiful woman with an attractive personality, and she had the reputation of being a refined and dignified woman who was an excellent housekeeper and cook. Her Methodist upbringing had helped her develop a great love of music."

She was about five feet, nine inches tall, used excellent English grammar, had dark hair and brown eyes and was a schoolteacher in the area. Joseph continued to court her over time and eventually asked her father for permission to marry her. He refused, expressing concerns about Joseph's lack of education and involvement with "gold digging." As a result, Joseph and Emma eloped and were married in South Bainbridge, New York, on January 18, 1827, after which they lived for a time with Joseph's parents in Manchester, New York. They stayed in Manchester until after Moroni delivered the gold plates to Joseph, on September 22, 1827. In fact, Emma accompanied her husband to the Hill Cumorah on that occasion and waited at the bottom of the hill while Joseph climbed up the hill to his meeting place with Moroni.

As soon as Joseph brought the gold plates home to his parent's house in Manchester, persecutions raged. Finally, with Emma's father's permission, Joseph and Emma moved back to Harmony, Pennsylvania, to her parent's home. A short time later, they moved to a small home on 13 acres near Emma's parents in Harmony.

When time permitted, Joseph worked on translating the gold plates and Emma served as his scribe. Susan Easton Black writes of the time after Joseph brought the plates to his parent's home and later of Emma's serving as a scribe during the translation, as follows:

"On 22 September 1827 Emma was privileged to be the first to know that Joseph had acquired the plates from the angel Moroni. The plates 'lay in a box under our bed for months,' she said, 'but I never felt at liberty to look at them.' Emma was a scribe for the Book of Mormon translation, and said of her experience, 'It is marvelous to me . . . when acting as his scribe, [he] would dictate to me hour after hour; and when returning after meals, or after interruptions, he could at once begin where he had left off, without either seeing the manuscript or having any portion of it read to him.' She bore a continuing testimony, even in her seventy-fourth year, of her husband's prophetic calling: 'I believe he was everything he professed to be'" (*Who's Who in the Doctrine and Covenants*, 273–74).

Once, while Emma was serving as Joseph's scribe as he was translating the gold plates, she said that he dictated something about the walls of Jerusalem, upon which he stopped and asked, "Emma, did Jerusalem have walls around it?" (Taken from a letter from Emma to her children, published in the *Saint's Herald*, 1884, Number 2, 31.) Thus, she bore record that her husband did indeed translate the Book of Mormon plates.

You may remember that the Book of Mormon translation was completed, with Oliver Cowdery serving as scribe, and the book was printed and available for sale on March 26, 1830. Afterward, Emma did considerable traveling with her husband during the months of April to July 1830 and felt the joy of the restored gospel as well as the wrath of persecutors who were constantly trying to thwart the Restoration.

At the time section 25 was given in July 1830, persecution was beginning to mount in Harmony, and the time was approaching when it would be necessary for Joseph and Emma to move to Fayette, New York, to escape it. Emma's Uncle Nathaniel (a minister) and others had tried to poison her mind regarding her "prophet" husband. Attempts were being made to persuade her to leave Joseph and stay in Harmony when he was forced to leave, where she would be well taken care of by family and friends. It is in this setting that she was given this revelation.

1 **HEARKEN unto the voice of the Lord your God, while I speak unto you, Emma Smith, my daughter** [*a term of tenderness and endearment*]; for verily I say unto you, **all those who receive my gospel are sons and daughters in my kingdom**.

The phrase "sons and daughters in my kingdom," in verse 1, above, is doctrinally significant vocabulary. It is one way of saying "are saved in the kingdom of heaven." In Mosiah 5:7, we see the same doctrine in slightly different wording as follows (**bold** added for emphasis):

Mosiah 5:7

And now, **because of the covenant which ye have made ye shall be called the children of Christ, his sons, and his daughters**; for behold, this day he hath spiritually begotten you; for ye say that **your hearts are changed through faith on his name**; therefore, ye are born of him and **have become his sons and his daughters.**

In summary, by way of doctrinal vocabulary, we find the following three classes of people referred to in the scriptures:

1. **Sons and daughters of God**—meaning those who have been baptized, are keeping covenants, and are heading for celestial glory. See D&C 76:24 and Moses 6:64–68.
2. **Sons and daughters of men**—meaning those who refuse to be baptized, and thus continue living according to the ways of the world. See Moses 8:14–15, and Genesis 6:2.
3. **Sons of perdition**—meaning those who sin to the extent that Cain did. See Moses 6:16–32 and D&C 76:30–38.

Continuing, in verse 2, next, the Lord gives Emma counsel to be faithful and He will preserve her life. This is no doubt especially meaningful in view of the threats and mobs that will confront her during her life. By the way, she died of natural causes, surrounded by family and friends, at the age of 74 on April 30, 1879, in Nauvoo, Illinois. Her last words, as recalled by her son Alexander, were "Joseph, Joseph, Joseph." Her son Joseph Smith III reported her last words as "Joseph! Yes, yes, I'm coming." (See *Zion's Ensign*, December 31, 1903.)

2 A revelation I give unto you concerning my will; and **if thou art faithful and walk in the paths of virtue before me**, I will preserve thy life, and **thou shalt receive an inheritance in Zion.**

3 Behold, **thy sins are forgiven thee**, and **thou art an elect lady**, whom I have called.

Joseph Smith explained the term "elect lady" in verse 3, above, as follows:

"I assisted in commencing the organization of 'The Female Relief Society of Nauvoo' in the Lodge Room. Sister Emma Smith, President, and Sister Elizabeth Ann Whitney and Sarah M. Cleveland, Counselors. I gave much instruction, read in the New Testament, and Book of Doctrine and Covenants, concerning the Elect Lady, and showed that the elect meant to be elected to a certain work . . . and that the revelation was then fulfilled by Sister Emma's election to the Presidency of the Society, she having previously been ordained to expound the Scriptures." (See *History of the Church*, 4:552–53.)

Verse 4, next, appears to be a reference to the gold plates and other things that Joseph saw but Emma didn't. The Lord assures her that He knows what He is doing by keeping these things from her.

4 **Murmur not because of the things which thou hast not seen**, for **they are withheld from thee** and from the world, **which is wisdom in me** in a time to come [*perhaps meaning that if Emma were to see these things, it would cause her extra trouble in the future*].

Next, we see some excellent marriage counsel. We need to include verse 9 in which Emma is told that "thy husband shall support thee."

5 And the office of thy calling shall **be** for **a comfort unto** my servant, Joseph Smith, Jun., **thy husband**, in his afflictions, **with consoling words, in the spirit of meekness**.

Only strong-willed, secure people are able to be meek, which, by definition, is strong but humble and not easily irritated.

Next, Emma is counseled to go with Joseph when he moves to Fayette. As mentioned in the background notes, above, she was being strongly pressured to use his leaving as a chance to leave him and live a peaceful, quiet life in the security and care of family and friends in Harmony.

She followed the counsel of the Lord given in verse 6, went with her husband, Joseph, and never saw her family again except for one brother in Nauvoo much later in life. The situation that was developing in Harmony at this time is described as follows:

"About this time a Methodist minister convinced Isaac Hale of many falsehoods about his son-in-law. As a result, life became unbearable for Joseph and his family in Harmony. Therefore, Joseph began to make preparations to permanently move to Fayette where he had been invited to live with Peter Whitmer Sr. again. In late August, Newel Knight took his team and wagon to Harmony to move Joseph and his family to Fayette" (*Church History in the Fulness of Times*, 1989, 77).

6 And **thou shalt go with him at the time of his going**, and be unto him for a scribe, while there is no one to be a scribe for him, that I may send my servant, Oliver Cowdery, whithersoever I will.

As mentioned previously, Emma was a school teacher. In verse 7, next, the Savior teaches her that she will be able to use her teaching talents, enhanced by the Holy Ghost, to strengthen members of the Church.

7 And **thou shalt be ordained** under his hand **to expound** [*explain and teach*] **scriptures**, and to **exhort** [*urge to be obedient*] the church, according **as it shall be given thee by my Spirit.**

Did you notice the word "ordain" in verse 7, above? Perhaps you've noticed that the doctrinal vocabulary of the Church has gradually developed over the years, and now, in many cases, we have more specifically defined words for specific practices and doctrines in the Church. In place of the word "ordained," as used in verse 7, we now use the phrase "set apart." Joseph Fielding Smith explained this as follows:

"The term 'ordain' was used generally in the early days of the Church in reference to both ordination and setting apart. . . . Men holding the Priesthood were said to have been 'ordained' to preside over branches and to perform special work. Sisters also were said to have been 'ordained' when they were called to some special duty or responsibility. In later years we developed a distinction between ordain and setting apart. Men are ordained to offices in the Priesthood and set apart to preside over stakes, wards, branches, missions, and auxiliary organizations. The sisters are set apart—not ordained—as presidents of auxiliary organizations, to missions, etc. This saying that Emma Smith was 'ordained' to expound scripture, does not mean that she had conferred upon her the Priesthood, but that she was set apart to this calling, which found its fulfillment in the Relief Society of the Church" (*Church History and Modern Revelation*, 1:126).

As we move on to verse 8, next, we note that Emma was baptized on June 28, 1830, but had not yet been confirmed. It may sound strange that they would wait so long for confirmation, but Emma, along with 12 others, had been baptized in Colesville, New York, on June 28, 1830, despite the attempts of a mob to prevent it. The mobs did succeed in preventing their confirmation that evening as summarized in research from the Joseph Smith Papers Project summarized in the *Doctrine and Covenants Student Manual,* 2018, as follows:

"In late June 1830, Joseph Smith, Emma Smith, Oliver Cowdery, David Whitmer, and John Whitmer traveled from Harmony, Pennsylvania, to visit Church members and other believers in Colesville, New York. On Saturday, June 26, a stream was dammed to prepare for baptisms the next day (Sunday), but a hostile mob destroyed the dam during the night. Early Monday morning, the dam was rebuilt and 13 people were baptized, including Emma

Smith. By the time the baptisms were completed, however, a mob of nearly 50 men gathered, insulting and threatening to harm the Saints. That evening, the Saints met to confirm those who had been baptized earlier that day, but before the confirmations could be performed, Joseph was arrested on charges of "being a disorderly person, of setting the country in an uproar by preaching the Book of Mormon" (in *The Joseph Smith Papers, Histories, Volume 1: Joseph Smith Histories, 1832–1844,* ed. Karen Lynn Davidson and others [2012], 396).

Thus, in verse 8, the Lord instructs Emma to be confirmed and receive the gift of the Holy Ghost. She will be confirmed in August 1830 after section 27 is given.

8 For **he shall lay his hands upon thee, and thou shalt receive the Holy Ghost**, and thy time shall be given to writing, and to learning much.

9 And **thou needest not fear, for thy husband shall support thee in the church** [*in your work in the Church*]; for unto them is his calling [*perhaps a reminder to Emma that Joseph will not become wealthy—see D&C 24:9—because his calling is to excel in spiritual things*], that all things might be revealed unto them [*he is to be the Prophet*], whatsoever I will, according to their faith.

10 And verily I say unto thee that **thou shalt lay aside the things of this world, and seek for the things of a better**.

At the end of verse 10, above, Emma is told basically the same thing her husband was told in D&C 24:9, namely that her priorities were to be spiritual rather than on the pursuit of worldly wealth.

Next, in verse 11, Emma is told that she will be given the ability and the assignment to make a selection of sacred hymns for the Church. This was in harmony with her talent in music and singing in her local choir as she grew up in Harmony.

11 And **it shall be given thee, also, to make a selection of sacred hymns**, as it shall be given thee, which is pleasing unto me, to be had in my church.

She accepted this calling, and in 1835, her hymnbook was published. This collection of sacred hymns was printed in a book that was four inches by three inches and a third-inch thick. It contained ninety hymns, thirty-four of which were written by Church members. No music was printed with the hymns, therefore, they were sung to popular melodies of the day, and in many cases, a given hymn could be sung to several different melodies.

Several of the hymns selected by Emma, with the help of W. W. Phelps, are still included in our present hymnbook, including the following:

1. "Gently Raise the Sacred Strain"
2. "Guide Us, O Thou Great Jehovah"
3. "He Died! The Great Redeemer Died!"
4. "How Firm a Foundation"
5. "I Know That My Redeemer Lives"
6. "Joy to the World"
7. "Know Then That Every Soul Is Free"
8. "Now Let Us Rejoice"
9. "O God, the Eternal Father"
10. "Redeemer of Israel"
11. "The Spirit of God Like a Fire Is Burning"

The title page to her hymnal was roughly as follows:

A COLLECTION
OF
SACRED HYMNS,
FOR THE
CHURCH
OF THE
LATTER DAY SAINTS.
SELECTED BY
EMMA SMITH.
Kirtland, Ohio:
Printed by
F. G. Williams & co.
1835

The Preface to her book of sacred hymns was as follows:

PREFACE

In order to sing by the Spirit, and with the understanding, it is necessary that the church of the Latter Day Saints should have a collection of "Sacred Hymns," adapted to their faith and belief in the gospel, and, as far as can be, holding forth the promises made to the fathers who died in the precious faith of a glorious resurrection, and a thousand years' reign on earth with the Son of Man in his glory. Notwithstanding the church, as it were, is still in its infancy, yet, as the song of the righteous is a prayer unto god, it is sincerely hoped that the following collection, selected with an eye single to his glory, may answer every purpose till more are composed, or till we are blessed with a copious variety of the songs of Zion.

Next, the Savior expresses His feelings about these hymns He has asked Emma to collect and publish. From His words, we learn that participating in singing the hymns of Zion is a form of prayer, and that we will be blessed for so doing.

Doctrine

Verse 12. When the righteous sing hymns, the Lord considers them to be prayers.

12 For **my soul delighteth in the song of the heart**; yea, **the song of the righteous is a prayer unto me**, and **it shall be answered with a blessing upon their heads**.

In the final verses of this section, Emma is invited to be happy and to stick with the covenants she has made, which would include her marriage vows to Joseph as well as her baptismal covenants. She is also counseled to beware of pride.

13 Wherefore, **lift up thy heart and rejoice**, and **cleave unto the covenants which thou hast made**.

14 **Continue in the spirit of meekness**, and **beware of pride**. Let thy soul delight in thy husband, and the glory which shall come upon him.

We will repeat verse 14, here, and **bold** some valuable marriage counsel given by the Lord to Emma, which can easily apply to many of us. It is that rather than being jealous of our spouse when he or she accomplishes things and receives praise for them, we should rejoice and be happy for them. This can certainly apply to parents also when their children succeed and garner praise, as well as to children when their parents succeed.

14 Continue in the spirit of meekness, and beware of pride. **Let thy soul delight in thy husband, and the glory which shall come upon him.**

Finally, Emma is counseled to keep the commandments. In terms of gospel vocabulary, the word "crown," in verse 15, next, refers to exaltation. We understand this from D&C 20:14 in which we read, "crown of eternal life." In the scriptures, the phrase "eternal life" always means exaltation, becoming gods. See also Revelation 2:10 and 3:11, as well as numerous other references in the Topical Guide under "Crown."

15 Keep my commandments continually, and a crown of righteousness thou shalt receive. And except thou do this, where I am you cannot come.

In verse 16, next, we are reminded that, in most cases, the counsel given by the Lord to one person in the scriptures can apply to all of us. Hence, the great value in our studying them.

16 And verily, verily, I say unto you, that **this is my voice unto all**. Amen.

SECTION 26

Background

This revelation was given to Joseph Smith, Oliver Cowdery, and John Whitmer, a son of

Peter Whitmer Sr., at Harmony, Pennsylvania, in July 1830. It is the last of the three revelations for which the basic background given for section 24 in this study guide applies.

This section is most commonly referred to as the basis for our sustaining of officers and teachers in our church meetings. It is known as the principle of "common consent" as given in verse 2. This principle of common consent is also used in sustaining actions of the Church, such as dividing wards and stakes, etc.

First, we will be reminded in verse 1 of the importance of all of us studying the scriptures throughout our lives as a basic foundation for our performing our duties in the Church.

1 BEHOLD, I say unto you that you shall **let your time be devoted to the studying of the scriptures**, and to **preaching**, and to **confirming the church** [*strengthening the Church; see context of Acts 15:41*] at Colesville, and to performing your labors on the land [*probably meaning to take care of their farms and crops*], such as is required, until after you shall go to the west [*to Fayette, New York*] to hold the next conference [*which was held in Fayette on September 26–27, 1830*]; and then it shall be made known what you shall do.

With respect to the phrase "studying of the scriptures," in verse 1, above, it could also be a reference to the Joseph Smith Translation of the Bible. It appears that the Prophet's study and translation of the Bible got under way about this time in the history of the Church. The earliest manuscripts of the JST (Joseph Smith Translation of the Bible) were written in the summer and fall of 1830 and are in the handwriting of John Whitmer and Oliver Cowdery. (See Robert J. Mathew's *Joseph Smith's Translation of the Bible*, page 27.)

Next, in verse 2, the Lord teaches the principle of common consent.

Doctrine

Verse 2. No one can hold a calling in the Church without being sustained by the people he or she will serve.

2 And **all things shall be done by common consent in the church**, by much prayer and faith, for all things you shall receive by faith. Amen.

The question sometimes comes up as to what would happen if you voted against an action being proposed by the person conducting a meeting of the Church.

The answer is that the presiding authority would acknowledge your negative vote and invite you to visit with him, your bishop, or your stake president after the meeting to discuss your concerns. If, for instance, the business at hand were the sustaining of a person to a calling in the Church, and you questioned their worthiness. The presiding officer might then hold up the ordination or setting apart until the matter was resolved.

On the other hand, if you just didn't like the person, you would be out of order in letting your personal feelings get in the way. Joseph Fielding Smith explained this as follows:

"I have no right to raise my hand in opposition to a man who is appointed to any position in this Church, simply because I may not like him, or because of some personal disagreement or feeling I may have, but only on the grounds that he is guilty of wrong doing, of transgression of the laws of the Church which would disqualify him for the position which he is called to hold" (*Doctrines of Salvation*, 3:124).

It is important for you to know that the use of the principle of common consent in the Church is a powerful safeguard against apostasy. In effect, it means that there are no secret ordinations, which often form the basis of apostate groups that have broken away from the Church. In fact, a person cannot hold an office in this church without the knowledge of the people. We will again use a quote from Joseph Fielding Smith from the *Doctrine and Covenants Student Manual* for institutes of religion, 1981, page 54:

"No man can preside in this Church in any capacity without the consent of the people. The Lord has placed upon us the responsibility of sustaining by vote those who are called to various positions of responsibility. No man, should the people decide to the contrary, could preside over any body of Latter-day Saints in this Church, and yet it is not the right of the people to nominate, to choose, for that is the right of the priesthood" (*Doctrines of Salvation*, 3:123; see also D&C 20:65).

Finally, once we have sustained a person in a calling, it is our responsibility to do our part to cooperate and help that person's responsibility move forward successfully.

SECTION 27

Background

This revelation was received by Joseph Smith near Harmony, Pennsylvania, in August 1830. The Prophet had set out to obtain wine for the sacrament when he was met by an angel and instructed not to secure wine from enemies of the Church (see heading to section 27 in your Doctrine and Covenants and also verse 3 of this section).

This section contains the revelation and instruction that provides the basis for our using water for the sacrament rather than wine.

The Prophet Joseph Smith provides background information for section 27 as follows:

"Early in the month of August Newel Knight and his wife paid us a visit at my place in Harmony, Pennsylvania; and as neither his wife nor mine had been as yet confirmed, it was proposed that we should confirm them, and partake together of the Sacrament, before he and his wife should leave us. In order to prepare for this I set out to procure some wine for the occasion, but had gone only a short distance when I was met by a heavenly messenger, and received the following revelation, the first four paragraphs of which were written at this time, and the remainder in the September following: [D&C 27]" (*History of the Church*, 1:106).

As you will see, this section consists of three distinct portions. Verses 1–4 deal with the matter of what to eat and drink when preparing and partaking of the sacrament. Verses 5–14 deal with a great sacrament meeting which will be held in conjunction with the meeting with Adam and the Savior at Adam-ondi-Ahman in Missouri prior to the Second Coming. Verses 15–18 counsel us to put on the "whole armor" of God.

In verse 1, Joseph is told that the heavenly messenger is representing the Savior on this occasion.

1 **LISTEN to the voice of Jesus Christ**, your Lord, your God, and your Redeemer, whose word is quick [*alive, living; symbolic of continuous revelation*] and powerful.

Next, in verse 2, Joseph is instructed that it does not matter what is used in partaking of the sacrament as long as it is done "with an eye single to my glory." In other words, with pure intent.

This is the basis for our using water rather than wine in our sacrament. It is also the reason that an isolated group of Latter-day Saints under unusual circumstances, such as a group of LDS servicemen and women, could use crackers and juice for the sacrament under the direction of their authorized group leader.

Obviously, such circumstances are unusual, and "variety" in the emblems of the sacrament is to be avoided. Otherwise, the focus of many members would be on what was being used for the sacrament that day rather than on the ordinance itself. As a matter of standard practice, we simply use bread and water.

Perhaps you've wondered if it is proper to use wheat bread rather than white bread. Good question. Answer: it is proper. There are many places on earth where white bread is not available. Also, what about those members who are allergic to wheat flour and thus must use bread or wafers made from rice?

In summary, it is the ordinance itself which is sacred, and components and settings should not detract from that.

Doctrine

Verse 2. It does not matter what is used for the sacrament as long as it is done with proper intent.

2 **For, behold, I say unto you, that it mattereth not what ye shall eat or what ye shall drink** when ye partake of the sacrament, **if it so be that ye do it with an eye single to my glory—remembering unto the Father my body which was laid down for you, and my blood which was shed for the remission of your sins.**

Ezra Taft Benson, who later became the President of the Church, gave an example of the meaning of verse 2, above, in a conference talk, when he explained basically that when bread is not available, a substitute may be used, such as potatoes or potato peelings, which were used by members of the Church in Europe during World War II (in Conference Report, Oct. 1952, 120).

3 Wherefore, a commandment I give unto you, that **you shall not purchase wine neither strong drink of your enemies**;

4 Wherefore, **you shall partake of none except it is made new** [*fresh*] **among you**; yea, in this my Father's kingdom which shall be built up on the earth.

Joseph Smith recorded the following, which serves as follow-up to verses 1–4, above:

"In obedience to the above commandment, we prepared some wine of our own making, and held our meeting, consisting only of five: Newel Knight and his wife, myself and my wife, and John Whitmer. We partook together of the Sacrament, after which we confirmed these two sisters [*Newel Knight's wife, Sally, and Emma Smith*] into the Church, and spent the evening in a glorious manner. The Spirit of the Lord was poured out upon us, [and] we praised the Lord God, and rejoiced exceedingly" (*History of the Church*, 1:108).

According to the Prophet, as quoted earlier, the remainder of this section was written down in September 1830. See also the heading to section 27 in your Doctrine and Covenants.

What follows in verses 5–14, next, is a most wonderful and marvelous revelation. It keys off of the statement of the Savior to His Apostles on the night of the Last Supper. He said, in reference to the sacrament which He had just introduced to them, "But I say unto you, I will not drink henceforth of this fruit of the vine, until that day when I drink it new with you in my Father's kingdom" (Matthew 26:29). Now, in section 27, we are given much more detail about the meeting at which this prophecy will be fulfilled. For instance, we are told the names of some prominent past prophets who will be in attendance. In addition, we are told that all those who are worthy of living with Christ forever will be in attendance. This is exciting! In order to point these people out, we will go through verses 5–14 and **bold** them. Then we will repeat these verses and do much more with them.

5 Behold, this is wisdom in me; wherefore, marvel not, for **the hour cometh that I will drink of the fruit of the vine with you** on the earth, **and with Moroni**, whom I have sent unto you to reveal the Book of Mormon, containing the fulness of my everlasting gospel, to whom I have committed the keys of the record of the stick of Ephraim;

6 And **also with Elias**, to whom I have committed the keys of bringing to pass the restoration of all things spoken by the mouth of all the holy prophets since the world began, concerning the last days;

7 And **also John** the son of Zacharias, which Zacharias he (Elias) visited and gave promise that he should have a son, and his name should be John, and he should be filled with the spirit of Elias;

8 Which John I have sent unto you, my servants, Joseph Smith, Jun., and Oliver Cowdery, to ordain you unto the first priesthood which you have received, that you might be called and ordained even as Aaron;

9 And **also Elijah**, unto whom I have committed the keys of the power of turning the hearts of the fathers to the children, and the hearts of the children to the fathers, that the whole earth may not be smitten with a curse;

10 And **also with Joseph** and **Jacob**, and **Isaac**, and **Abraham**, your fathers, by whom the promises remain;

11 And **also with** Michael, or **Adam**, the father of all, the prince of all, the ancient of days;

12 And **also with Peter**, and **James**, and **John**, whom I have sent unto you, by whom I have ordained you and confirmed you to be apostles, and especial witnesses of my name, and bear the keys of your ministry and of the same things which I revealed unto them;

13 Unto whom I have committed

the keys of my kingdom, and a dispensation of the gospel for the last times; and for the fulness of times, in the which I will gather together in one all things, both which are in heaven, and which are on earth;

14 And also **with all those whom my Father hath given me out of the world.**

As stated previously, we will now go through verses 5–14 again and do much more with them by way of study. First of all, by way of additional background, we will quote from *Millennial Messiah*, by Bruce R. McConkie (**bold** added for emphasis):

"With reference to the use of sacramental wine in our day, the Lord said to Joseph Smith: 'You shall partake of none except it is made new among you; yea, in this my Father's kingdom which shall be built up on the earth.' In so stating, he is picking up the language he used in the upper room [at the Last Supper in Jerusalem, before His crucifixion]. Then he says: 'The hour cometh that I will drink of the fruit of the vine with you on the earth.' **Jesus is going to partake of the sacrament again with his mortal disciples on earth. But it will not be with mortals only**. He names **others who will be present** and who will participate in the sacred ordinance. These include **Moroni, Elias, John the Baptist, Elijah, Abraham, Isaac, Jacob, Joseph** (who was sold into Egypt), **Peter, James, and John**, 'and also with **Michael, or Adam**, the father of all, the prince of all, the ancient of days.' Each of these is named simply by way of illustration. **The grand summation of the whole matter comes in these words: 'And also with all those whom my Father hath given me out of the world.'** (D&C 27:4–14.) **The sacrament is to be administered** in a future day, on this earth, when the Lord Jesus is present, and when all the righteous of all ages are present. **This, of course, will be a part of the grand council at Adam-ondi-Ahman**" (*The Millennial Messiah*, 587).

Elder McConkie summarized this great sacrament meeting as follows: **"Every faithful person in the whole history of the world, every person who has so lived as to merit eternal life in the kingdom of the Father will be in attendance and will partake, with the Lord, of the sacrament"** (*The Promised Messiah*, 595).

This certainly answers the question you hear asked as to who is going to attend the meeting held at Adam-ondi-Ahman before the Second Coming (see section 116).

With this as background, we will now continue verse by verse repeating verses 5–14 and adding more commentary. In verse 5, next, we learn that Jesus gave Moroni the "keys" of bringing the

Book of Mormon to earth in the last days.

5 Behold, this is wisdom in me; wherefore, marvel not, for the hour cometh that I will drink of the fruit of the vine with you on the earth, and with **Moroni, whom I have sent unto you to reveal the Book of Mormon, containing the fulness of my everlasting gospel, to whom I have committed the keys of the record of the stick of Ephraim** [*the Book of Mormon; see Ezekiel 37:15–17*];

Next, we must define the term "Elias" or verse 6 will leave us confused. We will use a quote from the *Doctrine and Covenants Student Manual*, 1981 edition, pages 55–56, as used in institute of religion classes of the Church. In it, we will be told that "Elias," as often used in the scriptures, is a term meaning "messenger from God." The quote is as follows (**bold** added for emphasis):

"Since Elias refers to more than one person, it is sometimes confusing. Elder Bruce R. McConkie explained: 'Correcting the Bible by the spirit of revelation, the Prophet restored a statement of John the Baptist which says that **Christ is the Elias** who was to restore all things. (Inspired Version [JST], John 1:21–28.) By revelation we are also informed that the **Elias** who was to restore all things **is the angel Gabriel** who was known in mortality as Noah. (D&C 27:6–7; Luke 1:5–25; *Teachings*, 157.) From the same authentic source we also learn that the promised **Elias is John the Revelator**. (D&C 77:9, 14.) Thus there are **three different revelations** which **name Elias as being three different persons**. What are we to conclude?

"'By finding answer to the question, by whom has the restoration been effected, we shall find who Elias is and find there is no problem in harmonizing these apparently contradictory revelations. Who has restored all things? **Was it one man? Certainly not**. Many angelic ministrants have been sent from the courts of glory to confer keys and powers, to commit their dispensations and glories again to men on earth. At least the following have come: Moroni, John the Baptist, Peter, James, and John, Moses, Elijah, Elias, Gabriel, Raphael, and Michael. (D&C 13; 110; 128:19–21.) Since it is apparent that no one messenger has carried the whole burden of the restoration, but rather that each has come with a specific endowment from on high, **it becomes clear that Elias is a composite personage. The expression must be understood to be a name and a title for those whose mission it was to commit keys and powers to men in this final dispensation**'"

(*Mormon Doctrine*, 221; see also D&C 110:12–16).

With the above quote as background, we will now proceed with verse 6.

6 And also with **Elias** [*a composite of many heavenly beings sent by God to earth*], **to whom I have committed the keys of bringing to pass the restoration of all things** spoken by the mouth of all the holy prophets since the world began, concerning the last days;

7 And also **John the son of Zacharias** [*John the Baptist*], which Zacharias he (Elias) [*Gabriel; in other words, Noah; see Bible Dictionary under "Gabriel"*] visited and gave promise that he should have a son, and his name should be John, and he should be filled with the spirit of Elias;

8 **Which John** [*the Baptist*] **I have sent unto you** [*on May 15, 1829; see D&C 13*], my servants, **Joseph Smith, Jun., and Oliver Cowdery, to ordain you** unto the first priesthood [*the Aaronic Priesthood; see D&C 13*] which you have received, that you might be called and ordained even as Aaron;

9 And also **Elijah** [*the prophet who was translated and taken up into heaven—see 2 Kings 2:11; he was resurrected with Christ—see D&C 133:55*], unto whom I have committed the keys of the power of turning the hearts of the fathers to the children, and the hearts of the children to the fathers [*the keys of sealing families together*], that the whole earth may not be smitten with a curse [*these keys will be restored to Joseph Smith and Oliver Cowdery in the Kirtland Temple on April 3, 1836—see D&C 110:13–15*];

10 And also with **Joseph** [*who was sold into Egypt*] and **Jacob**, and **Isaac**, and **Abraham**, your fathers [*ancestors*], by whom the promises remain [*in other words, through whom the blessings of Abraham are to be carried to the whole earth—see Abraham 2:9–11*];

11 And also with **Michael, or Adam**, the father of all [*the ancestor of all; the first man—see D&C 84:16*], the prince of all, **the ancient of days** [*the first mortal on earth*];

The phrase, "the prince of all," in verse 11, above, implies authority and power to rule. Joseph Fielding Smith taught that Adam has authority over all people on earth, directly under Christ, as follows (**bold** added for emphasis):

"Michael, who is **Adam, holds the keys of salvation for the human family, under the direction and counsel of Jesus Christ**, who is the Holy One of Zion [see D&C 78:15–16]. **Adam will**, when the earth is cleansed and purified and becomes a celestial globe, **preside over the children of men, who are of his posterity**. He is Adam, 'the prince, the arch-angel.' In the eternities before this earth was formed he was the archangel. He became Adam when he came to this earth to be the father of the human family. (D&C 107:54–57.)

"The Prophet Joseph Smith said of Adam: 'Commencing with Adam, who was the first man, who is spoken of in Daniel as the "Ancient of Days," or in other words, the first and oldest of all, the great progenitor of whom it is said in another place is Michael. . . . **Adam holds the keys of all the dispensations** of the fulness of times, i.e. the dispensations of all times have been and will be revealed through him from the beginning'" (*Teachings of the Prophet Joseph Smith*, 167–68; *Church History and Modern Revelation*, 1:309).

Next, as the Savior continues to list names of those from the past who will attend this meeting with Him, He verifies that Peter, James, and John have already restored the Melchizedek Priesthood to the earth in this dispensation.

Perhaps you will recall that Joseph Smith did not record the exact date of this great event, which appears to have taken place between the restoration of the Aaronic Priesthood on May 15, 1829 (see D&C 13), and the end of June 1829 (see D&C 18:9; see also background notes to section 18 in this study guide). The Lord apparently did not choose to bring the exact date back to his mind, and thus, the fact that we do not have the date is a reminder to us of Joseph's honesty.

12 And also with **Peter**, and **James**, and **John**, **whom I have sent unto you, by whom I have ordained you and confirmed you to be apostles, and especial witnesses of my name, and bear the keys of your ministry and of the same things which I revealed unto them**;

There is another precious truth that we can glean from verse 12, above. Did you notice that the Savior said, in effect, that He ordained them to the Melchizedek Priesthood? In other words, when an authorized servant of the Lord places his hands upon our heads, it is the same as if the Savior, Himself, were doing it!

Next, Jesus reiterates that He personally gave Peter, James, and John their priesthood keys and authority.

13 **Unto whom I have committed the keys of my kingdom**, and a dispensation of the gospel for the last times [*this is the last time the gospel will be restored, before the*

Second Coming]; and for the fulness of times [*the "dispensation of the fulness of times"*], in the which I will gather together in one all things, both which are in heaven, and which are on earth [*in other words, all things have been restored in our last days*];

As we finish the topic dealt with in verses 5–14, verse 14, next, tells us, in effect, that all the righteous who qualify for celestial glory will attend this "sacrament meeting" with the Savior.

14 And **also with all those whom my Father hath given me out of the world**.

Verse 14, above, obviously includes all the righteous, living and dead. In other words, this will be a rather large meeting. Daniel saw this in vision and speaks of it and the numbers attending it. We will quote him and use **bold** to point things out:

Daniel 7:9–13

9 I [*Daniel*] beheld till the thrones were cast down, and **the Ancient of days** [*Adam*] **did sit**, whose garment *was* white as snow, and the hair of his head like the pure wool: **his throne *was like* the fiery flame**, *and* his wheels *as* burning fire.

10 A fiery stream issued and came forth from before him: **thousand thousands** [*millions*] ministered unto him, and **ten thousand times ten thousand** [*a hundred million*] stood before him: the judgment was set, and the books were opened.

11 I beheld then because of the voice of the great words which the horn [*the power of heaven; "horn" symbolizes power, in Biblical symbolism*] spake: I beheld *even* till the beast [*symbolic of the devil*] was slain, and his body destroyed [*symbolic of Satan's kingdom*], and given to the burning flame [*destroyed by the power of Christ's glory*].

12 As concerning the rest of the beasts [*Satan's evil hosts, both mortal and evil spirits*], they had their dominion taken away: yet their lives were prolonged for a season and time [*they had their "glory days" of evil and wickedness in the last days before the coming of Christ*].

13 I [*Daniel*] saw in the night visions, and, behold, *one* like **the Son of man came** [*Christ came*] with the clouds of heaven, and came **to the Ancient of days**, and they brought him [*Adam*] near before him [*Christ*].

In concluding our consideration of verses 5–14, we will add one more quote as follows (**bold** added for emphasis):

"Before the Lord Jesus descends openly and publicly in the clouds of glory, attended by all the hosts of heaven; before the great and dreadful day of the Lord sends terror and destruction from one end of the earth to the other; before he stands on Mount Zion, or sets his feet on Olivet, or utters his voice from an American Zion or a Jewish Jerusalem; before all flesh shall see him together; before any of his appearances, which taken together comprise the second coming of the Son of God—before all these, there is to be a secret appearance to selected members of his Church. He will come in private to his prophet and to the apostles then living. Those who have held keys and powers and authorities in all ages from Adam to the present will also be present. And further, **all the faithful members of the Church then living and all the faithful saints of all the ages past will be present. It will be the greatest congregation of faithful saints ever assembled on planet earth. It will be a sacrament meeting**. It will be a day of judgment for the faithful of all the ages. And it will take place in Daviess County, Missouri, at a place called Adam-ondi-Ahman" (*The Millennial Messiah*, 578).

In verses 15–18, next, the Lord tells us how we can prepare to attend the great meeting spoken of in verses 5–14.

15 Wherefore, **lift up your hearts and rejoice** [*be happy; let the joy the gospel brings show on your faces and in your lives*], and **gird up your loins** [*prepare for action; dress your lives in the gospel of Jesus Christ*], and **take upon you my whole armor**, that ye may be able to withstand the evil day, having done all, that ye may be able to stand.

16 **Stand, therefore, having your loins girt about with** [*being dressed in*] **truth**, having on the breastplate of **righteousness**, and your feet shod with the preparation of **the gospel of peace**, which I have sent mine angels to commit unto you;

17 **Taking the shield of** [*protect yourselves with*] **faith** wherewith ye shall be able to quench all the fiery darts of the wicked;

18 And take **the helmet of salvation**, and the **sword of my Spirit** [*the Holy Ghost can cut through falsehood and deception*], which I will pour out upon you, and **my word** which I reveal unto you, and **be agreed as touching all things whatsoever ye ask of me** [*work together in harmony*],

and **be faithful** until I come, and ye shall be caught up [*you will be caught up to meet Christ, whether alive or dead—see D&C 88:96–98*], that where I am ye shall be also. Amen.

SECTION 28

Background

This section is a revelation given through Joseph Smith at Fayette, New York, in September 1830. Among other things, it deals with two important principles for Latter-day Saints that can protect them against deception. First, the Lord will not let His prophet lead the people astray. Second, the prophet is the only one who can receive revelation for the whole Church. Those who follow the living Prophet faithfully are fully assured of entrance into the celestial kingdom.

By way of background, Hiram Page, who was born in 1800, who studied medicine and traveled widely practicing it, and who was baptized into the Church on April 11, 1830 (five days after its organization), had found a stone that he considered to give him powers to receive revelations. He began using it and convinced others, including some members of the Whitmer family and Oliver Cowdery, that he was receiving revelations for the Church. These revelations included the supposed location of Zion and the proper order of the Church.

It is also helpful to know a bit about Hiram and Oliver and the Whitmer family. Hiram had married Catherine Whitmer, the oldest daughter of Peter Whitmer Sr., and Oliver had married her sister, Elizabeth Ann. So, they were all part of the same family.

Most of the people in that area of the country at the time were Congregationalists and believed that any person could receive revelation and pronounce doctrine for a whole congregation or any groups or individuals. Section 28 will preach correct doctrine with respect to the true Church of Jesus Christ; namely, that only one man is authorized to receive revelation and commandments for the whole church. That man is the living Prophet.

This "seer stone," or "peep stone" as it has variously been called, was handed down from generation to generation in the Whitmer family. It is now in the possession of what was known as the Reorganized Church of Jesus Christ of Latter Day Saints, which is now known as the Community of Christ Church. Cecil E. McGavin was permitted to examine it and described it as follows:

"The Page 'peep stone,' however, was preserved as a souvenir. It is now in the possession of the Reorganized Church. The writer was permitted to examine it. It is a flat stone about seven inches long, four wide, and one-quarter inch in thickness. It is dark gray in color with waves of brown and purple gracefully interwoven across the surface. A small hole has been drilled through one end of it as if a string had been threaded through it. It is simply impressive enough to make a good paper weight, yet it became a tool through which the adversary attempted to stir up strife and create a schism in the Church" (McGavin, *Historical Background of the Doctrine and Covenants* and Otten, *Historical Background and Setting for each section of the Doctrine and Covenants*).

Newel Knight, son of Joseph Knight Sr., recorded some valuable background to section 28 in his diary, as follows:

"After arranging my affairs at home, I again set out for Fayette, to attend our second conference, which had been appointed to be held at Father Whitmer's where Joseph then resided. On my arrival I found Brother Joseph in great distress of mind on account of Hyrum [Hiram] Page, who had managed to get up some dissension of feeling among the brethren by giving revelations concerning the government of the Church and other matters, which he claimed to have received through the medium of a stone he possessed. He had quite a roll of papers full of these revelations, and many in the Church were led astray by them. Even Oliver Cowdery and the Whitmer family had given heed to them, although they were in contradiction to the New Testament and the revelations of these last days. Here was a chance for Satan to work among the little flock, and he sought by this means to accomplish what persecution failed to do. Joseph was perplexed and scarcely knew how to meet this new exigency. That night I occupied the same room that he did and the greater part of the night was spent in prayer and supplication. After much labor with these brethren they were convinced of their error, and confessed the same, renouncing the revelations as not being of God, but acknowledged that Satan had conspired to overthrow their belief in the true plan of salvation. In consequence of these things Joseph enquired of the Lord before conference commenced and received the revelation published on page 140 of the Doctrine and Covenants [section 28], wherein God explicitly states His mind and will concerning the receiving of revelations.

"Conference having assembled, the first thing done was to consider the subject of the stone in connection with Hyrum Page, and after considerable investigation and discussion, Brother Page and all the members of the Church present renounced the stone, and the revelations connected with it, much to our joy and satisfaction." (Journal History, 26 Sept. 1830. See also *Doctrine and Covenants Student Manual*, 1981, 57.)

Sometime during this same summer, prior to the conference mentioned above by Newel Knight, Oliver Cowdery had written a letter to Joseph Smith in which he commanded him to change the wording of verse 37 of section 20 of the Doctrine and Covenants. Joseph, who was working at the time on arranging the revelations received so far for eventual publication, wrote of this as follows (**bold** added for emphasis):

"I began to arrange and copy the revelations, which we had received from time to time; in which I was assisted by John Whitmer, who now resided with me.

"Whilst thus employed in the work appointed me by my Heavenly Father, **I received a letter from Oliver Cowdery**, the contents of which gave me both sorrow and uneasiness. Not having that letter now in my possession, I cannot of course give it here in full, but merely an extract of the most prominent parts, which I can yet, and expect long to, remember.

"**He wrote to inform me that he had discovered an error in one of the commandments**—Book of Doctrine and Covenants [20:37]: **'And truly manifest by their works that they have received of the Spirit of Christ unto a remission of their sins.'**

"The above quotation, he said, was erroneous, and added: **'I command you in the name of God to erase those words, that no priestcraft be amongst us!'**

"I immediately wrote to him in reply, in which I asked him by what authority he took upon him to command me to alter or erase, to add to or diminish from, a revelation or commandment from Almighty God.

"A few days afterwards I visited him and Mr. Whitmer's family, when I found the family in general of his opinion concerning the words above quoted, and it was not without both labor and perseverance that I could prevail with any of them to reason calmly on the subject. However, Christian Whitmer at length became convinced that the sentence was reasonable, and according to Scripture; and finally, with his assistance, I succeeded in bringing, not only the Whitmer family, but also Oliver Cowdery to acknowledge that they had been in error, and that the sentence in dispute was in accordance with the rest of the commandment. And thus was this error rooted out, which having its rise in presumption and rash judgment, was the more particularly calculated (when once fairly understood) to teach each and all of us the necessity of humility and meekness before the Lord, that He might teach us of His ways, that we might walk in His paths, and live by every word that proceedeth forth from His mouth" (*History of the Church*, 1:104–5).

One of the things we see in all of

this is that the Lord waited until the need arose in the minds and hearts of the members and then taught principles of Church government that are vital to all of us today. We will now study this section. Notice how gentle the Lord is with Oliver, even though he has caused much anguish and concern for Joseph as well as others. In verse 1, next, He assures this "second elder" (D&C 20:3) of the Church that he is still important.

1 BEHOLD, I say unto thee, Oliver, that it shall be given unto thee that **thou shalt be heard by the church in all things whatsoever thou shalt teach them by the Comforter, concerning the revelations and commandments which I have given.**

Next, the Savior teaches the principle of having one man, the living Prophet, at the head of the Church, and the principle that no one is authorized to receive revelation for the whole Church except him.

2 But, behold, verily, verily, I say unto thee, **no one shall be appointed to receive commandments and revelations in this church excepting my servant Joseph Smith, Jun.**, for he receiveth them even as Moses [*he is the living Prophet now, just like Moses was then*].

3 And **thou** [*Oliver Cowdery*] **shalt be obedient unto the things which I shall give unto him**, even as Aaron, to **declare** [*explain and teach*] **faithfully** [*don't change them one bit, because of your own personal opinions*] **the commandments and the revelations, with power and authority unto the church.**

An important cross-reference for verse 2, above, is found in D&C 43:3–4, where the Lord teaches clearly that He will never allow the living Prophet to lead us astray. He thus bears testimony to us that there is complete safety and reliability in following the living Prophet.

Next, in verses 4 and 5, Oliver is told that he may speak and teach and even command under the direct supervision of the Holy Ghost, but he is not to write commandments to the Church. That is the Prophet's job. The Prophet is the only one who should give commandments and have them written down so that members can refer to them and abide by them.

This is an important distinction. Even elders can command the water to be calmed or an evil spirit to leave when clearly and definitely inspired to do so by the Holy Ghost. But written commandments and new doctrines are the specific jurisdiction of the living Prophet.

4 And **if thou art led at any time by the Comforter** [*the Holy Ghost*] **to speak or teach, or** at all times **by** the **way of commandment unto the church**, thou mayest do it.

5 But **thou shalt not write by way of commandment**, but by wisdom;

Verse 6, next, appears to be a direct reference to the incident, quoted in the background notes above, in which Oliver Cowdery had written to the Prophet, commanding him to delete the words "and truly manifest by their works that they have received of the Spirit of Christ unto a remission of their sins" from D&C 20:37.

6 And **thou shalt not command him who is at thy head, and at the head of the church**;

In verse 7, we are taught that the living Prophet is the only one on earth who has all the priesthood keys and is authorized to use them. (The counselors in the First Presidency and the members of the Quorum of the Twelve Apostles all have the keys—given to each one upon being ordained an Apostle—but they must use them under the direction of the President of the Church.)

Doctrine

Verse 7. The living Prophet is the only one on earth authorized to exercise all the priesthood keys available to man on earth today.

7 For **I have given him the keys** of the mysteries, and the revelations which are sealed, **until I shall appoint unto them another in his stead** [*in other words, the next Prophet*].

Next, Oliver Cowdery is called to go on a mission to the Lamanites. He will be joined by Peter Whitmer Jr. (D&C 30:5), Parley P. Pratt, and Ziba Peterson (D&C 32:2–3). This will be a dangerous and difficult journey of about 1,500 miles into the western frontier (just west of Missouri at that time). We will talk more about it when we get to section 32. Once again, Oliver is counseled not to take over as Prophet by writing commandments.

8 And now, behold, I say unto **you that you shall go unto the Lamanites and preach my gospel unto them**; and inasmuch as they receive thy teachings thou shalt cause my church to be established among them; and **thou shalt have revelations, but write them not by way of commandment**.

In the background notes to this revelation, we mentioned that one of the purported revelations claimed by Hiram Page apparently was that of giving the location of the city of Zion. We now know that it is to be located in Independence, Missouri, because the Lord revealed it to Joseph Smith on July 20, 1831, as recorded in D&C 57:2–3. But verse 9, next, informs Oliver that there has been no revelation from God yet on that matter. Thus, the source of Hiram Page's "revelations" becomes obvious.

9 And now, behold, I say unto you that **it is not revealed, and no man knoweth where the city Zion shall be built**, but it shall be given hereafter [*D&C 57:2–3*]. Behold, I say unto you that it shall be on the borders by the Lamanites.

10 Thou shalt not leave this place [*Fayette, New York*] until after the conference [*the second conference of the Church, scheduled to be held at the Peter Whitmer Sr. home in Fayette on September 26, 1830*]; and **my servant Joseph shall be appointed to preside over the conference** by the voice of it [*and will be sustained again by the members at the conference; similar to what we do in general, stake, and ward conferences*], **and what he saith to thee thou shalt tell** [*yet another reminder to Oliver to follow the Prophet and not go off on his own on doctrine and commandments*].

Next, we are taught a kind principle, namely, keep it as private as possible when it becomes our responsibility to correct another person. It is gratifying to know that Hiram Page accepted counsel, renounced the stone he was using to receive false revelations, and supported the Prophet at the conference.

11 And again, **thou shalt take thy brother, Hiram Page, between him and thee alone**, and tell him that **those things which he hath written from that stone are not of me and that Satan deceiveth him**;

Just a bit more information derived from the Joseph Smith Papers research that shows how Satan deceived Hiram Page with his stone. We will use a quote from the *Doctrine and Covenants Student Manual*, 2018, chapter 11.

"In northwestern New York during the early 1800s, many people believed individuals could receive knowledge supernaturally through an instrument such as a stone or a divining rod. Hiram Page claimed that words would appear on the stone he possessed. He said that after he dictated the words and had them copied to paper, the words would disappear from the stone and others would appear (see *The Joseph Smith Papers,*

Documents: Volume 1: July 1828–June 1831, ed. Michael Hubbard MacKay and others [2013], 184). The Lord denounced Hiram Page's false revelations."

Next, the Lord continues advising Oliver as to what to say to Hiram.

12 For, **behold, these things have not been appointed unto him** [*it is not his stewardship to receive revelation for the Church*], **neither shall anything be appointed unto any of this church contrary to the church covenants** [*no member of the Church will ever be given power and authority that goes contrary to the order established by God*].

13 For **all things must be done in order, and by common consent in the church**, by the prayer of faith.

14 And **thou** [*Oliver*] **shalt assist to settle all these things, according to the covenants of the church** [*according to the proper order of the true Church*], before thou shalt take thy journey among the Lamanites.

15 And it shall be given thee from the time thou shalt go, until the time thou shalt return, what thou shalt do [*you will be inspired to know what to do as you go on your missionary journey to the Lamanites—verse 8*].

Last of all, the Lord gives Oliver counsel about being willing to preach wherever he goes, having a good attitude about it, and making sure that his preaching reflects the positive nature of the gospel to those who heed it.

16 And thou must **open thy mouth at all times**, declaring my gospel **with the sound of rejoicing**. Amen.

SECTION 29

Background

This revelation was given through the Prophet Joseph Smith at Fayette, New York, in September 1830, some days before the conference mentioned in section 28, verse 10. This next conference would be the second conference of the Church since its organization on April 6, 1830, and was to be held in the Whitmer home. It would last for three days.

As already mentioned, this revelation, known now as section 29, was given some days prior to the conference. It was given through the Prophet in the presence of six elders, Oliver Cowdery, David Whitmer, John Whitmer, Peter Whitmer, Samuel H. Smith, and Thomas B. Marsh, along with three other members of the Church (see *The Joseph Smith Papers, Documents, Volume 1: July 1828–June 1831*, ed. Michael Hubbard MacKay and others [2013], 177–78).

It is filled with specific doctrines of the gospel. Perhaps you remember that the Lord showed Nephi in vision that he was going to restore many "plain and precious things" (1 Nephi 13:40) through "other books" (1 Nephi 13:39). One of these "other books" is the Doctrine and Covenants, in which the Lord said that He would "bring to light the true points of my doctrine" (D&C 10:62). Section 29 brings together many of these "points of doctrine."

We will first go through the entire section with no notes added, using **bold** to highlight many of these teachings and doctrines, so that you can see at a glance how powerful section 29 is. You may want to just read the **bolded** words and phrases this time through. Then we will repeat the section, adding several notes as we go.

1 LISTEN to the voice of **Jesus Christ**, **your Redeemer**, the **Great I AM**, whose **arm of mercy hath atoned for your sins**;

2 Who **will gather** his people even as a hen gathereth her chickens under her wings, even **as many as will hearken to my voice** and **humble themselves** before me, and **call upon me in mighty prayer**.

3 Behold, verily, verily, I say unto you, that **at this time your sins are forgiven you, therefore ye receive these things**; but remember to **sin no more, lest perils shall come upon you**.

4 Verily, I say unto you that **ye are chosen out of the world to declare my gospel** with the sound of rejoicing, as with the voice of a trump.

5 Lift up your hearts and be glad, for **I am in your midst**, and am **your advocate with the Father**; and it is his good will to give you the kingdom.

6 And, as it is written—**What-soever ye shall ask in faith, being united in prayer according to my command, ye shall receive**.

7 And **ye are called to bring to pass the gathering of mine elect**; for **mine elect hear my voice and harden not their hearts**;

8 Wherefore the decree hath gone forth from the Father that **they shall be gathered** in unto one place upon the face of this land, **to prepare** their hearts and be prepared **in all things against the day when tribulation and desolation are sent forth upon the wicked**.

9 For **the hour is nigh** and the day soon at hand when the earth

is ripe; and **all the proud and they that do wickedly shall be as stubble**; and **I will burn them up**, saith the Lord of Hosts, that wickedness shall not be upon the earth;

10 For **the hour is nigh**, and that which was spoken by mine apostles must be fulfilled; for as they spoke so shall it come to pass;

11 For **I will reveal myself from heaven with power and great glory**, with all the hosts thereof, and **dwell in righteousness with men on earth a thousand years**, and the wicked shall not stand.

12 And again, verily, verily, I say unto you, and it hath gone forth in a firm decree, by the will of the Father, that mine apostles, **the Twelve** which were with me in my ministry at Jerusalem, **shall stand at my right hand at the day of my coming** in a pillar of fire, being **clothed with robes of righteousness**, with **crowns upon their heads**, in glory even as I am, **to judge the whole house of Israel**, even **as many as have loved me and kept my commandments, and none else**.

13 For **a trump shall sound both long and loud**, even as upon Mount Sinai, and **all the earth shall quake**, and **they shall come forth**—yea, even **the dead which died in me**, to **receive a crown of righteousness**, and to be **clothed upon, even as I am**, to **be with me**, that we may be one.

14 But, behold, I say unto you that **before this great day** shall come the **sun shall be darkened**, and the **moon shall be turned into blood**, and the **stars shall fall** from heaven, and **there shall be greater signs** in heaven above and in the earth beneath;

15 And **there shall be weeping and wailing** among the hosts of men;

16 And there shall be **a great hailstorm** sent forth to destroy the crops of the earth.

17 And it shall come to pass, **because of the wickedness of the world**, that **I will take vengeance upon the wicked**, for they will not repent; for **the cup of mine indignation is full**; for behold, **my blood shall not cleanse them if they hear me not**.

18 Wherefore, I the Lord God will send forth **flies** upon the face of the earth, which shall take hold of the inhabitants thereof, and shall eat their flesh, and shall cause **maggots** to come in upon them;

19 And their **tongues shall be**

stayed that they shall not utter against me; and **their flesh shall fall from off their bones**, and their **eyes from their sockets**;

20 And it shall come to pass that **the beasts of the forest and the fowls of the air shall devour them up.**

21 And **the great and abominable church**, which is **the whore of all the earth**, shall be **cast down** by devouring fire, according as it is spoken by the mouth of Ezekiel the prophet, who spoke of these things, which have not come to pass but surely must, as I live, for abominations shall not reign.

22 And again, verily, verily, I say unto you that **when the thousand years are ended**, and **men again** begin to **deny their God**, then will I spare the earth but for **a little season**;

23 And **the end shall come**, and the heaven and the earth shall be consumed and pass away, and there shall be a **new heaven** and a **new earth**.

24 For **all old things shall pass away**, and **all things shall become new**, even the **heaven** and the **earth**, and all the fulness thereof, both **men** and **beasts**, the **fowls** of the air, and the **fishes** of the sea;

25 And **not one hair**, neither mote, **shall be lost**, for it is the workmanship of mine hand.

26 But, behold, verily I say unto you, **before the earth shall pass away, Michael, mine archangel, shall sound his trump**, and then shall **all the dead awake**, for their graves shall be opened, and they shall come forth—yea, **even all**.

27 And **the righteous shall be gathered on my right hand unto eternal life**; and **the wicked on my left hand will I be ashamed to own before the Father**;

28 **Wherefore I will say unto them—Depart from me, ye cursed, into everlasting fire, prepared for the devil and his angels**.

29 And now, behold, I say unto you, never at any time have I declared from mine own mouth that they should return, for **where I am they cannot come**, for they have no power.

30 But remember that **all my judgments are not given unto men**; and as the words have gone forth out of my mouth even so shall they be fulfilled, that **the first shall be last, and that the last shall be first** in all things whatsoever I have created by the

word of my power, which is the power of my Spirit.

31 For **by the power of my Spirit created I** them; yea, **all things both spiritual and temporal**—

32 **First spiritual, secondly temporal**, which is the beginning of my work; and again, **first temporal, and secondly spiritual**, which is the last of my work—

33 Speaking unto you that you may naturally understand; but unto myself **my works have no end, neither beginning**; but it is given unto you that ye may understand, because ye have asked it of me and are agreed.

34 Wherefore, verily I say unto you that **all things unto me are spiritual**, and not at any time have I given unto you a law which was temporal; neither any man, nor the children of men; neither **Adam, your father**, whom I created.

35 Behold, **I gave unto him that he should be an agent unto himself**; and I gave unto him commandment, but no temporal commandment gave I unto him, for **my commandments are spiritual**; they are **not natural nor temporal, neither carnal nor sensual**.

36 And it came to pass that **Adam**, being **tempted of the devil**—for, behold, **the devil** was before Adam, for he **rebelled against me**, saying, Give me thine **honor**, which **is my power**; and also a **third part** of the hosts of heaven **turned he away from me because of their agency**;

37 And they were thrust down, and **thus came the devil and his angels**;

38 And, behold, **there is a place prepared for them** from the beginning, which place is **hell**.

39 And **it must needs be that the devil should tempt the children of men, or they could not be agents unto themselves**; for **if they never should have bitter they could not know the sweet**—

40 Wherefore, it came to pass that **the devil tempted Adam**, and **he partook of the forbidden fruit** and transgressed the commandment, wherein **he became subject to the will of the devil**, because he yielded unto temptation.

41 Wherefore, I, the Lord God, caused that he should be **cast out from the Garden of Eden**, from my presence, because of his transgression, wherein he became **spiritually dead**, which is **the**

first death, even that same death which is **the last death**, which is spiritual, which **shall be pronounced upon the wicked** when I shall say: Depart, ye cursed.

42 But, behold, I say unto you that **I, the Lord God, gave unto Adam and unto his seed, that they should not die as to the temporal death, until I**, the Lord God, should send forth angels to **declare unto them repentance and redemption, through faith on the name of mine Only Begotten Son**.

43 And **thus did I, the Lord God, appoint unto man the days of his probation**—that **by his natural death he might be raised in immortality unto eternal life**, even as many as would believe;

44 And **they that believe not unto eternal damnation**; for they cannot be redeemed from their spiritual fall, because they repent not;

45 For **they love darkness rather than light**, and their deeds are evil, and **they receive their wages** of whom they list to obey.

46 But behold, I say unto you, that **little children are redeemed** from the foundation of the world through mine Only Begotten;

47 Wherefore, **they cannot sin**, for **power is not given unto Satan to tempt little children, until they begin to become accountable before me;**

48 For it is given unto them even as I will, according to mine own pleasure, that great things may be required at the hand of their fathers.

49 And, again, I say unto you, that **whoso having knowledge, have I not commanded to repent?**

50 And **he that hath no understanding, it remaineth in me to do according as it is written**. And now I declare no more unto you at this time. Amen.

As stated previously, we will now repeat all fifty verses of section 29 and take a closer look at the doctrines and teachings of the gospel and the plan of salvation that are given in them by the Lord. Basically, you could preach the entire gospel using this section as a springboard.

We will begin by pointing out what is known as "divine investiture." We will use verse 1 in combination with verses 42 and 46 to define this term. "Divine investiture" is probably not a term that you will have to recall and explain in order to make it through the final judgment successfully, but as you will see, it can be helpful to know what it means.

Perhaps you've been confused occasionally as to who is speaking in scripture—the Father or the Son. Some of this confusion comes from the fact that Jesus often quotes His Father without first telling us that He is going to do so. This is called "divine investiture." In other words, Christ is authorized or "invested" with the right to speak for the "Divine" Father, and when He does so, it is binding on us, just as if the Father had spoken it. There is nothing strange about His doing this, because He and His Father are "one." It just sometimes throws us off a bit.

"Divine investiture" can also refer to when the Holy Ghost is speaking for Christ, as in Moses 5:9, or when an angel is speaking for Christ, as if He were speaking, as is the case in Judges 2:1–3. Let's look now at our example of Christ speaking as if the Father were speaking. We will put the three verses together here, which we need in order to demonstrate this. We will **bold** words and phrases that point out the transition from when Christ is speaking for Himself and when He begins to speak directly for the Father.

D&C 29:1, 42 and 46

1 **LISTEN to the voice of Jesus Christ**, your Redeemer, the Great I AM, whose arm of mercy hath atoned for your sins;

42 But, behold, I say unto you that I, the Lord God, gave unto Adam and unto his seed, that they should not die as to the temporal death, until I, the Lord God, should send forth angels to declare unto them repentance and redemption, **through faith on the name of mine Only Begotten Son**.

46 But behold, I say unto you, that little children are redeemed from the foundation of the world **through mine Only Begotten**;

We see this same thing in Moses 1:6, where the Savior addresses Moses and speaks for the Father. By way of summary for the topic of "divine investiture," Joseph Fielding Smith explains:

"CHRIST MAY SPEAK AS THE FATHER. In giving revelations our Savior speaks at times for himself; at other times for the Father, and in the Father's name, as though he were the Father, and yet it is Jesus Christ, our Redeemer who gives the message. So, we see, in Doctrine and Covenants 29:1, that he introduces himself as 'Jesus Christ, your Redeemer,' but in the closing part of the revelation he speaks for the Father, and in the Father's name as though he were the Father, and yet it is still Jesus who is speaking, for the Father has put his name on him for that purpose" (*Doctrines of Salvation,* 1:27).

Next, we will point out more doctrine contained in verse 1.

Doctrine

Verse 1. Jesus Christ is the God (Jehovah) of the Old Testament, the God who gave commandments to Abraham, Moses, and others.

1 **LISTEN to the voice of Jesus Christ**, your Redeemer, **the Great I AM**, whose arm [*symbolic of power in scriptural symbolism*] of mercy hath atoned for your sins;

"I AM" is an Old Testament name for Jehovah, which is another name for the premortal Jesus Christ. During Jehovah's appearance at the burning bush, when Moses asked Him who he should tell the people gave him authority to be their prophet, Jesus told him to tell them that it was "I AM" who sent him. (See Exodus 3:14.)

Doctrine

Verse 2. It is time for the final gathering of Israel before the Second Coming.

2 **Who will gather his people** [*it is time for the last days' gathering of Israel*] **even as a hen gathereth her chickens under her wings** [*symbolic of the warmth, comfort, and security of the gospel*], even as many as will hearken to my voice and humble themselves before me, and call upon me in mighty prayer.

One of the great blessings of the Atonement is that we don't have to wait until Judgment Day to find out if our sins are forgiven. As illustrated in verse 3, next, as well as elsewhere in the scriptures, through proper repentance, we can receive forgiveness enroute. This means that we are clean, but we are obviously not yet perfect.

Doctrine

Verse 3. Sins can be and are forgiven as we strive to go through life on the covenant path. It is a merciful way of giving us encouragement enroute to exaltation.

3 **Behold, verily, verily, I say unto you, that at this time your sins are forgiven you**, therefore [*this is why*] ye receive these things; but **remember to sin no more**, lest perils shall come upon you.

In verses 4 and 5, next, we are reminded to be upbeat and pleasant as we take the gospel to others.

Doctrine

Verses 4 and 5. We are to be primarily upbeat and pleasant about preaching the gospel.

4 Verily, I say unto you that ye are chosen out of the world to declare my gospel with the sound of rejoicing, as with the voice of a trump [*symbolizing that the gospel is a clear, easy to recognize, pure message*].

5 **Lift up your hearts and be glad**, for **I am in your midst**, and am your advocate with the Father; and it is his good will to give you the kingdom.

Did you notice in verse 5, above, that the Savior is in our midst and that the Father loves to give His children His kingdom?

Doctrine

Verse 5, above. The Savior is not an "absentee" God. Rather, He spends much time in our midst.

Next, we are taught the importance of unity and harmony as we pray together for desired blessings.

Doctrine

Verse 6. There is much power in working together in harmony, as far as influencing the powers of heaven for desired blessings is concerned.

6 And, as it is written—Whatsoever ye shall ask in faith, **being united in prayer** according to my command, ye shall receive.

Doctrine

Verse 7. The "elect," those whose hearts are pure, recognize the gospel message when they hear it.

7 And ye are called to bring to pass the gathering of mine elect; for mine elect hear my voice and harden not their hearts;

Verse 8, next, tells us that there is one gathering place for the early Saints (when the Church was just starting out), but there are many "gathering places" now; namely, the stakes of Zion. (See D&C 115:6.)

8 Wherefore the decree hath gone forth from the Father that **they shall be gathered in unto one place upon the face of this land, to prepare their hearts** and be prepared in all things against the day when tribulation and desolation are sent forth upon the wicked.

There is an important message to us in verse 8, above, as to how best to prepare for the trouble and devastations of the last days. Did you notice the key word in verse 8? It is "hearts." Symbolically, our hearts are the center of our feelings and emotions. The Spirit often speaks to our heart, giving us feelings and testimony concerning the gospel. We tend to act according to our feelings, even more so than according to our minds. Thus, a major preparation for remaining strong and loyal to God during times of trial and trouble comes in the form of having the word of God and the testimony of the Spirit written in our hearts. This type of spiritual nourishment comes in large measure from scripture study, listening to the words of the living prophets, meeting with other Saints whose values and standards reflect the Lord, sincere prayer, serving others, and so on.

Doctrine

Verse 9. The wicked will be burned at the time of the Second Coming.

9 For **the hour is nigh** [*getting close*] and the day soon at hand **when the earth is ripe** [*when the majority of people on earth are fully wicked*]; and all **the proud** and **they that do wickedly shall be as stubble** [*very flammable stalks of dry straw*] ; and **I will burn them up**, saith the Lord of Hosts, that **wickedness shall not be upon the earth** [*for the beginning of the Millennium*];

A quote from the 2018 *Doctrine and Covenants Student Manual* for institutes of religion in the Church informs us that the wicked will not be able to survive the intensity of the Savior's glory when He comes. Therefore, they will be consumed by it. (**Bold** added for emphases.)

"The Lord warned that those who are 'proud and they that do wickedly shall be as stubble' and burn at His coming (D&C 29:9). While pride is a common sin that affects everyone to some degree, in this case 'the proud' refers to **those who cannot abide the Lord's glory because of wickedness**. In a later revelation, the Lord clarified that this group includes 'they who are liars, and sorcerers, and adulterers, and whoremongers, and whosoever loves and makes a lie. These are they who suffer the wrath of God on earth' (D&C 76:103–4)."

That the glory of the Savior at His coming will be the cause of the burning of the wicked is confirmed by D&C 5:19, as well as 2 Nephi 12:10, 19, and 21.

10 For **the hour is nigh, and that which was spoken by mine apostles** [*the "signs of the times," especially the prophecies about the Second Coming and the destruction of the wicked*] **must be fulfilled**; for **as they spoke so shall it come to pass** [*their prophecies will be fulfilled*];

Doctrine

Verse 11. The Savior's Coming ushers in the beginning of the Millennium, which will last for 1000 years. Also, there will be no wicked people at the beginning of the Millennium.

11 **For I will reveal myself from heaven with power and great glory**, with all the hosts thereof, **and dwell in righteousness with men on earth a thousand years**, and **the wicked shall not stand.**

Doctrine

The Twelve Apostles, who ministered with the Savior at Jerusalem, will assist the Savior in judging the righteous people of the House of Israel.

12 And again, verily, verily, I say unto you, and it hath gone forth in a firm decree, by the will of the Father [*this is all done under the direction of the Father*], that mine apostles, **the Twelve which were with me in my ministry at Jerusalem**, shall stand at my right hand [*symbolic of covenants; symbolic of personal righteousness and qualifying to enter celestial glory*] at the day of my coming in a pillar of fire [*with glory*], being clothed with robes of righteousness [*symbolic, among other things, of having kept temple covenants*], with crowns [*symbolic of the power and authority of gods, in exaltation*] upon their heads, **in glory even as I am** [*with the same glory that Christ has*], **to judge the whole house of Israel**, even **as many as have loved me and kept my commandments** [*the Twelve will judge the righteous of the House of Israel*], and **none else**.

As you can see, verse 12, above, is set in the context of the time of the Second Coming. This will usher in the Millennium. The Savior explains that the Twelve will only be involved with judging the righteous (see end of verse 12). This makes sense, since only the righteous dead will be resurrected at that time. Bruce R. McConkie gives added explanation as follows (**bold** added for emphasis):

"Be it remembered that the Twelve Apostles of the Lamb, who were with the Lord in his ministry in Jerusalem, shall judge the whole house of Israel, **meaning that portion of Israel who have kept the commandments**, 'and none else.' (D&C 29:12.) There will be a great hierarchy of judges in that great day, of whom Adam, under Christ, will be the chief of all. **Those judges will judge the righteous ones** under their jurisdiction, **but Christ himself, he alone, will judge the wicked** (*The Millennial Messiah*, 584).

Doctrine

Verse 13. The righteous who have died since the resurrection of Christ will be resurrected at the time of the Savior's Second Coming (except for Peter, James, and Moroni, who have already

been resurrected). They will be "clothed upon" (verse 13) with power and authority to rule and reign with Christ during the Millennium (see also Revelation 20:4).

13 For **a trump shall sound** both long and loud, even as upon Mount Sinai [*announcing the presence of the Lord—see Exodus 19:16–20*], and **all the earth shall quake**, and **they shall come forth**—yea, even **the dead which died in me** [*those who died faithful to Christ*], **to receive a crown of righteousness** [*these righteous people will have power and authority to rule and reign with the Savior during the Millennium; they will also know that they are heading toward celestial glory because they are included in this resurrection*], and **to be clothed upon, even as I am** [*perhaps also including the imagery of being clothed in personal righteousness—see Revelation 19:8*], **to be with me, that we may be one**.

Doctrine

Verses 14–21. Many signs of the times (prophecies that will be fulfilled as the Second Coming gets closer and finally arrives) will take place, alerting the righteous who study the scriptures and listen to the living prophets that the Second Coming is getting close.

14 But, behold, I say unto you that before this great day shall come [*before the Second Coming and the destruction of the wicked*] **the sun shall be darkened**, and the **moon shall be turned into blood**, and the **stars shall fall from heaven**, and there shall be **greater signs in heaven above and in the earth beneath**;

15 And **there shall be weeping and wailing** [*there will be much of agony and distress, gloom and doom*] **among the hosts of men**;

16 And there shall be **a great hailstorm** sent forth to destroy the crops of the earth.

17 And it shall come to pass, **because of the wickedness of the world**, that **I will take vengeance upon the wicked, for they will not repent**; for the cup of mine indignation [*righteous anger*] is full [*mercy cannot hold justice back any longer*]; for behold, **my blood shall not cleanse them if they hear me not** [*if they do not listen to and obey the gospel*].

18 Wherefore, **I the Lord God will send forth flies** upon the face of the earth, which shall take

hold of the inhabitants thereof, and shall eat their flesh, and shall cause **maggots** to come in upon them;

19 And **their tongues shall be stayed** [*perhaps they will be speechless because of horror; can also mean that the destruction of the wicked will stop their blasphemy against God*] that they shall not utter against me; and **their flesh shall fall from off their bones**, and **their eyes from their sockets** [*indicating horrible conditions on earth prior to the Second Coming*];

20 And it shall come to pass that **the beasts of the forest and the fowls of the air shall devour them up.**

21 And **the great and abominable church** [*the "church of the devil" (1 Nephi 14:10), "kingdom of the devil" (1 Nephi 22:22–23)*], which is **the whore** [*a highly symbolic word, meaning one who perverts that which is right and holy and good for evil purposes; thus symbolic of Satan and his evil hosts*] **of all the earth**, shall be **cast down by devouring fire**, according as it is spoken by the mouth of Ezekiel the prophet [*see Ezekiel 38:22 and 39:6; see also heading for Ezekiel 38 as background*], who spoke of these things, **which have not come to pass** [*yet in 1830, at the time of this revelation*] **but surely must**, as I live, for abominations shall not reign [*wickedness will not ultimately rule the earth*].

Doctrine

Verse 22. After the end of the Millennium, there will be a "little season," during which many will again turn wicked and deny God.

22 And again, verily, verily, I say unto you that when the thousand years are ended, and **men again begin to deny their God**, then will I spare the earth but for **a little season**;

Joseph Fielding Smith wrote of this "little season" as follows, telling us that there would be many sons of perdition during that time (**bold** added for emphasis):

"After the thousand years Satan will be loosed again and will go forth again to deceive the nations. Because men are still mortal, Satan will go out to deceive them. Men will again deny the Lord, but in doing **so they will act with their eyes open and because they love darkness rather than light, and so they become sons of perdition**. Satan will gather his hosts, both those on the earth and the wicked dead who will eventually also be brought forth in the resurrection. Michael, the prince,

[Adam] will gather his forces and the last great battle will be fought. Satan will be defeated with his hosts. Then will come the end. Satan and those who follow him will be banished into outer darkness" (*Doctrines of Salvation*, 1:87).

Doctrine

Verses 23–25. The heaven and the earth and everything on it will die and be resurrected. This includes pets.

23 And **the end** [*of the 7,000 years of this earth's temporal existence—see D&C 77:6*] **shall come**, and the **heaven and the earth shall be consumed and pass away** [*die—see D&C 88:26*], and **there shall be a new heaven and a new earth** [*not new in the sense of being replaced; rather, new in the sense of being renewed, or celestialized—see D&C 130:9*].

24 For **all old things shall pass away**, and **all things shall become new**, even the **heaven** and the **earth**, and **all the fulness thereof** [*everything on the earth*], both **men** and **beasts**, the **fowls of the air**, and the **fishes of the sea**;

25 And **not one hair, neither mote, shall be lost, for it is the workmanship of mine hand.**

We will give a quote from the *Doctrine and Covenants Student Manual*, 1981, used previously by our institutes of religion, by way of follow-up on verses 23–25, above (**bold** added for emphasis):

"President Joseph Fielding Smith explained that this passage '**does not mean that this earth shall pass away and another take its place**, and the heaven thereof shall pass away, and another heaven take its place, but that the earth and its heaven shall, after passing away through death, be renewed again in immortality. **This earth is living and must die**, but since it keeps the law it shall be restored through the resurrection by which **it shall become celestialized** and the abode of celestial beings. The next verse of this revelation explains this as follows: [D&C 29:24–25]

'So we see that the Lord intends to save, not only the earth and the heavens, not only man who dwells upon the earth, but all things which he has created. The animals, the fishes of the sea, the fowls of the air, as well as man, are to be recreated, or renewed, through the resurrection, for they too are living souls.' (In Conference Report, Oct. 1928, 99–100; see also D&C 88:17–19, 25–26.)" [As quoted in *Doctrine and Covenants Student Manual*, 1981, 62.]

Doctrine

Verse 26. There will be a final resurrection after the end of

the Millennium that will be the resurrection of the wicked (see also D&C 88:100–102).

26 But, behold, verily I say unto you, **before the earth shall pass away**, Michael [*Adam*], mine archangel, shall sound his trump, and **then shall all the dead awake**, for their graves shall be opened, and **they shall come forth** [*will be resurrected*]—**yea, even all**.

Although the Lord will reveal more details, especially in section 76 about the three degrees of glory and perdition, and in section 88, concerning the various resurrections, at this point in time (verses 27–29, next), He uses the Biblical imagery of being on God's "right hand" or "left hand" to emphasize that the righteous will gain eternal life and the wicked will not be privileged to live with God.

"Right hand," in this context, means that you are righteous, having made and kept covenants with God. "Right hand" symbolizes making covenants with God. "Left hand" means that a person is wicked, having refused to repent, and having either made and then violated covenants with God or refused to make such covenants.

27 And **the righteous shall be gathered on my right hand unto eternal life**; and **the wicked on my left hand** will I be ashamed to own before the Father;

28 Wherefore [*this is why*] I will say unto them—**Depart from me, ye cursed, into everlasting fire** [*hell*], **prepared for the devil and his angels**.

29 And now, behold, I say unto you, **never at any time have I declared from mine own mouth that they should return**, for **where I am they cannot come**, for **they have no power**.

30 But **remember that all my judgments are not given unto men** [*perhaps meaning that the Lord has not explained everything to us yet and does not give all His reasons to us for what He does; He doesn't have to explain to us in order to proceed with His work*]; and as the words have gone forth out of my mouth even so shall they be fulfilled, that **the first shall be last, and that the last shall be first** in all things whatsoever I have created by the word of my power, which is the power of my Spirit.

The Joseph Smith Translation of the Bible rendition of Mark 10:31 (which is Mark 10:30 in the JST) helps us understand the phrase "the first shall be last, and . . . the last shall be first" in verse 30, above. We will quote it here, with **bold** added for emphasis:

JST Mark 10:30

But **there are many who make themselves first, that shall be last**, and the last first. [*In other words, those who are prideful and make themselves priority, even above God's commandments, will find themselves in "last place" on Judgment Day.*]

Verses 31 and 32, next, sometimes confuse members of the Church a bit. While there are many things that could be done with these verses, we will take a simple approach. In effect, what the Lord is saying first is that He initially created all things in spirit form and then in physical form in conjunction with the Fall of Adam and Eve. This was the creation or "beginning" of the earth. Then, He speaks of the "last of my work" (verse 32), which could be understood to mean the final stage of our progression before Judgment Day, beginning with our mortal life and continuing to resurrection and final judgment.

Doctrine

Verses 31 and the first part of verse 32. God created all things in spirit form before they were created physically. (See also Moses 3:5.)

31 For by the power of my Spirit **created** I them; yea, **all things both spiritual and temporal** [*having to do with mortality, earthly time, earthly things*]—

32 **First spiritual, secondly temporal** [*all things were first created in spirit form in premortality and then created in physical form on earth in conjunction with the Fall of Adam and Eve*], which is the beginning of my work [*"to bring to pass the immortality and eternal life of man" (See Moses 1:39)*]; and **again, first temporal, and secondly spiritual** [*meaning, perhaps, among other things that the final phase of our progression toward Judgment Day and exaltation begins with mortality and then proceeds to the spirit world, the Second Coming, our work and progress during the Millennium, and on to final judgment, which are all designed to help us become more spiritual*], **which is the last of my work** [*which is the final part of the Savior's work before He turns all things back over to the Father—see D&C 76:107–8*]—

As the Lord continues, He explains that He is speaking in terms that we can understand as mortals, because, in fact, His works do not have a beginning, neither do they have an end. Also, since all that He does is designed to promote our spirituality and eternal well-being, everything is "spiritual" to Him, whereas we tend to make a distinction between physical things and spiritual things.

33 **Speaking unto you that you may naturally** [*as mortals*] **understand**; but unto myself my works have no end, neither beginning; but it is given unto you [*I'm speaking to you in this simpler way*] that ye may understand, because ye have asked it of me and are agreed [*are united together in asking Me*].

34 Wherefore, verily I say unto you that **all things unto me are spiritual** [*are designed to promote your spirituality*], and **not at any time have I given unto you a law which was temporal**; neither any man, nor the children of men; **neither Adam**, your father [*first ancestor*], whom I created.

35 Behold, **I gave unto him that he should be an agent unto himself** [*Adam was given agency*]; and I gave unto him commandment [*so that he had an environment of knowledge in which to exercise his agency*], but no temporal commandment gave I unto him, for **my commandments are spiritual; they are not natural nor temporal, neither carnal nor sensual**.

We will add one quote here from the *Doctrine and Covenants Student Manual*, 1981, in conjunction with verses 31–35:

"When the Lord created the earth, he first created all things spiritually (Moses 3:5–9). After the Fall all things became temporal (D&C 77:6). At the end of the earth, the temporal will again become spiritual (Articles of Faith 1:10). Thus, in the beginning things were spiritual first and temporal second. In the end things will be temporal first and spiritual second (McConkie, *Doctrinal New Testament Commentary*, 1:669). These expressions are given by the Lord only for the sake of man's understanding in mortality, however. From God's point of view there is neither beginning nor end, and all things are spiritual.

"Man makes a distinction between temporal and spiritual laws, and some are very much concerned about keeping the two separate. To the Lord everything is both spiritual and temporal, and the laws He gives are consequently spiritual because they concern spiritual beings. When He commanded Adam to eat bread in the sweat of his brow, or Moses to strike the rock that the people might drink, or the Prophet Joseph to erect the Nauvoo House, or the Saints in Utah to build fences and roads, such laws were for their spiritual welfare as well as physical. To obey such laws, when given, is a spiritual duty. One who performs his daily labor 'as to the Lord, and not to men' (Eph. 6:7) derives spiritual benefit from whatever his duties are (Smith and

Sjodahl, *Commentary*, 156)."

Doctrine

Verse 36. The ultimate source of God's power is His honor and integrity.

36 And it came to pass that Adam, being tempted of the devil—for, behold, **the devil was before Adam** [*Lucifer became the devil before Adam was placed on earth*], for he **rebelled against me, saying, Give me thine honor, which is my power**; and also a third part of the hosts of heaven turned he away from me **because of their agency;**

Doctrine

Verse 36, above. We had agency in premortality.

Some people wonder to what extent we had agency in our premortal life as spirit children of our Heavenly Parents (see *The Family: A Proclamation to the World*, September 23, 1995, second paragraph). The answer is obviously "yes," since Lucifer and the spirits who followed him exercised their agency to rebel against God. Thus, it is clear that we were given knowledge and agency there such that we could make choices, make mistakes, repent, be forgiven, and thus make progress there. In other words, our situation there was very similar to our situation here in mortality. It had to be in order for us to progress. A summary of this is given in the New Testament student manual, used in our institutes of religion, as follows (**bold** added for emphasis):

"**We were given laws** and **agency**, and **commandments to have faith** and **repent** from the wrongs that we could do there." "**Man could and did in many instances, sin before he was born** . . ." *(Life and Teachings of Jesus and His Apostles*, New Testament student manual, used by the institutes of religion, 336).

In conjunction with the above quote, it is important to note that the Atonement of Christ is infinite. It works in the present, past, and future and thus operated for us there in premortality also. A quote from Elder Jeffrey R. Holland, in which he speaks of things we might think about during the sacrament, verifies this as follows (**bold** added for emphasis):

"We could remember that even in the Grand Council of Heaven [*held in premortality*] He loved us and was wonderfully strong, that **we triumphed even there by the power of Christ and our faith in the blood of the Lamb**" ("This Do in Remembrance of Me," *Ensign*, Nov. 1995).

As the Lord continues the instructions given in section 29, we are taught that Lucifer and the rebellious spirits from our premortal life became the devil and his evil spirits.

Doctrine

Verse 37. Lucifer and the spirits who rebelled with him in premortality were thrust down to earth. Thus, Lucifer became the devil and they became his evil spirit followers.

37 And **they were thrust down** [*to earth—see Revelation 12:4*], **and thus came the devil and his angels**;

Doctrine

Verse 38. The plan of salvation, which was taught us in premortality, included a final place for the devil and those who follow him completely.

38 And, behold, **there is a place prepared for them from the beginning** [*in other words, as explained to us in the council in heaven in our premortality*], which place is **hell** [*perdition, outer darkness*].

Doctrine

Verse 39. Temptation is necessary in order for us to exercise our agency and progress.

39 **And it must needs be** [*it is necessary*] **that the devil should tempt the children of men** [*people*], **or they could not be agents unto themselves**; for if they never should have bitter they could not know the sweet—

In our battle against Satan and the evil spirits who follow him, it is important to know that people with physical bodies have power over those who do not. We will quote from the 2018 *Doctrine and Covenants Student Manual*, chapter 12, to show this.

"President James E. Faust (1920–2007) of the First Presidency explained: We need not become paralyzed with fear of Satan's power. He can have no power over us unless we permit it. He is really a coward, and if we stand firm, he will retreat. The Apostle James counseled: 'Submit yourselves therefore to God. Resist the devil, and he will flee from you' [James 4:7]. And Nephi states that 'he hath no power over the hearts' of people who are righteous [1 Nephi 22:26].

"We have heard comedians and others justify or explain their misdeeds by saying, 'The devil made me do it.' I do not really think the devil can make us do anything; certainly he can tempt and he can deceive, but he has no authority over us which we do not give him.

"The power to resist Satan may

be stronger than we realize. The Prophet Joseph Smith taught: 'All beings who have bodies have power over those who have not. The devil has no power over us only as we permit him. The moment we revolt at anything which comes from God, the devil takes power' [*Teachings of the Prophet Joseph Smith*, sel. Joseph Fielding Smith (1976), 181]. He also stated, 'Wicked spirits have their bounds, limits, and laws by which they are governed' [in *History of the Church*, 4:576]. So Satan and his angels are not all-powerful. . . ."

Doctrine

Verses 40–41. The Fall of Adam was a necessary part of the plan of salvation.

40 Wherefore [*this is why*], it came to pass that **the devil tempted Adam, and he partook of the forbidden fruit** and **transgressed the commandment, wherein he became subject to the will of** [*temptations of*] **the devil**, because he yielded unto temptation. [*In other words, by partaking of the forbidden fruit, Adam and Eve got things going for us on earth, including the necessary element of being subject to the temptations of the devil.*]

Because of our agency, we "own" the consequences of our own actions. So it was with Adam and Eve, because they were taught sufficiently to be accountable for their choices. Elder John A. Widtsoe, of the Quorum of the Twelve, explained this as follows (**bold** added for emphasis):

"Such was the problem before our first parents: to remain forever at selfish ease in the Garden of Eden, or to face unselfishly tribulation and death, in bringing to pass the purposes of the Lord for a host of waiting spirit children. They chose the latter . . . This they did with open eyes and minds as to consequences. The memory of their former estates may have been dimmed, but **the gospel had been taught them during their sojourn in the Garden of Eden** . . . the choice that they made raises Adam and Eve to preeminence among all who have come on earth" (*Evidences and Reconciliations*, 193–94).

Also, from the *Encyclopedia of Mormonism* we read (**bold** added for emphasis):

"Satan was present to tempt Adam and Eve, much as he would try to thwart others in their divine missions: 'and he sought also to beguile Eve, for he knew not the mind of God, wherefore he sought to destroy the world' (Moses 4:6). **Eve faced the choice between selfish ease and unselfishly facing tribulation and death** (Widtsoe, 193). As befit her calling, **she** realized that there was no other way and **deliberately**

chose mortal life so as to further the purpose of God and bring children into the world" (*Encyclopedia of Mormonism*; see "Eve").

One more note here. Elder Joseph Fielding Smith, of the Quorum of the Twelve, discussed the topic as to whether or not Adam's transgression was a sin and whether or not Adam and Eve got cursed as follows:

Was Adam and Eve's partaking of the fruit a sin? (Genesis 3:6, Moses 4:12)

Answer

"What did Adam do? The very thing the Lord wanted him to do; and I hate to hear anybody call it a sin, for it wasn't a sin . . . I see a great difference between transgressing the law and committing a sin." (Joseph Fielding Smith, "Fall, Atonement, Resurrection, Sacrament," in *Charge to Religious Educators*, 124, quoted in *Doctrines of the Gospel Student Manual*, 20).

If it wasn't a sin, then why did the Lord "curse" them for doing it? (Gen. 3:13–19.)

Answer

He didn't curse Adam and Eve. Read Genesis 3:13–19 more carefully. He cursed the serpent (verse 14) and the ground (verse 17). In fact, the ground was cursed "for thy sake"; i.e., it was a blessing for them. Joseph Fielding Smith explained this as follows:

"When Adam was driven out of the Garden of Eden, the Lord passed a sentence upon him. Some people have looked upon that sentence as being a dreadful thing. It was not; it was a blessing. In order for mankind to obtain salvation and exaltation it is necessary for them to obtain bodies in this world, and pass through the experiences and schooling that are found only in mortality . . . The fall of man came as a blessing in disguise, and was the means of furthering the purposes of the Lord in the progress of man, rather than a means of hindering them" (*Doctrines of the Gospel Student Manual*, 1981, 21).

41 **Wherefore** [*this is why*], **I, the Lord God, caused that he should be cast out from the Garden of Eden**, from my presence, **because of his transgression, wherein he became spiritually dead** [*cut off from the direct presence of God*], which is **the first death**, even **that same death which is the last death** [*which those who refuse to repent will suffer, meaning that they will be cut off from the presence of God forever*], which is spiritual, [*the "death" of their spirituality*] **which shall be pronounced upon the wicked when I shall say: Depart, ye cursed** [*at the final judgment—see verse 28, above*].

Next, in verse 42, the Savior quotes His Father, explaining our "probationary period" or "testing period" here on earth. First, He emphasizes the necessity of our having knowledge of the plan of salvation.

42 But, behold, I say unto you that **I, the Lord God, gave unto Adam and unto his seed** [*posterity*], **that they should not die as to the temporal death** [*physical death*], **until I**, the Lord God, **should send forth angels to declare** [*teach and explain*] **unto them repentance and redemption, through faith on the name of mine Only Begotten Son**.

__Doctrine__

Verse 43. Physical death is a necessary part of the plan of salvation. Without it, we could not gain resurrected bodies, nor would we have the opportunity to attain eternal life, which is exaltation, which is having our own family unit forever, becoming gods, having spirit children, and creating worlds to send them to.

43 And thus did I, the Lord God, appoint unto man the days of his probation—that by his natural death [*physical death*] **he might be raised in immortality** [*living forever as resurrected beings*] unto **eternal life**, even as many as would believe;

__Doctrine__

Verse 44. Those who refuse to come unto Christ will still be resurrected but will be damned, which means "stopped in their progression."

44 And they that believe not unto [*will be resurrected unto*] **eternal damnation** [*those who refuse to believe in Christ will still be resurrected but will be damned*]; for **they cannot be redeemed from their spiritual fall, because they repent not**;

Next, we are taught why some people refuse to be saved.

45 For **they love darkness rather than light**, and **their deeds are evil**, and they receive their wages [*rewards*] of whom they list [*desire*] to obey. [*In other words, they choose to be rewarded by the devil.*]

Next, in verses 46 and 47, we are given powerful doctrine regarding the salvation of little children. Among other things that come from these two verses, we understand that parents have the first eight years of their children's lives to teach them without Satan's direct temptations entering into their minds. Obviously, children can be tempted and influenced by others and conditions in their environment, so parents and others need to do their best to minimize such bad influences and teach their children to walk uprightly before the Lord.

Doctrine

Verses 46–47. Little children are saved. Little children cannot commit sin. Satan is not allowed to tempt little children.

46 But behold, I say unto you, that little children are redeemed from the foundation of the world [*according to the plan that was presented in the premortal council*] **through mine Only Begotten**;

47 Wherefore, **they cannot sin**, for **power is not given unto Satan to tempt little children, until they begin to become accountable** before me;

Perhaps you have wondered if the above means that little children will be saved in the celestial kingdom's lowest degree or if they will gain exaltation. The answer is that they will receive exaltation, which is the highest degree of glory in the celestial kingdom. President Joseph F. Smith taught that they "will inherit their exaltation." (See *Gospel Doctrine*, 453.) Thus, we understand that they will have the opportunity to choose a spouse (perhaps in the spirit world or during the Millennium), will be sealed together by proxies in temples during the Millennium, will enter celestial exaltation as husbands and wives in their own family units, and live forever as gods, having their own spirit offspring and creating worlds for them.

Next, the Lord emphasizes that because of being given this period of time during which Satan cannot directly put temptation into their children's minds (until the age of accountability, which is eight; see D&C 68:25), He expects great things of their parents!

48 For it is given unto them even as I will, according to mine own pleasure, **that great things may be required at the hand of their fathers**.

Next, we are reminded that those who are accountable and have knowledge are under obligation to repent.

49 And, again, I say unto you, that **whoso having knowledge, have I not commanded to repent?**

Finally, in this doctrinally packed section, we have a beautiful and merciful doctrine that applies, among other things, to the intellectually handicapped and others whose minds are not capable of full accountability.

Doctrine

Verse 50. The intellectually handicapped and others whose minds are not capable of full accountability are treated by the same rules and blessings as little children who are not accountable. Thus, their exaltation is assured.

50 And **he that hath no understanding, it remaineth in me to do according as it is written** [*for instance, in the Book of Mormon, Moroni, chapter 8, concerning the redemption of little children*]. And now I declare no more unto you at this time. Amen.

SECTION 30

Background

This revelation was given through Joseph Smith to David Whitmer (who was one of the Three Witnesses to the Book of Mormon), Peter Whitmer Jr. (who was one of the Eight Witnesses), and John Whitmer (who was also one of the Eight Witnesses). It was given at Fayette, New York, in September 1830, following the three-day conference of the Church that began on September 26, 1830.

As you can see in the heading to section 30 in your Doctrine and Covenants, this material was originally published as three revelations for the Book of Commandments but was later combined by the Prophet Joseph into one section for the 1835 edition of the Doctrine and Covenants. He gave some background to these revelations as follows:

"At length our conference assembled [September 26–28, 1830]. The subject of the stone previously mentioned [see Historical Background for D&C 28] was discussed, and after considerable investigation, Brother Page, as well as the whole Church who were present, renounced the said stone, and all things connected therewith, much to our mutual satisfaction and happiness. We now partook of the Sacrament, confirmed and ordained many, and attended to a great variety of Church business on the first and the two following days of the conference, during which time we had much of the power of God manifested amongst us; the Holy Ghost came upon us, and filled us with joy unspeakable; and peace, and faith, and hope, and charity abounded in our midst" (in *The Joseph Smith Papers, Histories, Volume 1: Joseph Smith Histories, 1832–1844,* ed. Karen Lynn Davidson and others [2012], 452).

As you will see in verses 1–4, David Whitmer is chastised by the Lord. From the context and historical background, we have reason to believe that he was thus scolded on account of his siding with his brother-in-law, Hiram Page, who was receiving false revelations by means of his seer stone (see notes for section 28).

As you have no doubt sensed, in the New England environment in which the Church was restored, it was quite a struggle to establish the principle of having only one person at the head of the Church; namely, the Prophet. In that same environment, it was a common belief that anyone could receive revelation for any group or individual. As the Lord instructs David Whitmer, we see firm instruction on these matters.

1 BEHOLD, I say unto you, **David**, that **you have feared man and have not relied on me** for strength as you ought.

2 But **your mind has been on the things of the earth more than on the things of me**, your Maker, and the ministry whereunto you have been called; and **you have not given heed unto my Spirit, and to those who were set over you** [*such as Joseph Smith*], **but have been persuaded by those whom I have not commanded** [*such as peer pressure from Hiram Page with his "peep stone" and family members who went along with him and opposed Joseph Smith as a result*].

Next, in verses 3 and 4, the Lord gives David some time to sort things out and ponder. Such time is often needed in order for real change to take place, especially change in one's heart and feelings about matters that have been a source of frustration and misunderstanding.

3 Wherefore [*for this reason*], **you are left to inquire for yourself at my hand** [*you need to do some praying about these matters and let Me help you understand*], and **ponder upon the things which you have received.**

4 And **your home shall be at your father's house, until I give unto you further commandments**. And you shall attend to the ministry in the church, and before the world, and in the regions round about. Amen.

Next, Peter Whitmer Jr. (David Whitmer's younger brother, born September 27, 1809, who never left the Church but remained faithful the rest of his life) is told to go on the mission to the Lamanites with Oliver Cowdery, who was called to this mission as recorded in D&C 28:8. Two others will be instructed by the Lord to join them (Parley P. Pratt and Ziba Peterson—see D&C 32). This will be a 1,500-mile journey that will start on October 18, 1830. We will do more with this mission when we study section 32.

5 Behold, I say unto you, **Peter**, that **you shall take your journey with your brother Oliver** [*on the mission to the Lamanites*]; for the time has come that it is expedient in me that you shall open your mouth to declare my gospel [*your preparation time is over and it is time for you to preach the gospel to the world*]; therefore, fear not, but give heed unto the words and advice of your brother [*Oliver Cowdery*], which he shall give you.

Next, we see some rather tender advice for missionary companions.

6 And **be you afflicted in all his afflictions, ever lifting up your heart unto me in prayer and faith, for his and your deliverance**; for I have given unto him [*Oliver Cowdery*] power to build up my church among the Lamanites;

Next, the Lord teaches another brief lesson about order and leadership in the Church. In this case, Oliver Cowdery is serving as "second elder" in the Church, next in authority to Joseph Smith, who is the "first elder" (see D&C 20:2–3).

7 And **none have I appointed to be his counselor over him in the church, concerning church matters, except it is his brother, Joseph Smith, Jun**.

8 Wherefore, give heed unto these things and be diligent in keeping my commandments, and you shall be blessed unto eternal life [*exaltation*]. Amen.

In the final revelation within this section, the Lord addresses John Whitmer, David Whitmer's older brother, born August 27, 1802. By the way, John will be called by the Lord to be the historian of the Church (D&C 47:1). He wrote 96 pages of history while actively serving in this position but refused to give them to the Church. This was one of the causes for his excommunication on March 10, 1838, in Missouri.

At the time of this revelation, John is given specific instructions to spend his time among the members of the Church in the area around Fayette, including in the home of Philip Burroughs, who was a neighbor of the Whitmers. There is no record indicating that Philip Burroughs was baptized, but his wife was (see *Doctrine and Covenants Student Manual*, 2018, chapter 13).

9 Behold, I say unto you, my servant **John**, that **thou shalt commence from this time forth to proclaim my gospel**, as with the voice of a trump.

10 And **your labor shall be at your brother Philip Burroughs', and in that region round about**,

yea, wherever you can be heard, **until I command you to go from hence** [*from here*].

11 And your whole labor shall be in Zion [*among the members of the Church*], **with all your soul**, from henceforth [*from this time forward*]; yea, you shall ever **open your mouth** in my cause, **not fearing what man can do**, for I am with you. Amen.

SECTION 31

Background

This revelation is given to Thomas B. Marsh through the Prophet Joseph Smith in September 1830 in Fayette, New York. Brother Marsh had been baptized on September 3, 1830, by David Whitmer in Seneca Lake, and had already been ordained an elder by Oliver Cowdery by the time of this revelation. He would become the first president of the Quorum of the Twelve Apostles.

Born on November 1, 1799, Thomas left his parents' home when he was 14 and wandered for many years from city to city. He finally tried to find success in the grocery business but failed. During this time, he joined the Methodist Church, but it never did seem to "take" in his soul. In the course of events, he ended up in western New York, where he heard of Joseph Smith. He pursued his interest in Joseph Smith and his "golden book" and finally ended up at E. B. Grandin's printing shop in Palmyra, New York, where the Book of Mormon was in the process of being printed. He met Martin Harris there, who gave him proof sheets of the first sixteen printed pages of the Book of Mormon.

Martin took Thomas to the Smith home in Manchester, next to Palmyra, where Oliver Cowdery spent the better part of two days telling Thomas about Joseph Smith and the restoration of the gospel. After this, Thomas returned to Boston, Massachusetts, where he taught his family what he had learned. Soon, the family moved with him to Palmyra, where he was baptized. In section 31, verse 3, he is called on a mission.

It will be helpful, by way of perspective and hindsight as we study section 31, to know that Brother Marsh was warned in advance by the Lord in this revelation, especially in verse 9, about keeping his own household in proper order and to "revile not against those that revile." If followed, this advice may well have kept him from leaving the Church and being excommunicated on March 17, 1839. He returned to the Church, although it was much later in his life, on July 16, 1857, in Florence, Nebraska. He came to the Salt Lake Valley and later settled in Ogden, about 35 miles north of Salt Lake City, where he died in poverty and broken health in January 1866.

A rather well-known incident in the life of Thomas Marsh that reflects the need for the counsel given in verse 9, was an argument that developed between His wife, Elizabeth, and Lucinda Harris, wife of George W. Harris, over milk strippings. Sister Marsh and Sister Harris made an agreement with each other in August 1838 to exchange milk, including the last of the milk, or "strippings" from their cows (which contains more cream than the first of the milking) so that each would have the cream needed for making cheese. Apostle George A. Smith, speaking of the importance of not letting little irritations in life develop into prideful battles, used this situation of milk strippings to illustrate his point as follows:

"You may think that these small matters amount to but little, but sometimes it happens that out of a small matter grows something exceedingly great. For instance, while the Saints were living in Far West, there were two sisters wishing to make cheese, and, neither of them possessing the requisite number of cows, they agreed to exchange milk.

"The wife of Thomas B. Marsh, who was then President of the Twelve Apostles, and sister Harris concluded they would exchange milk, in order to make a little larger cheese than they otherwise could. To be sure to have justice done, it was agreed that they should not save the strippings, but that the milk and strippings should all go together. Small matters to talk about here, to be sure, two women's exchanging milk to make cheese.

"Mrs. Harris, it appeared, was faithful to the agreement and carried to Mrs. Marsh the milk and strippings, but Mrs. Marsh, wishing to make some extra good cheese, saved a pint of strippings from each cow and sent Mrs. Harris the milk without the strippings.

"Finally it leaked out that Mrs. Marsh had saved strippings, and it became a matter to be settled by the Teachers. They began to examine the matter, and it was proved that Mrs. Marsh had saved the strippings, and consequently had wronged Mrs. Harris out of that amount.

"An appeal was taken from the Teacher to the Bishop, and a regular Church trial was had. President Marsh did not consider that the Bishop had done him and his lady justice, for they decided that the strippings were wrongfully saved, and that the woman had violated her covenant.

"Marsh immediately took an appeal to the High Council, who investigated the question with much patience, and I assure you they were a grave body. Marsh being extremely anxious to maintain the character of his wife, as he was the President of the Twelve Apostles, and a great man in Israel, made a desperate defense, but the High Council finally confirmed the Bishop's decision.

"Marsh, not being satisfied, took an appeal to the First Presidency of the Church, and Joseph and his Counsellors had to sit upon the case, and they approved the decision of the High Council.

"This little affair, you will observe, kicked up a considerable breeze, and Thomas B. Marsh then declared that he would sustain the character of his wife, even if he had to go to hell for it.

"The then President of the Twelve Apostles, the man who should have been the first to do justice and cause reparation to be made for wrong, committed by any member of his family, took that position, and what next? He went before a magistrate and swore that the 'Mormons' were hostile towards the State of Missouri.

"That affidavit brought from the government of Missouri an exterminating order, which drove some 15,000 Saints from their homes and habitations, and some thousands perished through suffering the exposure consequent on this state of affairs.

"Do you understand what trouble was consequent to the dispute about a pint of strippings?" (Talk by George A. Smith, *Journal of Discourses*, 3:283).

Remember, Brother Marsh did return to the Church, a reminder that the mercy of the Lord is constantly extended to us, but he paid a bitter price for pride and for not following the Lord's counsel regarding his family in this revelation. We are reminded that although we obtain promises from the Lord by way of blessings, including patriarchal blessings, there is still an obligation for us to do our part in order for the blessings to be fulfilled.

We will now proceed to study section 31.

1 **THOMAS**, my son [*a term of tenderness and endearment*], blessed are you because of your faith in my work.

2 Behold, **you have had many afflictions because of your family**; nevertheless, **I will bless you and your family**, yea, your little ones; and the day cometh that they will believe and know the truth and be one with you in my church.

3 Lift up your heart and rejoice, for **the hour of your mission is come**; and your tongue shall be loosed [*you will be given power and skill in teaching and preaching*], and **you shall declare glad tidings of great joy unto this generation**.

4 You shall declare the things

which have been revealed to my servant, Joseph Smith, Jun. You shall begin to preach from this time forth, yea, to reap in the field which is white already to be burned.

5 Therefore, thrust in your sickle with all your soul, and **your sins are forgiven you** [*you are given a fresh start*], and **you shall be laden with sheaves upon your back** [*you will have a good harvest of souls brought into the Church*], for the laborer is worthy of his hire [*the laborers in the Church must earn their keep*]. Wherefore, your family shall live.

"Sheaves," in verse 5, above, are grain stalks at harvest time, which have been bundled in order to make it easier to carry them to the threshing floor for harvest. They are symbolic of the "harvest" of souls being brought into the Lord's Church, as well as souls in the Church being brought to Christ.

6 Behold, verily I say unto you, go from them [*your family*] only for a little time, and declare my word [*preach the gospel*], and I will prepare a place for them.

7 Yea, **I will open the hearts of the people, and they will receive you**. And I will establish a church [*branches of the Church*] by your hand;

8 And **you shall strengthen them and prepare them** against the time [*for the time*] when they shall be gathered.

As mentioned previously, following the counsel of the Lord, given in verse 9, next, would have spared Thomas B. Marsh much agony.

9 **Be patient in afflictions, revile not against those that revile. Govern your house in meekness, and be steadfast.**

10 Behold, I say unto you that you shall be a physician unto the church, but not unto the world [*the worldly*], for they will not receive you.

11 Go your way whithersoever I will, and **it shall be given you by the Comforter** [*the Holy Ghost*] **what you shall do and whither you shall go.**

12 **Pray always, lest you enter into temptation and lose your reward**.

13 **Be faithful unto the end**, and lo, I am with you. **These words are not of man nor of men, but of me, even Jesus Christ**, your Redeemer, by the will of the Father [*Jesus always gives credit to the Father*]. Amen.

SECTION 32

Background

Section 32 is a revelation given through the Prophet Joseph Smith in October 1830 to Parley P. Pratt and Ziba Peterson. In verses 2 and 3, these two men will be called to join with Oliver Cowdery and Peter Whitmer Jr., who have already been called to prepare to go on a mission to the Lamanites (see D&C 28:8 and 30:5). These faithful brethren will depart on their mission from Fayette, New York, on October 18, 1830, for what will be about a 1,500-mile journey to Independence, Missouri, and a little beyond to the Indian lands. Among many others, Sidney Rigdon will be brought into the Church as a result of this mission.

Parley Parker Pratt was born April 12, 1807, and was baptized by Oliver Cowdery early in September 1830 after having read the Book of Mormon straight through. He was ordained an elder shortly after his baptism.

Some years prior to this, while still in his teens, Parley had become disgusted with society, purchased a Bible and an axe, and had moved west to the frontier, where he spent the winter alone, eating venison, studying his Bible, and reading about the Lewis and Clark expedition.

The Lord managed to get Parley back into society by having him think of a girl he liked back home in New York. He went to see her, and they married and moved back to his cabin. The frontier continued moving west, and so society caught up with him and his wife. They turned the cabin into a pleasant home and met others as they came west and settled in the area.

Among others, Parley met a Campbellite preacher and minister named Sidney Rigdon, whose views about religion matched his very nicely. Sidney felt strongly that there needed to be a return to the New Testament Church established by Christ. He also had a concern as to whether or not the proper authority to perform ordinances was even upon the earth any more. They became good friends and often studied and preached together. On this mission to the Lamanites, Parley would meet his old friend Sidney, who, by this time, was minister to a large congregation in Mentor, Ohio, not far from Kirtland. Sidney Rigdon and a large number of his congregation would be converted to the gospel, and in fact, as a result, the center of population for the Church would soon end up being in the Kirtland area. (For more information and fascinating reading, see *Autobiography of Parley P. Pratt*, edited by Parley P. Pratt Jr., Deseret Book, 1985.)

Ziba Peterson was baptized on April 18, 1830, and was probably in his late teens or early twenties at the time. He was ordained an elder not long thereafter, at least by June 1830.

As mentioned above, Parley Pratt and Ziba Peterson would be called by the Lord to join with Oliver Cowdery and Peter Whitmer Jr. in preaching to the Indians in western lands.

1 AND **now concerning my servant Parley P. Pratt**, behold, I say unto him that as I live **I will that he shall declare my gospel and learn of me, and be meek and lowly of heart**.

2 And that which I have appointed unto him is that **he shall go with my servants, Oliver Cowdery and Peter Whitmer, Jun., into the wilderness among the Lamanites**.

3 And **Ziba Peterson also shall go with them**; and **I myself will go with them and be in their midst**; and I am their advocate with the Father, and nothing shall prevail against them.

It is most comforting and encouraging, in verse 3, above, to learn that the Savior spends time with His missionaries.

Next, in verses 4 and 5, the Savior gives counsel that applies to all missionaries today; namely, to stick with the scriptures in their teaching.

4 And they shall **give heed to that which is written**, and **pretend to no other revelation**; and they shall pray always that I may unfold the same to their understanding.

5 And they shall **give heed unto these words** and **trifle not**, and I will bless them. Amen.

Here we will include a summary of this missionary journey to the Lamanites, taken from the Sunday School Gospel Doctrine teacher's supplement for 1978:

"The Lamanite missionaries commenced their work with the Cattaraugus tribe near Buffalo, New York. Here they were fairly well received, and after leaving copies of the Book of Mormon they continued their journey west. They took a slight detour to teach the gospel to a minister friend of Parley P. Pratt and his congregation near Kirtland, Ohio . . . What must have been thought to be a diversion from their mission turned out to be a major accomplishment. Here lived Sidney Rigdon, a Reformed Baptist preacher. Parley P. Pratt was apparently convinced that with the feelings and beliefs that Sidney Rigdon held he would respond to the gospel message. He was not disappointed.

"Not only Sidney Rigdon but many of his congregation joined the Church. In a short period of time, 130 people were baptized into the

Church in that area, making it the largest single group of Latter-day Saints on the earth at the time. After introducing Sidney Rigdon and the others to the gospel, the missionaries pursued their journey west toward more populous Lamanite tribes. The missionaries now numbered five, with the addition of a convert from Kirtland, Frederick G. Williams. Their missionary labors were temporarily delayed with the arrest of Parley P. Pratt [*as part of the attempt to prevent the missionaries from further successes*] . . .

"The missionaries visited the Wyandot tribe at Sandusky, Ohio. From here they commenced the most difficult part of their journey through the wilderness, to the frontier village of Independence, Missouri . . .

"Upon arriving at Independence, two of the missionaries took work to help finance their mission while the other three continued a short distance to the Indian lands. Here it appeared they would have their greatest success among the Delaware Indians. Although the Indians were at first suspicious of the missionaries because they had been exploited by some previous Christian missionaries, this suspicion was soon alleviated by the moving address delivered by Oliver Cowdery . . .

"Chief Anderson of the Delaware Tribe was very impressed and asked the missionaries to remain during the winter and teach them the Book of Mormon. Success appeared imminent, but it was shattered when other Christian missionaries influenced the Indian agent to evict the Mormon elders from Indian lands. Asked to leave, the disappointed missionaries made their way back to Independence. Here they stayed, with the exception of Parley P. Pratt, who was chosen to report their labors to Joseph Smith and to visit the Saints they had left behind in Kirtland" (Doctrine and Covenants, section 1 through 102 [Sunday School Gospel Doctrine teacher's supplement, 1978], 69–70).

SECTION 33

Background

This section is a revelation given through Joseph Smith to Ezra Thayre and Northrop Sweet in October 1830 at Fayette, New York.

As you can see, at this point in the Restoration, the Lord is gathering individuals and giving them specific instructions as they embark to spread the gospel, establish the Church, and gather Israel for the last time in preparation for the Second Coming.

Ezra Thayre was born October 14, 1791, and was 14 years older than Joseph Smith. He was converted by the preaching of Hyrum Smith and was baptized by Parley P. Pratt in October 1830. After much faithful service in building the kingdom, accompanied by periods when he was out of harmony with the leaders of the Church, Ezra Thayre refused to follow the Twelve after the martyrdom of the Prophet Joseph Smith and ultimately ended up a high priest in the Reorganized Church of Jesus Christ of Latter Day Saints. (See Susan Easton Black's *Who's Who in the Doctrine and Covenants*, pages 318–21.)

We know very little about Northrop Sweet, other than that he was born in 1802 and was baptized in October 1830. He apostatized in 1831 and formed his own church, which had six members including himself, and which never grew beyond that number.

In this revelation, we will see a number of things that apply to us. We will bold them now and then come back to do a bit more.

1 BEHOLD, I say unto you, my servants Ezra and Northrop, **open ye your ears** and **hearken to the voice of the Lord your God**, whose word is quick and powerful, sharper than a two-edged sword, to the dividing asunder of the joints and marrow, soul and spirit; and is a discerner of the thoughts and intents of the heart.

2 For verily, verily, I say unto you that ye are called to **lift up your voices** as with the sound of a trump, to declare my gospel unto a crooked and perverse generation.

3 For behold, the field is white already to harvest; and **it is the eleventh hour**, and **the last time that I shall call laborers into my vineyard**.

4 And **my vineyard has become corrupted every whit**; and **there is none which doeth good save it be a few**; and **they err in many instances because of priestcrafts**, all having corrupt minds.

5 And verily, verily, I say unto you, that **this church have I established** and called forth out of the wilderness.

6 And **even so will I gather mine elect** from the four quarters of the earth, even as many as will believe in me, and hearken unto my voice.

7 Yea, verily, verily, I say unto you, that **the field is white already to harvest**; wherefore, thrust in your sickles, and reap with all your might, mind, and strength.

8 **Open your mouths** and they shall be filled, and you shall become even as Nephi of old, who journeyed from Jerusalem in the wilderness.

9 **Yea, open your mouths** and

spare not, and you shall be laden with sheaves upon your backs, for lo, I am with you.

10 Yea, **open your mouths** and they shall be filled, saying: Repent, repent, and prepare ye the way of the Lord, and make his paths straight; for the kingdom of heaven is at hand;

11 Yea, repent and be baptized, every one of you, for a remission of your sins; yea, be baptized even by water, and then cometh the baptism of fire and of the Holy Ghost.

12 Behold, verily, verily, I say unto you, this is my gospel; and remember that they shall have faith in me or they can in nowise be saved;

13 And upon this rock I will build my church; yea, upon this rock ye are built, and if ye continue, the gates of hell shall not prevail against you.

14 And **ye shall remember the church articles and covenants to keep them**.

15 And **whoso having faith you shall confirm** in my church, by the laying on of the hands, **and I will bestow the gift of the Holy Ghost upon them**.

16 And **the Book of Mormon and the holy scriptures are given of me for your instruction**; and the power of my Spirit quickeneth all things.

17 Wherefore, **be faithful, praying always, having your lamps trimmed and burning, and oil with you**, that you may be ready at the coming of the Bridegroom—

18 For behold, verily, verily, I say unto you, that **I come quickly**. Even so. Amen.

We will now repeat the above verses and add some notes and commentary. As you perhaps noticed, there are a number of words and phrases that require a person to be familiar with the scriptures already in order to best understand them. We will add notes in brackets for a number of these.

1 BEHOLD, I say unto you, my servants Ezra and Northrop, **open ye your ears** [*listen carefully; pay attention*] and **hearken to the voice of the Lord your God**, whose word is quick [*living; consists of on-going revelation*] and powerful, sharper than a two-edged sword [*symbolic of being effective in all directions*], to the dividing asunder [*cutting apart*] of the joints and marrow [*literally, butchering an animal; symbolically, getting to the very essence of life*], soul and spirit;

and is a discerner [*one who knows*] of the thoughts and intents of the heart.

2 For verily, verily, I say unto you that ye are called to **lift up your voices** [*preach the gospel; let others hear your testimony*] as with the sound of a trump [*symbolic of pure, easy to understand, easy to pick out from the "noise" of the world*], **to declare my gospel unto a crooked and perverse generation** [*wicked people who pervert truth and do not walk the "strait and narrow" path*].

3 For behold, the field is white already to harvest; and **it is the eleventh hour** [*the Second Coming is getting close*], and **the last time that I shall call laborers into my vineyard** [*this is the last Restoration before the Second Coming*].

4 And **my vineyard** [*the world*] **has become corrupted every whit** [*every bit*]; and **there is none which doeth good save it be a few**; and **they err in many instances because of priestcrafts** [*in other words, they don't have the truth available to them*], all having corrupt minds.

5 And verily, verily, I say unto you, that **this church have I established** and called forth out of the wilderness [*out of apostasy*].

6 And **even so will I gather mine elect** [*among other things, those who are the noble and great from the premortal life who have been "planted" throughout the earth and will respond to the gospel message and gather with the Saints*] from the four quarters of the earth [*from all over the world*], **even as many as will believe in me, and hearken** [*listen and obey*] **unto my voice**.

7 Yea, verily, verily, I say unto you, that **the field is white already to harvest**; wherefore, thrust in your sickles [*go to work harvesting*], and reap with all your might, mind, and strength.

Next, in verses 8–10, the Lord reminds all of us of the importance of our being willing to "open our mouths" and teach the gospel. Many baptisms have been delayed because an acquaintance was afraid to "open his or her mouth." Notice that in the next three verses, the Savior says "Open your mouths" three times. In Biblical symbolism, saying something three times means that it is most important!

8 **Open your mouths** and they shall be filled [*with what you should say, by the Holy Ghost*], and you shall become even as Nephi of old [*a most powerful promise!*], who journeyed from Jerusalem in the wilderness.

9 **Yea, open your mouths** and spare not [*don't hold back*], and you shall be laden with sheaves upon your backs [*you will have much success, a bounteous "harvest" of souls; see Alma 26:5*], for lo, I am with you.

Since the phrase "laden with sheaves" is often used in scripture, we will take a moment and quote from Alma (as Ammon rejoices in the missionary work accomplished during their missions to the Lamanites) in order to explain this imagery. It deals with harvesting.

Alma 26:5

Behold, the field was ripe [*the missionary opportunities were abundant*], and blessed are ye, for ye did thrust in the sickle [*you went on missions*], and did reap [*harvest*] with your might, yea, all the day long did ye labor; and **behold the number of your sheaves** [*look at your bounteous harvest*]! And they [*the converts*] shall be gathered into the garners [*the storage bins, the Lord's barns; in other words, the celestial kingdom, to be with God forever*], that they are not wasted.

10 Yea, **open your mouths** and they shall be filled, saying: Repent, repent, and prepare ye the way of the Lord, and make his paths straight [*apply the ways of God in your lives; walk the "strait and narrow"*]; for the kingdom of heaven is at hand [*the gospel is here now and available to you*];

11 Yea, **repent and be baptized**, every one of you, **for a remission of your sins**; yea, be baptized even by water, and **then cometh the baptism of fire** [*symbolic of the Holy Ghost's burning the sin and impurities out of you*] **and of the Holy Ghost**.

12 Behold, verily, verily, I say unto you, **this is my gospel** [*repentance, baptism, gift of the Holy Ghost, faith (mentioned next, in this verse)*]; and remember that they shall have **faith in me** or they can in nowise be saved;

13 And upon this rock [*the gospel of Jesus Christ; Christ Himself*] I will build my church; yea, upon this rock ye are built [*you are building your lives upon the true Church*], and if ye continue, the gates of hell shall not prevail against you [*Satan and his evil hosts will not ultimately take you away from God*].

14 And **ye shall remember the church articles and covenants** [*the things given in section 20*] **to keep them**.

Next, these missionaries are reminded that they have the authority to confirm baptized converts as members of the Church, by the laying on of hands, and to bestow the gift of the Holy Ghost.

15 And whoso having faith **you shall confirm** in my church, **by the laying on of the hands** [*a specific, tangible ordinance, rather than just a "feeling"*], **and I will bestow the gift of the Holy Ghost upon them.**

We need to be aware that when we are confirmed and given the gift of the Holy Ghost, it still doesn't necessarily come upon us until we "receive" it and the Lord gives it to us. In other words, the gift of the Holy Ghost is not necessarily "automatic" after hands have been laid upon our heads. The Bible Dictionary, at the back of your LDS Bible, addresses this issue as follows:

Bible Dictionary under "Holy Ghost"

"The gift of the Holy Ghost is the right to have, whenever one is worthy, the companionship of the Holy Ghost."

16 And the Book of Mormon and the holy scriptures are given of me for your instruction; and the power of my Spirit quickeneth all things [*makes all things come alive in our understanding*].

17 Wherefore, **be faithful, praying always, having your lamps** [*symbolic of our lives*] **trimmed** [*a reference to the Parable of the Ten Virgins in Matthew 25:1–13*] **and burning, and oil with you, that you may be ready at the coming of the Bridegroom** [*the coming of Christ*]—

Perhaps you've noticed when you've read the Parable of the Ten Virgins, that all ten of the virgins had oil in their lamps. The problem came when five of them did not have a reserve supply of oil. These "reserves" come from faithfully living and keeping covenants. Those who do so have the "reserve" strength and spiritual stamina to remain faithful when it takes longer than they thought for the Savior to come into their lives and rescue them from difficulties.

18 For behold, verily, verily, I say unto you, that **I come quickly** [*not "I come soon"; rather, "when I come, it will be quickly, and there will be no time left for you to prepare to meet Me"*]. Even so. Amen.

SECTION 34

Background

This revelation was given through Joseph Smith to Orson Pratt, younger brother of Parley P. Pratt, in the Peter Whitmer Sr. home on November 4, 1830, at Fayette,

New York. Orson was born September 19, 1811, was baptized on his 19th birthday, September 19, 1830, and had been a member of the Church just six weeks when this revelation was given.

The Prophet recorded the following as background to this section:

"In the fore part of November, Orson Pratt, a young man nineteen years of age, who had been baptized at the first preaching of his brother, Parley P. Pratt, September 19th (his birthday), about six weeks previous, in Canaan, New York, came to inquire of the Lord what his duty was, and received the following answer [section 34]:" (*History of the Church,* 1:127–28).

Orson Pratt wrote in his journal about receiving this revelation as follows:

"In October, 1830, I traveled westward over two hundred miles to see Joseph Smith the Prophet. I found him in Fayette, Seneca County, New York, residing at the home of Mr. Whitmer. I soon became intimately acquainted with this good man, and also with the witnesses of the Book of Mormon. By my request, on the 4th of November, the Prophet Joseph inquired of the Lord for me and received the revelation published in the Doctrine and Covenants, Section 34" (Journal History, Nov. 1830, 1).

In verses 1–3, the Savior personally introduces Himself to Orson Pratt.

1 **MY son Orson, hearken and hear and behold what I, the Lord God, shall say unto you, even Jesus Christ your Redeemer**;

2 **The light and the life of the world, a light which shineth in darkness and the darkness comprehendeth it not**;

3 **Who so loved the world that he gave his own life, that as many as would believe might become the sons of God** [*"sons of God" is a scriptural term that means "exalted"; see Mosiah 5:7, D&C 76:24, D&C 25:1, Moses 6:64–68*]. **Wherefore you are my son**;

Next, in verses 4–6, the Lord issues the call for Orson Pratt to serve as a missionary.

4 And **blessed are you because you have believed**;

5 And more blessed are you [*you are going to receive additional blessings*] because **you are called of me to preach my gospel**—

6 To lift up your voice as with the sound of a trump, both long and loud, **and cry repentance unto a crooked and perverse generation, preparing the way**

of the Lord for his second coming.

Next, in verse 7, we are taught that the Second Coming of Christ is getting close.

7 For behold, verily, verily, I say unto you, **the time is soon at hand that I shall come in a cloud with power and great glory.**

Perhaps you've wondered why the scriptures say that Christ will come in a "cloud." In scriptural symbolism, "cloud" represents the presence and glory of the Lord, as in Exodus 13:21, where the Children of Israel were led by a cloud during the day, and as in Exodus 16:10, where the glory of the Lord appeared in the cloud. Also, when the Savior ascended into heaven, He was taken up into a cloud, and His Apostles were told that He would "so come in like manner as ye have seen him go into heaven." (See Acts 1:9–11. In D&C 84:5, the "cloud" is the "glory of the Lord.")

Thus, when we read that the Savior will come in clouds of glory, the clouds symbolize His presence and His glory.

Next, in verse 8, we see that, in context, the "great day" spoken of at the time of the Lord's coming will be, in effect, a "great day" of trouble for the wicked; or, in other words, a "day of great fear and trembling."

8 And it shall be **a great day** at the time of my coming, **for all nations shall tremble.**

Next, the Savior reminds Orson Pratt that many signs of the times will be fulfilled before His coming. Remember, "signs of the times" are prophecies that will be fulfilled in the last days, alerting the faithful that the Second Coming is indeed getting close.

9 But **before that great day** shall come, the **sun shall be darkened**, and the **moon** be **turned into blood**; and the **stars shall refuse their shining**, and **some shall fall**, and **great destructions await the wicked.**

Having shown Orson why the world needs the gospel so badly, the Savior now calls him on a mission.

10 Wherefore [*for this reason*], **lift up your voice and spare not** [*don't hold back*], for the Lord God hath spoken; therefore **prophesy**, and it shall be given **by the power of the Holy Ghost.**

As you are aware, the blessings promised us by the Lord have an "if," reminding us that we, too, have things to do in order for them to be fulfilled. We see this in the Lord's instruction to Orson Pratt in verse 11, next.

11 And **if** you are faithful, behold, **I am with you** until I come—

12 And verily, verily, I say unto
you, I come quickly. I am your
Lord and your Redeemer. Even
so. Amen.

SECTION 35

Background

This revelation was given to Joseph Smith and Sidney Rigdon in the Fayette, New York, area in December 1830.

Sidney Rigdon was born on February 19, 1793, and was about 12 years older than the Prophet. Thus, at the time of this revelation, Joseph was about 25 years old and Sidney was 37. Brother Rigdon was described as being about five feet, nine and one-half inches tall, and at one time weighed about 215 pounds.

In the background to section 32, we mentioned that a highly successful and popular minister by the name of Sidney Rigdon, in Mentor, Ohio (near Kirtland), had been converted to the gospel, along with around 120–130 of his congregation. When approached by his old friend, Parley P. Pratt, and Parley's three missionary companions, who were enroute on their mission to the Lamanites, Sidney had accepted a copy of the Book of Mormon. In so doing, he told Parley not to push him, rather, that he would read the book and determine whether or not it was of God. He read it and was converted. He was baptized on November 14, 1830.

Once converted, Sidney realized that he would lose his lucrative job as a preacher in the Kirtland area. He asked his wife, Phoebe, if she was willing to follow him in this new religion, saying, "My Dear you have followed me once into poverty, are you again willing to do the same[?]" She responded, "I have weighed the matter, I have contemplated on the circumstances in which we may be placed, I have counted the cost, and I am perfectly satisfied to follow you. [Y]ea, it is my desire to do the will of God, come life or come death" (in *The Joseph Smith Papers, Documents, Volume 1: July 1828–June 1831*, 213, note 91).

Soon after his baptism, he traveled to Fayette, New York, along with another convert from his congregation, Edward Partridge, to see the Prophet Joseph Smith. At this time, the Prophet was working on the translation of the Bible (which we know today as the Joseph Smith Translation of the Bible or the "JST"). Oliver Cowdery and John Whitmer had been serving as scribes for Joseph during this work of translation but had both been called on missions (Oliver Cowdery in D&C 28:8, John Whitmer in D&C 30:9–11), which left the Prophet without a scribe. In verse 20 of this section, Sidney Rigdon is called to fill this vacancy and serve as scribe.

As has been previously stated, Sidney was a very effective preacher and a successful minister, having attracted large numbers of people to his congregation, many of whom joined the Church when he did. Thus, in verse 4 of this section, Brother Rigdon is compared to John the Baptist, having prepared the way for Joseph Smith in the same sense that John the Baptist prepared the way for the Savior.

In verses 1 and 2, the Savior introduces Himself to Sidney Rigdon.

1 **LISTEN to the voice of the Lord your God**, even Alpha and Omega [*the "A" and "Z" of the Greek alphabet*], the beginning and the end, whose course is one eternal round [*He always uses the same gospel to bring salvation to people; the same principles of faith, repentance, baptism, gift of the Holy Ghost, ordinances, and so on*], the same today as yesterday, and forever.

2 **I am Jesus Christ**, the Son of God, who was crucified for the sins of the world, even as many as will **believe on my name** [*part of the "one eternal round" spoken of in verse 1, above*], **that they may become the sons of God** [*a scriptural term meaning attaining exaltation*], even one in me [*united in complete harmony with Christ*] as I am one in the Father [*united, working in complete harmony with the Father*], as the Father is one in me, that we may be one.

Next, the Savior reminds Sidney that He has been watching over him and knows of his past accomplishments. He has heard his prayers (no doubt including his prayers as to whether or not the Book of Mormon is true). He informs him that He has been preparing him for the work that now lies before him.

3 Behold, verily, verily, I say unto my servant Sidney, **I have looked upon thee and thy works. I have heard thy prayers, and prepared thee for a greater work**.

Imagine how Sidney Rigdon must have felt as he heard the next words addressed to him by the Savior! The Lord tells him, in verses 4–5, next, that he has been preparing the way, just like John the Baptist did for Jesus, but Sidney wasn't aware of it. This is a reminder to all of us that we are often prompted and led by the Lord to do something without even being aware that we are being inspired.

4 Thou art blessed, for thou shalt do great things. Behold **thou wast sent forth, even as John** [*John the Baptist*], **to prepare the way before me, and before Elijah** which should come, **and thou knewest it not**.

Did you notice in verse 4, above, that the Savior also mentioned that Sidney was sent to prepare the way for Elijah to come? He appeared in the Kirtland Temple on April 3, 1836, and restored the keys of sealing (D&C 110:13–15).

Next, the Lord addresses the issue of proper priesthood authority to perform saving ordinances of the gospel.

5 **Thou didst baptize by water** unto repentance, **but they received not the Holy Ghost**;

6 But **now** [*as a member of the Church, with proper priesthood authority*] I give unto thee a commandment, that **thou shalt baptize by water, and they shall receive the Holy Ghost** by the laying on of the hands, even as the apostles of old.

Joseph Fielding Smith wrote about verses 5 and 6 as follows:

"The Lord told Sidney that he had looked upon him and his works, having reference to his ministry as a Baptist and later as one of the founders of the 'Disciples' with Alexander Campbell and Walter Scott. During those years the hand of the Lord was over him and directing him in the gathering of many earnest souls who could not accept the teachings of the sects of the day. His prayers in which he sought further light than the world was able to give, were now to be answered. The Lord informed him that he had been sent to prepare the way, and in the gathering of his colony and the building up of his congregation in and around Kirtland, the hand of the Lord was directing him, and the way for the reception of the fulness of truth was being prepared. It should be carefully noted that a great number of forceful, intelligent men who became leaders in the Church had been gathered by Sidney Rigdon, with the help of the Lord, in this part of the land. Without any question, the Spirit of the Lord had rested upon these men, as it did on Sidney Rigdon and Parley P. Pratt, to direct them to gather in Kirtland at that early day. When, therefore, Parley P. Pratt, Ziba Peterson and their companions came to Kirtland they found the way prepared for them through the preaching, very largely, of Sidney Rigdon, so that it was not a difficult matter for these missionaries to convince this group of the truth. While Sidney was preaching and baptizing by immersion without authority, which the Lord informed him in this revelation, yet it all resulted in good when the Gospel message reached them. These men were not only convinced and ready for baptism, but were in a condition by which the Priesthood could be given them, and this was done" (*Church History and Modern Revelation*, 1:160).

Next, the Lord gives Sidney a perspective of the magnitude and importance of the Restoration, in which Sidney would now be a significant participant.

7 And it shall come to pass that **there shall be a great work in the land**, even **among the Gentiles**, for their folly and their abominations shall be made manifest in the eyes of all people.

The word "Gentile," as used in verse 7, above, generally refers to anyone who does not have the true gospel of Jesus Christ. Let's look at the Bible Dictionary in the back of our Latter-day Saint scriptures for the definition of Gentile.

Bible Dictionary, under "Gentile"

"As used throughout the scriptures it has a dual meaning, sometimes to designate peoples of non-Israelite lineage and **other times to designate nations that are without the gospel, even though there may be some Israelite blood therein.** This latter usage is especially characteristic of the word as used in the Book of Mormon."

You may wish to read more definitions of "Gentile" in your Bible Dictionary.

8 For I am God, and mine arm is not shortened [*I haven't lost My power*]; and **I will show miracles, signs, and wonders, unto all those who believe on my name.**

Elder Dallin H. Oaks taught about two types of miracles as follows: "First, miracles worked by the power of the priesthood are always present in the true Church of Jesus Christ. The Book of Mormon teaches that 'God has provided a means that man, through faith, might work mighty miracles' (Mosiah 8:18). The 'means' provided is priesthood power (see James 5:14–15; D&C 42:43–48), and that power works miracles through faith (see Ether 12:12; Moro. 7:37). . . .

"A second type of genuine miracle is the miracle worked through the power of faith, without specifically invoking the power of the priesthood. Many of these miracles occur in our Church, such as by the prayers of faithful women, and many occur outside it. As Nephi taught, God 'manifesteth himself unto all those who believe in him, by the power of the Holy Ghost; yea, unto every nation, kindred, tongue, and people, working mighty miracles, signs, and wonders, among the children of men according to their faith' (2 Ne. 26:13; see also 1 Ne. 7:12; James 5:15)" ("Miracles," *Ensign*, June 2001, 8–9).

Elder Oaks further explained why some miracles may not happen even when our faith is sufficient:

"I have been speaking of miracles that happen. What about miracles that don't happen? Most of us have offered prayers that were not answered with the miracle we requested at the time we desired. Miracles are not available for the asking. . . . The will of the Lord is always paramount. The priesthood of the Lord cannot be used to work a miracle contrary to the will of the Lord. We must also remember that even when a miracle is to occur, it will not occur on our desired schedule. The revelations teach that miraculous experiences occur 'in his own time, and in his own way' (D&C 88:68)" ("Miracles," 9).

As the Savior continues to give Brother Rigdon this perspective of the latter-day work that is about to come forth, He reminds him that the same miracles that followed the true Church in past dispensations will be present in this last dispensation.

9 And whoso shall ask it in my name in faith, **they shall cast out devils**; they shall **heal the sick**; they shall **cause the blind to receive their sight**, and **the deaf to hear**, and **the dumb** [*a person who is unable to talk*] **to speak**, and **the lame to walk.**

10 And the time speedily cometh that **great things are to be shown forth** unto the children of men [*in other words, there will be plenty of evidence for the honest in heart that the gospel is true*];

The word, "faith," in verse 11, next, must be looked upon as "faith in the Lord Jesus Christ" in order to make sense in this context. The basic message is that without faith in Christ, which involves following Him and keeping His commandments, nothing is ultimately left for society except wickedness and disaster.

11 But **without faith shall not anything be shown forth except desolations upon Babylon** [*symbolic of Satan's kingdom and the intense wickedness that goes with it*], the same **which has made all nations drink of the wine of the wrath of her fornication.**

We will take a moment to analyze the phrase "drink of the wine of the wrath of her fornication," in verse 11, above. "Fornication," in this context, means perverting the ways of God and being thus involved in deep and gross wickedness. Its definition comes from "fornication," as in sexual transgression, in which the powers of procreation (which are holy, good, and proper within the protective bonds of marriage) are perverted, misused, and put to evil designs and purposes, leading to destruction of spirituality.

The word "adultery" is also often used the same way in the scriptures; that is, meaning wickedness and breaking God's commandments. We will quote from the Bible Dictionary in the back of your LDS Bible (**bold** added for emphasis):

Bible Dictionary under "Adultery"

"**Adultery.** The unlawful association of men and women. Although generally having reference to illicit activity of married persons, the scripture often does not distinguish between the married and the unmarried. While adultery is usually spoken of in the individual sense, **it is sometimes used to illustrate the apostasy of a nation or a whole people from the ways of the Lord**, such as Israel forsaking her God and going after strange gods and strange practices (Ex. 20:14; Jer. 3:7–10; Matt. 5:27–32; Luke 18:11; D&C 43:24–25). Severe penalties were given in the O.T. for adultery (Lev. 20:10); and unrepentant adulterers will suffer the judgments of God in the world to come (Heb. 13:4; Rev. 18:3–18; D&C 76:103)."

Now, with the above definitions in place, we will repeat the last half of verse 11, adding notes.

Verse 11, last half

. . . **the same** [*Satan's kingdom, Babylon*] **which has made all nations** [*the wicked throughout the world, throughout history*] **drink** [*participate in*] **of the wine** [*the temptations*] **of the wrath** [*the destructive power*] **of her** [*Satan's kingdom, the "whore of all the earth" (1 Nephi 14:10)*] **fornication** [*sin, wickedness, rebellion, etc.; Satan's intentional perversion of righteousness*].

Finally, we will just mention that Babylon was a huge, wicked city in ancient times, and thus came to be symbolic of Satan's kingdom. The city of Babylon was surrounded by 56 miles of walls that were 335 feet high and 85 feet wide. See Bible Dictionary under "Babylon or Babel."

Continuing, in verses 12 through 15, next, the Lord explains that He will use "the weak things of the world" to spread His gospel, and that they will be successful. This is a comforting reminder that all of us, regardless of intellect and educational background, can be effective instruments in the hands of the Lord.

12 And there are none that doeth good except those who are ready to receive the fulness of my gospel, which I have sent forth unto this generation [*the Restoration through the Prophet Joseph Smith*].

13 Wherefore, **I call upon the weak things of the world**, those who are unlearned and despised, to thrash the nations by the power of my Spirit;

14 And **their arm shall be my arm**, and **I will be their shield and their buckler**; **and I will gird up their loins** [*I will prepare them for battle*], and they shall fight manfully for me; and **their enemies shall be under their feet** [*they will succeed; the gospel will go forth*]; and **I will let fall the sword in their behalf** [*I will defend them*], and **by the fire of mine indignation** [*the Lord's righteous anger*] **will I preserve them.**

15 And **the poor and the meek shall have the gospel preached unto them**, and they shall be looking forth for the time of **my coming**, for it **is nigh at hand**—

Next, the Lord uses a parable that Sidney Rigdon no doubt knows well. Perhaps he has used it in his preaching over many years. It deals with how people can know that the Second Coming of Christ is getting close. Sidney would know what it means when the Lord says, "summer is nigh."

16 And they shall learn **the parable of the fig-tree**, for even now already **summer is nigh**.

We will take a moment and quote the parable of the fig-tree. It is a reference to the signs of the times, which will alert the faithful that the Second Coming is getting close. There are several places in scripture where this parable is given. We will use Matthew (**bold** added for emphasis):

Matthew 24:32–33

32 Now learn a parable of **the fig tree**; **When** his branch is yet tender, and **putteth forth leaves, ye know that summer *is* nigh**:

33 So likewise ye, **when ye shall see all these things, know that it** [*the Second Coming of Christ*] **is near, *even* at the doors.**

With this in mind, Sidney Rigdon can sense the urgency of the work to which he is now being called by the Savior; namely, to assist Joseph Smith in the spreading forth of the restored gospel of Jesus Christ. Sidney will be reminded, in verses 17–19, next, that Joseph has weaknesses too.

As you can imagine, it might be difficult for an accomplished gospel scholar and minister like Sidney Rigdon, who is 37 years old, to work under the direction of a 25-year-old Prophet whose weaknesses and inexperience he may well notice. This is certainly a reminder for all of us that our leaders are not perfect, yet we are commanded to sustain them and support them in the work to which they have been called. It is perhaps one of the greatest miracles of all that in the work of saving souls, the Lord does a perfect work with imperfect people.

17 And **I have sent forth the fulness of my gospel by the hand of my servant Joseph**; and **in weakness have I blessed him**;

18 And **I have given unto him the keys** [*he is the Prophet*] of the mystery of those things which have been sealed [*such as the Book of Mormon*], even things which were from the foundation of the world, and the things which shall come from this time until the time of my coming [*I will continue to reveal things to My Prophet*], **if he abide in me** [*if he remains faithful*], and **if not, another will I plant in his stead.**

Did you notice that we have a guarantee from the Lord, Himself, in verse 18, above, that He will not let the Prophet lead us astray? In effect, at the last of verse 18, we are taught that if the Prophet were ever to depart from the Lord, He would remove him and replace him. Thus, we are always completely safe in following our living Prophet.

Next, we feel the tenderness of the Lord as He instructs the much older and much more experienced Sidney Rigdon to "watch over" His young Prophet.

19 Wherefore, **watch over him** that his faith fail not, and it shall be given by the Comforter, the Holy Ghost [*you will be helped in "watching over him" by the Holy Ghost*], that knoweth all things [*including Joseph's needs*].

Next, Sidney Rigdon will be called by the Lord to serve as a scribe for the Prophet as he continues to work on the Joseph Smith Translation of the Bible. Can you imagine how fascinating it would be for Sidney, who no doubt had come upon many questions about the Bible during his own studies of it, to sit in the presence of the Prophet of God and hear corrections to the Bible? Just think how many of his questions would be answered during this process!

20 And a commandment I give unto thee—that **thou shalt write** [*serve as a scribe*] **for him**; and the scriptures [*the inspired translation of the Bible*] shall be given, even as they are in mine own bosom [*the way that I gave them originally*], **to the salvation of mine own elect** [*the honest in heart, who recognize and respond to the gospel when they hear it; this also includes members of the Church as they continue to study the gospel*];

21 For **they will hear my voice**, and **shall see me**, and **shall not be asleep** [*as was the case in the parable of the 10 virgins (see Matthew 25:1–13), in other words, will not be caught unprepared*], and **shall abide the day of my coming** [*they will not be burned at the Second Coming*]; **for they shall be purified** [*by the gospel and the Atonement, such that they can be in His presence when He comes in full glory*], **even as I am pure** [*through the Atonement of Christ, we can become as pure and clean as the Savior Himself*].

Next, Sidney is instructed to remain for a time in Fayette with the Prophet and to accompany him in his travels.

22 And now I say unto you, **tarry with him**, and he shall journey with you; **forsake him not**, and surely these things [*the things spoken of in this revelation*] shall be fulfilled.

Next, Sidney is given a brief but concise lesson in what the Prophet's role is and what his own role is. Joseph can "prophesy," but Sidney is limited to "preaching" and explaining what the living Prophet has revealed.

Perhaps you've noticed that it is the same today. The role of our living Prophet includes that of revealing new doctrine, whereas, all others are limited to explaining and clarifying existing revealed doctrine. This is one of the very significant safeguards for us to prevent deception. It is often the case that apostates claim new doctrines and revelations that change existing doctrines and the current order of the Church.

23 And inasmuch as ye do not write [*when you are not involved in being a scribe for the Prophet*], behold, **it shall be given unto him** [*Joseph Smith*] **to prophesy**; and **thou shalt preach** my gospel and call on the holy prophets [*use your knowledge of the teachings of ancient prophets in the Bible and the Book of Mormon*] **to prove his words**, as they shall be given him.

Next, the Lord gives Sidney an inkling of his potential for good if he follows this counsel.

24 **Keep all the commandments and covenants** [*including baptism*] **by which ye are bound**; and **I will cause the heavens to shake for your good**, and **Satan shall tremble** and **Zion shall rejoice upon the hills** [*symbolic of getting closer to heaven and God*] **and flourish**;

"Israel," as used in verse 25, next, refers to the "house of Israel," which means "descendants of Jacob (Israel)," which means "descendants of Abraham, Isaac, and Jacob," who are the Lord's covenant people (see Abraham 2:9–11). All who come into the Church by baptism, whether direct descendants of Israel or not, become covenant Israel and are on the covenant path that leads to exaltation.

25 And **Israel shall be saved** in mine own due time [*when the time is right*]; and **by the keys** [*the keys of the priesthood*] **which I have given shall they be led**, and **no more be confounded** [*confused or stopped in their progression toward exaltation*] **at all.**

26 **Lift up your hearts and be glad**, your redemption draweth nigh.

Have you noticed how many times the Lord tells these early Saints to be happy? This is counter to a commonly held notion, especially in the New England environment of Joseph Smith's day, that truly religious people were unsmiling and sour of disposition.

27 **Fear not, little flock**, the kingdom is yours until I come [*you will run the Church until I come to rule on earth for a thousand years*]. Behold, I come quickly. Even so. Amen.

SECTION 36

Background

This revelation was given to Edward Partridge through the Prophet Joseph Smith, near Fayette, New York, in December 1830. In the background notes given in this study guide for section 35, we mentioned that Sidney Rigdon was accompanied by Edward Partridge in coming to Fayette to meet the Prophet Joseph Smith personally.

Edward Partridge was born August 27, 1793, and thus was 37 years old when he met the 25-year-old Prophet in Fayette. By profession, he was a hatter (a maker of hats), having served a four-year apprenticeship and having become a journeyman hatter in Clinton, New York, by age twenty. He eventually moved to Painesville, Ohio, where he married his wife, Lydia, and owned his own hat shop, plus other property. He was a respected family man and business owner in 1830 when Oliver Cowdery, Parley P. Pratt, Peter Whitmer Jr., and Ziba Peterson came through on their 1,500-mile mission to the Lamanites, preaching the gospel as they went along.

Lydia was baptized, but Edward was not favorably impressed at first by the message of these missionaries. However, he did send an employee to get a copy of the Book of Mormon for him to read. As he read, he was converted, but did not agree to be baptized at this point.

After traveling with Sidney Rigdon to Fayette and meeting Joseph

Smith there, he listened to a talk by the Prophet and then agreed to be baptized if Joseph would baptize him. The Prophet agreed. Edward Partridge was thus baptized on December 11, 1830, and ordained an elder four days later on December 15. Within three days of his return to his home in Ohio, near the first of February 1831, he would be called to be the first Bishop of the Church (see D&C 41:9).

The Prophet gave a brief description of Edward Partridge as follows (**bold** added for emphasis):

"In December Sidney Rigdon came to inquire of the Lord, and with him came **Edward Partridge**, the latter was **a pattern of piety**, and **one of the Lord's great men.** Shortly after the arrival of these two brethren, thus spake the Lord [*sections 35 and 36 follow*]:" (*History of the Church,* 1:128).

We will now proceed with section 36. Verse 1, next, contains two major messages for Edward Partridge. First, he is forgiven of sins, which will give him confidence to do the work of the Lord. Second, he is called to preach the gospel.

1 **THUS saith the Lord God, the Mighty One of Israel** [*another "name-title" for Christ*]: Behold, I say unto you, **my servant Edward**, that **you are blessed**, and **your sins are forgiven you**, and **you are called to preach my gospel** as with the voice of a trump;

Another part of the symbolism, which is a part of the word "trump," in verse 1, above (in addition to its being a clear, simple message, easy to pick out from the noise of the world), is that the sounding of a horn is a clear signal to gather, to rally together for a common cause. In this case, it symbolizes, among other things, the gathering of Israel in the last days.

Next, as the Lord instructs Edward to be confirmed a member of the Church, we are taught that when a worthy priesthood holder places his hands upon our head, it is the same as if the Lord were placing His hands upon our heads and blessing us. We are also taught about the benefit of receiving the gift of the Holy Ghost.

2 And **I will lay my hand upon you by the hand of my servant Sidney Rigdon**, and **you shall receive** my Spirit, **the Holy Ghost**, even **the Comforter** [*another "name-title" for the Holy Ghost, which reminds us of His role in bringing peace and comfort to us*], **which shall teach you the peaceable things of the kingdom**;

As you can see from the last part of verse 2, above, one of the major roles of the Holy Ghost is to teach us the gospel. This role of the Holy Ghost as our teacher was also emphasized in John, as follows:

John 14:26

But the Comforter, which is the Holy Ghost, whom the Father will send in my name, he shall teach you all things, and bring all things to your remembrance, whatsoever I have said unto you.

Moving forward with section 36, the Savior continues to instruct Edward Partridge about his missionary service.

3 And you shall **declare it** [*the gospel message*] **with a loud voice**, saying: **Hosanna**, blessed be the name of the most high God.

The word "Hosanna," as used in verse 3, above, is a special word for the followers of God. It is used in many settings, including in our dedication services for new temples. And President Russell M. Nelson led members of the Church worldwide in the Hosanna Shout during the April 2020 general conference. Basically, it means "Lord, save us now, please" or "Lord, grant us salvation." See Bible Dictionary, under "Hosanna." Yet another way of defining it would be "Come now, O thou great Jehovah, deliver us, O we plead!"

The waving of palm leaves (which symbolized triumph and victory in Biblical cultures) often accompanied the shouting of Hosanna. In *Mormon Doctrine*, under "Hosanna Shout," Bruce R. McConkie mentions the waving of white handkerchiefs in conjunction with the Hosanna Shout during our temple dedications. Our waving of white handkerchiefs is symbolic of the waving of palm branches. We invite the Savior to come into our lives and save us, thus giving us triumph and victory over all things that could prevent us from returning to the presence of God forever.

Next, the Lord tells Edward Partridge that what He is saying applies to all who go forth in missionary service. As you know, this period in the restoration of the gospel was a time when the Lord inspired many of the great and noble, who had been sent to earth at that time, to join the Church and go forth in missionary service. We have been watching them "gather" for the last several sections of the Doctrine and Covenants. As they gather to the Prophet, they are then sent forth to gather others.

4 And now **this calling and commandment** give I unto you **concerning all men**—

5 That **as many as shall come before my servants Sidney Rigdon and Joseph Smith, Jun.**, embracing this calling and commandment, shall be ordained [*"ordained" can mean to be ordained to an office in the priesthood, or, it can mean "set apart" to serve*] and **sent forth**

to preach the everlasting gospel among the nations—

6 **Crying repentance**, saying: Save yourselves from this untoward [*rebellious, wicked, unruly*] generation, and come forth out of the fire [*come away from the fires of hell*], hating even the garments [*clothing*] spotted with the flesh [*symbolic of lives dirtied by the wickedness of the world*].

7 And this commandment shall be given unto the elders of my church, that **every man which will embrace it with singleness of heart may be ordained and sent forth** [*sent on missions*], even as I have spoken.

8 **I am Jesus Christ, the Son of God**; wherefore, gird up your loins [*prepare for action*] and I will suddenly come to my temple. Even so. Amen.

SECTION 37

Background

As previously mentioned, the population center of the Church began switching from New York to the Kirtland, Ohio, area with the conversion of Sidney Rigdon and over 100 members of his congregation in Mentor, Ohio, and the Kirtland, Ohio, area. In this revelation, given to Joseph Smith and Sidney Rigdon near Fayette, New York, in December 1830, the Lord instructs the Church to gather in Ohio (see especially verse 3). At this time, there were about 200 members of the Church in New York.

First, though, in verse 1, the Lord instructs Joseph and Sidney to stop work on the Joseph Smith Translation of the Bible (the JST) for now. After they relocate to Ohio, they will resume the work of translating the Bible. You may wish to look at the map of the Ohio area in the back of your Doctrine and Covenants to get oriented as to where "the Ohio" (verses 1 and 3) is. If you look at your map, "the Ohio" is basically the area in and around Kirtland.

1 BEHOLD, I say unto you that **it is not expedient** [*necessary*] in me **that ye should translate** [*translate the Bible, which will become the JST*] **any more until ye shall go to the Ohio** [*the Ohio River Valley area in northeastern Ohio*], and this because of the enemy [*including the enemies of the Church in New York*] and for your sakes [*it will be to your advantage*].

Next, though, in verse 2, the Lord instructs them not to rush off to Ohio before they have completed their current callings to preach the gospel in New York, etc.

2 And again, I say unto you **that ye shall not go until ye have preached my gospel in those parts**, and have **strengthened up the church** whithersoever it is found, and more **especially in Colesville**; for, behold, they pray unto me in much faith.

Next, in verse 3, the Savior tells them that He wants them in Ohio by the time that Oliver Cowdery and his companions get back from their mission to the Lamanites (see D&C 28:8, 30:5, 32:1–3). These missionaries left on October 18, 1830, for their 1,500-mile missionary journey to the western frontier and points in between. (See notes for section 32 in this study guide.)

3 And again, a commandment I give unto the church, that it is expedient in me [*necessary according to My knowledge*] that they should **assemble together at the Ohio, against the time that my servant Oliver Cowdery shall return unto them**.

4 Behold, here is wisdom [*there is wisdom in following My counsel*], and let every man choose for himself [*you now have knowledge and are invited to use your agency*] until I come. Even so. Amen

SECTION 38

Background

This revelation was given through Joseph Smith at the third conference of the Church, held in Fayette, New York, on January 2, 1831. Members from the branches of the Church in various locations in New York gathered for this conference in the home of Peter Whitmer Sr. During the conference, several members asked about the commandment to move to Ohio.

As you saw in section 37, the Lord had commanded the members of the Church in the New York area to move some 300 miles west to Ohio in the dead of winter. In fact, it seems that every time they have to relocate, it is in the cold and misery of winter—New York to Kirtland, Kirtland to Missouri, Missouri to Nauvoo, Nauvoo to the Salt Lake Valley. Perhaps it was a kindness to them since it was less convenient for their enemies and persecutors to follow them under such miserable conditions.

During the conference, Joseph Smith prayed to the Lord in the presence of those in attendance and received this revelation. Here, in section 38, among other things, they will be told why they have been commanded to move to Ohio, especially in verse 32, where they are informed that they will be given the "law" in Ohio (section 42) and be "endowed with power from on high" (in the Kirtland Temple, which they will yet build).

This section is filled with powerful teachings and gospel doctrine, including much of doctrinal vocabulary. At this point in time, the Church has only been organized for about 9 months. It is a credit to the new converts to the restored gospel that the Lord is able to give them so much at this time. It would take humble and grateful people to change their ways and accept so much that was new to them.

There are many approaches that can be taken to study this section. First, we will simply go through it, using **bold** to point out several of the teachings, doctrines, and important gospel vocabulary words and phrases contained in it. This way, you can see "at-a-glance" what a precious and power-packed revelation this is for these early Saints, as well as for us. Then, we will repeat the section again, demonstrating just one approach to gospel study, and yet again, adding a number of notes.

As a suggestion, you may wish to read only the **bolded** segments this time through and see how many of them you understand.

1 THUS saith **the Lord your God**, even **Jesus Christ**, the **Great I AM, Alpha and Omega**, the **beginning and the end**, **the same which looked upon the wide expanse of eternity**, **and all the seraphic hosts of heaven, before the world was made**;

2 The same **which knoweth all things**, for **all things are present before mine eyes**;

3 **I** am the same which **spake, and the world was made**, and **all things came by me.**

4 **I am the same which have taken the Zion of Enoch into mine own bosom**; **and** verily, I say, **even as many as have believed in my name,** for **I am Christ, and in mine own name, by the virtue of the blood which I have spilt, have I pleaded before the Father for them**.

5 But behold, **the residue of the wicked have I kept in chains of darkness** until the **judgment** of the great day, which **shall come at the end of the earth**;

6 And even so will I cause the wicked to be kept, that will not hear my voice but harden their hearts, and **wo, wo, wo**, is their doom.

7 But behold, verily, verily, I say unto you that **mine eyes are upon you**. **I am in your midst** and ye cannot see me;

8 But the day soon cometh that ye shall see me, and know that I

am; for **the veil of darkness shall soon be rent**, and **he that is not purified shall not abide the day**.

9 Wherefore, **gird up your loins** and be prepared. Behold, **the kingdom is yours**, and the enemy shall not overcome.

10 Verily I say unto you, **ye are clean, but not all**; and there is none else with whom I am well pleased;

11 For **all flesh is corrupted before me**; and **the powers of darkness prevail upon the earth**, among the children of men, in the presence of all the hosts of heaven—

12 **Which causeth silence to reign**, and all **eternity is pained**, and the **angels are waiting** the great command **to reap down the earth**, to **gather the tares** that they may be burned; and, behold, **the enemy is combined**.

13 And now **I show unto you a mystery, a thing which is had in secret chambers, to bring to pass even your destruction** in process of time, and ye knew it not;

14 But now I tell it unto you, and ye are blessed, not because of your iniquity, neither your hearts of unbelief; for verily some of you are guilty before me, but **I will be merciful unto your weakness**.

15 Therefore, **be ye strong** from henceforth; **fear not, for the kingdom is yours**.

16 And for your salvation I give unto you a commandment, for I have heard your prayers, and the poor have complained before me, and the rich have I made, and all flesh is mine, and **I am no respecter of persons**.

17 And **I have made the earth rich**, and behold **it is my footstool**, wherefore, **again I will stand upon it.**

18 And **I hold forth and deign to give unto you greater riches**, even a land of promise, **a land flowing with milk and honey**, upon which there shall be no curse when the Lord cometh;

19 And I will give it unto you for **the land of your inheritance**, if you seek it with all your hearts.

20 And this shall be **my covenant** with you, **ye shall have it for the land of your inheritance**, and for the inheritance of your children forever, **while the earth shall stand**, and **ye shall possess it again in eternity**, no more to pass away.

21 But, verily I say unto you that

in time ye shall have no king nor ruler, for I will be your king and watch over you.

22 Wherefore, **hear my voice and follow me**, and you shall be a free people, and **ye shall have no laws but my laws when I come**, for **I am your lawgiver**, and **what can stay my hand?**

23 But, verily I say unto you, **teach one another** according to the office wherewith I have appointed you;

24 And **let every man esteem his brother as himself**, and **practice virtue** and **holiness** before me.

25 And again I say unto you, **let every man esteem his brother as himself**.

26 For what man among you having twelve sons, and is no respecter of them, and they serve him obediently, and he saith unto the one: Be thou clothed in robes and sit thou here; and to the other: Be thou clothed in rags and sit thou there—and looketh upon his sons and saith **I am just**?

27 Behold, this I have given unto you as a parable, and it is even as I am. I say unto you, be one; and **if ye are not one ye are not mine**.

28 And again, I say unto you that **the enemy in the secret chambers seeketh your lives**.

29 **Ye hear of wars in far countries**, and you say that there will soon be great wars in far countries, but **ye know not the hearts of men in your own land**.

30 I tell you these things because of your prayers; wherefore, **treasure up wisdom in your bosoms**, lest the wickedness of men reveal these things unto you by their wickedness, in a manner which shall speak in your ears with a voice louder than that which shall shake the earth; but **if ye are prepared ye shall not fear**.

31 And that ye might escape the power of the enemy, and be gathered unto me a righteous people, **without spot and blameless**—

32 Wherefore, for this cause I gave unto you the commandment that ye should go to the Ohio; and there I will give unto you **my law** [*section 42*]; and there you shall be **endowed with power from on high**;

33 And from thence, whosoever I will shall go forth among all nations, and it shall be told them what they shall do; for I have a great work laid up in store, for **Israel shall be saved**, and I will lead

them whithersoever I will, and **no power shall stay my hand**.

34 And now, I give unto the church in these parts a commandment, that certain men among them shall be appointed, and they shall be **appointed by the voice of the church**;

35 And **they shall look to the poor and the needy, and administer to their relief** that they shall not suffer; and send them forth to the place which I have commanded them;

36 And this shall be their work, to govern the affairs of the property of this church.

37 And they that have farms that cannot be sold, let them be left or rented as seemeth them good.

38 See that all things are preserved; and when men are endowed with power from on high and sent forth, all these things shall be **gathered unto the bosom of the church**.

39 And **if ye seek the riches which it is the will of the Father to give unto you**, ye shall be the richest of all people, for ye shall have **the riches of eternity**; and **it must needs be** that the riches of the earth are mine to give; but **beware of pride**, lest ye become as the Nephites of old.

40 And again, I say unto you, I give unto you a commandment, that every man, both elder, priest, teacher, and also member, go to with his might, with the labor of his hands, to prepare and accomplish the things which I have commanded.

41 And **let your preaching be** the warning voice, every man to his neighbor, **in mildness and in meekness**.

42 And **go ye out from among the wicked**. Save yourselves. **Be ye clean that bear the vessels of the Lord**. Even so. Amen.

As mentioned above, there are many important messages and teachings contained in this section. For instance, one of the principles in section 38 that is taught often in talks and lessons in the Church by using the last phrase of verse 30 is the value of preparation. It says, "If ye are prepared ye shall not fear." This section also often serves as a springboard for a talk or sermon based on the last part of verse 42 in which the Lord says, "Be ye clean that bear the vessels of the Lord."

Yet another vital message is that of avoiding being abrasive and harsh in our gospel teaching and preaching. This counsel is given in verse 41, wherein the Lord counsels to "let your preaching be the warning voice . . . in mildness and in meekness."

There are also many approaches to studying the scriptures. We will take time to demonstrate one here. It is to select a theme or topic and then go through a section or block of scripture picking out only those verses, words, and phrases that tie in with that theme. For instance, section 38 lends itself well to picking out what we might call "the ten commandments of good teaching." We will take the time and space here to repeat verses 22 to 42 again, but this time we will only **bold** those passages associated with effective and inspired teaching. You will no doubt be able to pick out other words and phrases that could be added to these rules of good teaching. We will place numbers from one to ten by each of these "commandments" and list ten of them, starting with verse 22. You will see that many of these suggestions for effective teaching have to do with the preparation of the teacher himself or herself.

Just one more bit of explanation. You will no doubt observe that some of the **bolded** items are not really well connected with the verses or context in which they lie. One of the points we are making is that under the direction of the Holy Ghost, you may find much inspiration and help as you read the scriptures, which does not really relate to the context of the passage of scripture at hand. Rather, words and concepts "jump out at you" in answer to your own specific needs. Such is the case demonstrated by these "ten commandments" of effective teaching.

So, suppose you are a newly called teacher in one of the church classes and are searching in the scriptures for help in fulfilling your new calling. By the help of the Spirit, these ten items "jump out at you." Remember, our first item is found in verse 22.

22 Wherefore, **hear my voice and follow me [*1. You must be following Christ yourself.*]**, and you shall be a free people, and ye shall have no laws but my laws when I come, for I am your lawgiver, and what can stay my hand?

23 But, verily I say unto you, **teach one another [*2. Some of the most important teaching in the Church is done when we teach and strengthen each other in gospel knowledge and principles and living.*]** according to the office wherewith I have appointed you;

24 And **let every man esteem his brother as himself [*3. We must respect those we teach.*]**, and **practice virtue and holiness before me [*4. You must have a deep, inner commitment to live the gospel.*].**

25 And again I say unto you, let every man esteem his brother as himself.

26 For what man among you having twelve sons, and is no respecter of them, and they serve him obediently, and he saith unto the one: Be thou clothed in robes and sit thou here; and to the other: Be thou clothed in rags and sit thou there—and looketh upon his sons and saith I am just?

27 Behold, this I have given unto you as a parable, and it is even as I am. I say unto you, **be one [*5. You must try to avoid contention in order to have the Spirit.*]**; and if ye are not one ye are not mine.

28 And again, I say unto you that the enemy in the secret chambers seeketh your lives.

29 Ye hear of wars in far countries, and you say that there will soon be great wars in far countries, but ye know not the hearts of men in your own land.

30 I tell you these things because of your prayers; wherefore, **treasure up wisdom in your bosoms [*6. Study the scriptures; learn wisdom and use wisdom in your teaching.*]**, lest the wickedness of men reveal these things unto you by their wickedness, in a manner which shall speak in your ears with a voice louder than that which shall shake the earth; but if ye are prepared ye shall not fear.

31 And that ye might escape the power of the enemy, and be gathered unto me a righteous people, without spot and blameless—

32 Wherefore, for this cause I gave unto you the commandment that ye should go to the Ohio; and there I will give unto you my law; and there you shall be endowed with power from on high;

33 And from thence, whosoever I will shall go forth among all nations, and it shall be told them what they shall do; for I have a great work laid up in store, for Israel shall be saved, and I will lead them whithersoever I will, and no power shall stay my hand.

34 And now, I give unto the church in these parts a commandment, that certain men among them shall be appointed, and they shall be appointed by the voice of the church;

35 And they shall look to the poor and the needy, and administer to their relief that they shall not suffer; and send them forth to the place which I have commanded them;

36 And this shall be their work, to govern the affairs of the property of this church.

37 And they that have farms that cannot be sold, let them be left or rented as seemeth them good.

38 See that all things are preserved; and when men are endowed with power from on high and sent forth, all these things shall be gathered unto the bosom of the church.

39 And if ye seek the riches which it is the will of the Father to give unto you, ye shall be the richest of all people, for ye shall have the riches of eternity; and it must needs be that the riches of the earth are mine to give; but **beware of pride [*7. Pride alienates others, including students, in a hurry.*]**, lest ye become as the Nephites of old.

40 And again, I say unto you, I give unto you a commandment, that every man, both elder, priest, teacher, and also member, go to with his might, with the labor of his hands, to **prepare [*8. Good teaching requires much preparation and study on your part.*]** and accomplish the things which I have commanded.

41 And **let your preaching be the warning voice**, every man to his neighbor, **in mildness and in meekness [*9. Be pleasant with your students and try not to alienate them.*]**.

42 And go ye out from among the wicked. Save yourselves. **Be ye clean that bear the vessels of the Lord [*10. strive to be clean in mind and body in order to teach effectively.*]**. Even so. Amen.

Having done the above, we will now go through the entire section again, adding several notes and teaching comments. Beginning with verse 1, next, we find three of the many "name-titles" for Jesus Christ. We will list them here:

1. **The Lord God**—the God of this world, under the direction of the Father.

2. **The Great I AM**—"I AM" means "the Living God" (as opposed to idols, etc., that are, of course, inanimate objects). "I AM" is another name for Jehovah, the name by which Christ is often known, as the God of the Old Testament. (See Exodus 3:14.)

3. **Alpha and Omega**—the first and last letters of the Greek alphabet, symbolizing that Jesus is in charge of all things under the direction of the Father. It also means that He was there in premortality, "in the beginning" helping us, and that He

will be there for us at the end on Judgment Day as our Advocate (see D&C 45:3–5), making those who are worthy completely free from sin and worthy to enter celestial glory.

In verses 1–6, after giving three of His names by which He is known in scripture, the Savior describes a number of His powers and functions.

1 THUS saith **the Lord your God**, even **Jesus Christ, the Great I AM, Alpha and Omega**, the beginning and the end [*in charge of all things under the direction of the Father*], the same [*the Creator*] which looked upon the wide expanse of eternity, and all the seraphic hosts of heaven [*including all the premortal spirit children of the Father*], before the world was made;

We will include a quote from the *Doctrine and Covenants Student Manual*, 1981, page 75, which gives added insight for the phrase "seraphic hosts of heaven" in verse 1, above:

"Seraphs are angels who reside in the presence of God. . . . it is clear that seraphs include the unembodied spirits of preexistence, for our Lord 'looked upon the wide expanse of eternity, and all the seraphic hosts of heaven, before the world was made' (D&C 38:1). Whether the name seraphs also applies to perfected and resurrected angels is not clear."

"In Hebrew the plural of seraph is seraphim" (*Mormon Doctrine*, 702–3).

2 The same which **knoweth all things**, for **all things are present before mine eyes**;

3 I am **the same which spake** [*I am the Creator*], **and the world was made**, and **all things came by me.**

Next, Jesus informs these early Saints that He is the God who caused the City of Enoch to be taken up to heaven.

4 **I am the same which have taken the Zion of Enoch into mine own bosom**; and verily, I say, even as many as have believed in my name, for I am Christ, and in mine own name, by the virtue of the blood which I have spilt, have I pleaded before the Father for them.

Verse 4, above, regarding the City of Enoch, is particularly significant in this context, because in December 1830, shortly before this conference of the Church (January 2, 1831), the Savior had revealed the seventh chapter of the Book of Moses (which is in the Pearl of Great Price). In Moses 7:69, the City of Enoch (Zion) is taken up. Can you imagine the excitement of these new members as they received the Book of Moses, which restores so much that had been left out of the Bible? And then to hear the Lord refer specifically to this as He introduced Himself to them during this conference, in this revelation!

By the way, the Lord began revealing the chapters of Moses to the Prophet Joseph Smith, which we have in the Pearl of Great Price, in June 1830 (as you can see if you look at the headings for each chapter of Moses) and finished by revealing Moses, chapter 8, in February 1831.

Next, the Lord continues telling these Saints about Himself and what He does. He refers to the captivity of wickedness, in which the rebellious find themselves, and to the final judgment. In a very real sense, the Savior is bearing witness here also that He respects agency so completely that He allows people to get themselves into real trouble.

5 But behold, the residue of the wicked have I kept in **chains of darkness** until the judgment of the great day, which shall come at the end of the earth [*after the Millennium is over, and after the "little season" (see D&C 88:111–14) that comes after the Millennium*];

Behaviors that lead up to being held captive in the "chains of darkness" are described in Alma as follows (**bold** added for emphasis):

Alma 12:11

And they that will harden their hearts [*reject the gospel*], to them is given the lesser portion of the word **until they know nothing concerning his mysteries** [*the basics of the gospel, which are "mysteries" to those who know nothing about Christ*]; and then they are taken captive by the devil, and led by his will down to destruction. Now **this is what is meant by the chains of hell**.

6 And even so will I cause the wicked to be kept, that will not hear my voice [*who refuse to pay attention to the gospel when it is brought to them*] but harden their hearts, and wo, wo, wo [*"wo" means, basically, "deep trouble"*], is their doom.

Next, the Savior assures these Saints that He knows their needs and is among them.

7 But behold, verily, verily, I say unto you that **mine eyes are upon you. I am in your midst** and ye cannot see me;

Perhaps you've seen or heard of the "all seeing eye" carved on the east center tower of the Salt Lake Temple. The symbolism of that, according to the architect, Truman O. Angell, is that of verse 7, above; namely, that the Lord can see us and knows how best to help and support us.

Also, concerning the statement, "I am in your midst and ye cannot see me," in verse 7, above: I recall, as a young missionary, attending the mission home in Salt Lake City where the Church Office Building now stands. Part of our training consisted of a meeting in an upper room of the Salt Lake Temple with Elder Harold B. Lee. He invited us to ask any questions we wanted to ask. A meeting similar to this is described by Elder Lee in the following quote (**bold** added for emphasis):

"I have a session with the missionary groups as they go out, in the temple, where they are permitted to ask intimate questions that wouldn't be proper to be discussed elsewhere. They sometimes ask, 'Could you tell us a certain place in the temple where the Savior has been seen?' My answer is, 'Keep in mind that this is the house of the Lord; this is the place that we try to keep as pure and holy and sacred as any building we have. This is the most likely place He would come when He comes on earth. Don't ask for a certain place because He has walked these halls. How do you know but what He is here in your midst?'" (In Conference Report, British Area Conference 1971, 135–36; or *Ensign*, Nov. 1971, 12–13).

8 But **the day soon cometh** [*the Second Coming*] **that ye shall see me**, and know that I am; for the veil of darkness shall soon be rent [*torn aside*], and **he that is not purified shall not abide the day** [*will not survive the Second Coming*].

In reference to the phrase "shall not abide the day," in verse 8, above, we will quote four verses contained in the scriptures that teach that the wicked will be burned by the glory of the coming Christ. We will add **bold** for emphasis.

D&C 5:19

For a desolating scourge shall go forth among the inhabitants of the earth, and shall continue to be poured out from time to time, if they repent not, until the earth is empty, and the inhabitants thereof are **consumed away and utterly destroyed by the brightness of my coming**.

2 Nephi 12:10, 19, 21

10 O ye wicked ones, enter into the rock, and hide thee in the dust, for the fear of the Lord and **the glory of his majesty shall smite thee**.

19 And they shall go into the holes of the rocks, and into the caves of the earth, for the fear of the Lord shall come upon them and **the glory of his majesty**

shall smite them, when he ariseth to shake terribly the earth.

21 To go into the clefts of the rocks, and into the tops of the ragged rocks, for the fear of the Lord shall come upon them and the majesty of **his glory shall smite them**, when he ariseth to shake terribly the earth.

Next, the Savior counsels to be prepared and explains that nothing can prevent faithful Saints from attaining celestial glory.

9 Wherefore, **gird up your loins** [*prepare for action*] and **be prepared**. Behold, **the kingdom is yours**, and **the enemy shall not overcome**.

In verse 10, next, the Lord encourages these humble members by telling them, in effect, that He is pleased with them even though they still have a distance to go in terms of gospel progress.

10 Verily I say unto you, **ye are clean, but not all**; and **there is none else with whom I am well pleased**;

Next, in verses 11 to 12, we are given a brief lesson on "cause and effect," in this case being why communication from heaven to the inhabitants of the earth has been curtailed so severely.

11 For **all flesh is corrupted before me**; and **the powers of darkness prevail upon the earth**, among the children of men, in the presence of all the hosts of heaven [*perhaps meaning "as witnessed by all the hosts of heaven"*]—

12 **Which causeth silence to reign** [*which cuts off communication from heaven to the inhabitants of the earth*], and **all eternity is pained** [*all the beings in heaven are very concerned about this*], and **the angels** [*the destroying angels*] **are waiting the great command to reap down the earth** [*to harvest the wicked on earth*], **to gather the tares** [*the wicked*] that they may be burned; and, behold, **the enemy is combined** [*all the forces of evil are combining together to destroy the spirituality of the inhabitants of the earth*].

Verse 12, above, is a reference to the parable of the Wheat and the Tares, given in Matthew 13:24–30, 36–43, and explained in D&C 86:1–7. Since an understanding of this parable is a must for understanding verse 12, above, we will take time to review the parable here. We will use a quote from *New Testament Made Easier*, part 1, 28–29.

The Parable of the Wheat and the Tares (Matthew 13:24–30, 36–43)

24 Another parable put he forth unto them, saying, The kingdom of heaven is likened unto a man [*Christ, see verse 37*] which sowed [*planted*] good seed [*faithful followers of Christ, verse 38*] in his field [*the world, verse 38*]:

25 But while men slept, his enemy [*the devil, verse 39*] came and sowed tares [*wicked people, verse 38*] among the wheat [*faithful members of the Church*], and went his way.

A tare is a weed that looks very much like wheat while it is growing. Often, the roots of tares intertwine with the roots of the wheat while both are growing.

26 But when the blade was sprung up, and brought forth fruit, then appeared the tares also.

27 So the servants of the householder [*Christ*] came and said unto him, Sir, didst not thou sow [*plant*] good seed [*wheat*] in thy field? from whence then hath it tares [*where did the tares come from*]?

28 He said unto them, An enemy hath done this. The servants said unto him, Wilt thou then that we go and gather them up [*would you like us to weed out the tares now*]?

29 But he said, Nay [*No*]; lest [*for fear that*] while ye gather up the tares, ye root up also the wheat with them.

There are several messages here in verse 29. One message might be that there are usually insincere and unrighteous members living among the righteous members of wards and branches of the Church. Another message could be that each of us has some "tares" in our own lives and personalities, and we would be wise to weed them out as our righteous attributes mature. Jacob 5:65–66 in the Book of Mormon reminds us that as the good in people grows, the bad can gradually be cleared away. See also D&C 86:6.

30 Let both grow together until the harvest: and in the time of harvest I will say to the reapers [*harvesters, angels in verse 39*], Gather ye together first the tares [*the wicked*], and bind them in bundles to burn them: but gather the wheat [*the righteous*] into my barn [*my kingdom*].

D&C 86:7 changes the order of the harvesting, as does JST Matt. 13:29. The correct order is that the wheat is gathered first, then the tares are gathered, bundled (bound), and burned. This is significant doctrinally, because it indicates that, at the Second Coming, the righteous will be taken up first (D&C 88:96), and then the wicked will be burned.

36 Then Jesus sent the multitude away, and went into the house: and his disciples came unto him, saying, Declare [*explain*] unto us the parable of the tares of the field [*verses 24–30*].

37 He answered and said unto them, He that soweth [*plants*] the good seed [*wheat; righteousness*] is the Son of man [*Christ; Son of Man of Holiness—see Moses 6:57*];

38 The field is the world; the good seed are the children of the kingdom [*faithful members of the Church; the righteous*]; but the tares are the children of the wicked *one* [*followers of Satan; the wicked*];

39 The enemy that sowed them is the devil; the harvest is the end of the world; and the reapers [*harvesters*] are the angels.

40 As therefore the tares [*the wicked*] are gathered and burned in the fire; so shall it be in the end of this world [*the wicked will be burned at the Second Coming*].

41 The Son of man [*Christ*] shall send forth his angels, and they shall gather out of his kingdom all things that offend, and them which do iniquity [*the wicked*];

42 And shall cast them into a furnace of fire [*the burning at the Second Coming—see note above*]: there shall be wailing [*bitter crying*] and gnashing [*grinding*] of teeth.

43 Then shall the righteous shine forth as the sun [*symbolic of celestial glory for the righteous Saints*] in the kingdom of their Father. Who hath ears to hear, let him hear [*those who are spiritually in tune will understand what I am saying*].

We will now continue with section 38. In verse 13, next, the Savior alerts these New York Saints that their enemies are in the process of hatching some plots and conspiracies to bring about their destruction.

13 And **now I show unto you** a mystery, **a thing which is had in secret chambers, to bring to pass even your destruction in process of time**, and ye knew it not;

There is a rather encouraging message for all of us in verse 14, next. It is that even though we have our weaknesses and faults, the Lord still extends mercy to us and blesses us, which fosters growth and progress in people whose hearts are honest.

14 But now I tell it unto you, and **ye are blessed**, not because of your iniquity, neither your hearts of unbelief; for verily **some of you are guilty before me, but I will be merciful unto your weakness**.

15 Therefore, **be ye strong from henceforth** [*use this as an opportunity to improve from now on*]; **fear not** [*fear is the opposite of faith and is an enemy to personal progress*], **for the kingdom is yours** [*if we allow God to keep working with us, we will ultimately "make it"*].

Next, at the end of verse 16, we are reminded that the Lord loves all people, and everyone, regardless of their status or financial state, will be given a completely fair chance to understand and accept or reject the gospel by using their individual agency (whether on earth or in the postmortal spirit world).

Doctrine

Verse 16. God is completely fair to all people.

16 And for your salvation I give unto you a commandment [*through which you can obtain all the blessings I have in store for you—see verses 23–27, below*], for I have heard your prayers, and the poor have complained before me, and the rich have I made, and all flesh is mine, and **I am no respecter of persons** [*the Lord treats all people fairly, and we must also if we expect to become like Him; this is part of the "setting" for the commandments given in verses 23–27*].

As we study verses 17–20, next, we will use a quote from the *Doctrine and Covenants Student Manual,* 1981, page 77, as background to what we will be taught.

"To better understand the Lord's promise in these verses, one needs to understand that the earth was designed by the Lord as a place of habitation for his children. The earth itself reflects the level of life that is lived on it. Elder Bruce R. McConkie described four of the stages the earth has gone through and will yet go through:

"Edenic earth. Following its physical creation, the earth was pronounced good. It was a terrestrial or paradisiacal state. There was no death either for man or for any form of life, and 'all the vast creation of animated beings breathed naught but health, and peace, and joy.' (2 Ne. 2:22; *Voice of Warning*, 89–91.)

"Telestial earth. When Adam fell, the earth fell also and became a mortal sphere, one upon which worldly and carnal people can live. This condition was destined to continue for a period of 6,000 years, and it was while in this state that the earth was baptized in water. (D&C 77:6–7, 12; *Man: His Origin and Destiny*, 415–36, 460–66.)

"Terrestrial earth. 'We believe . . . that the earth will be renewed and receive its paradisiacal glory.' (Tenth Article of Faith.) Thus, the earth is to go back to the primeval, paradisiacal, or terrestrial state that prevailed in the days of the Garden of Eden. Accompanying this transition to its millennial status the earth is to be burned, that is, receive its baptism of fire. It will then be a new heaven and a new earth, and again health, peace, and joy will prevail upon its face. (D&C 101:23–32; Isa. 65:17–25; Mal. 3:1–6; 4:1–6; *Man: His Origin and Destiny*, 380–97.)

"Celestial earth. Following the millennium plus 'a little season' (D&C 29:22–25), the earth will die, be resurrected, and becoming like a 'sea of glass' (D&C 130:7), attain unto 'its sanctified, immortal, and eternal state.' (D&C 77:1–2.) Then the poor and the meek—that is, the godfearing and the righteous—shall inherit the earth; it will become an abiding place for the Father and the Son, and celestial beings will possess it forever and ever. (D&C 88:14–26, 111.) (*Mormon Doctrine*, 211.)

"The statement that there will be no curse on the land when the Lord comes (see D&C 38:18) refers to the terrestrial earth during the Millennium, whereas the promise that the Saints will possess it during eternity (see D&C 38:18) reflects the earth's eventual celestial state."

With the above quote from the *Doctrine and Covenants Student Manual* as background, we will proceed with verses 17–20.

17 And **I have made the earth rich** [*there is plenty for all; it is man's mismanagement that causes problems; compare with D&C 104:17*], and behold it is my footstool [*this earth is Christ's; see D&C 130:9, end of verse*], wherefore, **again I will stand upon it** [*during the Millennium, and then on through eternity, after it is celestialized; see D&C 130:9–11*].

18 And **I hold forth** [*have in mind*] **and deign** [*plan*] **to give unto you greater riches, even a land of promise, a land flowing with milk and honey** [*the very best; the celestial earth*], **upon which there shall be no curse** [*during the Millennium, when the earth is once again a paradise, like it was before the Lord cursed it at the time of the Fall of Adam*] **when the Lord cometh** [*for the Millennium*];

19 And **I will give it unto you for the land of your inheritance,**

if you seek it with all your hearts [*you will obtain celestial glory and live on this earth forever, as it becomes your celestial planet; see D&C 130:9*].

Doctrine

Verse 20. The righteous will live on this earth forever.

20 And this shall be my covenant with you, ye shall have it for the land of your inheritance, and **for the inheritance of your children forever**, while the earth shall stand, and **ye shall possess it again in eternity** [*when the earth is celestialized*], no more to pass away.

21 But, verily I say unto you that in time [*during the Millennium*] ye shall have no king nor ruler, for **I will be your king and watch over you.**

22 Wherefore, **hear my voice and follow me** [*listen carefully to what the Savior says as He describes the commandment mentioned in verse 16, above, which, if followed, will gain you all the millennial and celestial blessings described above*], and **you shall be a free people**, and **ye shall have no laws but my laws when I come** [*during the Millennium*], **for I am your lawgiver**, and what can stay my hand [*what can stop the hand of the Lord*]?

Next, the Savior describes some of the components of the "commandment" that He said He would give these Saints in verse 16, above.

23 But, verily I say unto you, **teach one another** according to the office wherewith I have appointed you;

24 And **let every man esteem his brother as himself, and practice virtue and holiness before me.**

25 And again I say unto you, **let every man esteem his brother as himself.** [*This is basically the "golden rule."*]

Next, using a parable, Jesus reasons with all of us, the point being that He is completely fair with all people. Thus, all who earn exaltation will be given it.

26 For **what man among you having twelve sons**, and is no respecter of them [*is not prejudiced for or against any of them*], **and they serve him obediently**, and he saith unto the one: Be thou clothed in robes [*symbolic of royalty; in other words, exaltation*] and sit thou here; and to the other: Be thou clothed in rags [*received much less than he earned*] and sit thou there—and looketh upon his sons and saith I am just [*completely fair*]?

27 Behold, **this I have given unto you as a parable**, and it is even as I am [*the parable represents the Savior and that He would never deprive any people of what they have earned*]. I say unto you, **be one** [*live in harmony; be united in righteousness; avoid contention*]; and **if ye are not one ye are not mine**.

> Now, the Lord returns to the topic of dangers that are developing against the Saints at this time in New York.

28 And again, I say unto you that **the enemy in the secret chambers** [*secret plots against you are developing*] **seeketh your lives.**

29 **Ye hear of wars in far countries**, and you say that there will soon be great wars in far countries, **but ye know not the hearts of men in your own land** [*there are dangers you are unaware of in your home areas*].

> Next, we are reminded that our prayers can be effective in helping save us from dangers.

30 **I tell you these things because of your prayers**; wherefore, treasure up wisdom in your bosoms [*take what the Lord says to heart*], lest the wickedness of men reveal these things unto you by their wickedness [*otherwise, you will find out the hard way*], in a manner which shall speak in your ears with a voice louder than that which shall shake the earth; **but if ye are prepared ye shall not fear**.

> Among the many lessons that could be taught from the last phrase of verse 30, above, is the fact that if we are prepared to meet the Savior, we need not fear anything else, even death at the hand of enemies. The righteous have a type of peace about them that the wicked can't have or understand.

> As the Lord continues, and with the above background in place, He answers the question on the minds of many members who are attending this conference of the Church. The question? Why were they commanded to move to Ohio (see D&C 37:3). The answer? Verses 31–33. In fact, the Lord gives five specific reasons for having the Saints move to Ohio.

31 And **(1) that ye might escape the power of the enemy**, and **(2) be gathered unto me a righteous people, without spot and blameless**—

32 Wherefore, **for this cause** [*for this reason*] **I gave unto you the commandment that ye should go to the Ohio**; and **(3) there I will give unto you my law** [*section 42*]; and **(4) there you shall be endowed with power from on**

high [*in the Kirtland Temple, after it is built; see especially D&C 110, which records the visits of Christ, Moses, Elias, and Elijah in the Kirtland Temple*];

33 And **(5) from thence, whosoever I will shall go forth among all nations** [*from Kirtland, Ohio, missionaries will go out to all the world*], and it shall be told them what they shall do; for I have a great work laid up in store, for **Israel shall be saved**, and I will lead them whithersoever I will, and **no power shall stay my hand**.

Next, instructions are given concerning the immediate problems faced by the members as they deal with leaving homes and property, or, in some cases, by those who do not have the means to move to Ohio.

34 And now, I give unto the church in these parts [*New York*] a commandment, that **certain men among them shall be appointed**, and they shall be appointed by the voice of the church [*they are to be sustained by the members of the Church*];

35 And **they shall look to the poor and the needy, and administer to their relief that they shall not suffer**; and send them forth to the place which I have commanded them;

36 And this shall be their work, **to govern the affairs of the property of this church**.

Next, the Savior teaches a lesson in priorities. If material things are standing in the way of following the commandments of God, leave material concerns and possessions behind.

37 And **they that have farms that cannot be sold, let them be left or rented** as seemeth them good.

38 See that all things are preserved; and **when men are endowed with power from on high and sent forth, all these things shall be gathered unto the bosom of the church** [*perhaps meaning that the time will come that the Church will prosper and much more than what is being left behind by members in New York will be owned by the Church and its members*].

In verse 39, we are reminded that true riches are the things of eternal value. These include the gospel, exaltation, and eternal families. However, in the last half of verse 39, it is noted that the wealth of the world is also available to members, but if they gain it, they must beware of pride.

39 And if ye seek **the riches which it is the will of the Father to give unto you**, ye shall be the richest of all people, for ye shall

have **the riches of eternity**; and it must needs be that **the riches of the earth are mine to give; but beware of pride**, lest ye become as the Nephites of old [*who were destroyed by the "prosperity, pride, wickedness, destruction" cycle of apostasy*].

In Jacob 2:18–19, we are taught the proper order of priorities regarding financial success and being loyal to God as follows (**bold** added for emphasis):

Jacob 2:18–19

18 But **before ye seek for riches, seek ye for the kingdom of God.**

19 And **after ye have obtained a hope in Christ** [*after you have proven that you can live the gospel no matter what*] **ye shall obtain riches, if ye seek them**; and **ye will seek them for the intent to do good**—to clothe the naked, and to feed the hungry, and to liberate the captive, and administer relief to the sick and the afflicted.

Before we leave verse 39, above, we will do just a bit more with the last warning, "beware of pride, lest ye become as the Nephites of old." Throughout the Book of Mormon, we see what is commonly known as the "cycle of apostasy." It is basically that when people prosper, they become prideful. Then they forget God and turn wicked. Then He has to humble them. After they get humbled by pestilence and destruction, they repent and start being righteous. As they become more righteous, they prosper. As they prosper, they become prideful and forget God. And the whole cycle starts over.

Of course, there is an easy way to avoid going round and round through this cycle. It is to remain humble and faithful to God when prosperity comes your way, and follow the pattern in Jacob 2:18–19, above. By doing this, you can avoid the "cycle of apostasy" and continue to enjoy the blessings of the gospel *and* prosperity.

As we return to section 38, we see in verse 40, next, that the Lord commands the priesthood holders as well as all members to do everything they can to fulfill the commandments He has given them in this section.

40 And again, I say unto you, **I give unto you a commandment**, that **every** man, both **elder**, **priest**, **teacher**, and also **member**, go to with his might, with the labor of his hands, to **prepare and accomplish the things which I have commanded.**

As all of us fulfill the commandment to share and spread the gospel, we are reminded that it is to be done in kindness and wisdom.

The Lord also reminds us in verse 41, next, that often the most likely candidates for joining the Church are our neighbors (those around us, whether in our neighborhoods, at work, school, etc.). Often, the best and most effective "preaching" is a good example.

41 And let your **preaching** be the warning voice, every man to his neighbor, **in mildness and in meekness**.

Perhaps you've noticed the symbolism in verse 42, next, in the actual moving of these Saints from New York to Ohio. They must physically flee the wicked in New York who are plotting to destroy them, just as all of us must "go out from among the wicked" in terms of avoiding the filth and spiritual corruption of our day in order to "save ourselves."

42 And **go ye out from among the wicked. Save yourselves**. Be ye clean that bear the vessels of the Lord. Even so. Amen.

The final phrase of verse 42, above, is a reference to the priesthood holders of ancient Israel whose responsibilities included handling the bowls, containers, instruments, and such that were used in the sacrifices and rituals of the Law of Moses. They were expected to keep themselves clean and worthy to officiate in these rites. So also today are those who officiate in the ordinances of salvation expected to keep themselves clean and worthy of doing the work of the Lord. In a broader sense, this applies to all members, who are expected to be worthy examples to all as they "bear" the gospel of Jesus Christ to all the world.

SECTION 39

Background

Sections 39 and 40 go together. They both deal with an elderly Methodist minister named James Covel. Section 39 was given to him in Fayette, New York, through the Prophet Joseph Smith, on January 5, 1831. Section 40 was given to Joseph Smith and Sidney Rigdon on the following day, January 6, 1831, regarding him.

Up until the 2013 edition of the Doctrine and Covenants, his name was given as "James Covill," but recent research, including that for *The Joseph Smith Papers* publications, shows that his name was "James Covel." You can see this by comparing the headings to section 39 in earlier editions and the 2013 edition. Also, recent research tells us that he was a Methodist minister rather than a Baptist minister as indicated in the heading of section 39 in previous editions of the Doctrine and Covenants

James had been a Methodist minister for about forty years at the time of his becoming interested in the Church. There is disagreement among historians as to when he was born, so we will simply note that he was probably somewhere near seventy years old when he received the revelation given him by the Lord as recorded in section 39. John Whitmer, one of the Eight Witnesses to the Book of Mormon, said that James Covel "covenanted with the Lord that he would obey any commandment that the Lord would give through his servant Joseph" (in *The Joseph Smith Papers, Documents, Volume 1: July 1828–June 1831*, 233–34).

In section 39, James Covel is told that if he listens to the Lord and gets baptized, he will receive blessings beyond his fondest dreams (see verse 10). He is called to do a great work, even at his age, and is told that he has tremendous potential for good. The sad thing about him is that he accepted the Church with great enthusiasm, and then, within a short time, rejected it and the marvelous promises of the Lord to him. We don't even know for sure if he was baptized.

There is much for us to learn from this revelation, including some significant comparisons to our patriarchal blessings, which we will point out along the way. As is the case with several previous revelations in the Doctrine and Covenants that were given to individuals or groups, the Lord will first introduce Himself to James Covel, particularly in verses 1–5. The Savior will use several Biblical words and phrases with which this Methodist minister is no doubt familiar.

1 HEARKEN and **listen to the voice of him who is** from all eternity to all eternity, **the Great I AM** [*Exodus 3:14; one of the many names for Jehovah, the God of the Old Testament, the premortal Jesus Christ*], even **Jesus Christ**—

2 **The light and the life of the world** [*compare with John 8:12, etc.*]; **a light which shineth in darkness and the darkness comprehendeth it not** [*John 1:5*];

3 **The same which came in the meridian of time** unto mine own, **and mine own received me not** [*compare with Isaiah 53:3*];

4 But **to as many as received me, gave I power to become my sons** [*John 1:12*]; and even so will I give unto as many as will receive me, power to become my sons [*a scriptural phrase meaning exaltation; see Mosiah 5:7, D&C 76:24, etc.*].

5 And verily, verily [*listen very carefully*], I say unto you, **he that receiveth my gospel receiveth me** [*compare with John 13:20*]; **and he that receiveth not my gospel receiveth not me.**

Next, the Savior teaches James Covel and all of us a brief course in some gospel basics, emphasizing the role of the gift of the Holy Ghost in teaching us throughout our lives after baptism and confirmation.

6 And **this is my gospel—repentance** and **baptism** by water, and **then cometh** the baptism of fire and **the Holy Ghost**, even the Comforter, **which showeth all things, and teacheth the peaceable things of the kingdom**.

Next, in verses 7–9, the Savior gets very personal with James Covel, encouraging him and telling him of concerns He has had about him in the past.

7 And now, behold, I say unto you, my servant James, I have looked upon thy works and **I know thee**.

8 And verily I say unto thee, **thine heart is now right before me at this time**; and, behold, **I have bestowed great blessings upon thy head** [*a reminder that God likes to bless all His children, whether members of the Church or not; perhaps referring also to the blessing of hearing the true gospel just recently*];

9 Nevertheless, thou hast seen great sorrow, for **thou hast rejected me many times because of pride and the cares of the world** [*a clear warning about weaknesses that have caused problems for him in the past. Unfortunately, they will yet lead him away from the great blessings that are now ready for him, as explained in verses 10–23*].

You will see the word "if" in both verses 10 and 11. Patriarchal blessings often have "ifs" in them, meaning that the promised blessings are conditional upon the person's faithfulness and obedience to the Lord. President Harold B. Lee spoke of "iffy" blessings as follows:

"I sat in a class in Sunday School in my own ward one day, and the teacher was the son of a patriarch. He said he used to take down the blessings of his father, and he noticed that his father gave what he called 'iffy' blessings. He would give a blessing, but it was predicated on . . . 'if you will cease doing that.' And he said, 'I watched these men to whom my father gave the "iffy" blessings, and I saw that many of them did not heed the warning that my father as a patriarch had given, and the blessings were never received because they did not comply.'

"You know, this started me thinking. I went back into the Doctrine and Covenants and began to read the 'iffy' revelations that have been given to the various brethren in the Church. If you want to have an exercise in something that will startle you, read some of the warnings that were given through the Prophet Joseph Smith to Thomas B. Marsh, Martin Harris, some of the Whitmer brothers, William E. McLellin—warnings which, had they heeded, some would not have fallen by the wayside. But because they did not heed, and they didn't clear up their lives, they fell by the wayside, and some had to be dropped from membership in the Church" (In Conference Report, Oct. 1972, 130; or *Ensign,* Jan. 1973, 107–8).

We will look at these "ifs" and at the great blessings promised to James Covel if he would follow the counsel of the Lord. But first, as mentioned previously in this study guide, the Doctrine and Covenants contains many "doctrines," but there are just a few "covenants." The covenants we make with God pertain to obtaining celestial glory and exaltation in the highest degree of glory thereof. These covenants include baptism and confirmation, sacrament, ordination to Melchizedek Priesthood for men, endowments, and celestial marriage. They also include covenants we make with the Lord through our priesthood leaders during temple recommend interviews, including payment of tithing, sabbath observance, and keeping the Word of Wisdom.

Two of these "covenants" mentioned now by the Savior to James Covel are those of baptism and confirmation, in verse 10. They are given in conjunction with the "ifs" in this revelation.

Covenants

Verse 10. Baptism and Confirmation

10 But, behold, the days of thy
deliverance are come [*you can be*
delivered from this pride, etc., now],
if thou wilt hearken to my voice,
which saith unto thee: Arise and
be baptized, and **wash away**
your sins, calling on my name,
and you shall **receive my Spirit**
[*receive the gift of the Holy Ghost*],
and a blessing so great as you
never have known.

11 And **if thou do** this, **I have pre-**
pared thee for a greater work
[*you will be able to do even greater*
things than you have in the past].
Thou shalt preach the fulness of
my gospel [*rather than the incom-*
plete gospel you have been preaching
in the past], which I have sent forth
in these last days, **the covenant**
[*that the Lord made that He would*
gather Israel in the last days] which I
have sent forth **to recover** [*gather*]
my people, which are of **the house**
of Israel [*the twelve tribes of Israel*].

12 And it shall come to pass that
power shall rest upon thee; **thou**
shalt have great faith, and **I will**

be with thee and go before thy face [*among other things, the Lord will prepare people to hear Brother Covel's preaching*].

13 **Thou art called to labor in my vineyard** [*the earth*], and to **build up my church**, and to **bring forth Zion** [*help establish the restored Church*], that it may rejoice upon the hills and flourish.

Next, the Lord specifically tells James Covel that He does not want him to do missionary work in the eastern United States. While we do not know, we have to wonder if that is where James Covel wanted to go, perhaps because he would be among former members of his congregations and other friends. Whatever the case, he is told to gather with the Saints in Ohio, which means that he would be leaving basically everything and starting over new. This was a real test of faith and of the depth of his commitment to the covenant (see background notes above) he had made with the Lord before this revelation, to follow whatever instructions were given him through Joseph Smith.

14 Behold, verily, verily, I say unto thee, **thou art not called to go into the eastern countries** [*eastern United States and perhaps Canada*], **but thou art called to go to the Ohio.**

Next, the Savior gives James Covel an idea of the great blessings that await him if he will gather with the Saints to Ohio.

15 And **inasmuch as** [*if*] **my people shall assemble themselves at the Ohio**, I have kept in store **a blessing such as is not known among the children of men**, and **it shall be poured forth upon their heads** [*among other things, they will build the Kirtland Temple and receive the tremendous blessings of the visits of the Savior, Moses, Elias, and Elijah; see D&C 110*]. And **from thence men shall go forth into all nations**.

Next, we are given an insight into the fact that people have agency, and if they use it to be disobedient, the Lord is obligated by eternal laws to punish them if they continue to refuse to repent, even though kind and merciful Saints continue to pray that He will hold back the punishments.

16 Behold, verily, verily, I say unto you, that **the people in Ohio call upon me in much faith, thinking I will stay my hand in judgment** [*thinking that I will hold back the punishments*] upon the nations, **but I cannot deny my word**.

Nephi was taught this same lesson (verse 16, above) early on in his life, at a time when he prayed fervently for Laman and Lemuel.

We will quote this short scripture block from First Nephi and use **bold** to point out this lesson:

<u>1 Nephi 2:17–21</u>

17 And **I spake unto Sam, making known unto him the things which the Lord had manifested unto me by his Holy Spirit**. And it came to pass that **he believed in my words**.

18 But, behold, **Laman and Lemuel would not hearken unto my words; and being grieved** because of the hardness of their hearts **I cried unto the Lord for them**.

19 And it came to pass that **the Lord spake unto me**, saying: **Blessed art thou, Nephi, because of thy faith**, for thou hast sought me diligently, with lowliness of heart.

20 And **inasmuch as ye shall keep my commandments, ye shall prosper**, and shall be led to a land of promise; yea, even a land which I have prepared for you; yea, a land which is choice above all other lands.

21 And **inasmuch as thy brethren shall rebel against thee, they shall be cut off from the presence of the Lord**.

As we continue with section 39, the Savior informs James Covel that there is one way in which the judgments (punishments) of God can be held back. If people like him accept the gospel and spread it successfully to others (verse 17), then the punishments will not come (verse 18).

17 Wherefore **lay to** [*go to work*] **with your might** and call faithful laborers into my vineyard [*bring others into the Church to join you*], that it [*the "vineyard," the inhabitants of the world*] may be pruned [*have false doctrines, false philosophies, pride, wickedness, etc. cut out of their thinking and their lives*] for the last time [*before the Second Coming of Christ*].

18 And **inasmuch as** [*if*] **they do repent and receive the fulness of my gospel, and become sanctified** [*made clean, pure, and fit to be in the presence of God*], **I will stay mine hand in judgment**.

Yet again, in verse 19, next, James Covel is instructed to go forward in missionary work. Imagine how the skills and knowledge he gained as a Methodist minister for over forty years would bless him and those he would teach in this effort!

19 Wherefore, **go forth** [*in this missionary work*], **crying with a loud voice, saying: The kingdom of heaven is at hand** [*the true gospel*

is now available to you]; crying: Hosanna! [*see notes about "Hosanna" after D&C 36:3 in this study guide*] blessed [*praised*] be the name of the Most High God.

If James Covel will obey the Lord's counsel to him in this revelation, he will be baptized and ordained to the Melchizedek Priesthood such that as he goes forth preaching, he can baptize converts and confirm them, giving them the gift of the Holy Ghost. He will then have proper priesthood authority to do this (which he did not have formerly, as a minister). In other words, the Lord is clearly telling him what his potential is, much the same as He tells us our potential in our patriarchal blessings.

20 **Go forth baptizing** with water [*by immersion*], preparing the way before my face for the time of my coming [*the Second Coming*];

In verse 21, next, we are reminded that no one knows the "day or the hour" when Christ will come in power and glory to start His millennial reign on earth, which will last for a thousand years.

Doctrine

Verse 21. No man knows the day or hour of the Second Coming.

21 **For the time is at hand** [*the Second Coming is getting close*]; **the day or the hour no man knoweth**; but it surely shall come.

It is interesting that some people can't seem to accept what the Lord said in verse 21, above, at face value. For instance, some teach that our living prophets, the First Presidency, and the Quorum of the Twelve Apostles will know the day and hour but will just not be allowed to tell us. Elder M. Russell Ballard of the Twelve addressed this issue in a BYU devotional on March 12, 1996, as follows (**bold** added for emphasis):

"Now with the Lord's help I would like to speak to you about a subject that is on a lot of people's minds. My intention is not to alarm or to frighten, but to discuss the significant and interesting times in which we are now living, to consider some of the events and circumstances we can anticipate in the future and to suggest a few things we can all do to fortify ourselves and our families for the challenges and trials that will surely come into all of our lives at one time or another."

Elder Ballard continued, reading from Matthew 24:3–7, reading and commenting, and then paused, saying, "I want to pause here for a moment and suggest to you, if you haven't been aware, that some of these things seem to be occurring with ever-increasing regularity. If you measured the natural disasters that have occurred in the world during the last 10 years and plotted that year-by-year, you would see an acceleration. The earth is rumbling, and earthquakes are occurring in 'divers places.' Human nature being what it is, we don't normally pay much attention to these natural phenomena until they happen close to where we are living. But when we contemplate what has happened during the past decade, not only with earthquakes but also with regards to hurricanes, floods, tornadoes, volcanic eruptions, and the like, you would see an accelerating pattern.

"So, can we use this scientific data to extrapolate that the Second Coming is likely to occur during the next few years, or the next decade, or the next century? Not really. I am called as one of the apostles to be a special witness of Christ in these exciting, trying times, and **I do not know when He is going to come again**. As far as I know, none of my brethren in the Council of the Twelve or even in the First Presidency knows. And I would humbly suggest to you, my young brothers and sisters, that **if we do not know, then nobody knows**, no matter how compelling their arguments or how reasonable their calculations."

We will now finish our study of section 39. In verse 22, next, we see, among other things, the commonly used phrase in the Church "in time and eternity," which means on this earth as well as throughout eternity.

22 And he that receiveth these things [*the blessings and message of the restored gospel*] receiveth me [*receives Christ*]; and they shall be gathered unto me **in time and in eternity**.

23 And again, it shall come to pass that on as many as ye shall baptize with water, **ye shall lay your hands, and they shall receive the gift of the Holy Ghost**, and shall be looking forth for the signs of my coming [*the signs of the times*], and shall know me.

24 Behold, **I come quickly** [*can mean that when the Savior comes, it will be quickly, worldwide, rather than meaning He is coming right away*]. Even so. Amen.

SECTION 40

Background

Section 40 goes together with section 39. Please refer to the background notes for section 39 in this study guide. By way of summary, James Covel, who had been a Methodist minister (see *Doctrine and Covenants Student Manual*, 2018 edition, chapter 14) for about forty years, had approached joining the Church with great enthusiasm, covenanting with the Lord that he would do whatever he was told to do by way of revelation through the Prophet

Joseph Smith. As a result, he was given the revelation contained in section 39 at Fayette, New York, on January 5, 1831, three days after the third general conference of the Church was held there.

But on the next day, James Covel abruptly left Fayette. This was no doubt a big disappointment to Joseph Smith and Sidney Rigdon. On this day, January 6, 1831, the Lord gave the revelation recorded in section 40 to Joseph and Sidney, explaining why James went back on his word and that He, the Lord, would handle the matter from that point on. The Prophet recorded the following regarding James Covel at this point:

"As James Covill [*Covel*] rejected the word of the Lord, and returned to his former principles and people, the Lord gave unto me and Sidney Rigdon the following revelation, explaining why he obeyed not the word: [D&C 40]" (*History of the Church,* 1:145).

Among the lessons we might learn from this very brief revelation is that agency plays a pivotal role in our lives. The Lord teaches us what our potential is, and then we use our agency to accept or reject it. This is the case with many patriarchal blessings. We are shown our potential and given great blessings and promises. But we are free to reject those blessings, and some do, as did James Covel.

Some people might be inclined to ask why the Lord would pronounce such a marvelous revelation upon this man, James Covel, when He knew that he would reject the gospel. The answer comes in the form of an important principle; namely that **the Lord does not withhold present blessings from us because of our future misbehavior** (see *Doctrine and Covenants Student Manual*, 1981, page 306).

Yet another lesson for us here might be that we should not try to second guess such people to any great degree; rather, we should hope and pray for the best for them and turn the matter over to the Lord (verse 3).

One more observation. As you know, it is possible for a person's heart to be right before the Lord, which opens the door to view available blessings. The door can be closed again through a change of heart. This principle is taught clearly in the parable of the sower (Matthew 13:3–9, 18–23).

1 BEHOLD, verily I say unto you, that **the heart of my servant James Covill was right before me**, for he covenanted with me [*before the revelation was given; see notes for section 39 in this study guide*] that he would obey my word.

2 And **he received the word with gladness**, but straightway [*right away*] Satan tempted him;

and the **fear of persecution** and the **cares of the world caused him to reject the word**.

3 Wherefore he broke my covenant, and **it remaineth with me to do with him as seemeth me good** [*in other words, the Lord will handle it from here*]. Amen.

SECTION 41

Background

This revelation was given to the members of the Church on February 4, 1831, at Kirtland, Ohio. It is the first of many revelations in the Doctrine and Covenants given in Ohio. By now a large number of members had gathered in Ohio according to the commandment of the Lord (D&C 37:1, 3; 38:32) with the central location for gathering being in Kirtland.

The Prophet Joseph Smith and his wife, Emma, along with Sidney Rigdon and Edward Partridge, arrived in Kirtland from New York in early February, a few days before this revelation was given. This 300-mile trip in winter cold was difficult for Emma, who had already moved seven times since their marriage four years before. To make things more trying, she was just recovering from a month of being sick and was six months pregnant with twins. Joseph Knight provided a good sleigh to make the trip a bit more bearable for her.

Upon their arrival, the sleigh stopped in front of a store owned by Newel K. Whitney. What followed is another testimony of the prophetic calling of Joseph Smith:

"About the first of February the sleigh pulled up in front of Newel K. Whitney's store in Kirtland. Joseph sprang from the sleigh and entered the store. 'Newel K. Whitney! Thou art the man,' he exclaimed, extending his hand cordially, as if to an old and familiar acquaintance. 'You have the advantage of me,' replied the merchant, . . . I could not call you by name as you have me.' 'I am Joseph the Prophet,' said the stranger smiling. 'You've prayed me here, now what do you want of me?' Joseph explained to the amazed merchant that back in New York he had seen Newel in a vision praying for him to come to Kirtland. The Whitney's received Joseph and Emma Smith with kindness and invited them to live temporarily with them. During the next several weeks the Smiths 'received every kindness and attention which could be expected, and especially from Sister Whitney'" (*Church History in the Fulness of Times*, 2003, 90–91).

The Prophet Joseph Smith gave background to this section as follows:

"The branch of the Church in this part of the Lord's vineyard, which had increased to nearly one hundred members, were striving to do the will of God, so far as they knew it, though some strange notions and false spirits had crept in among them. With a little caution and some wisdom, I soon assisted the brethren and sisters to overcome them. The plan of 'common stock,' which had existed in what was called 'the family,' whose members generally had embraced the everlasting Gospel, was readily abandoned for the more perfect law of the Lord; and the false spirits were easily discerned and rejected by the light of revelation.

"The Lord gave unto the Church the following: [D&C 41]" (*History of the Church*, 1:146–47).

One other bit of background for understanding this section, as well as section 42, is that many of the members in the Kirtland area had been living a type of "united order" prior to joining the Church. In other words, they had all things in common. Joseph Smith had succeeded in persuading these new converts to leave this order and told them that the Lord would reveal to them the proper form of the law of consecration. A first step toward the proper order of the Lord with respect to this matter was the appointing of the first bishop of the Church (Edward Partridge in verse 9).

As we begin our study of the verses in this section, we find some strong wording against hypocrites in verse 1. It is a strong contrast between faithful Saints, who do their best to obey the Lord, and others, who claim membership in the Church, but who do not really want to live the gospel.

Doctrine

Verse 1. The Lord loves to bless us.

1 HEARKEN and hear, O ye my people, saith the Lord and your God, ye whom I delight to bless with the greatest of all blessings, ye that hear me [*listen and obey*]; and **ye that hear me not** [*disregard the Lord's commandments*] **will I curse, that have professed my name** [*who claim to be members but don't follow the Lord's commandments; in other words, you who are hypocrites*], with the heaviest of all cursings.

You may recall that in the New Testament, the Savior was patient toward all kinds of sinners, with the exception of those who were deeply hypocritical, whom He called "whited sepulchres." We will quote this verse from Matthew:

Matthew 23:27

Woe unto you, scribes and Pharisees, **hypocrites**! for ye are like unto **whited sepulchres** [*whitewashed graves*], which indeed **appear beautiful outward, but are within** [*inside*] **full of dead *men's* bones, and of all uncleanness.**

Next, in verses 2–3, the Lord teaches these members the importance of unity and harmony as preparation to receive revelation from God.

2 Hearken, O ye elders of my church whom I have called, behold **I give unto you a commandment**, that ye shall **assemble yourselves together to agree upon my word**;

3 And **by the prayer of your faith ye shall receive my law** [*which will be given in section 42*], **that ye may know how to govern my church and have all things right before me.**

It is hoped that from this section you will sense the importance of what the Lord reveals in section 42. The main purpose of section 41 is to prepare the Lord's people for what He gives them in section 42, which is often referred to as "The Law."

Next, especially in verse 5, you can sense that with the added knowledge that is coming to these early members of the Church, comes a considerable increase in accountability.

4 And I will be your ruler when I come [*for the Millennium*]; and behold, I come quickly, and **ye shall see that my law is kept.**

5 **He that receiveth my law and doeth it, the same is my disciple** [*a true follower of Christ*]; and **he that saith he receiveth it and doeth it not, the same is not my disciple, and shall be cast out from among you** [*otherwise, they will ruin the harmony and unity that are required in order to become a "Zion" people*];

6 **For it is not meet** [*good, proper, appropriate*] **that the things which belong to the children of the kingdom** [*faithful members of the Church*] **should be given to them that are not worthy** [*in other words, who are hypocritical and don't desire to live the gospel*], or to dogs [*a reference to Matthew 7:6*], or the pearls [*precious gospel truths, experiences, testimonies, etc.*] to be cast before swine [*see Matthew 7:6*].

In verses 7–8, the members are instructed to provide a house for Joseph and Emma. They will build a small frame house for them on the Isaac Morley farm. The instruction for Sidney Rigdon's accommodations is a bit different, perhaps because he is from this area and has many friends and acquaintances. In fact, Leman Copley, who has a large farm about 20 miles east of Kirtland, will offer to provide a house and supplies for Sidney and his wife, Phoebe.

7 And again, it is meet [*needed*] that my servant **Joseph Smith, Jun., should have a house built, in which to live and translate** [*resume work on translating the Bible, which will become the Joseph Smith Translation of the Bible or JST*].

8 And again, it is meet that my servant **Sidney Rigdon should live as seemeth him good**, inasmuch as he keepeth my commandments.

Next, Edward Partridge is called to be the first Bishop of the Church. Among other things, this is an important step in setting things in place for the Saints to live the law of consecration. Notice that the law of "common consent," established in section 26, is now firmly in place in the Church.

9 And again, I have called my servant **Edward Partridge**; and I give a commandment, that he should be appointed [*sustained*] **by the voice of the church** [*by the members of the Church, according to the law of common consent*], and ordained a **bishop unto the church**, to leave his merchandise [*his hat shop (he was a journeyman hatter) and other property*] and to **spend all his time in the labors of the church**;

10 **To see to all things** as it shall be appointed unto him **in my laws** in the day that I shall give them.

As you can see, based on the end of verse 10, above, the Lord is telling these members that He is going to reveal much more concerning the law of consecration and other laws and principles soon.

As this revelation draws to a close, the Lord pays Edward Partridge a high complement.

11 And this because **his heart is pure before me**, for **he is like unto Nathanael of old** [*see John 1:47*], **in whom there is no guile** [*deceit; selfish motives; fraud*].

Finally, the Lord warns them not to change or alter the words of this revelation. We are also reminded that accountability increases with additional knowledge of the gospel. Of course, it is worth it, but it is good to be reminded of the consequences of sinning against knowledge. See D&C 82:3.

12 **These words are given unto you, and they are pure before me**; wherefore, **beware how you hold them**, for they are to be answered upon your souls [*you are accountable to live by them*] in the day of judgment. Even so. Amen.

SECTION 42

Background

This revelation is often referred to as "The Law" or "The Law of the Lord." If you truly want to be a disciple of Christ and return to the Father in celestial exaltation, you will follow the principles and commandments taught in this section.

The Lord promised the Saints that He would give them this "law" in Ohio (D&C 38:32).

Given through the Prophet Joseph Smith, section 42 was actually revealed in two parts. Verses 1 through 72 were given February 9, 1831, in the presence of twelve elders (see heading to section 42 in your Doctrine and Covenants), and verses 74–93 were given two weeks later on February 23, 1831. Verse 73 was added by Joseph Smith at the time the Doctrine and Covenants was published. (See institutes of religion, *Doctrine and Covenants Student Manual*, 2018, chapter 16.)

An additional quote from the 2018 *Doctrine and Covenants Student Manual*, chapter 16, is also helpful in setting the stage for our study of section 42:

"In obedience to the Lord's direction recorded in Doctrine and Covenants 41:2–3, the Prophet Joseph Smith and 12 elders met on February 9, 1831, and prayed together, supplicating the Lord to manifest His law. These brethren asked the Lord about five matters in particular: (1) whether the various communities of Saints should gather in one place or remain separate for the time being, (2) what the Lord's law was for governing and regulating the Church, (3) how they should care for the families of those called to serve as missionaries, (4) how the Saints living under the principles of consecration should deal with nonmembers, and (5) what preparations should be made in order to care for the Saints arriving from the East (see *The Joseph Smith Papers, Documents, Volume 1: July 1828–June 1831,* ed. Michael Hubbard MacKay and others [2013], 246–47, note 42). In response, the Prophet received the revelation recorded in Doctrine and Covenants 42:1–72, which is a composite of revelatory answers that the Lord gave these brethren in answer to the first three questions. The revealed answers to the remaining questions were not published as part of the Doctrine and Covenants.

"Two weeks later, on February 23, 1831, Joseph Smith and seven elders approached the Lord with further questions regarding implementing the law of the Church. The Lord gave these men additional direction. This direction was added to the February 9 revelation and is now recorded in Doctrine and Covenants 42:74–93. The additional details recorded in Doctrine and Covenants 42:73 were added later by the Prophet at the time the

Doctrine and Covenants was prepared for publication. It is important to note that the Prophet Joseph Smith occasionally made changes or additions to previously recorded revelations to clarify or reflect additional understanding that the Lord had revealed. These inspired revisions illustrate the ongoing nature of revelation and are an example of the right and authority of the Lord and His prophet to amend or clarify previous revelation."

This section is one of the great doctrinal revelations from the Lord, as explained by Apostle George Q. Cannon as follows:

"Altogether this was a most important revelation. It threw a flood of light upon a great variety of subjects and settled many important questions. Faithful men and women were greatly delighted at being members of a Church which the Lord acknowledged as His own, and to which He communicated His word through his inspired Prophet as he did at this time" (*Life of Joseph Smith*, Good Press, 109).

We will first go through this section, using **bold** to point out several of the many "laws" contained in this revelation. Then we will repeat the verses, doing yet more as we go through again.

The Law of Listening and Obeying

1 HEARKEN, O ye elders of my church, who have assembled yourselves together in my name, even Jesus Christ the Son of the living God, the Savior of the world; inasmuch as ye believe on my name and **keep my commandments**.

2 Again I say unto you, **hearken** and **hear** and **obey** the law which I shall give unto you.

The Law of Unity

3 For verily I say, as ye have assembled yourselves together according to the commandment wherewith I commanded you, and are agreed as touching this one thing, and have asked the Father in my name, even so ye shall receive.

The Law of Missionary Work

4 Behold, verily I say unto you, I give unto you this first commandment, that **ye shall go forth in my name**, every one of you, excepting my servants Joseph Smith, Jun., and Sidney Rigdon.

5 And I give unto them a commandment that they shall go forth for a little season, and it shall be given by the power of the Spirit when they shall return.

6 And ye shall **go forth in the power of my Spirit**, preaching my gospel, **two by two**, in my

name, lifting up your voices as with the sound of a trump, declaring my word like unto angels of God.

7 And ye shall go forth **baptizing with water, saying: Repent ye, repent ye, for the kingdom of heaven is at hand**.

8 And from this place ye shall go forth into the regions westward; and inasmuch as ye shall find them that will receive you ye shall **build up my church in every region**—

9 **Until the time shall come when it shall be revealed unto you from on high, when the city of the New Jerusalem shall be prepared**, that ye may be gathered in one, that ye may be my people and I will be your God.

The Law of Replacing Church Leaders Who Transgress

10 And again, I say unto you, that my servant Edward Partridge shall stand in the office whereunto I have appointed him. And it shall come to pass, that **if he transgress another shall be appointed in his stead**. Even so. Amen.

The Law of No Secret Ordinations

11 Again I say unto you, that **it shall not be given to any one to go forth to preach my gospel, or to build up my church, except he be ordained by some one who has authority, and it is known to the church that he has authority and has been regularly ordained by the heads of the church**.

The Law of Teaching

12 And again, the elders, priests and teachers of this church shall **teach the principles of my gospel, which are in the Bible and the Book of Mormon**, in the which is the fulness of the gospel.

13 And they shall **observe the covenants and church articles** [*Doctrine and Covenants, section 20*] **to do them**, and **these shall be their teachings, as they shall be directed by the Spirit**.

The Law of Obtaining the Spirit in Order to Teach

14 And **the Spirit shall be given unto you by the prayer of faith**; and **if ye receive not the Spirit ye shall not teach**.

The Law of Continuing Revelation and Additional Scripture

15 And **all this ye shall observe to do as I have commanded concerning your teaching, until the fulness of my scriptures is given**.

16 And as **ye shall lift up your voices by the Comforter, ye shall speak and prophesy as seemeth me good**;

17 For, behold, **the Comforter knoweth all things, and beareth record of the Father and of the Son**.

The Law of Avoiding Going to Telestial Glory

18 And now, behold, I speak unto the church. **Thou shalt not kill** [*intentional murder*]; and he that kills shall not have forgiveness in this world, nor in the world to come.

19 And again, I say, thou shalt not kill; but he that killeth shall die.

20 **Thou shalt not steal**; and he that **stealeth and will not repent** shall be cast out.

21 Thou shalt **not lie**; he that lieth and will **not repent** shall be cast out.

22 Thou shalt **love thy wife with all thy heart, and shalt cleave unto her and none else**.

23 And **he that looketh upon a woman to lust after her shall deny the faith, and shall not have the Spirit**; and **if he repents not he shall be cast out**.

24 **Thou shalt not commit adultery**; and he that **committeth adultery, and repenteth not, shall be cast out**.

25 **But he that has committed adultery and repents with all his heart, and forsaketh it, and doeth it no more, thou shalt forgive**;

26 But if he doeth it again, he shall not be forgiven, but shall be cast out.

27 **Thou shalt not speak evil of thy neighbor**, nor **do him** any **harm**.

28 Thou knowest my laws concerning these things are given in my scriptures; he that sinneth and **repent**eth **not** shall be cast out.

The Law of Obtaining Celestial Glory

29 If thou **lov**est **me** thou shalt **serve me** and **keep all my commandments**.

30 And behold, thou wilt **remember the poor**, and **consecrate of thy properties for their support** that which thou hast to impart unto them, with a covenant and a deed which cannot be broken.

31 And inasmuch as ye **impart of your substance unto the poor**, ye will do it unto me; and they shall be laid before the bishop of my church and his counselors, two of the elders, or high priests, such as he shall appoint or has appointed and set apart for that purpose.

32 And it shall come to pass, that after they are laid before the bishop of my church, and after that he has received these testimonies concerning the consecration of the properties of my church, that they cannot be taken from the church, agreeable to my commandments, every man shall be made accountable unto me, a steward over his own property, or that which he has received by consecration, as much as is sufficient for himself and family.

33 And again, if there shall be properties in the hands of the church, or any individuals of it, more than is necessary for their support after this first consecration, which is a residue to be consecrated unto the bishop, it shall be kept to administer to those who have not, from time to time, that every man who has need may be amply supplied and receive according to his wants.

34 Therefore, the residue shall be kept in my storehouse, to administer to the poor and the needy, as shall be appointed by the high council of the church, and the bishop and his council;

35 And for the purpose of purchasing lands for the public benefit of the church, and building houses of worship, and building up of the New Jerusalem which is hereafter to be revealed—

36 That my covenant people may be gathered in one in that day when I shall come to my temple. And this I do for the salvation of my people.

37 And it shall come to pass, that he that sinneth and repenteth not shall be cast out of the church, and shall not receive again that which he has consecrated unto the poor and the needy of my church, or in other words, unto me—

38 For **inasmuch as ye do it unto the least of these, ye do it unto me**.

39 For it shall come to pass, that which I spake by the mouths of

my prophets shall be fulfilled; for I will consecrate of the riches of those who embrace my gospel among the Gentiles unto the poor of my people who are of the house of Israel.

40 And again, **thou shalt not be proud in thy heart**; let all thy garments be plain, and their beauty the beauty of the work of thine own hands;

41 And **let all things be done in cleanliness before me**.

The Law of Work

42 **Thou shalt not be idle**; for he that is idle shall not eat the bread nor wear the garments of the laborer.

The Law of Healing

43 And **whosoever among you are sick**, and **have not faith to be healed, but believe**, shall be **nourished with** all **tenderness**, with **herbs** and **mild food,** and that not by the hand of an enemy.

44 And the **elders of the church, two or more**, shall be called, and shall pray for and **lay their hands upon them in my name**; and **if they die they shall die unto me, and if they live they shall live unto me.**

45 **Thou shalt live together in love**, insomuch that thou shalt **weep for the loss of them that die**, and **more especially for those that have not hope of a glorious resurrection**.

46 And it shall come to pass that **those that die in me shall not taste of death, for it shall be sweet unto them**;

47 And **they that die not in me**, wo unto them, for **their death is bitter**.

The Law of Faith

48 And again, it shall come to pass that he that hath **faith in me to be healed**, and is **not appointed unto death, shall be healed**.

49 He who hath **faith** to see shall see.

50 He who hath **faith** to hear shall hear.

51 The lame who hath **faith** to leap shall leap.

52 And **they who have not faith to do these things, but believe in me, have power to become my sons** [*can be saved in celestial glory also*]; and inasmuch as they break not my laws thou shalt bear their infirmities.

The Law of Consecration

53 **Thou shalt stand in the place of thy stewardship**.

54 **Thou shalt not take thy brother's garment**; thou shalt **pay for that which thou shalt receive of thy brother**.

55 And **if thou obtainest more than that which would be for thy support, thou shalt give it into my storehouse**, that all things may be done according to that which I have said.

The Law of Continuing with the Work of Translating the Bible (the JST)

56 Thou shalt **ask, and my scriptures shall be given** as I have appointed, and they shall be preserved in safety;

57 And it is expedient that thou shouldst hold thy peace concerning them, and **not teach them until ye have received them in full**.

58 And I give unto you a commandment that **then ye shall teach them unto all men**; for they shall be taught unto **all nations, kindreds, tongues and people**.

59 Thou shalt take the things which thou hast received, which have been given unto thee in my scriptures for a law, to be my law to govern my church;

The Law of Being Saved

60 And **he that doeth according to these things shall be saved**, and **he that doeth them not shall be damned if he so continue**.

The Law of Gaining Additional Knowledge

61 **If thou shalt ask, thou shalt receive** revelation upon revelation, knowledge upon knowledge, that thou mayest know the mysteries and peaceable things—that which bringeth joy, that which bringeth life eternal.

62 **Thou shalt ask**, and it shall be revealed unto you in mine own due time where the New Jerusalem shall be built.

The Law of Missionary Work (continued)

63 And behold, it shall come to pass that **my servants shall be sent forth to the east** and to the **west**, to the **north** and to the **south**.

64 And even now, let him that goeth to the east teach them that shall be converted to flee to the west, and this in consequence of that which is coming on the earth, and of secret combinations.

The Law of Knowing the Mysteries **(details of the gospel, which are a mystery to those caught up in the ways of the world)**

65 Behold, thou shalt **observe all these things**, and **great shall be thy reward; for unto you it is given to know the mysteries of the kingdom**, but unto the world it is not given to know them.

66 Ye shall **observe the laws which ye have received and be faithful**.

67 And **ye shall hereafter receive** church **covenants, such as shall be sufficient to establish you**, both here and in the New Jerusalem.

68 Therefore, **he that lacketh wisdom, let him ask of me, and I will give him liberally and upbraid him not**.

69 Lift up your hearts and rejoice, for unto you the kingdom, or in other words, the keys of the church have been given. Even so. Amen.

The Law of Using Consecrated Property to Support Church Officers

70 **The priests and teachers shall have their stewardships**, even as the members.

71 And **the elders or high priests who are appointed to assist the bishop** as counselors in all things, **are to have their families supported out of the property which is consecrated to the bishop**, for the good of the poor, and for other purposes, as before mentioned;

72 **Or they are to receive a just remuneration for all their services**, either a stewardship or otherwise, as may be thought best or decided by the counselors and bishop.

73 **And the bishop, also, shall receive his support, or a just remuneration for all his services in the church**.

The Law for Dealing with Divorce Because of Fornication

74 Behold, verily I say unto you, that **whatever persons among you, having put away their companions for the cause of fornication**, or in other words, **if they shall testify before you in all lowliness of heart that this is the case, ye shall not cast them out from among you**;

The Law for Dealing with Divorce Because of Adultery

75 **But if ye shall find that any persons have left their**

companions for the sake of adultery, and **they themselves are the offenders**, and their companions are living, they **shall be cast out from among you**.

76 And again, I say unto you, that ye shall be watchful and careful, with all inquiry, that ye **receive none such among you if they are married**;

The Law of Allowing Persons Guilty of Sexual Sin into Membership in the Church

77 And **if they are not married, they shall repent of all their sins or ye shall not receive them.**

The Law of Maintaining Good Standing in the Church

78 And again, every person who belongeth to this church of Christ, shall observe to keep all the commandments and covenants of the church.

The Law for Dealing with Murderers

79 And it shall come to pass, that **if any persons among you shall kill they shall be delivered up and dealt with according to the laws of the land**; for remember that he hath **no forgiveness**; and it shall be proved according to the laws of the land.

The Law for Dealing with Members Who Commit Adultery

80 And **if any man or woman shall commit adultery, he or she shall be tried before two elders of the church, or more**, and **every word shall be established** against him or her **by two witnesses of the church**, and not of the enemy; but **if there are more than two witnesses it is better**.

81 But **he or she shall be condemned by the mouth of two witnesses**; and **the elders shall lay the case before the church, and the church shall lift up their hands against him or her**, that they may be dealt with according to the law of God.

82 And **if it can be, it is necessary that the bishop be present also**.

83 And thus ye shall do in all cases which shall come before you.

The Laws of Dealing with Members Who Steal, Rob, Lie.

84 And if a man or woman shall **rob**, he or she shall be **delivered up unto the law of the land.**

85 And if he or she shall **steal**, he or she shall be **delivered up unto the law of the land**.

86 And if he or she shall **lie**, he or she shall be **delivered up unto the law of the land**.

The Law of Final Judgment by God

87 And **if he or she do any manner of iniquity, he or she shall be delivered up unto the law, even that of God**.

The Law Governing How Members Are to Deal with Those Who Have Offended Them

88 And if thy brother or sister offend thee, thou shalt **take him or her between him or her and thee alone**; and **if he or she confess thou shalt be reconciled**.

89 And **if he or she confess not** thou shalt **deliver him or her up unto the church**, not to the members, but **to the elders** [*turn the matter over to the leaders of the branch or ward, etc.*]. And it shall be done **in a meeting**, and that **not before the world** [*keep it as private as possible*].

90 And **if** thy brother or sister **offend many**, he or she shall be **chastened before many**.

91 And **if** any one **offend openly**, he or she shall be **rebuked openly**, that he or she may be ashamed. And **if** he or she **confess not**, he or she shall be **delivered up unto the law of God**.

92 **If** any shall **offend in secret**, he or she shall be **rebuked in secret, that he or she may have opportunity to confess in secret to him or her whom he or she has offended, and to God**, that the church may not speak reproachfully of him or her [*so that there is not a lot of gossip about him or her*].

93 And **thus shall ye conduct in all things**.

We will now repeat section 42, adding additional notes and commentary. As is the case in previous revelations, the Savior identifies Himself as the one giving this revelation.

1 **HEARKEN**, O ye elders of my church, who have assembled yourselves together in my name, even **Jesus Christ the Son of the living God** [*as opposed to "dead" or inanimate gods, idols, etc.*]**, the Savior of the world**; inasmuch as ye believe on my name and keep my commandments.

2 Again I say unto you, **hearken** and **hear** and **obey the law** which I shall give unto you.

3 For verily I say, **as ye have assembled yourselves together**

according to the commandment wherewith I commanded you [*in D&C 41:2–3*], **and are agreed** as touching this one thing [*are unified and in harmony on this matter of seeking the "Law of the Lord"*], and have asked the Father in my name, even so **ye shall receive**.

It is crucial that the membership of the Church increase rapidly at this point in the beginnings of the Restored Church. Perhaps you have noticed that the Lord had a great many people in place to accept the gospel. The first commandment the Savior gives here has to do with this need for rapid membership growth.

4 Behold, verily I say unto you, I give unto you **this first commandment**, that **ye shall go forth in my name, every one of you, excepting** my servants **Joseph Smith, Jun.,** and **Sidney Rigdon**.

Perhaps one of the reasons Joseph Smith and Sidney Rigdon were told not to spend much time in missionary efforts in verse 4, above, and in verse 5, next, was that they were to continue with the translation of the Bible (corrections, revisions, etc.), as commanded in verse 56. Joseph was the translator and Sidney was the scribe in this important work that will become The Joseph Smith Translation of the Bible, commonly referred to as the JST.

5 And I give unto them a commandment that **they shall go forth for a little season**, and it shall be **given by the power of the Spirit when they shall return**.

The Savior continues explaining and instructing regarding His commandment to go forth on missions in verses 6–9, next.

6 And ye shall **go forth in the power of my Spirit, preaching** my gospel, **two by two**, in my name, lifting up your voices as **with the sound of a trump** [*a clear, easy-to-pick-out sound as compared to all the confusion about religion in the world*], **declaring my word like unto angels of God**.

In the New England of the day, as is the case in our day, there was much controversy among various religions as to whether or not literal baptism was even necessary, let alone whether or not it could properly be done by sprinkling or should be done by immersion.

7 And ye shall go forth **baptizing with water** [*by immersion*], **saying: Repent ye**, repent ye, for **the kingdom of heaven is at hand** [*meaning, among other things, that the gospel is now being made available to you*].

8 And from this place [*Kirtland*] ye shall **go forth into the regions westward**; and inasmuch as ye

shall find them that will receive you ye shall **build up my church in every region**—

Next, in verse 9, it is made clear that Kirtland, Ohio, is a temporary gathering place. It will be a headquarters and gathering place for about five years (see D&C 64:21), and then the Saints will gather to Missouri, including Independence, Missouri, the location where the New Jerusalem will be built (see D&C 57:1–3).

Doctrine

Verse 9. A city called "New Jerusalem" will be built.

9 **Until the time shall come** when it shall be revealed unto you from on high, **when the city of the New Jerusalem shall be prepared, that ye may be gathered** in one, **that ye may be my people and I will be your God.**

Next, the Lord explains that Church leaders are not above the laws of the Lord, and if they transgress seriously, they must be replaced.

10 And again, I say unto you, that my servant Edward Partridge shall stand in the office whereunto I have appointed him [*as the first Bishop of the Church. See section 41, verse 9*]. And it shall come to pass, that **if he transgress another shall be appointed in his stead** [*in his place*]. Even so. Amen.

It may be that relatively few members realize how important the law of common consent (raising our hands to sustain those called to positions, etc.; see D&C 26:2) is to the stability and security of the Church. Among other things, it protects against apostasy by assuring that there are no secret ordinations in the Church.

For instance, anyone who presides over a group in the Church must have been sustained by that group and ordained or set apart by one who has the proper authority and who has likewise been sustained by members. A number of break-off groups from the Church claim secret ordinations as the source of their authorization to create a new church. Verse 11, next, teaches this principle of having no secret ordinations in the Lord's true Church.

11 Again I say unto you, that **it shall not be given to any one** to go forth to preach my gospel, or **to build up my church, except** [*unless*] **he be ordained by some one who has authority, and it is known to the church that he has authority** and has been **regularly ordained** by the heads of the church.

Next, in verse 12, those who teach the gospel are instructed to stick with the scriptures in their teaching.

12 And again, the elders, priests and teachers of this church shall **teach the principles of my gospel, which are in the Bible and the Book of Mormon**, in the which is the fulness of the gospel.

Next, those who teach the gospel are counseled to live the gospel themselves and to follow the Spirit as to what to teach.

13 And **they shall observe the covenants and church articles** [*another name for section 20; see background notes to section 20 in this study guide*] to **do them**, and **these shall be their teachings, as they shall be directed by the Spirit**.

14 And **the Spirit shall be given unto you by the prayer of faith; and if ye receive not the Spirit ye shall not teach**.

There are at least two ways to look at verse 14, above. One is to understand that it is saying that if you do not have the Spirit with you, don't try to teach. The other way is to consider it to be saying that if you try to teach without the Spirit, your efforts will be unsuccessful. Either way, without the Spirit, your teaching will be ineffective.

15 And **all this ye shall observe to do as I have commanded concerning your teaching**, until the fulness of my scriptures is given.

16 And as ye shall **lift up your voices by the Comforter** [*as directed by the Holy Ghost*], ye shall speak and prophesy as seemeth me good;

<u>Doctrine</u>

Verse 17. The Holy Ghost knows all things.

17 For, behold, the Comforter [*the Holy Ghost*] **knoweth all things, and beareth record of the Father and of the Son.**

Next, in verses 18–28, the Lord reinforces the fact that the Ten Commandments are still in force today. This message is badly needed in our world.

The word "kill," as used in the context of verse 18, next, means the intentional murdering of another human being by one who has sufficient knowledge of the gospel to be accountable for the deed. The Prophet Joseph Smith taught about murderers as follows:

"A murderer, for instance, one that sheds innocent blood, cannot have forgiveness" (*Teachings of the Prophet Joseph Smith*, 339).

The *Doctrine and Covenants Student Manual*, used by our institutes of religion, 1981 edition, page 83, teaches the following about murder:

"There is no forgiveness in this world or in the world to come, because the Atonement of Christ does not cover murder committed by one who has joined the Church—a murderer must suffer for the sin himself (see Smith, *Teachings of the Prophet Joseph Smith*, 339)."

We will now read verses 18 and 19.

Doctrine

Verses 18–28. The Ten Commandments are still in force today.

18 **And now, behold, I speak unto the church. Thou shalt not kill**; and **he that kills shall not have forgiveness in this world, nor in the world to come.**

19 And again, I say, thou shalt not kill; but he that killeth shall die [*according to D&C 42, footnote 19b, this is a reference to capital punishment; verse 79 instructs that murderers are to be dealt with by the laws of the land*].

20 **Thou shalt not steal**; and he that stealeth and will not repent shall be cast out.

21 **Thou shalt not lie**; he that lieth and will not repent shall be cast out.

Verse 22, next, gives counsel for successful marriage. It is interesting to note that there is only one other person, in addition to our spouse, whom we are commanded to love "with all our heart"; namely, the Lord (Matthew 22:37). That puts spouses in a high and exclusive category as well as priority.

22 **Thou shalt love thy wife with all thy heart**, and shalt cleave unto her and none else.

Did you notice also, in verse 22, above, that the Lord leaves absolutely no room for flirting on the part of married people? Spencer W. Kimball taught this subject as follows:

"There are those married people who permit their eyes to wander and their hearts to become vagrant, who think it is not improper to flirt a little, to share their hearts, and have desire for someone other than the wife or the husband, the Lord says in no uncertain terms: [D&C 42:22 quoted]

"And, when the Lord says *all* thy heart, it allows for no sharing nor dividing nor depriving. And, to the woman it is paraphrased: 'Thou shalt love thy husband with *all* thy heart and shalt cleave unto him and none else.' The words *none else* eliminate everyone and everything. The spouse then becomes pre-eminent in the life of the husband or wife, and neither social life nor occupational life nor political life nor any other interest nor person nor thing shall ever take precedence over the companion spouse. We sometimes find women who absorb and hover over the children at the expense of the husband, sometimes even estranging them from him. The Lord says to them: '. . . Thou shalt cleave unto *him* and none else.'" (*Improvement Era*, December 1962, 65:928).

"Marriage presupposes total allegiance and total fidelity. Each spouse takes the partner with the understanding that he or she gives totally to the spouse all the heart, strength, loyalty, honor, and affection, with all dignity. Any divergence is sin; any sharing of the heart is transgression. As we should have 'an eye single to the glory of God,' so should we have an eye, an ear, a heart single to the marriage and the spouse and family" (*Faith Precedes the Miracle*, 142–43).

Next, in verse 23, we learn the dangers and penalties of entertaining lustful thoughts. "Entertaining" means to intentionally continue in engaging in lustful thinking rather than getting such thoughts out of your mind.

A student once asked me why it was such a "big deal" to abstain from sex outside of marriage since the medical technology is readily available to prevent conception. The class, as you can imagine, was at full attention. I complemented her for asking the question and then invited the class to turn to D&C 42:23 to find the answer. (Obviously, if one is involved in sex outside of marriage, that person's mind is entertaining lustful thoughts.) Verse 23 points out two major dangers.

Doctrine

Verse 23. Sexual immorality drives the Spirit away.

23 **And he that looketh upon a woman to lust after her shall deny the faith**, and **shall not have the Spirit**; and if he repents not he shall be cast out.

Referring back to verse 23, above, denying the faith or rejecting your loyalty to God is a most serious consequence of lustful thinking. In addition, driving the Spirit away through intentionally continuing in lustful thinking leaves you wide open to Satan's temptations and input into your mind. Thus, it leaves you vulnerable to much damage from the devil.

Next, in verses 24–26, the issue of adultery and Church disciplinary action (probation, disfellowship, or excommunication) are addressed.

24 **Thou shalt not commit adultery**; and **he that committeth adultery, and repenteth not, shall be cast out** [*subject to Church discipline*].

25 **But he that has committed adultery and repents with all his heart**, and **forsaketh it** [*stops doing it*], and **doeth it no more**, thou shalt **forgive**;

26 But **if he doeth it again**, he shall not be forgiven, but shall be **cast out**.

Sometimes a misunderstanding results from misreading verse 26, above. It is that if a person has committed adultery more than once, he or she must be excommunicated. This is not necessarily the case. That decision is left up to what the Spirit tells the presiding authority (for example, the bishop or stake president) who is conducting the disciplinary council.

The following First Presidency statement from Heber J. Grant, J. Reuben Clark, and David O. McKay is instructional concerning the Church and sexual transgression of members (**bold** added for emphasis):

"To us in this Church the Lord has declared that adulterers should not be admitted to membership (D&C 42:76); that adulterers in the Church, if unrepentant should be cast out (D&C 42:75) but if repentant should be permitted to remain (D&C 42:74, 42:25) and, He said, 'By this ye may know if a man repenteth of his sins—behold, he will confess them and forsake them' (D&C 58:43).

"In the great revelation on the three heavenly glories, the Lord said, speaking of those who will inherit the lowest of these, or the telestial glory: 'These are they who are liars, and sorcerers, and adulterers, and whoremongers, and whosoever loves and makes a lie' (D&C 76:103).

"The doctrine of this Church is that sexual sin—the illicit sexual relations of men and women—stands, in its enormity, next to murder. (Alma 39:3–5)

"The Lord has drawn no essential distinctions between fornication and adultery and harlotry or prostitution. Each has fallen under His solemn and awful condemnation.

"You youths of Zion, you cannot associate in nonmarital, illicit sex relationships, which is fornication, and escape the punishments and the judgments which the Lord has declared against this sin. The day of reckoning will come just as certainly as night follows day. They who would palliate this crime and say that such indulgence is but a sinless gratification of a normal desire, like appeasing hunger and thirst, speak filthiness with their lips. Their counsel leads to destruction; their wisdom comes from the Father of Lies.

"You husbands and wives who have taken on solemn obligations of chastity in the Holy Temples of the Lord and who violate those sacred vows by illicit sexual relations with others, you not only commit the vile and loathsome sin of adultery, but you break the oath you yourselves made with the Lord himself before you went to the altar for your sealing. You become subject to the penalties which the Lord has prescribed for those who breach their covenants with Him. . . .

"But they who sin may repent and they repenting, God will forgive them, for the Lord has said, "Behold, he who has repented of his sins, the same is forgiven and I, the Lord, remember them no more" (D&C 58:42).

"By virtue of the authority in us vested as the First Presidency of the Church, we warn our people who are offending of the degradation, the wickedness, the punishment that attend upon unchastity; we urge you to **remember the blessings which flow from the living of the clean life**; we call upon you to keep, day in and day out, the way of strictest chastity, through which only can God's choice gifts come to you and His Spirit abide with you.

"How glorious is he who lives the chaste life. He walks unfearful in the full glare of the noon-day sun, for he is without moral infirmity. He can be reached by no shafts of base calumny, for his armor is without flaw. His virtue cannot be challenged by any just accuser, for he lives above reproach. His cheek is never blotched with shame for he is without hidden sin. He is honored and respected by all mankind, for he is beyond their censure. He is loved by the Lord, for he stands without blemish. The exaltations of eternities await his coming" (In Conference Report, October 1942, 10–12).

Next, the Lord reminds us that if we want to be true disciples, we will treat others with kindness.

27 **Thou shalt not speak evil of thy neighbor, nor do him any harm.**

Finally, as far as the above scripture block is concerned, the Savior bears witness that the Bible and Book of Mormon contain His commandments concerning the above sins.

28 Thou knowest **my laws concerning these things are given in my scriptures**; he that sinneth and repenteth not shall be cast out.

As we move on to the next several verses, we are taking a large step from the avoiding of telestial behaviors to the living of celestial law, including the law of consecration in a "Zion" society, which involves treating others the way the Savior would treat them.

Perhaps you have wondered whether or not you could live successfully and comfortably in the celestial kingdom in the presence of God. The personal qualities needed for living the law of consecration are evident, and the "ground rules" for living in a Zion environment are given in the next several verses. You may be interested in evaluating your own preparation for celestial glory against these criteria.

Before we continue, we will quote just one verse from the Doctrine and Covenants that deals with the above:

D&C 105:5

And **Zion** cannot be **built up** unless it **is by the principles of the law of the celestial kingdom**; otherwise I cannot receive her unto myself.

Verses 30–42, next, give some details of how to administer and live the law of consecration. Remember that many more details will be added in later revelations. We will use **bold** to point out celestial traits and law of consecration details.

29 If thou lovest me thou shalt serve me and **keep all my commandments** [*since none of us are perfect, we understand this to mean to earnestly strive to keep all of God's commandments*].

30 And behold, thou wilt **remember the poor**, and **consecrate of thy properties for their support** [*be generous*] **that which thou hast** [*your surplus, after your own needs and wants—see D&C 51:3—are taken care of*] to impart unto them, with a covenant and a deed [*willing to deed your properties to the Church*] which cannot be broken.

31 And **inasmuch as ye impart of your substance unto the poor, ye will do it unto me** [*when you are generous with the poor, it is the same as being generous with God*]; and **they shall be laid before the bishop** of my church and his counselors [*the bishop is the main administrator of the law of consecration*], two of the elders, or high priests, such as he shall appoint or has appointed and set apart for that purpose.

32 And it shall come to pass, that **after they** [*the properties that have been deeded to the Church by members willing to live the law of consecration*] **are laid before the bishop of my church**, and after that he has received these testimonies [*written deeds*] concerning the consecration of the properties of my church, that **they cannot be taken from the church** [*if a person "quits" this "united order," he or she does not get the property back that was originally deeded to the Church*], agreeable to my commandments, **every man shall be made accountable unto me, a**

steward over his own property [*everyone will be deeded—see D&C 51:4—some property back*], or that which he has received by consecration [*deeded to him by the bishop*], as much as is sufficient for himself and family [*according to his family's needs*].

As you no doubt noticed, in verse 32, above, **private ownership of property is a major part of living the true law of consecration**. Most people do not understand this. Private ownership of property was one of the major differences between the "united order" that some of Sidney Rigdon's congregation had been living on Isaac Morley's farm in the Kirtland area, and the proper "united order" set up according to the Lord's rules.

By now you can see that unselfishness and generosity would be major personality traits needed by participants in living the law of consecration. These are celestial qualities.

Next, in verses 33–35, the Lord instructs further that if, after all participating members have deeded their property to the Church (the initial step in living the law of consecration), and after the bishop has deeded back to each family according to their needs, there is still some left over, it is to be kept by the bishop for assisting the poor, helping members now and then when their needs exceed their resources, for purchasing public lands for the Church, building churches, and so on.

33 And again, **if there shall be properties in the hands of the church**, or any individuals of it, **more than is necessary** for their support **after this first consecration**, which is a residue to be consecrated unto the bishop, **it shall be kept to administer to those who have not, from time to time**, that **every man who has need may be amply supplied and receive according to his wants**.

34 Therefore, **the residue shall be kept in my storehouse, to administer to the poor and the needy**, as shall be appointed by the high council of the church, and the bishop and his council;

35 And **for the purpose of purchasing lands for the public benefit of the church**, and **building houses of worship**, and **building up of the New Jerusalem** which is hereafter to be revealed [*the location will be revealed as being in Independence, Jackson County, Missouri; see D&C 57:2–3*]—

36 That my covenant people may be gathered in one in that day when I shall come to my temple. And **this I do for the salvation of my people**.

Next, the Lord instructs concerning what to do about members who join in with the law of consecration but later drop out and leave the Church. They do not receive back the properties they originally deeded to the Church.

37 And it shall come to pass, that he that sinneth and repenteth not shall be cast out of the church, and **shall not receive again that which he has consecrated unto the poor and the needy of my church, or in other words, unto me**—

38 For **inasmuch as ye do it unto the least of these, ye do it unto me** [*another principle of living the law of consecration*].

39 For it shall come to pass, that which I spake by the mouths of my prophets shall be fulfilled; for **I will consecrate of the riches of those who embrace my gospel among the Gentiles unto the poor of my people who are of the house of Israel.**

Have you noticed how much the Church is doing today to fulfill the Savior's prophecy, **bolded** in verse 39, especially through tithing, fast offerings, missionary donations, the Humanitarian Fund, and the Perpetual Education Fund? In some very real ways, we are living the law of consecration today with very gratifying results!

In verses 40–42, next, the Lord gives added instructions for living the law of consecration, including that those who are lazy cannot be a part of such groups.

40 And again, **thou shalt not be proud in thy heart; let all thy garments be plain** [*this can be carried to extremes; it was designed to avoid the fashion "caste system" which often exists in society*], and their beauty the beauty of **the work of thine own hands** [*in other words, the clothes they made were to have individual beauty and reflect the individuality of the owner; this point was missed by some in early "united orders"*];

41 And **let all things be done in cleanliness** before me.

42 **Thou shalt not be idle**; for he that is idle shall not eat the bread nor wear the garments [*clothing*] of the laborer.

In verses 43–52, next, the Lord gives much counsel and direction concerning the healing of the sick. First, he counsels those who do not have faith to be healed but who still believe in God. You will see that He treats them with kindness rather than criticism for their lack of faith.

43 And whosoever among you are **sick, and have not faith to be healed, but believe, shall be**

nourished with all tenderness, with herbs and mild food, and that not by the hand of an enemy [*in other words, members should take care of their own*].

Next, instructions are given for administering to the sick.

44 And **the elders of the church, two or more, shall be called**, and shall pray for **and lay their hands upon them in my name; and if they die they shall die unto me, and if they live they shall live unto me** [*in other words, they will be fine either way; the Lord has a different perspective on death than most people*].

45 **Thou shalt live together in love**, insomuch that thou shalt **weep for the loss of them that die**, and **more especially for those** [*the wicked*] **that have not hope of a glorious resurrection**.

The counsel given in the last half of verse 45, above, is somewhat difficult to follow for those who tend to "rejoice" when a wicked leader or cruel terrorist is killed or dies. This would seem to be an additional lesson for us from the Lord on developing Christlike love for all people, regardless of how offensive they might be, if we desire someday to enter celestial glory.

Next, we are taught that dying holds no fear for the righteous.

46 And it shall come to pass **that those that die in me** [*who have been faithful to the Lord*] **shall not taste of death, for it shall be sweet unto them**;

Brigham Young gives a perspective on dying that is truly enlightening:

"We shall turn round and look upon it [the valley of death] and think, when we have crossed it, why this is the greatest advantage of my whole existence, for I have passed from a state of sorrow, grief, mourning, woe, misery, pain, anguish and disappointment into a state of existence, where I can enjoy life to the fullest extent as far as that can be done without a body. My spirit is set free, I thirst no more, I want to sleep no more, I hunger no more, I tire no more, I run, I walk, I labor, I go, I come, I do this, I do that, whatever is required of me, nothing like pain or weariness, I am full of life, full of vigor, and I enjoy the presence of my heavenly Father" (*Journal of Discourses*, 17:142).

President Joseph F. Smith taught the following:

"All fear of this death has been removed from the Latter-day Saints. They have no dread of the temporal death, because they know that as death came upon them by the transgression of Adam, so by the righteousness of

Jesus Christ shall life come unto them, and though they die, they shall live again. Possessing this knowledge, they have joy even in death, for they know that they shall rise again and shall meet again beyond the grave. They know that the spirit dies not at all; that it passes through no change, except the change from imprisonment in this mortal clay to freedom and to the sphere in which it acted before it came to this earth" (*Gospel Doctrine*, 428).

And finally, Spencer W. Kimball gave the following concerning death:

"If we say that early death is a calamity, disaster or a tragedy, would it not be saying that mortality is preferable to earlier entrance into the spirit world and to eventual salvation and exaltation? If mortality be the perfect state, then death would be a frustration but the Gospel teaches us there is no tragedy in death, but only in sin" ("Tragedy or Destiny," Brigham Young University Speeches of the Year [Dec. 6, 1955], 3).

As we continue, the Lord teaches, in effect, that death is not sweet for the wicked.

47 And they **that die not in me, wo unto them, for their death is bitter.**

Next, we are taught the importance of faith in the healing of the sick.

48 And again, it shall come to pass that **he that hath faith in me to be healed, and is not appointed unto death, shall be healed.**

Spencer W. Kimball taught the following regarding the phrase "appointed unto death" in verse 48, above:

"If not 'appointed unto death' and sufficient faith is developed, life can be spared. But if there is not enough faith, many die before their time. It is evident that even the righteous will not always be healed and even those of great faith will die when it is according to the purpose of God. Joseph Smith died in his thirties as did the Savior. Solemn prayers were answered negatively.

"If he is not 'appointed unto death!' That is a challenging statement. I am confident that there is a time to die. I am not a fatalist. I believe that many people die before 'their time' because they are careless, abuse their bodies, take unnecessary chances, or expose themselves to hazards, accidents, and sickness. . . .

"God can control our lives. He guides and blesses us, but gives us our agency. We may live our lives in accordance with His plan for us or we may foolishly shorten or terminate them.

"I am positive in my mind that the Lord has planned our destiny. We can shorten our lives but I think we cannot lengthen them very much. Sometime we'll understand fully, and when we see back from the vantage point of the future we shall be satisfied with many of the happenings of this life which seemed too difficult for us to comprehend" ("Tragedy or Destiny," 6, 9, 11–12).

Wilford Woodruff gave a rather fascinating discourse on the phrase, "appointed unto death," as follows:

"The Prophet Joseph Smith held the keys of this dispensation on this side of the veil, and he will hold them throughout the countless ages of eternity. He went into the spirit world to unlock the prison doors and to preach the Gospel to the millions of spirits who are in darkness, and every Apostle, every Seventy, every Elder, etc., who has died in the faith, as soon as he passes to the other side of the veil, enters into the work of the ministry, and there is a thousand times more to preach there than there is here. I have felt of late as if our brethren on the other side of the veil had held a council, and that they had said to this one, and that one, 'Cease thy work on the earth, come hence, we need help,' and they have called this man and that man. It has appeared so to me in seeing the many men who have been called from our midst lately. Perhaps I may be permitted to relate a circumstance with which I am acquainted in relation to Bishop Roskelley, of Smithfield, Cache Valley. On one occasion he was suddenly taken very sick—near to death's door. While he lay in this condition, President Peter Maughan, who was dead, came to him and said: 'Brother Roskelley, we held a council on the other side of the veil. I have had a great deal to do, and I have the privilege of coming here to appoint one man to come and help. I have had three names given to me in council, and you are one of them. I want to inquire of your circumstances.' The Bishop told him what he had to do, and they conversed together as one man would converse with another. President Maughan then said to him: 'I think I will not call you. I think you are wanted here more than perhaps one of the others.' Bishop Roskelley got well from that hour. Very soon after, the second man was taken sick, but not being able to exercise sufficient faith, Brother Roskelley did not go to him. By and by this man recovered, and on meeting Brother Roskelley he said: 'Brother Maughan came to me the other night and told me he was sent to call one man from the ward,' and he named two men as had been done to Brother Roskelley. A few days afterwards the third man was taken sick and died. Now, I name this to show a principle. They have work on the other side of the veil; and they want men, and they call them. And that was my view in regard to Brother George A. Smith. When he was almost at death's door, Brother Cannon administered to him, and in thirty minutes he was up and ate breakfast with his family. We labored with him in this way, but ultimately, as you know, he died. But it taught me a lesson. I felt that man was wanted behind the veil. We labored also with Brother Pratt; he, too, was wanted behind the veil.

"Now . . . those of us who are left here have a great work to do. We have been raised up of the Lord to take this kingdom and bear it off. This is our duty; but if we neglect our duty and set our hearts upon the things of this world, we will be sorry for it (*Journal of Discourses*, 22:333–34).

Next, more examples of the principle of faith are given.

49 **He who hath faith to see shall see.**

50 **He who hath faith to hear shall hear.**

51 **The lame who hath faith to leap shall leap.**

In verse 52, next, the Savior comforts those who do not have sufficient faith to be healed by telling them that they can still attain exaltation. This puts "faith to be healed" into a proper perspective as compared to being true to covenants and living the gospel.

52 And **they who have not faith to do these things, but believe in me, have power to become my sons** [*"power to become my sons (and daughters)" means power to attain exaltation; see Mosiah 5:7, D&C 76:24, etc.*]; and inasmuch as they break not my laws thou shalt bear their infirmities.

53 **Thou shalt stand in the place of thy stewardship** [*take care of your stewardship (properties, callings, etc.) with diligence, honor, and integrity*].

Before you read the next verse, it will be helpful to have a bit more background. Before the conversion of Sidney Rigdon and many of his rather large congregation (he was a successful minister and preacher on the western frontier in Ohio), several former members of his congregation were living in a type of "united order" in which all things were owned in common. They had set it up according to their understanding of Acts 2:44–45 and 4:32. There was no private ownership of property, and some problems developed. We will quote some commentary on this from the institute of religion student manual, *Church History in the Fullness of Times*, 1989, page 95 (**bold** added for teaching purposes):

"Now settled in Kirtland, the Prophet was eager to know the Lord's will concerning the economic salvation of the Saints, many of whom were impoverished, particularly those who had left their homes in New York. His interest in the Lord's economic program was aroused when he arrived in Ohio and discovered a group of about fifty people who had established a cooperative venture based on their interpretation of statements in the book of Acts, describing the early Saints as having all things in common (see Acts 2:44–45; 4:32). This group, known as 'the family,' formerly followers of Sidney Rigdon, were members of the Church living on Isaac Morley's farm near the village of Kirtland. When John Whitmer arrived in mid-January, he noted that what they were doing created many problems. For example, **Heman Bassett took a pocket watch belonging to Levi Hancock and sold it. When asked why, Heman replied, 'Oh, I thought it was all in the family.' Levi responded that he did not like such 'family doing'** and would not endure it any longer."

With the above as specific context, verse 54, next, is even more meaningful as a principle of the law of consecration.

54 **Thou shalt not take thy brother's garment**; thou shalt **pay for that which thou shalt receive of thy brother**.

Perhaps you've noticed that nowhere in the specific instructions given so far by the Lord regarding the law of consecration does He define for these Saints what "surplus" is. In other words, it is up to them to determine what it is. This would definitely require "celestial" type generosity and integrity on the part of the people involved. But just in case you are thinking that it would be extremely difficult to be "that good," have you noticed that the leaders of our Church today apply the same principle to our tithes and offerings? In fact, they even apply it to our temple attendance. They don't tell us how often to go to the temple, they don't tell us how much fast offering to pay, and they don't tell us how to calculate our tithing, other than to quote D&C 119:3, which says tithing is to be paid on "one tenth of all their interest annually." They have defined "interest" as being "income."

In summary, all of these things involve the consecration of our time and money, and it is up to the individuals to determine how much fast offering they pay, how they calculate their tithing, and how much of their time they dedicate to temple attendance. So, being a faithful Saint in our day requires celestial qualities also. This principle is given again in verse 55, next.

55 And **if thou obtainest more than that which would be for thy support, thou shalt give it into my storehouse**, that all things may be done according to that which I have said.

Next, in verses 56–58, the topic

is the translation of the Bible. See D&C 42, footnote 56a, as well as 45:60–61. This translation is now referred to as the Joseph Smith Translation of the Bible, or the JST.

56 Thou shalt **ask, and my scriptures** [*the inspired translation of the Bible*] **shall be given as I have appointed** [*according to the instructions of the Lord, for instance in D&C 35:20*], and **they shall be preserved in safety** [*possibly a reference to the lost 116 manuscript pages of the translation from the gold plates that were lost by Martin Harris; in other words, be very careful not to lose the translation notes from your work on the Bible*];

57 And it is expedient [*necessary*] that thou shouldst **hold thy peace concerning them** [*don't start preaching about them yet*], and not teach them until ye have received them in full.

One significant way in which the JST is being taken to all the world as instructed in verse 58, next, is in our Latter-day Saint edition of the Bible, which contains numerous footnotes using the JST, as well as a section in the back for longer excerpts from the JST.

58 And I give unto you a commandment that then ye shall teach them unto all men; for **they shall be taught unto all nations, kindreds, tongues and people.**

Verses 59–60, next, are a "straight to the point" summary of the importance of taking these laws seriously. Such things raise our accountability level as well as our opportunities for growth.

59 **Thou shalt take the things which thou hast received**, which have been given unto thee **in my scriptures for a law**, to be my law **to govern my church**;

60 And **he that doeth according to these things shall be saved**, and **he that doeth them not shall be damned** if he so continue [*unless he repents*].

Next, these Saints are encouraged to keep asking questions and learning. The benefits far outweigh the risks of additional accountability.

61 **If thou shalt ask, thou shalt receive revelation upon revelation, knowledge upon knowledge, that thou mayest know the mysteries** [*spiritual truths; see Bible Dictionary under "Mystery"*] **and peaceable things—that which bringeth joy, that which bringeth life eternal** [*exaltation in the highest degree of glory in the celestial kingdom*].

Next, the topic turns briefly to the future New Jerusalem.

62 Thou shalt **ask, and it shall be revealed** unto you **in mine own due time where the New Jerusalem shall be built**.

New Jerusalem is often referred to as the City of Zion and will be built in Independence, Jackson County, Missouri (see D&C 57:2–3). The following quote from the Bible Dictionary points this out (**bold** added for emphasis):

Zion

"The word *Zion* is used repeatedly in all the standard works of the Church, and is defined in latter-day revelation as 'the pure in heart' (D&C 97:21). Other usages of Zion have to do with a geographical location. For example, Enoch built a city that was called Zion (Moses 7:18–19); Solomon built his temple on Mount Zion (1 Kgs. 8:1; cf. 2 Sam. 5:6–7); and Jackson County, Missouri, is called Zion in many of the revelations in the D&C, such as 58:49–50; 62:4; 63:48; 72:13; 84:76; 104:47. **The city of New Jerusalem, to be built in Jackson County, Missouri, is to be called Zion** (D&C 45:66–67). The revelations also speak of 'the cause of Zion' (D&C 6:6; 11:6). In a wider sense all of North and South America are Zion (HC 6:318–19). For further references see 1 Chr. 11:5; Ps. 2:6; 99:2; 102:16; Isa. 1:27; 2:3; 4:3–5; 33:20; 52:1–8; 59:20; Jer. 3:14; 31:6; Joel 2:1–32; Amos 6:1; Obad. 1:17, 21; Heb. 12:22–24; Rev. 14:1–5; and many others. (In the N.T., *Zion* is spelled *Sion*.)"

The Book of Mormon has a number of references to the New Jerusalem, including in Third Nephi as follows:

3 Nephi 20:22

22 And behold, this people will I establish in this land, unto the fulfilling of the covenant which I made with your father Jacob; and it shall be a **New Jerusalem**. And the powers of heaven shall be in the midst of this people; yea, even I will be in the midst of you.

Apostle Bruce R. McConkie explains more about "New Jerusalem":

"'We believe . . . that Zion (the New Jerusalem) will be built upon the American continent.' So specified the seer of latter days in our Tenth Article of Faith. Zion, the New Jerusalem, on American soil! And we hasten to add, so also shall there be Zions in all lands and New Jerusalems in the mountains of the Lord in all the earth. But the American Zion shall be the capital city, the source whence the law shall go forth to govern all the earth [*during the Millennium*]. It shall be the city of the Great King. His throne shall be there, and from there he shall reign gloriously over all the earth" (*The Millennial Messiah*, 301).

In 1879, Apostle Orson Pratt gave a brief description of the temple that will be built in conjunction with the New Jerusalem:

"There [*New Jerusalem*] . . . we expect to build a temple different from all other temples in some respects. It will be built much larger, cover a larger area of ground, far larger than this Tabernacle covers and this Tabernacle will accommodate from 12,000 to 15,000 people. We expect to build a temple much larger, very much larger, according to the revelation God gave to us forty years ago in regard to that temple. But you may ask in what form will it be built? Will it be built in one large room, like this Tabernacle? No; there will be 24 different compartments in the temple that will be built in Jackson County. The names of these compartments were given to us some 45 or 46 years ago; the names we still have, and when we build these 24 rooms, in a circular form and arched over the centre, we shall give the names to all these different compartments just as the Lord specified through Joseph Smith. . . . Perhaps you may ask for what purpose these 24 compartments are built. I answer not to assemble the outside world in, nor to assemble the Saints all in one place, but these buildings will be built with a special view to the different orders, or in other words the different quorums or councils of the two Priesthoods that God has ordained on the earth. That is the object of having 24 rooms so that each of these different quorums, whether they be High Priests or Seventies, or Elders, or Bishops, or lesser Priesthood, or Teachers, or Deacons, or Patriarchs, or Apostles, or High Councils, or whatever may be the duties that are assigned to them, they will have rooms in the temple of the Most High God, adapted, set apart, constructed, and dedicated for this special purpose. . . . But will there be any other buildings excepting those 24 rooms that are all joined together in a circular form and arched over the center—are there any other rooms that will be built—detached from the temple? Yes. There will be tabernacles, there will be meeting houses for the assembling of the people on the Sabbath day. There will be various places of meeting so that the people may gather together; but the temple will be dedicated to the Priesthood of the Most High God, and for the most sacred and holy purposes" (*Journal of Discourses,* 25:24–25).

The Tenth Article of Faith refers to the yet-to-be-built New Jerusalem as follows:

10 We believe in the literal gathering of Israel and in the restoration of the Ten Tribes; that **Zion (the**

New Jerusalem) will be built upon the American continent; that Christ will reign personally upon the earth; and, that the earth will be renewed and receive its paradisiacal glory.

We will learn more about the coming New Jerusalem when we study section 45. The instruction in verses 63–64, next, seems to apply especially to these early Saints. They are to go on missions in all directions, but those who go east to New York and the surrounding area are to counsel their converts to go west and gather with the Saints in Ohio.

63 And behold, it shall come to pass that my servants shall be sent forth to the east and to the west, to the north and to the south.

64 And even now, **let him that goeth to the east teach them** that shall be converted to flee to the west, and this in consequence of that which is coming on the earth, and of secret combinations [*see D&C 38:13 and 28–29*].

In verses 65–66, next, we all learn, again, the lesson that obedience brings great blessings. Perhaps this is the reason that obedience is sometimes referred to as "the first law of heaven."

65 Behold, **thou shalt observe** [*obey*] **all these things, and great shall be thy reward**; for unto you it is given to know the mysteries [*spiritual truths, simple basics of the gospel—see verse 61, above*] of the kingdom, but unto the world [*those who reject the gospel and thus remain "worldly"*] it is not given to know them.

66 **Ye shall observe the laws which ye have received and be faithful.**

Can you see the "progression" in these verses? First, the Lord has reminded the Saints of the value of obedience (verses 65 and 66, above). Then, in verse 67, next, He tells them that if they are obedient to what they have been given, they will receive more! This process of going from one level up to the next, and then to the next and so on, will continue for the faithful until they qualify for exaltation.

67 And **ye shall hereafter receive church covenants, such as shall be sufficient to establish you, both here and in the New Jerusalem.** [*Those in the New Jerusalem will be "Zion" people; in other words, worthy of celestial glory and living in the presence of the Savior; see 3 Nephi 20:22.*]

Next, the Savior encourages all of us to continue seeking wisdom, which, among other things, can be defined as planning wisely for a pleasant future.

68 Therefore, **he that lacketh wisdom, let him ask of me**, and I will give him liberally and upbraid him not.

The word "upbraid," in verse 68, above, is familiar to Latter-day Saints since it is also used in James 1:5, which led Joseph Smith to go into the grove to pray, which led to the First Vision. It means "to scold" and is derived from the practice in ancient times of disciplining disobedient children by taking hold of their braids and jerking upward.

In verse 69, next, the Savior invites the Saints to cheer up and be happy. Remember, they are facing many hardships and sacrifices. Many of them have recently relocated from New York to Kirtland in wintertime, and many more hardships are yet to come, especially as the Saints make their way west.

69 **Lift up your hearts and rejoice**, for unto you the kingdom, or in other words, the keys of the church have been given. Even so. Amen.

Verses 70–73, next, are additional instructions as to the use of consecrated properties to support those who are called to serve full time in the Church.

70 The priests and teachers shall have their stewardships, even as the members.

71 And **the elders or high priests who are appointed to assist the bishop** as counselors in all things, **are to have their families supported out of the property which is consecrated to the bishop**, for the good of the poor, and for other purposes, as before mentioned;

72 **Or they are to receive a just remuneration** [*payment*] **for all their services**, either a stewardship or otherwise, as may be thought best or decided by the counselors and bishop.

73 And **the bishop, also, shall receive his support**, or a just remuneration for all his services in the church.

As mentioned at the beginning of the background notes for section 42 in this study guide, verses 74–93 were given two weeks later than verses 1–72. (Verse 73 was added later by Joseph Smith at the time the Doctrine and Covenants was published.) Verses 74–93 are instructions about dealing with transgressors in the Church. We will study about disciplinary councils when we get to section 102.

In the meantime, keep in mind that in these next verses, the Lord is setting up the proper order for helping members guilty of serious sin get their lives back in order with the help of the Atonement of Jesus Christ. It is a kindness and a show of love to help people straighten out their lives before Judgment Day.

President N. Eldon Tanner, of the First Presidency, spoke on this subject as follows:

"Every mission president, stake president, and bishop is directed and instructed how to investigate and handle all cases of transgression. A person who is guilty of a serious transgression cannot progress, and he is not happy while the guilt is upon him. Until he has confessed and repented he is in bondage. The transgressor who is dealt with as he should be, with love and with proper discipline, will later express his appreciation for your concern, your interest, and your leadership. As he is properly dealt with, he is in a position to repent and come back to full activity. But he must be dealt with.

"It has been reported to me that some bishops and even stake presidents have said that they never have excommunicated or disciplined anyone and that they do not intend to. This attitude is entirely wrong. Judges in Israel have the responsibility to sit in righteous judgment where it becomes necessary. Let me read from the twentieth section of the Doctrine and Covenants an important reminder to those who have the responsibility of judging: 'Any member of the Church of Christ transgressing, or being overtaken in a fault, shall be dealt with as the scriptures direct.' (D&C 20:80.)

"Brethren, study the scriptures and the handbook and do as they direct and discipline the members of the Church when necessary. Remember that it is no kindness to a transgressor for his local authority to ignore or overlook or try to cover up his iniquity" (In Conference Report, Oct. 1974, 110; or *Ensign*, Nov. 1974, 78).

In verses 74–75, next, instructions are given for dealing with divorces caused by sexual transgression.

74 Behold, verily I say unto you, that whatever persons among you, **having put away** [*divorced*] **their companions for the cause of fornication**, or in other words, **if they shall testify before you in all lowliness of heart that this is the case** [*if they repent humbly*], **ye shall not cast them out** from among you [*don't excommunicate them*];

75 But if ye shall find that any persons have **left their companions for the sake of** [*divorced because of*] **adultery**, and **they themselves are the offenders**, and their companions are living, **they shall be cast out** [*excommunicated*] from among you.

Next, instructions are given with

respect to letting such transgressors join the Church.

76 And again, I say unto you, that ye shall **be watchful and careful**, with all inquiry, **that ye receive none such among you if they are married**;

Keep in mind that these instructions, above, were given at the beginnings of the Church. Be aware that an overriding principle in disciplinary action is that the Holy Ghost reveals to the presiding priesthood authority what type of disciplinary action is best suited to help the transgressor return to good standing with the Lord.

Verse 77, next, reminds us that it is possible to repent completely of sexual sin.

77 And if they are not married, **they shall repent of all their sins or ye shall not receive them**.

78 And again, **every person who belongeth to this church of Christ, shall observe to keep all the commandments and covenants of the church**.

In verses 79–87, we are reminded that there are limits to the jurisdiction of Church discipline, and that some situations must be dealt with by civil courts according to the laws of the land. This is a strong example of the principle of separation of church and state.

79 And it shall come to pass, that **if any persons among you** [*members of the Church*] shall **kill** [*murder*] **they shall be delivered up and dealt with according to the laws of the land**; for remember that he hath no forgiveness [*D&C 42:18*]; and it shall be proved according to the laws of the land.

Next, in verses 80–83, the Lord instructs that being disciplined properly for sexual immorality comes under the jurisdiction of the Church.

80 And **if any man or woman shall commit adultery, he or she shall be tried before two elders of the church, or more**, and every word shall be established against him or her by two witnesses of the church, and not of the enemy; but if there are more than two witnesses it is better.

81 But he or she shall be condemned by the mouth of two witnesses; and the elders shall lay the case before the church, and the church shall lift up their hands against him or her, that they may be **dealt with according to the law of God**.

82 And **if it can be, it is necessary that the bishop be present also.**

83 And thus ye shall do in all cases which shall come before you.

Verses 84–86 specify more situations which must be dealt with by the laws of the land. In other words, the Church can't put people in jail or fine them.

84 **And if a man or woman shall rob**, he or she shall be **delivered up unto the law of the land**.

85 And **if he or she shall steal**, he or she shall be **delivered up unto the law of the land**.

86 And **if he or she shall lie**, he or she shall be **delivered up unto the law of the land.**

We must not miss the point made by the Lord in verse 87, next, that all of the above, including sins that are to be handled by the laws of the land, are also sins against God and against the covenants of baptism and so forth. Therefore, as you have no doubt seen, members of the Church who commit serious crimes against society also must face Church disciplinary action as part of their repentance process.

87 And **if he or she do any manner of iniquity, he or she shall be delivered up unto the law, even that of God**.

Finally, as this tremendous revelation on the "Law" comes to a close, the Lord gives instructions regarding the handling of both personal offenses and offenses against large numbers of people. First of all, the Lord is concerned about protecting the privacy of the offender wherever possible. This obviously helps avoid gossip and unnecessary additional pain.

88 And **if thy brother or sister offend thee**, thou shalt **take him or her between him or her and thee alone** [*handle it in private*]; and **if he or she confess thou shalt be reconciled** [*if they confess and apologize, forgive them and let it go*].

Obviously, some refuse to confess and ask forgiveness when invited to do so, thus continuing their abusive behavior. Next, the Savior gives instructions for dealing with this situation among members.

89 And **if he or she confess not thou shalt deliver him or her up unto the church** [*turn him or her over to the Church, usually the bishop or branch president*], not to the members, but to the elders [*the presiding priesthood authority*]. And it shall be done in a meeting, and that not before the world [*still keep it as private as possible*].

If the transgression of a member has hurt the feelings and testimonies of many members, the above-given "privacy rules" do not apply, as explained next in verses 90–91.

90 **And if thy brother or sister offend many, he or she shall be chastened** [*disciplined*] **before many** [*as many as need to be informed about the disciplinary action*].

91 And **if any one offend openly, he or she shall be rebuked openly**, that he or she may be ashamed. And **if he or she confess not** [*if he or she does not acknowledge being in the wrong*]**, he or she shall be delivered up unto the law of God** [*this can mean at least two things; namely, be subject to disciplinary action of the Church, or be dealt with by the Lord on or before Judgment Day; see D&C 40:3 and 64:11*].

It is significant that the Lord, as He brings this instructional session to a close, chooses to emphasize that whenever possible, the privacy of persons who have sinned should be maintained. It is a strong reminder to us of the "worth of souls" (D&C 18:10) and strong counsel to each of us in our personal relationships with others.

92 **If any shall offend in secret, he or she shall be rebuked in secret, that he or she may have opportunity to confess in secret to him or her whom he or she has offended, and to God**, that the church [*members of the Church*] may not speak reproachfully of [*gossip about*] him or her.

93 And thus shall ye conduct in all things.

Bonus Section

A
Brief Chronology
of
Major Characters
in
Early Church History

By David J. Ridges

Introduction

Who was Where, When, in Early Church History?

Years ago, I got to wondering where other significant players in the Restoration were and what they were doing about the time Joseph Smith had the First Vision in the spring of 1820. I wondered how the Lord got them prepared and in the right place at the right time to do their part in the marvelous work that was coming forth. With some research, I found, for instance, that:

John Taylor, who would become the third president of the Church, was twelve years old, in England, working on his father's farm. Four years later, he would join the Methodist Church in England. During this period of his life, he would see a vision of an angel in heaven with a trumpet and a message to all nations. In five years, he would have strong thoughts come into his mind of preaching the gospel in the Americas.

Wilford Woodruff, who would become the fourth president of the Church, was thirteen years old and had already suffered through eleven serious accidents (that obviously didn't kill him). They, among other things, seemed to toughen him up to issue the Manifesto stopping the practice of plural marriage.

Sidney Rigdon was twenty-seven years old, already on the western frontier in Ohio, and would marry Phebe Brooks in June 1820.

Lorenzo Snow, who would become the fifth president of the Church, was six years old and wanted to be a soldier. His older sister was Eliza R. Snow.

The Peter Whitmer Sr. Family by 1820 had already lived in Fayette, New York, for eleven years. They were Pennsylvania Germans and attended German church services (Anderson, *Investigating the Book of Mormon Witnesses*, 67). In ten years, on April 6, 1830, the true Church would be organized in their home.

Martin Harris was thirty-seven years old and an established farmer, textile manufacturer, and civic leader in Palmyra, New York. He was respected and meticulous, known for his integrity, and thus would make a reliable witness to the Book of Mormon.

Parley P. Pratt was thirteen years old and had already read much of the Bible. The previous year he had read Revelation chapter 20 in the Bible, which concerns the First Resurrection (the resurrection of those who will attain celestial glory), and had a fervent desire to be a part of that resurrection. In a few years, he would become disgusted with all white men and their corrupt society, would move a bit beyond the western frontier of civilization, and would meet a frontier preacher named Sidney Rigdon.

Now, let's go chronologically, starting with Martin Harris, and watch the Lord prepare and move these people around geographically to be where they were needed, when they were needed for the work of the Restoration.

1783—Martin Harris is born in New York (thirty-seven years before the First Vision and twenty-two years before Joseph Smith is born). Martin will be highly respected and prominent in the community affairs of Palmyra, New York. He will also be known as one who constantly reads the scriptures and can quote the Bible at surprising length (Anderson, *Investigating the Book of Mormon Witnesses*, chapter 7). He will come to Utah at age eighty-seven and die at age ninety-two.

1793—Sidney Rigdon is born in Pennsylvania on February 19. He will love books, the Bible, and history. His father, a strict Baptist, will strongly oppose young Sidney's constant reading but will not be able to stop him. He will be five feet, nine and one-half inches tall, and later in life will weigh 215 pounds. He will be twelve years older than Joseph Smith and will be instructed to watch over him in D&C 35:19. Joseph Smith will be twenty-five and Sidney Rigdon thirty-seven when they meet. Sidney will be told that his role is similar to that of John the Baptist (D&C 35:4).

1800—A respected friend of Wilford Woodruff's parents, "Father" Robert Mason, receives a vision concerning the Restoration. In thirty years, he will tell his young friend, twenty-three-year-old Wilford Woodruff, about it (*Teachings of Presidents of the Church*, 1–3). Mason taught Wilford Woodruff much during his youth, including that true authority did not exist on earth and that the day was near when God would again restore His Church.

1801—Brigham Young is born in Vermont, the ninth child in the family. He will be four years older than Joseph Smith. He will be five feet, ten inches tall, with red hair and freckles (Susan Easton Black lecture, summer 1985).

1802—Joseph Smith's mother-to-be, Lucy Mack Smith, comes down with "a heavy cold, which caused a severe cough. A hectic fever set in which threatened to prove fatal" (Proctor, *Revised and Enhanced History of Joseph Smith*, 47). The doctors gave up on saving her. One night, as her husband sat by her side, expecting her to die, she begged and pled with the Lord to spare her life so she could bring up her children and so that her husband would be comforted. She "covenanted with God that if he would let me live, I would endeavor to get that religion that would enable me to serve him right, whether it was in the Bible or wherever it might be found, even if it was to be obtained from heaven by prayer and faith. At last a voice spoke to me and said, 'Seek, and ye shall find; knock, and it shall be opened unto you. Let your heart be comforted. Ye believe in God, believe also in me'" (ibid., 48). From that time forward, she gained strength, and when her health had returned sufficiently, she began to diligently search for "some pious person who knew the ways of God to instruct me in the things of heaven" (ibid.). In this search, she was repeatedly disappointed, which finally led her to say in her heart, "There is not on earth the religion which I seek. I must again turn to my Bible, take Jesus and his disciples for an example. I will try to obtain from God that which man cannot give nor take away" (ibid., 50). Surely these feelings and conclusions in Mother Smith's heart and mind prepared her to support her son when he was called to restore the gospel.

1803—Lucy Mack Smith has a dream in which she is told that the "pure and undefiled gospel of the Son of God . . . will be made available when her husband . . . was more advanced . . . in life" (Proctor, *Revised and Enhanced History*, 58–60). This great lady was well prepared to be the mother of the prophet of the Restoration.

1804—Emma Hale is born in Harmony, Pennsylvania, on July 10 (one and one-half years before Joseph Smith is born), the seventh child in the family. She will grow to be a beautiful young woman, five feet, nine inches tall, with dark hair and brown eyes (Black, *Who's Who in the Doctrine and Covenants*, 273). She will have a good singing voice and will be intelligent, capable, and particular with grammar and her choice of words, never using slang expressions. She will be a meticulous housekeeper and an excellent cook. She will also be a "rural schoolteacher" (Anderson, *Investigating the Book of Mormon Witnesses*, 5).

Brigham Young's parents move to eastern New York. In those days, a man could be fined five schillings for kissing his wife on Sunday (Rebecca Cornwall and Richard F. Palmer, "The Religious and Family Background of Brigham Young," *BYU Studies*, vol. 18:3, spring 1978, 288). Sometime in Brigham's young life he will be taught that dancing and violin music are evil. Later, as a prophet, he will be given D&C 136:28, in which the members of the Church are told to "praise the Lord with singing, with music, with dancing, and with a prayer of praise and thanksgiving."

Joseph Smith Sr. moves his family to eastern New York, not far from where Brigham Young is living.

1805—Joseph Smith Sr. moves back to Vermont.

Joseph Smith is born on December 23 in Vermont (the fourth of ten children in the Smith Family—Alvin, Hyrum, Sophronia, Joseph Smith Jr., Samuel, Ephraim (died in infancy), William, Catherine, Don Carlos, and Lucy, who was born in 1821, after the First Vision).

1806—Oliver Cowdery is born on October 3 in Vermont, the youngest of eight children. His mother will die when he is about three years old. He has brown eyes and will be five feet, five inches tall (Lang, *History of Seneca County (Ohio)*, 365). His oldest brother, Warren, will join the Church late in 1831, will hold responsible positions, but will leave the Church in 1838 (the same year Oliver is excommunicated) and never return (Black, *Who's Who in the Doctrine and Covenants*, 77). Oliver's father, William Cowdery, will join the Church in February 1836.

1807—Wilford Woodruff is born on March 1 in Connecticut. His mother will die when he is not quite one year old. He will be toughened up by life, having had numerous life-threatening accidents, and will be well prepared to handle the tough task of issuing the Manifesto stopping polygamy. He will write a journal of nine volumes with more than seven thousand pages, including a "Chapter on Accidents." He will live ninety-one years.

Parley P. Pratt is born April 12. In twenty-three years, he will be ready for baptism (1830). He will be murdered while on a mission in Arkansas on May 13, 1857, at age fifty.

1808—Joseph Smith will turn three on December 23.

Martin Harris will marry his first cousin Lucy Harris in March. They will have three children.

John Taylor is born November 1 in England. He will grow to more than six feet tall. Parley P. Pratt will preach to him in Canada, and he will be baptized in 1836. He will carry a bullet from Carthage to the time of his death. He will be a double martyr. He will nearly die in Carthage Jail, when the Prophet Joseph is martyred. He will die at age 78, on July 25, 1887, of congestive heart failure while in hiding in Davis County, Utah, unable to get proper medical help because of persecutors.

Wilford Woodruff's mother dies of spotted fever on January 11 when she is twenty-eight years old. Wilford is not quite one year old.

1809—Oliver Cowdery's mother dies. He is three years old.

The Whitmers move from Pennsylvania to Fayette, New York. They will be well established in twenty-one years, when the Lord will use their home for the organization of the Church on April 6, 1830.

1810—Wilford Woodruff falls into a cauldron of scalding water. He is three years old, and it will be nine months before he will be out of danger of dying from this accident (*Teachings of Presidents of the Church—Woodruff*, 6).

Sidney Rigdon's father dies. Sidney is seventeen years old and must support his mother on the farm. He doesn't like farming.

1811—Joseph Smith Sr. has a vision closely paralleling Lehi's dream (Smith, *History of Joseph Smith*, 48–50). This is one of at least seven visions this great father had. No wonder he supported his son! Joseph's parents were well prepared to be the parents of a prophet, just as others like Elizabeth and Zacharias (John the Baptist), Abraham and Sarah (Isaac), and Joseph and Mary (Jesus). Joseph, of course, was not the Savior's father, but was well prepared through dreams and visions to help raise Him.

1812—Twenty-nine-year-old Martin Harris serves in the War of 1812 against Britain. He is wealthy enough to hire a substitute but doesn't (Anderson, *Investigating the Book of Mormon Witnesses*, 99). He is a man of high principles.

1812–1813—When he is five and six, Wilford Woodruff has many accidents.

He will fall from the top of a barn flat on his face on the bare floor. Later, he will fall from the top to the bottom of the stairs but will only break one arm in one place.

Wilford is feeding a pumpkin to his favorite cow when a bull leaves his own pumpkin, pushes away the cow that young Wilford likes, and starts eating her pumpkin. Wilford is furious, picks up the pumpkin and marches toward his cow to give it to her. The bull sees him carrying the pumpkin and lunges toward him. Wilford starts running but does not drop the pumpkin despite his father's frantic shouts to do so. The enraged bull is upon him—he trips and falls, the pumpkin rolls away, and the bull jumps over little Wilford, gores the pumpkin, and tears it to shreds. Wilford escapes.

Wilford falls from his uncle's porch and breaks his other arm. Wilford hasn't yet broken a leg, so he does that. He lies in pain in the house for nine hours before help arrives. Wilford gets kicked in the abdomen by an ox. (If he hadn't been standing so close, he probably would have been killed. As it was, he was thrown more than kicked, probably saving his life.) Later, a wagon load of hay tips on top of him, but he suffers no harm (Cowley, *Wilford Woodruff*, 6–8).

1813—Joseph Smith Jr., going on eight, has bone surgery on his left leg. Fourteen pieces of bone will work their way to the surface before the wound heals. He will use crutches for three years and walk with a slight limp in later life (LeRoy S. Wirthlin, "Joseph Smith's Boyhood Operation: An 1813 Surgical Success," *BYU Studies,* vol. 21, no. 2, 153). By the time he has the First Vision, he will already be familiar with overcoming obstacles.

1814—Lorenzo Snow is born in Mantua, Ohio. As he grows up, he will want to pursue a military career. His sister Eliza R. Snow and the Lord have other plans for him.

Parley P. Pratt, seven years old, reads selections from the Old Testament under the direction of his mother.

1815—Brigham Young's mother dies. He is fourteen. Wilford Woodruff's mother, Oliver Cowdery's mother, and Sidney Rigdon's Father have all died by now.

Wilford Woodruff is about eight years old and still alive, but his horse has bolted, tipping the wagon over on top of him and his father. Later this year, Wilford climbs an elm tree and steps on a dry limb when he is fifteen feet up. It breaks and he falls, landing flat on his back on the ground. The fall knocks the wind out of him. A cousin runs and tells Wilford's folks that Wilford is dead. He isn't. A Baptist revival this year in Farmington, Connecticut, gets his hopes up with respect to religion, but he is disappointed. It seems to him that preachers don't preach a living gospel (Cowley, *Wilford Woodruff*, 21).

1816—Brigham Young's father moves farther west, settling in Genoa, New York, which is about sixty miles southeast of Palmyra.

1817—Sidney Rigdon, about twenty-four years of age, joins with the United Baptists in Pennsylvania.

1818—Joseph Smith starts earnestly seeking the truth concerning God and which church to join. He is twelve years old and will search diligently for two years, encountering much frustration.

Sidney Rigdon becomes a licensed Baptist preacher. He is five feet, nine inches tall, will weight up to 215 pounds, and is an excellent preacher and speaker. Later, on the western frontier, he will bring many to him who will eventually join the true Church. He will be a type of John the Baptist for the Prophet Joseph Smith (see D&C 35:4).

1819—Twelve-year-old Parley P. Pratt reads Revelation 20 in the Bible, which concerns the First Resurrection. He has an urgent desire to secure for himself a place in the resurrection of the just.

Sidney Rigdon moves to Warren, Ohio, to preach as an apprentice to Adamson Bentley. This gets Sidney closer to the western frontier, where he will need to be in eleven years when Elder Parley P. Pratt and his three missionary companions come through Kirtland, Ohio. Sidney and many of his congregation at that time will be converted.

Twelve-year-old Wilford Woodruff is drowning in thirty feet of water. A man saves him. He suffers much as he is revived (Cowley, *Wilford Woodruff*, 7).

1820—Joseph Smith is visited by the Father and the Son in the First Vision.

John Taylor, age twelve, is working on his father's farm in England.

Sidney Rigdon marries Phebe Brooks in Ohio on June 12. They are on the western frontier.

Thirteen-year-old Wilford Woodruff is freezing to death. Hypothermia has set in. He is asleep in the hollow of a large apple tree. A man in the distance, who sees him crawl into the hollow, comes to his aid. He has much difficulty waking him but saves his life.

1821—Sidney Rigdon becomes an ordained Baptist minister, attracting large crowds wherever he preaches. During the summer of this year, he will visit Alexander Campbell and be converted to Campbell's ways of thinking, which include faith, repentance, baptism by immersion, and the gift of the Holy Ghost. Later this year, Sidney will move back to Pittsburgh, Pennsylvania, to accept a position as pastor for a Campbellite congregation.

Wilford Woodruff has accidently sunk an ax into his left instep, passing nearly through his foot. It will be nine months before it is healed. He is fourteen years old (Cowley, *Wilford Woodruff*, 8).

1822—Parley Pratt is working on a farm. He is fifteen years old and away from home.

Wilford Woodruff is fifteen years old and has just been bitten on the hand by a dog with rabies. The dog did not draw blood, and Wilford is spared again.

1823—Moroni visits Joseph Smith the first time.

Brigham Young joins the Methodist Reform Church (some think it was in 1824), but it will not satisfy his desire for truth.

Sixteen-year-old Parley P. Pratt is living with his Aunt VanCott and is able to attend a few months of school. He does well, and his teacher holds him up as an exemplary student, a fact he mentions in his autobiography: "I made such extraordinary progress that the teacher often spoke of me to the whole school, and exhorted them to learn as Parley Pratt did" (Pratt, *Autobiography*, 1938, 21).

John Taylor, 15, has decided to be a cooper (barrel maker) in England. Little does he know what God has in mind!

Martin Harris will win eight prizes this year at the fair for cloth manufacturing. He produces linen, cotton, wool ticking, blankets, and worsted and flannel fabrics (Anderson, *Investigating the Book of Mormon Witnesses*, 99).

1824—Sixteen-year-old John Taylor joins the Methodist Church in England. This year he will see a vision of an angel in the heavens with a trumpet and a message to all nations. He wonders what the dream means. (See Revelation 14:6–7.)

Parley P. Pratt is working with his father to clear seventy acres in New York, above Palmyra, as a homesite for his father's family. While working with his father, he asks why there are so many discrepancies between the biblical church and churches now. Where are the simple doctrines of repentance, baptism, and the gift of the Holy Ghost? He is much perplexed over these matters. Furthermore, he wonders if the authority of God is even on earth. His father can't give satisfactory answers.

Joseph Smith visits Moroni as scheduled. He is being taught by other Book of Mormon prophets as well.

Sidney Rigdon has been fired as a pastor for teaching too many of his own doctrines. He is working as a tanner in Pittsburgh and will continue to do so through 1826.

Wilford Woodruff has just been dislodged from the saddle on a runaway horse careening wildly down a hillside. He has slid up the horse's neck and is on its head, hanging onto its ears for dear life as it continues to plummet down a steep, rocky hillside. The horse slams into a breast-high boulder, stopping it dead in its tracks, and Wilford flies through the air, landing on his feet almost one rod (sixteen feet) in front of the horse (otherwise he would have been killed instantly). He breaks one leg in two places and displaces both ankles. The dazed horse almost rolls over him as it attempts to get up. In eight weeks, he will be able to walk with the aid of crutches.

1825—John Taylor, in England, is strongly impressed that he will someday preach the gospel in America. He is seventeen years of age and will preach his first sermon this year for the Methodists.

Parley P. Pratt, eighteen, is baptized into the Baptist Church.

Joseph Smith continues to be taught by Moroni and others.

1826—Parley Pratt has become disgusted with corrupt white-man society. He buys a Bible and leaves the civilized world. He later buys a gun, earns an ax, and moves a bit past the western frontier, where he builds a shack in the forest about thirty-two miles west of Cleveland, Ohio (Sidney Rigdon territory). Parley is nineteen. He is now in a position to meet Sidney Rigdon, who teaches faith, repentance, baptism, and the gift of the Holy Ghost.

Sidney Rigdon moves to Mentor, Ohio, near Cleveland, to become pastor of a congregation there.

Joseph Smith continues his visits and discussions with Moroni. He is getting so familiar with Book of Mormon places, architecture, dress styles, and so forth that his parents and brothers and sisters often gather around him in the evening and listen to him tell stories of ancient American history.

Joseph and Emma wish they could get her parents' permission to marry.

Parley P. Pratt is sitting in a shack in the forest, eating venison, reading the Bible, and reading about the Lewis and Clark expedition. Once in a while he will have a refreshing conversation with a red man, whom he still respects, but he wants nothing to do with white men because of their generally corrupt ways.

1827—Joseph Smith elopes with Emma Hale on January 18. They are married in South Bainbridge, New York, by a justice of the peace. Nine children will come (see information sheet at the end of this section), and four will live to maturity. Three will live a few hours, one fourteen months, and one will be stillborn. In addition, they will adopt twins.

Parley P. Pratt, still living on the western frontier, clears an area for a farm and replaces his shack with a house, which triggers thoughts about the girl he left behind in New York. He is now twenty, tanned by the sun and weather, and has a heavy growth of whiskers. On July 4, he finds himself in Canaan, Columbia, New York, near the house where the girl of his dreams, Thankful Halsey, lived the last time he saw her three years before. She is home! Later that evening he proposes to her with the following words: "If you still love me and desire to share my fortune you are worthy to be my wife." She accepts. They will marry on September 9 (Pratt, *Autobiography,* 29).

Joseph Smith brings the gold plates home to his parent's place in Palmyra from the Hill Cumorah.

Martin Harris sends his wife, Lucy, and his daughter, Lucy, to the Smiths to investigate whether Joseph really has obtained the gold plates. He is a careful man and wants to be sure before he gets involved. Lucy and Lucy are allowed to heft the box the plates are in. It convinces them, and they report as much to Martin. They say that the plates must weigh close to sixty pounds.

In December, Joseph and Emma move to Harmony, Pennsylvania, to live with her parents.

Wilford Woodruff is twenty years old and still alive, but he is standing on a water wheel, clearing away ice. Another worker, unaware that Wilford is there, opens the water head gate, which starts the wheel in motion. Wilford falls off and narrowly escapes being crushed in the machinery.

1828—Oliver Cowdery, who will become one of the Three Witnesses to the Book of Mormon, comes to Manchester, near Palmyra, where Joseph Smith's parents live, to teach school (his brother, Lyman, got the job in the first place but wasn't able to keep his commitment, so Oliver was cleared by Hyrum Smith and others on the board of education to take his place). Thus, Oliver meets the Smith family. Also, he finds himself quite impressed by one of his students in the school. She is Elizabeth Ann Whitmer, the sister of David Whitmer. Oliver will marry her in 1832. They will have six children: five girls and one boy. Only one will live to maturity, a girl. She will marry but will have no children.

David Whitmer, who will also become one of the Three Witnesses, comes to Palmyra on business and becomes fast friends with Oliver Cowdery. They discuss various rumors they've heard about the gold plates. They are both curious about the matter.

Martin Harris, who likewise will become one of the Three Witnesses, visits Joseph Smith in Harmony, Pennsylvania, where Joseph and Emma are living. He obtains a copy of some of the characters from the plates and takes them to a professor of ancient languages, Dr. Charles Anthon, in New York City, who will initially confirm their authenticity. In April, Martin begins serving as scribe for Joseph, and by June 14, 116 pages of the translation will be completed. Martin will plead with Joseph to let him take the 116 pages of translation home to Palmyra to show them to his wife, Lucy, in order to counter her caustic criticism of his spending time and wasting money on foolish pursuits with Joseph Smith, and also in order to stop the wagging tongues about him among the citizens in Palmyra. The 116 manuscript pages will soon be lost.

Because of the loss of 116 pages, Joseph loses the gift of translation for a season. Moroni takes the Urim and Thummin and the plates. He will return them to Joseph on September 22.

1829—Parley P. Pratt meets Sidney Rigdon near the western frontier and is excited about Sidney's preaching of faith, repentance, baptism, and the gift of the Holy Ghost. Parley joins with Sidney but is still uncomfortable about the matter of authority to perform ordinances.

Oliver Cowdery decides he must visit Joseph Smith in Harmony, Pennsylvania, to investigate the gold plates. He stops along the way and talks to his friend, David Whitmer, in Fayette, New York, and agrees to write and tell David what he finds out. He arrives in Harmony and within two days (April 7) he begins as scribe in the work of translation.

Brigham Young and his wife move to Mendon, New York, fifteen miles from Palmyra. At Palmyra, he hears rumors regarding a man named Joe Smith and a gold Bible he dug out of a mountain.

In early spring of this year, Oliver writes to the Whitmers, informing them that Joseph is indeed involved in the work of the Lord. Moved by Oliver's statements, Peter Whitmer Sr. and some members of his family journey to Harmony and meet Joseph personally. David Whitmer is apparently not with them on this visit.

Later, David Whitmer brings a wagon to Harmony and transports Joseph and Oliver to Fayette to complete the work of translation. Emma will follow shortly. In fact, Emma's Uncle Nathaniel has tried to talk her into not going with Joseph. Instead, she will follow the Lord's counsel given later (in D&C 25:6) and join Joseph in Fayette. She never saw her family again except for one brother in Nauvoo. Moroni transports the plates to Fayette, meets Joseph in the garden there, and returns the plates to him.

John the Baptist restores the Aaronic Priesthood by conferring it upon Joseph Smith and Oliver Cowdery.

Peter, James, and John restore the Melchizedek Priesthood.

The Book of Mormon is completed, and a printer is hired.

1830—Robert Mason tells young Wilford Woodruff of the coming Restoration of the true Church, and that Wilford will play a major role in it. It will be two years before Wilford hears about the Latter-day Saints and three years before he is baptized. Wilford will be baptized for Robert Mason in the Nauvoo Temple. Much later in his life, he will have the signers of the Declaration of Independence and others appear to him in the St. George Temple and will supervise work for the dead for them.

By March 26, the first copies of the Book of Mormon are printed.

The Church is organized at the Whitmer home in Fayette, New York, on April 6.

Parley P. Pratt is impressed to search the scriptures and pray for understanding. He is impressed to sell the farm and return with his wife to New York. He does. When they arrive at Rochester, he is impressed to change plans and head south from there. He bids his wife "goodbye," says he will catch up to her later, and heads south. He obtains a copy of the Book of Mormon from a Baptist Deacon named Hamlin, who happens to have one. He then reads it through, hardly stopping for food or sleep. He then hurries to the Palmyra area, finds Hyrum Smith, and keeps him up all night asking about the gospel. Shortly thereafter, on September 1, he is baptized by Oliver Cowdery.

Sidney Rigdon is baptized after being visited by the newly baptized Parley P. Pratt, who, with his missionary companions, is on his way to the western frontier to fulfill his mission to the Lamanites (D&C 32).

Wilford Woodruff concludes that the only real peace of mind or true happiness comes through righteousness and service to God (Cowley, *Wilford Woodruff*, 26).

Samuel Smith gives a copy of the Book of Mormon to John P. Greene, who gives it to his wife, who gives it to her brother, Brigham Young, who is one of Heber C. Kimball's best friends. Brigham will not be an instant baptism. He will study and compare the Book of Mormon and the Bible for almost two years before baptism. Brigham's father reads and believes it too.

1831—Lorenzo Snow hears Joseph Smith preach at Hiram, Ohio. Lorenzo is seventeen years old.

Brigham Young and Heber C. Kimball listen to LDS missionaries in Phineas Young's home.

Wilford Woodruff has another bout with a water wheel. He survives again. He wonders why no apostles are on earth. He has desired baptism but doubts the authority of Christian ministers. He is twenty-four years old. He finally talks a Baptist minister into baptizing him on condition that he does not have to join the minister's church.

1832—John Taylor moves to Canada with his parents. He is twenty-four years old, is a skilled wood turner, and serves as a Methodist Sunday school teacher. He meets Leonora Cannon, George Q. Cannon's sister. (George Q. Cannon will become a counselor to John Taylor, Wilford Woodruff, and Lorenzo Snow in the First Presidency.) John Taylor proposes to Leonora, but she says, "No." That night she has a dream in which she sees herself married to John Taylor. Consequently, she accepts his proposal. John will get into trouble with his church by comparing it with the Bible and sticking to Bible teachings.

Brigham Young is baptized on April 14. He is instrumental in converting all of his brothers and sisters, his father, and his dying wife (Barrett, *Joseph Smith and the Restoration*, 210). Heber C. Kimball takes care of his children. Heber Kimball is baptized June 15. He is over six feet tall with a barrel chest that measures the same from front to back as from side to side (ibid., 210–11).

Wilford Woodruff, age twenty-five, reads about Joseph Smith and the new church in a slanderous newspaper article. He is deeply impressed and has a strong desire to meet some Latter-day Saints, who claim to possess gifts of the Spirit as in Bible times (Cowley, *Wilford Woodruff*, 30).

Oliver Cowdery and Elizabeth Ann Whitmer are married in Jackson County, Missouri, where the Whitmer family has immigrated. He is twenty-six, she is almost eighteen. Of their children, three will live less than a month, one will live five months, and the remaining child will live six and one-half years.

Brigham Young meets Joseph Smith in September in Kirtland, Ohio.

1833—Brigham Young marries Mary Ann Angell. (She is buried with him in Salt Lake City.) She will move alone from Far West. Her child will be run over in a wagon accident and will be miraculously healed.

Wilford Woodruff, age twenty-six, is baptized on December 31, two days after first hearing missionaries preach. "The snow was about three feet deep, the day was cold, and that water was mixed with ice and snow, yet I did not feel the cold," he wrote (Cowley, *Wilford Woodruff*, 35). That same day, his horse with newly caulked shoes kicks Wilford's hat off his head, missing his head by just two inches. Ten minutes later, Wilford has hitched the horse with another to a sled and is driving away. Some loose boards on the sled slide forward, slip end first to the ground, and fly up endwise, picking Brother Woodruff up and pitching him forward between the horses. The frightened animals run down the hill, dragging him under the sled behind them. He escapes without injury.

1834—Wilford Woodruff and Brigham Young are marching with Zion's Camp. Wilford is nearly shot by a rifle ball that is accidently discharged by a camp member. The ball passes through three tents with a dozen men in each without hurting anyone and passes within inches of Wilford's chest (Cowley, *Wilford Woodruff*, 9).

A musket, heavily loaded with buckshot and pointing directly at Wilford Woodruff's chest, is accidently snapped but misfires.

1835—Lorenzo Snow enters Oberlin College. He is disenchanted with organized religion. He is twenty-one. His sister, Eliza R. Snow, invites him to Kirtland to study Hebrew. He will rub shoulders with many of the Church leaders and become especially fond of Joseph Smith Sr.

1836—John Taylor has been converted in Canada by Parley P. Pratt and is baptized.

1837—Wilford Woodruff marries Phoebe Carter.

1838—Wilford Woodruff baptizes his father, Aphek Woodruff, on July 1.

1839—In April, Wilford Woodruff is pinned in a wagon accident and dragged by the frightened team for about half a mile with his head and shoulders dragging on the ground. Despite his awkward position, he manages somehow to steer the frightened horses into the corner of a high fence, where he and the team land in a pile together. Of this incident he said, "I was considerably bruised, but escaped without any broken bones, and after one day's rest was able to attend to my labors again" (Cowley, *Wilford Woodruff*, 10).

1846—On October 15, while cutting down a tree a couple of miles outside of Winter Quarters, Nebraska (just across the western border of Iowa), Wilford Woodruff is struck by the tree, knocked into the air, and thrown against an oak tree. His left thigh, hip, and left arm are badly bruised, and his breastbone and three left ribs are broken. His lungs, internal organs, and left side are badly bruised. He must ride his horse two and one-half miles over rough road to get back to the settlement. Pain forces him off the horse twice. Upon arriving back at Winter Quarters, men carry him in a chair to his wagon. Before putting him in bed, Brigham Young, Heber C. Kimball, Willard Richards, and others bless him. He lays upon his bed, unable to move until his breastbone begins to knit together. In about twenty days he begins to walk, and in thirty days, he returns to his normal duties.

Of his accidents, Wilford said, "I have broken both legs, one of them in two places; both arms, both ankles, my breastbone, and three ribs. I have been scalded, frozen and drowned. I have been in two water wheels while turning under a full head. I have passed through a score of other hairbreadth escapes" (Cowley, *Wilford Woodruff*, 11).

Taught By Whom?

(Heavenly Messengers Who Taught Joseph Smith)

The Prophet Joseph Smith was taught by many from beyond the veil. President John Taylor, in various talks, mentioned many of these "teachers" of the Prophet. The following combined quotes from some of his talks help us realize how many heavenly personages were involved:

"When God selected Joseph Smith to open up the last dispensation . . . the **Father** and the **Son** appeared to him . . . **Moroni** came to Joseph. . . . Then comes another personage, whose name is **John the Baptist**. . . . Afterwards came **Peter**, **James** and **John**. . . . Then we read again of **Elias** or **Elijah**, . . . who committed to him the powers and authority associated with his position. Then **Abraham**, who had the Gospel, the Priesthood and Patriarchal powers in his day; and **Moses** who stood at the head of the gathering dispensation in his day. . . . We are informed that **Noah**, who was a Patriarch, **and all in the line of the Priesthood, in every generation back to Adam**, who was the first man, possessed the same. Why was it that all these people . . . could communicate with Joseph Smith? Because he stood at the head of the dispensation of the fullness of times. . . . If you were to ask Joseph what sort of a looking man **Adam** was, he would tell you at once; he would tell you his size and appearance and all about him. You might have asked him what sort of men **Peter**, **James** and **John** were, and he could have told you. Why? Because he had seen them." (*Journal of Discourses*, 18:325–26).

"And when Joseph Smith was raised up as a Prophet of God, **Mormon**, **Moroni**, **Nephi** and others of the ancient Prophets who formerly lived on this Continent, and **Peter** and **John** and others who lived on the Asiatic Continent, came to him and communicated to him certain principles pertaining to the gospel of the son of God" (*Journal of Discourses*, 17:374).

"I know of what I speak for I was very well acquainted with him (Joseph Smith) and was with him a great deal during his life, and was with him when he died. The principles which he had, placed him in communication with the Lord, and not only with the Lord, but with the ancient apostles and prophets; such men, for instance, as **Abraham**, **Isaac**, **Jacob**, **Noah**, **Adam**, **Seth**, **Enoch**, and **Jesus** and the **Father**, and the **apostles that lived on this continent** as well as **those who lived on the Asiatic Continent**. He seemed to be as familiar with these people as we are with one another" (*Journal of Discourses*, 21:94).

Appendix

Children of Joseph Smith Sr and Lucy Mack Smith

Name	Birth Date	Place of Birth	Death Date
1. Child	about 1797	Tunbridge, VT	about 1797
2. Alvin	11 Feb. 1798	Tunbridge, VT	19 Nov. 1823
3. Hyrum	9 Feb. 1800	Tunbridge, VT	27 June 1844
4. Sophronia	16 May 1803	Tunbridge, VT	about 1876
5. Joseph Jr.	23 Dec. 1805	Sharon, VT	27 June 1844
6. Samuel Harrison	13 March 1808	Tunbridge, VT	30 July 1844
7. Ephraim	13 March 1810	Royalton, VT	24 March 1810
8. William	13 March 1811	Royalton, VT	13 Nov. 1893
9. Catherine	28 July 1812	Lebanon, NH	1 Feb. 1900
10. Don Carlos	25 March 1816	Norwich, VT	7 Aug. 1841
11. Lucy	18 July 1821	Palmyra, NY	9 Dec. 1882

(See *Church History in the Fulness of Times*, 21.)

Children of Joseph Smith and Emma Hale Smith

1. Alvin—Born and died on June 15, 1828, at Harmony, Pennsylvania. Some historians say his name was Alva.
2. Louisa—Born April 30, 1831, at Kirtland, Ohio. A girl, one of the twins, lived about three hours.
3. Thaddeus—Born April 30, 1831, at Kirtland, Ohio. A boy, one of the twins, lived about three hours.
4. Joseph Smith III—Born November 6, 1832, at Kirtland, Ohio. Died December 10, 1914, at Independence, Missouri.

5. Frederick G. Williams—Born June 20, 1836, at Kirtland, Ohio. Died April 13, 1862, at Nauvoo.
6. Alexander Hale—Born June 2, 1838, at Far West, Missouri. Died August 12, 1909, at Nauvoo.
7. Don Carlos—Born June 13, 1840, at Nauvoo. Died August 15, 1841, at 14 months at Nauvoo, Illinois.
8. A boy—Born December 26, 1842, at Nauvoo. He did not survive his birth.
9. David Hyrum—Born November 17, 1844, at Nauvoo. Died August 29, 1904, in Elgin, Illinois.

Adopted Children

10. Joseph Smith Murdock—A twin, born April 30, 1831, at Kirtland, Ohio. Died one year later on March 29, 1832.
11. Julia Murdock—A twin, born April 30, 1831, at Kirtland, Ohio. Died in 1880 near Nauvoo.

Final Situation of the Five Surviving Children of Joseph and Emma

1. **Julia Murdock**. Twins were born to John Murdock's wife the same day that Emma Hale Smith gave birth to twins, a boy and a girl. Emma's infants did not survive their birth. Sister Murdock passed away, leaving her twins motherless. John Murdock asked that Joseph and Emma raise his infants in place of their lost twins. The boy died after a year. The girl survived.

Julia grew up in the Smith household and at about age eighteen married Elisha Dixon. They resided in Nauvoo for some years. The couple later moved to Texas, where Elisha was killed in a boiler explosion on a steamship trafficking the Red River. Still in her early twenties, Julia returned to Nauvoo. She subsequently married John J. Middleton and moved with him to St. Louis. John was a Catholic, and she joined his faith. He became a chronic alcoholic. Julia left him and returned to Nauvoo, where she lived in the Mansion House until the death of Emma in 1879. Sick, penniless, and suffering from breast cancer, Julia passed away in 1880 at the home of Mr. and Mrs. James Moffatt, near Nauvoo.

2. **Joseph Smith III**. The eldest son was not yet twelve years old when his father, the Prophet Joseph Smith, was martyred, on June 27, 1844. His mother, Emma Smith, elected not to move the family to the west with the body of Saints, and so Joseph grew up in Nauvoo. As a young man he studied law and held various offices of public trust. At twenty-four, Joseph married Emmeline Griswold and subsequently two other wives, Ada Rachel Clark and Bertha Madison. Seventeen children were born to Joseph and his three wives.

He was contacted in 1856 by a church body calling itself the "New Organization." Its members requested that he assume the presidency of their church, but he declined. However, in his twenty-eighth year, he wrote to William Marks, former Nauvoo stake president and a leader in the "New Organization," stating that he was now ready to take his father's place as the head of the Reorganized Church. William Marks, W. W. Blair, and Israel Rogers visited Joseph in Nauvoo and discussed the proposed reorganization. Consequently, Joseph and his Mother, Emma Smith, attended a special conference at Amboy, Illinois, April 6, 1860, where, under the hands of Zenos H. Gurley, William Marks, Samuel Powers, and W. W. Blair, he was ordained prophet, seer, and revelator and successor to his father.

Joseph Smith III retained his office as president of the Reorganized Church of Jesus Christ of Latter Day Saints until his death on December 10, 1914. Frederick G. Smith, third child of Joseph and Bertha Madison, succeeded his father.

3. **Frederick G. Williams Smith**. The Prophet's second living son married Annie Marie Jones when he was twenty-one years old. They lived in Nauvoo for many years, where he was a farmer and merchant. Only one daughter was born to them, Alice Fredericka. Alice was contacted in Chicago by missionaries from the Church in Utah and was baptized into the faith of the "Utah Mormons" on January 6, 1915. However, her family prevailed upon her to give up this affiliation, and she returned to the Reorganized Church. Frederick Granger Williams Smith passed away in Nauvoo at the age of twenty-six on April 13, 1863.

4. **Alexander Hale Smith**. The prophet's third living son married Elizabeth Kendall and became the father of four sons and five daughters. He farmed near Nauvoo for many years and was recognized as a skilled wrestler, hunter, and marksman. Alexander gave his full support to his elder brother in the work of the Reorganized Church. He became one of the most popular ministers of the organization, traveling extensively in America and in many foreign lands. Alexander served as an apostle and as a counselor to the president. His last years were spent as the presiding patriarch. While visiting

Nauvoo, he passed away in the old Mansion House at age seventy-one on August 12, 1909.

5. **David Hyrum Smith**. The prophet's last son was born five months after the Martyrdom, receiving the name his father had suggested at the time of his leaving for Carthage. David and his brother, Alexander, were sent as missionaries to Utah in 1869. At the age of twenty-six, he married Clara Hartshorn, and they had one son named Elbert. Elbert served as a counselor to his Uncle Joseph and later to President Frederick M. Smith. Subsequently he was called as presiding patriarch of the Reorganized Church. David Hyrum was a popular missionary, preacher, hymn writer, and poet for the Reorganized Church. Early in his mature life, his activity was curtailed by illness. He died at age sixty in the State Mental Hospital at Elgin, Illinois.

SOURCES

Anderson, Richard Lloyd. *Investigating the Book of Mormon Witnesses*. Salt Lake City: Deseret Book, 1981.

Barrett, Ivan J. *Joseph Smith and the Restoration*. Provo, UT: Brigham Young University, 1982.

Black, Susan Easton. *Who's Who in the Doctrine and Covenants*. Salt Lake City: Bookcraft, 1997.

Cannon, George Q. *Life of Joseph Smith the Prophet*. Good Press, 1888.

———. *Life of Joseph Smith the Prophet*. Salt Lake City: Deseret News Press, 1907.

Church History in the Fulness of Times. Salt Lake City: The Church of Jesus Christ of Latter-day Saints (Institutes of Religion), 1989, 2003.

Clark, James R. (Compiler.) *Messages of the First Presidency of The Church of Jesus Christ of Latter-day Saints*. 6 vols. Salt Lake City: Bookcraft, 1965–75.

Conference Reports of The Church of Jesus Christ of Latter-day Saints. Salt Lake City: The Church of Jesus Christ of Latter-day Saints, 1898 to the present.

Cowley, Matthias F. *Wilford Woodruff: History of His Life and Labors*. 2d ed. Salt Lake City: Bookcraft, 1964.

Doctrine and Covenants Student Manual. Salt Lake City: The Church of Jesus Christ of Latter-day Saints (Institutes of Religion), 1981, 2018.

Doctrines of the Gospel Student Manual. Salt Lake City: The Church of Jesus Christ of Latter-day Saints (Institutes of Religion), 1981.

Doxey, Roy W. (Compiler.) *Latter-day Prophets and the Doctrine and Covenants*. Salt Lake City: Deseret Book, 1978.

"The Family: A Proclamation to the World." *Ensign or Liahona*, Nov. 2010, 129.

Hancock, Levi Ward. Autobiography. Typescript. L. Tom Perry Special Collections, Harold B. Lee Library, Brigham Young University, Provo, Utah.

Joseph Smith Papers, The. Salt Lake City: Church Historian's Press. (These books consist of several volumes now [2020] and will consist of more than 30 volumes when they are complete.)

Journal of Discourses. 26 vols. London: Latter-day Saints' Book Depot, 1854–86.

Kimball, Spencer W. *The Teachings of Spencer W. Kimball*. Edited by Edward L. Kimball. Salt Lake City: Bookcraft, 1982.

Lang, W. *History of Seneca County [Ohio], from the Close of the Revolutionary War to July, 1880*. Woburn, MA: Unigraphic, 1973.

Latter-day Saints' Millennial Star, The. Manchester, Liverpool, and London, England: The Church of Jesus Christ of Latter-day Saints, 1840–1970.

Life and Teachings of Jesus and His Apostles: New Testament Student Manual, The. Salt Lake City: The Church of Jesus Christ of Latter-day Saints, 1979.

Ludlow, Daniel H. *Encyclopedia of Mormonism.* Edited by Daniel H. Ludlow. 5 vols. New York: Macmillan, 1992.

Lundwall, N. B. *Temples of the Most High.* Salt Lake City: Bookcraft, 1971.

Matthews, Robert J. *A Plainer Translation: Joseph Smith's Translation of the Bible—A History and Commentary.* Provo, Utah: Brigham Young University Press, 1975.

McConkie, Bruce R. *Doctrinal New Testament Commentary.* 3 vols. Salt Lake City: Bookcraft, 1965–73.

———. *The Millennial Messiah: The Second Coming of the Son of Man.* Salt Lake City: Deseret Book, 1982.

———. *Mormon Doctrine.* 2d ed. Salt Lake City: Bookcraft, 1966.

———. *The Mortal Messiah: From Bethlehem to Calgary.* 4 vols. Salt Lake City: Deseret Book, 1979–81.

———. *The Promised Messiah: The First Coming of Christ.* Salt Lake City: Deseret Book, 1978.

McGavin, Cecil E. *Historical Background of the Doctrine and Covenants.* Salt Lake City: Literary Licensing, 2011.

Otten, L. G. *Historical Background and Setting for each section of the Doctrine and Covenants.* Privately published, 1970.

Pratt, Parley P. *Autobiography of Parley P. Pratt.* Salt Lake City: Deseret Book, 1938–1985.

Proctor, Scott and Maurine. *The Revised and Enhanced History of Joseph Smith by His Mother.* Salt Lake City: Bookcraft, 1996.

Roberts, B. H. *A Comprehensive History of The Church of Jesus Christ of Latter-day Saints, Century One.* 6 vols. Salt Lake City: Deseret Press, 1930.

Smith, Hyrum M. and Janne M. Sjodahl. *Doctrine and Covenants Commentary.* Salt Lake City: Deseret Book, 1951.

Smith, Joseph. *History of The Church of Jesus Christ of Latter-day Saints.* Edited by B. H. Roberts. 2d ed. rev., 7 vols. Salt Lake City: The Church of Jesus Christ of Latter-day Saints, 1932–51.

———. *Teachings of the Prophet Joseph Smith.* Selected by Joseph Fielding Smith. Salt Lake City: Deseret Book, 1976.

Smith, Joseph F. *Gospel Doctrine.* Salt Lake City: Deseret Book, 1939.

Smith, Joseph Fielding. *Answers to Gospel Questions.* Compiled by Joseph Fielding Smith Jr. 5 vols. Salt Lake City: Deseret Book, 1957–66.

———. *Church History and Modern Revelation—A Course Study for Melchizedek Priesthood Quorums.* Salt Lake City: The Council of the Twelve Apostles of The Church of Jesus Christ of Latter-day Saints, 1946.

———. *Doctrines of Salvation.* Compiled by Bruce R. McConkie. 3 vols. Salt Lake City: Bookcraft, 1954–56.

———. *Way to Perfection.* Salt Lake City: Deseret Book, 1975.

Smith, Lucy Mack. *History of Joseph Smith by His Mother, Lucy Mack Smith.* Salt Lake City: Bookcraft, 1958.

Talmage, James E. *The Articles of Faith.* Salt Lake City: Deseret Book, 1984.

Teachings of Presidents of the Church—Wilford Woodruff. Salt Lake City: The Church of Jesus Christ of Latter-day Saints, 2004.

———. *Jesus the Christ.* Salt Lake City: Deseret Book, 1977.

Times and Seasons. Commerce (later Nauvoo), Illinois, 1839–46.

Widtsoe, John A. *Evidences and Reconciliations.* Salt Lake City: Bookcraft, 1943.

———. *The Message of the Doctrine and Covenants.* Salt Lake City: Bookcraft, 1978.

———. *The Word of Wisdom: A Modern Interpretation.* Salt Lake City: Deseret Book, 1938.

Young, Brigham. *Discourses of Brigham Young.* Selected by John A. Widtsoe. Salt Lake City: Deseret Book, 1954.

Additional sources for the notes given in this work are as follows:

- The Standard Works of The Church of Jesus Christ of Latter-day Saints.
- Footnotes in the Latter-day Saint version of the King James Bible.
- The Joseph Smith Translation of the Bible.
- The Bible Dictionary in the back of the Latter-day Saint version of the King James Bible.

- Various dictionaries.
- Various student manuals provided for our institutes of religion.
- Other sources as noted in the text.

About the Author

David J. Ridges was raised in southeastern Nevada until his family moved to North Salt Lake City, Utah, when he was in fifth grade. He is the second of eight children.

Brother Ridges graduated from Bountiful High, served a two-and-a-half-year German-speaking mission to Austria, attended the University of Utah and BYU, and then graduated from BYU with a major in German and a physics minor. He later received a master's degree in educational psychology with a Church History minor from BYU.

He taught seminary and institute of religion as his chosen career for thirty-five years. He taught BYU Campus Education Week, Especially for Youth, Adult Religion, and Know Your Religion classes for over twenty-five years.

Brother Ridges has served as a Sunday School and seminary curriculum writer. He has had many callings, including Gospel Doctrine teacher, bishop, stake president, and patriarch. He and Sister Ridges have served two full-time, eighteen-month CES missions. He has written over forty books, which include several study guides for the standard works, Isaiah, Revelation, and many doctrinal publications on gospel topics such as the signs of the times, plan of salvation, and temples.

Brother and Sister Ridges met at the University of Utah. They were married in the Salt Lake Temple, are the parents of six children, and have sixteen grandchildren and one great-granddaughter so far. They make their home in Springville, Utah.

Scan to visit

www.davidjridges.com

Notes

Notes

Notes

NOTES